LOCKDOWN AMERICA

LOCKDOWN AMERICA

AMERICA

Police and Prisons in the Age of Crisis

CHRISTIAN PARENTI

VERSO

London • New York

First published by Verso 1999
© Christian Parenti 1999
All rights reserved
Reprinted 2000

The moral rights of the author have been asserted

Verso
UK: 6 Meard Street, London, London W1V 3HR
US: 180 Varick Street, New York, NY 10014—4606

Verso is the imprint of New Left Books

ISBN 1—85984—718—8

British Library Cataloguing in Publication Data
A catalogue record for this book is available from the British Library

Library of Congress Cataloging-in-Publication Data
A catalog record for this book is available from the Library of Congress

Typeset by The Running Head Limited, www.therunninghead.com
Printed in the USA by R. R. Donnelley & Sons Co.

for the rock solid comrade
Rose Braz

and for my dear mother
Susan Parenti

That justice is a blind goddess
Is a thing to which we poor are wise:
her bandage hides two festering sores
That once, perhaps, were eyes.

Langston Hughes

CONTENTS

ACKNOWLEDGMENTS

First and foremost I would like to thank Rose Braz, without whom this book would never have been written. Her knowledge of the criminal law helped me find my way, just as her love, support, and editorial comments kept me going. My aunt Jeanne Mahon proofread the dyslexic carnage of my first drafts and made useful comments on content and style. Steve Duncombe gave me the necessary nudge forward and entrée with Verso, all of which led to the initiation of this project. I am also deeply thankful for Steve's thoughtful editing. (I still owe you one.) Lilly Garbel assisted with much of the most important research; her skill and discipline were both helpful and inspiring. Michael Yaki of the New College of California Library helped my research efforts in numerous ways and gave access to library resources that made the job much easier. Colin Robinson was a gracious publisher and a supportive, careful editor. Rachel Guidera and Niels Hooper, also of Verso, made things happen on time and were always willing to answer my silly questions. Craig Gilmore gave clear advice on how to navigate the world of publishing and bookselling, and I learned much from my conversations with Ruthie Gilmore. Co-teaching with Sheila Tully helped push my thinking forward. Likewise many thanks to: John Manshall, whose platinum-wired mind has kept me on my intellectual toes for more than ten years; Chris D. Cook, who always knew how to fix the clotted phrase and reframe the muddled idea, even over the phone; and my comrade Rene Pointevin, who read the rough draft. Thanks also to Neeli Cherkovski, Bill Cole, David Downes, David Meltzer, Jose Palafox, Dan Pens, Andy Pratt, Elspeth Slayter, James Tracy, Paul Wright, and many others; and to my students at New College who, whether they know it or not, helped "educate the educator." No doubt

I should have taken more advice from all these wonderful folks; if I had, this book would perhaps carry fewer flaws. As for the intellectual and stylistic blemishes that remain, I plead guilty.

PREFACE

Shortly before starting to write this book a strange – or not so strange – thing happened. I was walking down the street in my neighborhood when a white guy dressed like a construction worker stepped into my path.

"Open your mouth! Open your mouth! Open your fucking mouth!" he roared, grabbing my throat and flashing a badge.

"Are you crazy?" Crunch went the grip on my larynx.

"You got that dope in your mouth! Open your mouth! Open your fucking mouth!"

Dope. Oh yeah. Finally realizing what was going on I opened my mouth, lifted my tongue. No baggies of heroin fell out.

"Whad ya do with that dope you're sell'n?" insisted the cop.

"Man, I don't even smoke pot anymore," was all I could muster.

Meanwhile a second and rather large undercover officer was restraining my companion.

"Leave him alone," she yelled, batting away the officer's hands.

"It's OK, they're cops," I said, immediately regretting my choice of words.

Up against the wall, hands on my head, I heard the cop, using standard police code for a suspicious person, mumble into his radio: "What was the description on that nine-seventeen?" After a pause a voice crackled back: "Green pants, black shirt with a stripe." Just what I was wearing.

"Did that shirt say anything?"

Another pause. "Uh yeah, it said BDK, over."

Mine didn't, plus I have white skin and a middle class accent, so the cops figured I wasn't the nine-seventeen. But every day thousands of folks are not so lucky. The above incident is not the only time police have momentarily mistaken me for a drug dealer or buyer. And like many Americans I've spent the stupid night or two in jail for petty offenses like hitchhiking and driving without a license.

Despite all this over-regulation and the many layers of criminal justice, America's violent crime rate still puts it in a league with countries like Venezuela and Colombia, as opposed to its presumed peers like France or the UK.

So what does the law-and-order regime achieve? And who is it really aimed at? One thing is crystal clear: poor people of color, particularly African Americans, are the main targets. By the year 2000 it is estimated that one in ten Black men will be in prison. Already, although African Americans make up only 13 percent of the total US population, *half* of all prisoners are Black.

The argument in the following pages is this: Beginning in the late sixties US capitalism hit a dual social and economic crisis, and it was in response to this crisis that the criminal justice buildup of today began. After a surge of expansion in the late sixties the growth of criminal justice plateaued in the late seventies, only to resume in earnest during the early and mid eighties with Reagan's war on drugs. Since then we've been on a steady path toward ever more state repression and surveillance.

Initially this buildup was in response to racial upheaval and political rebellion. The second part was/is more a response to the vicious economic restructuring of the Reagan era. This restructuring was itself a right-wing strategy for addressing the economic crisis which first appeared in the mid and late sixties. To restore sagging business profits, the welfare of working people had to be sacrificed. Thus the second phase of the criminal justice crackdown has become, intentionally or otherwise, a way to manage rising inequality and surplus populations. Throughout this process of economic restructuring the poor have suffered, particularly poor people of color. Thus it is poor people of color who make up the bulk of American prisoners.

The first section of the book deals with the recent history of American political economy and the origins of the current criminal justice buildup. The second explores some important forms of policing, like New York–style zero tolerance, SWAT teams, and the Immigration and Naturalization Service (INS) war on immigrants. The third deals with prison: the politics of life inside (gangs, rape, and brutality) and incarceration's role in reproducing the US economic and social order. This book is written with a linear, broadly historical narrative, but readers should feel free to digest the chapters in any order they wish.

PART I

CRISIS

CHAPTER ONE

NIXON'S SPLENDID LITTLE WAR: SOCIAL CRISIS AND CONTAINMENT

The revolution revolutionizes the counter-revolutionaries.
Régis Debray

[President Nixon] emphasized that you have to face the fact that
the whole problem is really the blacks. The key is to devise a
system that recognizes this while not appearing to.
H. R. Haldeman

How bleak the world must have been for those with political and economic power during the late sixties and early seventies. Order seemed to be
unraveling: massive anti-war protests on the Mall; a war effort bogged down
and hemorrhaging in the mud of Southeast Asia; economic stagnation and
declining profit rates; and, in the cities, skyrocketing crime coupled with
some of the most violent riots since the Civil War.

The crisis had two primary fault lines: race and the war. The civil rights
movement had radicalized and transmogrified into more militant, nationalist, and explicitly anti-capitalist forms. The Panthers – Black Marxists and
fully armed – stormed the California state capitol. In Newark, Watts, and
Chicago, Black people shot back at cops and National Guardsmen; in Detroit,
African American snipers were joined by transplanted urban "hillbillies."[1] In
New Mexico, armed Chicanos fired on a county court house, trying to kill

the sheriff. Chants of "Black Power," "Brown Power," and "Red Power" rose from all quarters. Gay men, routinely pilloried as "sissies," were knocking out cops during the pitched battles following a police raid on the Stonewall bar in New York City. Meanwhile, women burnt bras and, more importantly, filed suits, protested against discrimination, and won the right to reproductive choice. Not even the US army could be trusted. In January 1968 the American embassy in Saigon came under direct attack. With that the *Wall Street Journal* called the war doomed; gung-ho officers in the field started getting "fragged" with terrifying regularity, as drug addiction, madness, and open insubordination became the norm among GIs. (In 1970, the military, which preferred to suppress news of rebellion in the ranks, gave a official "fragging count" of 363 for that year alone.)[2]

Back in the belly of the beast, the Weather Underground was – as Che put it, "waging the most important struggle of all" – bombing the Pentagon, Congress, IBM, police stations, the headquarters of the New York Department of Corrections, and scores of other targets. By the early seventies a version of this same breakdown had metastasized to the shop floor. Sabotage, drug abuse, and wildcat strikes began biting into Fordist production regimes; costs began to rise as quality and profits slumped. It was not just alienated and pampered white youth who were "dropping out." America's whole social fabric seemed to be coming apart. Every structure of authority and obedience was breaking down. Though garnished with youthful nudity and flowers, the crisis of the late sixties and early seventies was more serious than is often acknowledged; the country was in the midst of a haphazard but deadly social revolution. It is from this political and economic crucible that today's emerging anti-crime police state and prison industrial complex were forged.

POLICE CRISIS

And where were the police during these convulsions? In hindsight they appear as masters of repression: murdering Fred Hampton in his sleep, framing activists, cracking heads at the Democratic convention in Chicago, and gunning down students at Jackson State. But consider the era from a different angle. Police had been swinging clubs, buying provocateurs, and worse since the march on Selma, yet protests and social upheaval only seemed to spread.

Martin Luther King's home had been fire-bombed as early as 1956, and by the late sixties Black militants were being killed as routine procedure, yet the protest and mass rioting continued. If the job of the police was to maintain order, they were failing. As a besieged and buffoonish Mayor Daley said during the debacle of the 1968 Democratic convention in Chicago: "Get the thing straight once and for all. The policeman isn't there to create disorder. The policeman is there to preserve disorder." Daley's malapropism was perhaps a Freudian slip which revealed a deeper truth: state repression *was not working*; it was failing to put the genie of social change and economic crisis back in the bottle. In fact, if the role of the Chicago PD is anything to go by, repression was making things *worse*. Repression – like the tear gas so liberally dispensed at demonstrations – was blowing back into "the Man's" own face.

Nor was the crisis confined to the realm of the overtly political. According to the FBI's Uniform Crime Reports (UCRs), both violent crime and crimes against property had been pitched on a steep incline since 1961.[3] Likewise, the spread of lifestyle "perversions" – homosexuality, miscegenation, free love, and drug use – were, in the eyes of many political and economic elites, dragging America towards some modern Sodom. Nothing the police did seemed to stop this. To make matters worse, Kennedy had booby-trapped the federal courts with liberal appointments. From 1963 on, the Warren court handed down a series of decisions which conservatives like Congressman Gerald Ford said would cause the "breakdown" of law and order.[4] First came *Gideon vs. Wainwright*, which guaranteed the poor a public defense. Then a year later came *Escobar vs. Illinois*, which gave defendants the right to have a lawyer present during interrogation. And finally in 1966 the coup de grace, *Miranda vs. Arizona*, required police to inform suspects of their legal rights upon arrest. Overnight an arsenal of "traditional" investigative methods had to be scrapped.

Forming the crucial backdrop to all this were the hundreds of riots which ravaged American cities between 1965 and 1968. Imagine the moment from the right-wing, racist vantage point of your average Southern senator: pencil-necked liberal judges giving away the goddam store, while Negroes burnt down the cities, and communists in pajamas kicked ass in Vietnam! What a nightmare.

It was in the midst of this storm that President Johnson, stubbornly losing the war in Southeast Asia, began edging towards a new war at home. In 1967 he took drug enforcement and regulation away from the Treasury and

FDA, respectively, and handed both to Attorney General Ramsey Clark at the Justice Department, creating a new agency called the Bureau of Narcotics and Dangerous Drugs (BNDD), the precursor of today's Drug Enforcement Administration (DEA). At the same time Johnson called on Congress to create a new "super agency" to strengthen ties between the federal government and local police. Over the next decade that body, the Law Enforcement Assistance Administration (LEAA), spent billions of dollars in an effort to reshape, retool, and rationalize American policing. Along with money, the federal government doled out military weaponry, communications technology, and special training.

Thus Johnson laid the initial groundwork for the tremendous combination of police power, surveillance, and incarceration that today so dominates domestic politics. But the rhetoric that would fuel the long criminal justice boom was first crafted by Sunbelt Republicans.

THE POLITICAL LEXICON OF FEAR

Senator Barry Goldwater, that desert photographer turned neoconservative demagogue, first dredged up crime as a presidential campaign issue in 1964. The Mann Act of 1910, the Harris Act of 1914, the Wickersham Commission, and Hale Boggs' mandatory minimums of 1951 had made crime a national political issue. But the vast majority of criminal justice policy was local and *not* the business of American presidents. Goldwater's rhetoric changed all that. "Security from domestic violence," said the senator, "no less than from foreign aggression is the most elementary form and fundamental purpose of any government." Goldwater promised that "enforcing law and order" would be central to his presidency.[5]

Around the same time another Sunbelt Republican began to experiment with the same fearmongering black science. Enter Richard Nixon: inveterate red-baiter, enforcer in the McCarthyite mob, and a former vice president, whose "political obituary" had been broadcast by ABC in the wake of his 1962 California gubernatorial race. Surveying the approaching cloudbursts of the late sixties, Nixon argued that "the deterioration [of respect for law and order] can be traced directly to the spread of the corrosive doctrine that every citizen possesses an inherent right to decide for himself which laws to obey and when to disobey them."[6] As Dan Baum has pointed out, Nixon, like many who would follow in his wake, was linking street crime to the civil disobedience of the civil rights movement. Likewise, Goldwater linked the redistributive efforts of the war on poverty to criminal violence:

> If it is entirely proper for the government to take away from some to give to others, then won't some be led to believe that they can rightfully take from anyone who has more than they? No wonder law and order has broken down, mob violence has engulfed great American cities, and our wives feel unsafe in the streets.[7]

Goldwater lost to Johnson, but the Goldwater message won. At the heart of this new type of politics was a very old political trope: white racism and the self-fueling fear bred by it. Crime meant urban, urban meant Black, and the war on crime meant a bulwark built against the increasingly political and vocal racial "other" by the predominately white state. The fear of crime became all-American; law and order were emerging as the new political currency with which to unite white voters of disparate classes. In fact, shortly before his presidential victory in 1968 Nixon wrote his mentor Dwight Eisenhower, noting both the power of anti-crime fearmongering and its racial content: "I have found great audience response to this [law-and-order] theme in all parts of the country, including areas like New Hampshire where there is virtually no race problem and relatively little crime."[8]

In observing the momentum of Nixon's vicious law-and-order stumping, *New York Times* columnist James "Scotty" Reston made a passing but prophetic remark. Nixon, he wrote, "undoubtedly will emphasize order in the cities, for that is his best issue . . . He thinks he can tame the ghettos and then reconstruct them, and he may very well make reconciliation with the Negro community impossible in the process."[9] Nixon's message was taking on a life of its own. By the summer of 1968, 81 percent of respondents to one Harris poll believed that law and order had broken down and blamed the chaos on "communists" and "Negroes who start riots."[10]

Amidst this climate the right was painting Johnson as soft on crime, and his young Attorney General Ramsey Clark, scion of an LBJ confederate and Texas state supreme court justice, wasn't helping matters with his fuzzy comments about "root causes."[11] In response, Johnson appointed a national commission on crime and another on riots, and started proposing legislation.

Then in the early spring of election year 1968, Dr. Martin Luther King was gunned down in Memphis, and hundreds of cities great and small exploded in frenzied and desperate rioting, some for the second time in less than five years. With billowing smoke from D.C.'s ghettos to concentrate their minds, Congress worked diligently on muscular criminal justice legislation. The hard work culminated in Johnson's Omnibus Crime Bill, which received its final changes just as Robert Kennedy followed King in early departure to the hereafter. The first big federal crime bill, the Omnibus Crime Control and Safe Streets Act of 1968, was passed in the House the very next day and was signed into law a few months later.

Against this backdrop and mounting casualties in Vietnam, Nixon announced a secret plan to bring "peace with honor" to the debacle in Southeast Asia. At the same time he ratcheted up his narco-phobic, anti-crime rhetoric: "I say that doubling the conviction rate in this country would do more to cure crime in America than quadrupling the funds for [Hubert] Humphrey's war on poverty."[12] It was this sort of right-wing rhetoric that shaped the Omnibus Crime Control and Safe Streets Act. In many ways the bill was a Frankenstein initiated by Johnson in the wake of the 1966 rioting season; the monster had been given more life than the administration wanted or expected, thanks to two years of haggling and pressure from congressional Republicans and Southern Democrats. Johnson got his LEAA and $75 million overall in funding, but the bill was also larded with draconian legal provisions and millions for riot control and police training which the president and many House liberals opposed. Johnson called the bill "unwise" and "potentially dangerous," prevaricated for two weeks, and then signed the act into law just as his veto ran out.

Among the Omnibus Crime Control and Safe Streets Act's most aggressive features was a weakening of *Miranda* rights in federal cases. Now "confessions" made by defendants in police custody would be admissible evidence, as long as such statements were made "voluntarily." More importantly, the law unleashed police to tap phones and plant bugs in a wide variety of cases. And when law enforcement officials felt an "emergency" existed, they were now free to intercept communications for up to forty-eight hours without a warrant. These were momentous changes. Previously legal wiretapping had been restricted to cases of "national security" only, and states for the most part did not have the right to tap phones. The change in federal law cleared the way for similar transformations at the state level.

NIXON GOES TO WAR

Once in office Nixon faced an interesting problem. Johnson's lame protes tations during the 1964 campaign against the fulminating Goldwater had in fact been correct: crime control was predominantly a local issue, beyond federal jurisdiction. So how was Nixon to deliver on his political hype and how was he to restore order? He had invoked the specter of street crime, political chaos, and narcotics abuse – much of which was thinly veiled code for "the race problem," namely African American migration and the politi- cal demolition of US apartheid. But could Nixon actually deal with the real- ity of rising crime? Delivering a drop in crime rates would be valuable political capital for Republicans in the next election. Most importantly, how could Nixon contain the growing threat of organized political rebellion and the culture of disobedience and disrespect that fed it?[13]

The mean young squares at the White House soon found a strategy. Narcotics would be the Trojan horse for deeper federal involvement in polic- ing. Since the Harris Act of 1914, the Feds had policed illegal drugs based on their constitutional right to tax. But this rather narrow entrance would not accommodate the onslaught of forces that Nixon was planning. So the new team slid federal prerogatives onto the more generous terrain of polic- ing interstate commerce by redefining narcotics trafficking as a violation of the Hobbs Interstate Commerce Act. The "war on drugs" would give the Feds the necessary latitude to beef up local policing and rationalize the nation's haphazard and often contradictory patchwork of criminal law. Thus the image of the evil dope fiend loomed large in the new administration's rhetoric, as it had during the campaign. Trafficking was targeted as "public enemy number one," while using was cast as the linchpin of rising crime rates, because as Nixon informed the nation, addicts "turn to shoplifting, mugging, burglary, armed robbery, and so on" to feed their habits. Six months after taking office, the president told Congress that

> Within the last decade, the abuse of drugs has grown from essentially a local police problem into a serious national threat to the personal health and safety of millions of Americans . . . A national awareness of the grav- ity of the situation is needed: a new urgency and concerted national pol- icy are needed at the federal level to begin to cope with this growing menace to the general welfare of the United States.[14]

Nixon was correct that drug use – that is, casual drug use, mostly in the form of smoking marijuana – was on the rise, but evidence of a national narcotics siege did not exist.[15] Nonetheless, Nixon's team went into action, haranguing the public about the evils of drugs at every opportunity and drawing up tough new legislation (all of it double-checked by a young right-wing attorney named William Rehnquist). The proposed legislation back-filled legal spaces that had been missed by crime hawks, or successfully defended by liberals, during the battle over the 1968 crime bill.

Among the most controversial new proposals was one creating "preventive detention," which allowed judges to deny bail to federal defendants despite the constitutional presumption of innocence. The bill also unveiled "no-knock" warrants, which allowed cops to kick in doors without warning. The American Civil Liberties Union (ACLU) called no-knock "excessive and unconstitutional." Congressional opponents called no-knock a violation of Fourth Amendment protections against unlawful search and seizure. Attorney General John L. Mitchell fired back: "We are dealing with clever and ruthless drug peddlers, who have no hesitation about taking the life of an agent." He went on to suggest that new rules might be more palatable if referred to simply as "quick entry" and urged Congress to give American families "an exciting 'back-to-school' present . . . letting them know that more effective tools for drug control are on the way."[16]

The battle of words raged throughout 1969 and 1970, as Nixon's legislative wish-list lingered in Congress without passage. (But Congress did quadruple LEAA funding from $59.4 million for fiscal year 1968 to $268 million for fiscal year 1970.)[17]

As Nixon's anti-crime legislation made its way through the House and Senate, congressional hearings provided a platform for law-and-order hawks to tutor the public about evil narcotics. Suddenly it seemed *all* of America's troubles were somehow drug related – even the horrors of Vietnam. A report on CBS showed US GIs in the verdant killing fields of Vietnam smoking pot through the barrel of a rifle, and even Bob Hope, Mr. Super-straight himself, was telling "pot" jokes to the troops during his annual Christmas tours of Indochina. As news of the massacre at My Lai finally broke, the demonization of drugs – particularly marijuana – reached fantastic new heights.

According to one eyewitness testifying before Congress, "At least 60 percent of the soldiers in Charlie Company, the unit involved in the My Lai incident, had smoked marijuana at least once. Some soldiers smoked marijuana the night before they went to My Lai on the day of the alleged massacre."[18] Senator Thomas Dodd, a Democrat from Connecticut, concluded that "in Vietnam dangerous drugs and even heroin are almost as available as candy bars." Ronald Ridenhour, the helicopter door-gunner who witnessed, researched, and then exposed the barbarism of My Lai, concurred; most troops in Vietnam smoked pot. But he denied that had anything to do with *why* Charlie Company massacred a village during Operation Song My: "Many Americans are looking for any reason other than a command decision." The real crimes were assiduously avoided. "Did the Viet Cong smoke marijuana?" asked a concerned Senator Dodd.[19] The parade of witnesses seemed to think not — yet another unfair advantage. The message was simple: America was under attack, and even its war crimes were just aberrations, animated by heroin and weed.

The months of hysterical talk fueled the smooth passage of the next big federal crime bill, the Comprehensive Drug Abuse Prevention and Control Act of 1970. This provided $189 million for expanded drug treatment during 1970–77; in the interest of getting crime rates down by the next election, even the toughest conservatives were willing to mix a "soft" approach with their $220 million booster shot to enforcement. The Bureau of Narcotics and Dangerous Drugs received 300 additional agents. That same year Congress allocated the LEAA $3.55 billion to be doled out to local and state law enforcement over the next three years.[20] For the rest of the decade the LEAA's annual budget routinely topped more than a billion dollars.

Simultaneous with Nixon's "war on drugs" the administration set afloat another canard to facilitate expansion of the state's police apparatus: the fight against "La Cosa Nostra." On October 15 Nixon signed the Organized Crime Control Bill — also known as the Racketeer Influenced and Corrupt Organizations (RICO) Act. Turning to his Attorney General John Mitchell and the malevolent FBI Director J. Edgar Hoover, Nixon said: "I give you the tools. You do the job."

"The job," as it turned out, was much more than cracking down on a few crime families. In fact the RICO "tools" were immediately turned on the left. Most pernicious among the law's new devices was the advent of secret "special grand juries" empowered to subpoena and interrogate *anyone* (including a defendant's attorney) about literally *anything*. These grand juries revolutionized the state's investigative powers and gave birth to a legal culture of mass snitching. Unlike previous grand juries, the secret RICO tribunals did not have to offer witnesses immunity. The new so-called "use-immunity" laws transformed immunity into a rare payoff for complete and total co-operation with the state, and thus greatly facilitated federal prosecutors' efforts to "flip" defendants – that is, turn them into government informants. Unlike witnesses before traditional grand juries, uncooperative RICO witnesses could be jailed for up to eighteen months. The new juries quickly became investigative tools used against the left, as federal prosecutors used them to trawl for evidence.

RICO also loosened the rules pertaining to the use of illegally obtained evidence by prosecutors; it created new categories of federal crime, including types of gambling and reinvesting allegedly ill-gotten lucre; it allowed the federal government to seize the assets of any organization deemed to be a criminal conspiracy; it created new penalties and policing powers over the use of explosives (a provision, tailor-made for the more energetic elements of the New Left, which had detonated over 350 bombs in the previous two years); and finally, it created 25-year-long sentences for "dangerous adult offenders."[21]

The New York Bar Association described the law as containing "the seeds of official repression." While the language of RICO invoked organized crime (its eponym is a character from an Edward G. Robinson gangster movie), the act's real targets were more often members of the New Left. "Nixon's Justice Department subpoenaed over 1,000 anti-war activists . . . [and] twenty-three leaders of the Vietnam Veterans Against the War were subpoenaed to appear before a grand jury on the day they were to hold a protest at the Democratic convention in Miami."[22] Thousands of journalists, Black Panthers, and the Puerto Rican *Independistas* were also hauled before RICO grand juries. These were Nixon's real enemies, and his ultimate goal was to put the militant representatives of the urbanized poor in check. This required a generalized buildup of police power, hardware, and organization. As Nixon's Chief of Staff H. R. Haldeman had written in his diary: "[President Nixon] emphasized that you have to face the fact that the whole problem is really the blacks. The key is to devise a system that recognizes this while not appearing to." That "system" was the war on crime and criminal justice buildup.[23]

It was in this same tendentious vein that Nixon attempted to shift the focus of BNDD enforcement efforts away from the higher levels of the

narcotics business and down to street level dealing. When the BNDD resisted, Nixon created a narco Praetorian Guard, the Office of Drug Abuse Law
Enforcement (ODALE), a special police agency directly accountable to the
White House. The new presidential drug cops would move against Black
people and the other dangerous demographics causing such chaos and so
terrifying Nixon's "forgotten" Americans. Such intervention was all the more
necessary because the growing political tumult was now joined by economic
stagnation and labor strife, which together posed real threats to the smooth
functioning of American capitalism. A generalized show of state force was
needed and ODALE would act as the flamboyant vanguard.

ODALE's 300 commandos – equipped with all the best gear and broad
new RICO powers – were deployed at ghetto listening posts with orders
to search and destroy. Staffed mostly by agents from the BNDD and
prosecutors from the Department of Justice, ODALE's mission was to hunt
down the "very vermin of humanity." Their field agents were the drug war
irregulars; free to "adopt [the] dress and tactics" of "drug people."[24] From
1972 through 1973 these ODALE squads – usually augmented with cross-
deputized officers from local forces – roamed their areas of operation at will,
using "no-knock warrants," preventive detention, and the special grand juries
to raise hell and make headlines on the streets of a few big cities. But the
press generated by ODALE bullying tactics was not all good.[25]

For example, in the spring of 1973 *Newsweek* reported that the outfit's
(admittedly loose) discipline completely unraveled during a night of ram-
paging in the working class suburb of Collinsville, Illinois, outside St. Louis,
Missouri. It seemed that two ODALE detachments had gone berserk and
vandalized a pair of all-American homes; kicking in the doors, the raiding
parties held their victims at gunpoint, calling the women "whores" and
threatening to kill the men as they ransacked the quarters. No dope was
found, and one traumatized non-combatant had to be evacuated to the local
psychiatric ward.[26]

Simultaneously, the crisis of Watergate was closing in and public tolerance for police state tactics was fraying. In response Nixon collapsed both
ODALE and the BNDD into a new agency called the Drug Enforcement
Administration. Congress and the administration began cooling to the crime
issue in 1973, but they did pass new anti-hijacking legislation, expanded the
role of the LEAA, and gave the agency another $3.25 billion funding to last
it through 1976.[27]

LEAA: ADDRESSING THE POLICE CRISIS

ODALE had been short-term pyrotechnics, but it cut the template for later task-force-style federal drug wars, and for that reason it is important. However, the Nixon administration's most significant legacy to domestic repression was manifest in Johnson's brainchild gone bad, the LEAA. For a few years in the early seventies this hybrid think-tank/slush fund/law enforcement bureaucracy was the fastest-growing agency in the federal government. In its early years, 50 percent of LEAA "action grants" went to police hardware and training, other moneys went to community corrections, drug rehab, and research. ODALE was largely funded with "repurposed" LEAA money.[28]

Though the LEAA was an effective catalyst in the Nixon-era buildup, its role as such was bitterly contested. Many congressional liberals and policy analysts opposed what they saw as a bastardization of the LEAA's originally intended function. Under Johnson, the LEAA had been launched to develop a broadly defined "reformist" approach to crime control and corrections. But under Nixon's "new federalism" – whereby the federal government increased aid to states without increasing its control over them – the LEAA became, in the eyes of many, "merely a conduit" for federal aid. As one critic from the non-profit legal sector put it, "The overall result is that the federal reform program has become a fiscal relief program . . ."[29] Other critics focused on the LEAA's cumbersome, sloppy, and chaotic bureaucracy. Despite the LEAA's problems it was the Johnny Appleseed of today's law-and-order militarization.

The LEAA's primary function during the first half of the seventies was to address the police failures of the sixties. That is, it was intended to forge an infrastructure capable of containing rising crime, protest, rioting, and cultural upheaval. In this respect the LEAA's mission was to rebuild the heart of the state's function: protecting powerful minorities from majorities. Recall that "every state is a 'special repressive force' for the suppression of the oppressed class. Consequently, *no* state is either 'free' or a 'people's state.'"[30]

What then were the causes of the policing crisis? One stood out above all others: America's police apparatus was hopelessly fragmented and uncoordinated. Whole regions of the country's law enforcement infrastructure were submerged in quagmires of nepotism, corruption, and incompetence; many metropolitan departments, despite decades of reform, were still ruled by recalcitrant, provincial, good ol' boys or corrupt municipal machine-style thugs.[31] In 1965 *only four* states mandated police training; more than twenty states did not even have *minimum* educational and literacy requirements for their recruits. A Department of Justice study noted with concern that both barbers and beauticians, on average, were required to train more than three times as long as the average American cop. In Detroit most officers came from the bottom 25 percent of their high school class, and this was not a unique situation. One regional LEAA administrator relayed the story of a sheriff in Missouri who was totally illiterate and signed his grant applications with an X.[32]

In 1967 the President's Commission on Law Enforcement and Justice Administration noted that: "the problem of personnel is at the root of most of the criminal justice system's problems . . . The system cannot operate swiftly and certainly unless its personnel are efficient and well informed."[33] The forces of law and order were in need of a "great leap forward."

Modernization necessitated massive retooling, reorganization, and re-training of law enforcement nationwide, along with building a new structure for regionally coherent, long-term law enforcement planning.

Police officials were some of the first to recognize the challenge. "Greater demands than ever before are being made on our police by American citizens for the preservation of law and order," read an article in a 1965 issue of the *FBI Law Enforcement Bulletin*.[34] Another warning claimed: "Our population increases daily, the crime rate rises steadily and the police line is stretched further. If the breaking point is reached, the cost in crime, property loss, and most of all liberty, will be the intolerable results."[35]

The young Daryl Gates (who went on to become chief of the LAPD), in a self-deprecating article on riot control, noted that "the police of America have not been overwhelmingly successful in their control of riots . . . [In Los Angeles] our initial efforts were pretty awful . . . Control strategy and street tactics have had to be developed and combat-tested almost simultaneously. Police ingenuity has been sorely tested under the most severe conditions. Some of the strategies employed have proven to be completely ineffective . . ." Turning the tide, argued Gates, "requires careful and precise planning. It requires talking to one another, and building upon our strengths, not lamenting past weaknesses."[36]

Gates was merely echoing a growing consciousness among law enforcement officials and policy analysts and their academic counterparts. Correcting the failure of policing required a new "military-corporate model."[37] As one expert put it: "The problem of crime demands the same kind of research techniques that have been so dramatically effective in other national programs; in the space program, in the fight against disease and in the defense effort."[38]

Policing needed the technological edge of the Defense Department, coupled with the managerial expertise of the large corporation. After all, the Presidential Crime Commission of 1967 had found that many departments were "not organized in accordance with well-established principles of modern business management."[39] Thus the dominant vision of change was rooted in modernist notions of society as machine, social problems as technical problems.

One of the first forces to embrace the corporate managerial model was that veritable laboratory of police innovation, the Los Angeles Police Department. (The LAPD and Sheriff's Department, like other California law enforcement agencies, had long maintained close links to research universities and the military, and as a result both had been on the cutting edge of policing for decades.) Chief William Parker sent emissaries to study the management training programs at Ford, Rockwell, IBM, and Union Oil. With LEAA funding, and lessons from corporate America, the LAPD set up a "Management Development Center." Other departments quickly followed suit, submerging their captains and lieutenants in courses like "Managerial Communications," "Creative Thinking," and "Speed Reading."[40]

As a result of the 1968 Omnibus Crime Control Act, these rationalizations at the departmental level were complemented by law enforcement planning at the state level.[41] In order to receive LEAA funds, each state was required to form a law enforcement state planning agency (SPA) and have this body approved by the LEAA. As the haphazard will of nature and the chaos of the city were conquered, so too would "modern planning" and "scientific organization" tame the new unruly social forces.

Enforced planning by the LEAA – an often overlooked feature of Nixon's war on crime – was an essential mechanism in producing law enforcement's rapid modernization. Among other things, state planning agencies played "an active role in initiating, drafting, and implementing state legislation."[42] Though relations between the planning agencies and the LEAA were often chaotic and choked with bureaucratic confusion (caused in part by the Nixon administration's eagerness to pump huge sums of federal cash to local cops as quickly as possible), such linkages nonetheless fostered autonomous state-level rationalization. The planning efforts forced local cops into more regular contact with the state bureaus of investigation, state police, and local FBI field offices. The SPAs created uniform training standards, state-wide academies, contingency plans, and special joint task forces that dealt with everything from traffic flows to guerrilla warfare.

Kentucky offers an illustration of the changes: "Before 1966, a great majority of Kentucky police and sheriffs departments afforded no training to their officers . . ." nor did they seek training from the FBI or state troopers. But starting in 1969 the new SPA, with LEAA money, established training standards, built a state police academy and a mobile training school, helped pass a new criminal code, and opened relations between police forces and the University of Kentucky.[43]

In the early sixties, the ultimate symbol of chaos had been the urban riot: for white America all bad things converged there. Consider the kaleidoscopic vision of the Los Angeles police chief: "We are living in an age of discontent and discord. We see rapid – almost daily – changes in social, economic, and philosophic values . . . We have 'love-ins,' 'be-ins,' 'sit-ins,' and other demonstrations, and they have gradually degenerated in riots . . ."[44]

With the onset of the seventies a more sinister specter haunted police. According to the FBI, "New tactics and techniques have been developed in the United States by a small number of criminals who style themselves urban guerrillas."[45] Counterinsurgency had always been close to the surface, but now it was coming to the fore. "[N]ever before in the history of American law enforcement," wrote J. Edgar Hoover in an article on urban guerrilla warfare, "has our profession faced such inflamed bitterness and hostility and such purposive intentions to wreak havoc against the police officers through injury, maiming and outright murder . . . Ideological and revolutionary violence in the nation is on the increase."[46]

Hyperbolic as Hoover may have sounded, policy and law enforcement elites were increasingly concerned with "militants," "extremists," "terrorists," and what seemed to be an increasingly organized war against order. Between 1967 and 1973 annual fatal assaults on law enforcement officers increased from 76 to 131. Most disturbing for authorities was the growing number of organized ambushes.[47] In the first nine months of 1970 sixteen police were killed in what appeared be unprovoked sniping, bombings, and point-blank executions; a dozen more were wounded. Real or imagined, the threat of warfare loomed large in the minds of police policymakers and pundits.[48]

As elements in the New Left turned toward the moral and strategic beacons of Che, Marighella, and Uncle Ho, so too did the authors of domestic repression borrow lessons from the Third World. Counterinsurgency techniques developed in Southeast Asia, Africa, and Latin America were now being openly repatriated to domestic policing. As early as 1966, articles intended to tutor American law enforcement in counterinsurgency and urban guerrilla warfare started appearing in the law enforcement trade press. One piece entitled "Police–Military Relations in a Revolutionary Environment," by an instructor from the US Army War College, made these recommendations:

> It is now generally agreed among counterinsurgency experts that one of the most important aspects of counter-insurgency operations is the control of population and resources . . . Techniques to control the people include individual and family identification, curfews, travel permits, static and mobile check point operations, and the prevention of assemblies or rallies.

The article went on to describe rising crime rates as a precursor to revolution, and to laud the "value of an effective police organization – both civil and military – in maintaining law and order, whether in California, Pennsylvania, Mississippi, or the rice paddies and jungles of Vietnam."[49]

COMPUTER SURVEILLANCE: BIRTH OF THE ELECTRONIC DRAGNET

Development of a nationwide law enforcement communications infrastructure was central to the mission of modernization and pacification. Police information systems had to be upgraded, rationalized, and computerized. Typed memos on carbon copy, filed in clumsy cabinets, had to go. Not only was each department urged to modernize its record keeping and surveillance files, but the LEAA, through a hybrid contractor called SEARCH, set about creating a unified national police information system with a massive database of criminal histories. America's patchwork, disparate, and sometimes overlapping police agencies had to be brought together into a single, coherent, smooth-running informational and surveillance network. It would be a monumental task.

In 1968, only ten states had automated state-level criminal justice information systems.[50] Four years and $90 million later, forty-seven states had functioning computerized criminal databases, all connected to the FBI's recently formed master system, the National Crime Information Center (NCIC). Started in 1967 as a database of wanted persons, firearms, stolen autos, and other property, the NCIC contained 500,000 files. By 1974 the future of policing was already hard at work; the NCIC included criminal histories and held a total of 4.9 million entries, handled 130,000 transactions daily, and was wired to ninety-four different federal, state, and large metropolitan law enforcement agencies, as well as all fifty-five FBI field offices.[51] Among the federal agencies contributing and receiving information from the NCIC in 1974 were the Secret Service, the Internal Revenue Service, Bureau of Alcohol, Tobacco and Firearms, US Bureau of Prisons, INS, US courts, and the US Marshals Service.

Previous to the massive infusion of federal cash, local enforcement agencies had to send for files by mail and wait two weeks to receive fingerprints and background checks from the FBI in Washington, D.C. As a result, wanted fugitives often slipped the leash before the appropriate documents could be forwarded. Likewise, fabricated identities often functioned as well as real ones.

The NCIC brought the nation one step closer to "achiev[ing] the ultimate goal of a law enforcement information system encompassing the entire United States."[52] For the NCIC to operate with maximum power, it required (and still requires) increasingly sophisticated surveillance and computer systems to feed it. Thus as the NCIC expanded, so too did police computer power at the regional, state, and local level. With the growth of these systems came the demand for ever more information, which meant increased emphasis on stopping and questioning the general population. In San Diego, "the source documents included in the system were traffic citations, traffic warnings, all traffic offense arrests, and field interrogation reports containing vehicle information. These contacts provide approximately 300,000 vehicle descriptions per year."[53]

Since its inception the NCIC has been used for employment background checks, immigration purposes, large-scale private investigations, and in routine police work. As the system's functions expand, society is rendered ever more transparent to the state and police power. While most NCIC "transactions" are innocuous enough, or in an immediate sense even enhance public safety, the larger long-term significance of a national computerized database is more ominous. A central police database in which anyone can appear is the axis around which any future police state will revolve. And the NCIC's voracious appetite for ever more input from local sources fosters new surveillance practices among subsidiary institutions, thus propelling us towards a "dossier society." Thus the NCIC logarithmically expands state power to control individuals and groups.

The advent of the NCIC, like so much of the policing infrastructure, was not without problems. In fact the system was vexed by the very issues it sought to overcome: First there were the technical limitations and vicious turf fights between the FBI and the bureaucrats controlling the LEAA. The more liberal (or at least publicly accountable) LEAA argued that any centralized computer network should have at its hub merely an index of local law enforcement files, not actual files. The idea was to avoid over-centralization and concentration of power in federal hands. And the LEAA argued that it should control the criminal history files of the new system and that its function should only be facilitating information flows between local agencies.

One LEAA idea that the Bureau saw as particularly inane was a proposal to allow individual citizens access to *their own files*. Needless to say, Hoover soon crushed this and other fuzzy-headed plans. He wanted more than just an index, he wanted a national database of complete files fed by local law enforcement and controlled by the FBI. And eventually that's what he got.[54]

Another problem for the NCIC was that many state and local law enforcement agencies were hesitant to cooperate with the FBI, or Feds of any sort. In fact many local police hated the FBI, especially its bullying and parsimonious chieftain Hoover. As early as 1956, police from California and seven other western states held a secret meeting to launch the Law Enforcement Intelligence Unit (LEIU), a private consortium designed to facilitate information sharing and avoid the prying of Hoover's G-men. According to one former member, the LEIU's founder, Captain Hamilton (then head of the Los Angeles Police Department's intelligence unit),

. . . wanted to take police intelligence away from the FBI. Police departments do the street-level work to collect information and Hamilton didn't like the idea of turning it over to the FBI and making them the monitor; so he formed the LEIU to circumvent the FBI's network. It was established to form an intelligence network independent of any Federal agency.[55]

By the early seventies, the LEIU involved police agencies from throughout the US and Canada and served as a hot-house of cross fertilization for local red squads, spooks and over-zealous law enforcement satraps.

But the Feds and the territorial locals, whether they knew it or not, still needed to integrate their intelligence systems and build a culture of collaboration if America was to conquer "disorder" as it had outer space and nature. So the LEAA had to sweeten interagency cooperation with hearty federal grants and the promise of subsidized technology transfers from the military. It worked, more or less, and by the mid seventies all fifty states were plugged into the NCIC grid.[56]

THE GEAR GIVEAWAY

The LEAA also helped build up the capillary levels of police communications, supplying local law enforcement agencies with the basic physical infrastructure of car radios, high-tech dispatch systems, and mobile command and control centers. (Even in the early seventies few foot cops had portable radio "transceivers" that connected them to headquarters. Beat cops used call-boxes, and car patrols could only communicate by radio when in their cruisers.) Today gadgetry such as "shoulder radios" may seem mundane, but for the riot-besieged cops of the sixties communications were all-important. One forward-looking officer described the confusion between local, state, and federal forces in Illinois as follows:

[B]ecause these various agencies operate on different radio frequencies, it has been impossible to mobilize all the police units involved under a single unified command. This has not only resulted in inefficient use of available police units, but it has also left many police units to operate without direction and without knowledge of the overall plan of action

. . . Inadequate communications have plagued law enforcement officials for many years, only in the last few has proper attention been given to the problem . . .[57]

Even the best equipped forces, like the LAPD, were shown to be unprepared when mass rioting erupted. In fact, it was a communications breakdown between the three forces attempting to quell the inchoate Watts rebellion in 1965 – the LAPD, California Highway Patrol, and L.A. County Sheriff's Department – that allowed the conflagration to grow so large. At first, scrambled radio communications led to confusion, then paralysis, and then – in the face of mounting violence and looting on the street – *a complete withdrawal of forces!*[58] Effective policing, like modern warfare, requires communications, proper organization, and a clear chain of command.

Computers, microfilm fingerprint files, and electronic maps (developed for use in Vietnam) were also part of the LEAA's modernist arsenal. Likewise, police forensic labs were stocked with technology for taking and matching dental files, processing samples of organic compounds, and so on. But the most spectacular new tool was the helicopter. The Watts riots of 1965 showed the sheriff's year-old helicopter program to be an indispensable command and control tool during civil disturbances. One LEAA case study found that

> Civil disturbances often result in a vast amount of confusion, particularly at night, with ground patrol units unable to identify the key points of difficulty, and participants often claiming they did not hear an order to disperse. *The helicopter's over all view of the scene, together with loud speakers and riot suppression equipment, will do much both tangibly and psychologically to bring the situation to a rapid and accepted conclusion.* [emphasis added][59]

Choppers were also noted to be effective in locating, spotting, and deterring night-time snipers; and floodlights helped support night-time operations by ground units.

Police choppers, when used with sufficient regularity, helped to create an urban panopticon, where citizens internalized the police gaze and made the effects of state power constant even when its application was sporadic. As the L.A. county sheriff explained it,

Concentrated patrol had not only demonstrated that visibility of the officers was vastly improved, *it also placed officers in a position where they were highly visible to offenders.* One of the most effective deterrents to crime is the "would be" offender observing a patrolman nearby. This two way visibility factor, coupled with the fact the helicopters would not become involved with the petty routine demands made on radio cars, presented the probability that helicopters could provide the sorely needed crime deterrent link sometimes missing in ground unit deployment. [original emphasis][60]

As a result of the L.A. experience, the National Highway Safety Act of 1966, as well as the LEAA, made police air power a new priority; on average the Feds were willing to pay 75 percent of the bill for police choppers.[61] By 1972 Bell and Hughes were selling 120 police helicopters a year. Fully decked out, these aircraft featured radio communications, high-intensity directional lights, powerful public address systems and in a few cases infrared scopes for night-time surveillance. This early seventies revolution in police equipment marked the first systematic and large-scale "technology transfers" from the military to the civilian police, and (as we shall see later) set an important precedent. The zenith of this new ethos, where military technology *and* organization met in perfect synthesis, was the advent of Special Weapons and Tactics (SWAT) teams.

Started in L.A. in 1966, and quickly duplicated throughout the country, SWAT teams were first designed to deal with snipers and hostage crises. Conceived by an ex-marine, and armed with M-16s or Colt AR-15s, body armor, and tear gas, SWAT teams were at first trained at Camp Pendalton, and then by the FBI. Usually backed up by mobile command centers, SWAT teams were and still are the vanguard of police militarization. In the eighties, SWAT teams would proliferate, and become even more central to routine policing.[62]

"TURNING ON" THE COMMUNITY TO LAW ENFORCEMENT

Along with LEAA-funded paramilitarization of policing, the buildup of the sixties and seventies had a soft side. Many experts saw that the policing crisis of the sixties was as much a matter of *too much* repression as *too little*. Indicative of this dilemma were the findings of the Kerner Commission on Civil Disturbances: "Invariably the incident that ignites disorder arises from police action. Harlem, Watts, Newark and Detroit – all major outbursts of recent years – were precipitated by routine arrests of Negroes for minor offenses by white police."[63] The sordid truth was that the belligerent and racist forces of order were in fact *destabilizing* America's cities; in every ghetto conflagration police brutality against Black people had been the fuse. This breakdown of social control was only the most dramatic example of a growing alienation between citizenry and police. Poor intelligence, lack of community cooperation, the increasing rates of assaults on police officers and miserably low "clear up" rates for many categories of crime were the less dramatic expressions of this problem.

The more sophisticated analysis of America's growing disorder suggested that the LEAA's military-corporate model alone would not restore a politics of obedience. The gendarmerie needed to become more thoroughly insinuated into the communities they policed. And law enforcement, traduced by a decade of its own misdeeds, was in need of re-legitimization.

But this "soft" side of the great leap forward borrowed just as heavily from the military, as did helicopter patrols, computer systems, SWAT teams, and regional anti-riot plans. As in Vietnam, so too in the cities the battle for "hearts and minds" was as essential as any satellite photo or high-tech fire power.

"Community relations efforts," explained one *FBI Bulletin,* "were born in the turbulent sixties as police concentrated on rebuilding their image, gaining community support and cooling the brush fires of violence."[64] At the forefront of this movement was a group of conservative criminologists – most notably James Q. Wilson, George Kelling, and Lawrence Sherman. These "community policing" experts were rather more cynical about crime and disorder than their friends the square-jawed, modernist police administrators and Nixon spin-doctors, who trumpeted a possible "end to crime." The "new criminologists" saw crime and rebellion as endemic in modern American society. The question for them was "what constitutes an effective law-enforcement and order maintenance system."[65]

Effective policing would require that cops re-engineer their social skills: the new school of thought called for sensitivity training and the creation of official communication and input channels for community members. The main intellectual base camp for this new line of reasoning was the Police Foundation in Washington, DC. Launched in 1970 with $30 million from the Ford Foundation, the Police Foundation began developing experiments in what was variously called "community sector policing," "team policing," the "beat commander project," or the "basic car plan." Syracuse, Los Angeles, New York, Cincinnati, Detroit, and Kansas City were some of the first cities to embrace the tactics.[66] In contrast to the professional "emergency response" model – in which cops, no longer walking the beat, answered 911 calls in cars – the "team policing" model pushed responsibility down the police hierarchy and kept beat cops in a (preferably small) regular geographic area. In many ways this was simply a return to the model of the beat cop in close contact with all aspects of community life, but with the added responsibility of initial investigation and a new layer of formal community relations with anti-crime groups, schools, business, and hospitals. Donald Santarelli, head of the LEAA, summed it up best: "there's an obvious need to turn the citizen on to the criminal justice system."[67]

If, in the police world-view, the much storied "militant Negro" was the domestic equivalent to the Viet Cong, then the soft community police strategies – like block watches and police community alliances – were domestic parallels to the "strategic hamlets" of South Vietnam (those militarized villages where a combination of land reform, urban planning, and ideological bombardment was used to pry the people away from the guerrillas). It was in the same spirit that police in the late sixties set about deliberately insinuating themselves into the social life of the ghetto.

Before the riots such efforts were rare; the police struggle for hearts and minds was almost non-existent. For example, the LAPD, like most forces, had no community relations program in the 1950s and early 1960s, not even youth programs. As LAPD's *caudillo* Chief Parker said, "I'm a policeman not a social worker." But when the lid blew off Watts, attitudes changed.

As the smoke cleared, Chief Parker reassigned one hundred staff to "community relations," ordered officers to "fraternize" with Blacks and Latinos, began sensitivity training, and even returned some cops to foot patrol. Despite internal confusion and a leadership struggle after Parker's death in 1966, one thing was clear: the ideological struggle for legitimacy and police penetration of targeted communities was not to be brushed off as mere "social work." By 1971 the department had seventy separate community relations programs including youth sports, partnerships with merchants, community patrols, and neighborhood watch groups.[68] Throughout the country other departments followed suit.

In San Francisco the Police Community Relations (PCR) unit – in direct competition with the Black Panther Party – started holding dances, parties, movies, sporting events, and even job fairs, in the isolated African American neighborhood of Hunter's Point. While the PCR made some inroads into the Black community, it failed in its more important task of schooling the SFPD: Chief Cahill called PCR "a secondary function," while the rank and file called it "Commie relations." And in 1966, when police killed an unarmed youth, Hunter's Point exploded in three days of fiery riots.[69]

As PCR units around the country were "pow-wowing" with "hostiles," police forces – with LEAA funding – set up neighborhood watch groups, block patrols, and civilian auxiliary forces. In St. Louis police set up a secret "Block Watchers" association designed to facilitate anonymous tip-offs; Toledo established REACT, a citizens' surveillance network that maintained radio contact with the police; Oakland set up a similar radio tip-off system, with private funding.[70]

In short, the early seventies saw a buildup in law enforcement's social-psychological arsenal as well as matériel. Of course all these programs had problems, and there were very real natural limits to the affinity between oppressor and oppressed. Unemployed Black youth and white suburbanite (often racist) "pigs" and "rollers" will never be strongly united. Likewise, "block captains" and the volunteer "eyes and ears" of law and order are notoriously flighty; after initial waves of enthusiasm, such civilian cooperation with the police usually wanes. Regardless of the long-term success of individual projects, the general effort to create formal, rationalized "police–community" relations was born – like so much of the present – in reaction to the rebellion and chaos of the sixties: as such it was an attempt to reimpose racial and class control.

STALEMATE: THE FORD AND CARTER YEARS

Watergate effectively marked the beginning of the end of the criminal justice buildup of the late sixties and early seventies. Suddenly the guardians of law and order were on the defensive, and during the second half of the seventies their project temporarily stalled.

The *Congressional Quarterly Almanac* noted that "it was an ironic twist on the 'law and order' theme of the first years of the Nixon administration: the crimes which drew the most attention in the administration's last years were those committed by or charged against the men who held some of the highest offices, including Nixon himself."[72] The siege began in earnest with the March 1973 indictment of Nixon's spooky retinue: Attorney General John Mitchell, former White House Chief of Staff H. R. Haldeman, and former presidential advisor John D. Ehrlichman. By late July 1974 the House Judiciary Committee had recommended impeachment and Nixon was forced to release more tapes which confirmed his involvement in at least the cover-up of the June 1972 break-in of the Democratic National Committee headquarters. With that the Nixon administration collapsed. "Faced with certain impeachment and probable conviction, Nixon resigned as president Aug. 9." A month later President Ford dragged Nixon from the fire with a full pardon.

The magnitude of the scandal put something of a damper on the Ford administration's ability to apply right-wing medicine on either the macro-economic front or in the realm of domestic social control. The LEAA continued its work, but no new pro-police legislative offensives were launched at the federal level. And as the economy continued to drift, public opinion turned away from the issues of crime, violence, and law enforcement, towards the more pressing issue of "economic concerns."[73] In fact, during the next six years significant progressive legislation passed at the federal level, designed to expose and curtail the power of police agencies. Behind it all loomed the specter of Watergate. First to fall was the "no-knock" provision of the 1970 Drug Abuse Prevention and Control Act. Senator Sam J. Ervin, a Democrat from North Carolina, said the laws had been enacted in a "period of hysteria," adding that "The Bill of Rights applies to everyone, even drug peddlers."[74] Later some wiretapping practices were also restricted.

The second half of the seventies also saw the LEAA come under increased criticism for being inept, wasteful, and uncoordinated. Pressure from liberals directed more LEAA money toward the soft side of criminal justice, to projects like public and private delinquency prevention programs and community-based alternatives to incarceration. During 1976 both the House and Senate spent considerable time and energy investigating domestic intelligence; the release of the full report of the Church Committee further damaged the image of America's police agencies. Municipal policing took a direct hit as the nation read of the Knapp Commission's investigation into mass corruption in the New York Police Department. Meanwhile the Ford administration was sounding downright liberal; the official 1976 "Federal Drug Strategy" made mention of poverty, unemployment, alienation, or lack of opportunity as causes of addiction, and noted that alcohol was linked to more violence and accidental death than any other drug. Finally, the Strategy called for "seriously studying" the decriminalization of marijuana.[75]

Carter went even further, announcing to Congress that "I support legislation amending federal law to eliminate all federal criminal penalties for the possession of up to one ounce of marihuana [sic]."[76] And twelve states did decriminalize possession. Carter's new Attorney General Griffin B. Bell spent most of his lobbying efforts on securing more funding for the courts and expanding the number of judges. This clearly facilitated further penetration of the law into everyday life, but it was a fairly innocuous agenda compared to doling out helicopters and new legal powers. The new ethos even pulled in the LEAA, which started directing much of its money towards the infrastructure of the courts and community corrections. By 1978 the LEAA was funding some of the movements it had helped repress. For example, it gave a $100,000 grant to a Black Panther–run youth program.[77]

At the same time, a torrent of revelations about domestic spying and abusive police culminated in the passage of the Foreign Intelligence Surveillance Act, which restricted the federal government's ability to spy on Americans suspected of aiding "foreign powers." The law hardly made amends for the crimes of Watergate, Wounded Knee, and the liquidation of the Panthers, but it was a distinct departure from the ideological and legislative onslaught of the Nixon era.

CHAPTER TWO

FROM CRISIS TO ROLLBACK

> Rising unemployment was a very desirable way of reducing the
> strength of the working classes . . . What was engineered – in
> Marxist terms – was a crisis in capitalism which re-created a
> reserve army of labor, and has allowed the capitalists to make
> high profits ever since.
> Alan Budd, chief economic advisor to Margaret Thatcher[1]

The Nixon-era criminal justice buildup was an attempt to re-engineer a socio-economic system in crisis, a system besieged from below and within. But why was there such a crisis and what exactly were its dimensions? We are all familiar with the story of the sixties. Or are we? As Tom Frank put it, "We understand 'the sixties' almost instinctively as the decade of the big change, the birthplace of our culture, homeland of hip . . ."[2] But "culture" is only one part of the story. There's another, systematically forgotten sixties. Beneath the bohemian boom, Summer of Love, Days of Rage, and May '68 lurks a less flamboyant nuts-and-bolts history of profound economic crisis.

The story of this near-meltdown begins three decades earlier, at the end of the last great economic calamity. With the onset of World War II, the US began a massive economic recovery that pulled the country out of the Depression and increased its industrial capacity by almost 100 percent between 1940 and 1945.[3] After the war, Europe and Japan (the world's two other most industrialized regions) were both devastated: economic recovery required heavy dependence on imports of US goods and capital. This further boosted US industry, which shifted from munitions production to feeding these hungry new markets. The Bretton Woods Agreement of 1944 made the

US dollar the world's dominant currency, allowing US business incredible buying power abroad. In 1946 the American economy produced fully *half* of world output, and by 1951 the US still produced one-third of the planet's commodities.[4]

The unusually high profits afforded by these conditions meant that US capital could buy off organized labor. The postwar boom was so bountiful for American industry that taxes, wages, and profits were all high. The contest between labor and capital of course continued; just after the war capital went on the offensive. One result was the Taft-Hartley Act of 1947, which limited organized labor's right to strike, prohibited secondary boycotts, and prevented communists from being officers in the American Federation of Labor and Congress of Industrial Organizations. Nonetheless the predominantly white industrial working class saw its quality of life improve dramatically after the war.

The postwar boom also caused a number of social and geographic changes that would later become factors in shaping the crisis of the sixties. First there was the baby boom, which meant more economic demand to absorb production, but by the late sixties the babies were becoming a swollen generation of young adults, many of them angry and alienated. Then there was mass, government-subsidized suburbanization, which meant increased living standards for many American workers, thus more consumption and more jobs. But it also meant white flight from the cities. In the South, accelerated mechanization of agriculture led to a huge new wave of African American migration to northern cities. When combined with job-site racism, government and private sector redlining, and white flight, this migration meant the formation of large urban ghettos. Beginning in the fifties and accelerating through the sixties, there was also increased immigration from Latin America and the Caribbean, which, coupled with the wider society's racism, translated into more ghettoization.

The first signs of economic trouble were evident by 1966, when, after two decades of unprecedented high growth rates and previously unheard-of profitability, the unique chemistry of the postwar boom began to turn sour. Importantly, Germany and Japan had recovered from their war-time devastation and had begun supplying their domestic markets as well as aggressively exporting. These new economic competitors had an added edge over the US: their wages were lower, and most of their capital stock was newer and more efficient; their factories were state-of-the-art replacements for old ones that had been bombed to smithereens.

"The fundamental problem faced by US business," write Armstrong *et al.*, "was that rivals in Europe and Japan were accumulating capital at a far faster rate and were doing so on the basis of far lower wage costs."[5] This was due in part to nationalist and social democratic industrialization strategies that quelled financial speculation and capital export, while encouraging businesses to fold their profits back into domestic infrastructure and capital stock, which further accelerated growth rates.[6]

In other words, European and Japanese business accumulated huge quantities of productive capital, which itself produced more of the same. "Between 1955 and 1970 the capital stock in US manufacturing rose by 74 percent; in the major European countries the rise was 115 percent, and in Japan it was 500 percent."[7] Of course war-ravaged Europe and Japan were both starting from a much smaller base, but the point still stands: their rates of growth and investment were higher than America's. In 1955, Japanese manufacturing capital per worker (an index of mechanization) was about $5,000 a head (in 1980 prices). By 1970, Japanese manufacturing capital per worker was around $13,000 per head. Though this was still only half the value of manufacturing capital per American worker, Japanese and European wages were much lower than in the States. This meant Japanese and European rates of productive output and profitability per hour of labor were increasing. In 1960 American hourly manufacturing labor costs, including social security contributions, were roughly *three times as high* as in Europe, and *ten times as high* as labor costs in Japan.[8]

These low wages meant intensified international competition for American manufacturing. For example, Bluestone and Harrison point out that "in 1960 the Japanese sold a total of 38,809 cars worldwide! By 1979 the Japanese were exporting nearly $26 billion worth of cars, stereos, video recorders, televisions, machine tools and other goods to the US."[9] By the late 1960s and early 1970s so-called newly industrialized countries (NICs) – such as Korea, Hong Kong, and Taiwan – started joining the game in force and began rapid export-oriented industrialization, thus further filling global markets with commodities of all sorts. Assisting America's new competitors was the high value of the dollar, which made imports comparatively cheap; this was due to the Bretton Woods Agreement of 1944, which fixed the dollar to the price of gold.

OVER-ACCUMULATION

What bounty. But was there enough demand? By the mid sixties consumer spending was tapering off; those classes that could buy mass-produced commodities could not keep up with the pace of output.

Some statistics may help clarify the dilemma: Between 1953 and 1987 the number of homes with air-conditioning and automatic dishwashers increased from 1.3 percent and 3 percent to 64 percent and 43 percent, respectively.[10] By 1970, 99 percent of American homes had refrigerators, electric irons, and radios; more than 90 percent had washing machines, vacuum cleaners, and toasters. In short the slowdown of the seventies was caused in large part by the saturation of markets for consumer durables, the very business lines that had been the heart of the postwar expansion. As one economist put it:

> Saturation in one market led to saturation in others as producers looked abroad when the possibilities for domestic expansion were exhausted. The results were simultaneous export drives by companies in all advanced countries, with similar, technologically sophisticated products going into one another's markets . . . Increasing exports . . . from developing countries such as Taiwan, Korea, Mexico and Brazil further increased the congestion of mass markets in the advanced economies.[11]

By the early seventies, all this postwar growth and industrialization meant chronic *excess capacity on a global scale*. It was a classic crisis of "over-accumulation." In other words, capitalism was suffocating from industrial success.

In this economic environment, American manufacturing and merchandising firms found it increasingly difficult to maintain their amazing (if not aberrant) postwar profitability.[12] With so many commodities already in existence, the price of new commodities necessarily declined. To maintain profits in an environment of declining prices, businesses had to expand output, which only drove down prices further. In short there was too much capital looking for profitable investment outlets, and not enough profitable investment opportunities. (Such conditions lend themselves to speculation and massive "debt formation," but more on that later.)

LABOR AND THE CRISIS

At the same time that the US economy began to slow under the weight of over-accumulation, surplus labor supplies began drying up. Unemployment rates were down and the amount of time unemployed workers had to spend between jobs was declining.

> The civilian unemployment rate fell from 5.5 percent at the 1959 business cycle peak to 3.8 percent at the 1966 peak. The average duration of unemployment (as calculated by the U.S. Bureau of Labor Statistics) fell from 14.4 weeks in 1959 to . . . its low of 7.8 weeks in 1969, set[ting] a historic record . . . [And] during the [1966–73] period, the rate of increase of total worker compensation per hour, including not only wages but all benefits, rose from 4.1 percent to 6.8 percent.[13]

Tight labor markets meant that wages continued to *rise* even as corporate revenues and profits *declined*.

It is axiomatic that low unemployment increases working class power in relation to employers. But it can be tricky measuring such power. However, Juliet Schor has created one useful indicator called "the cost of job loss," that is, the amount of income (measured in terms of potentially missed wages) that the average worker loses between jobs. Another indicator of "the cost of job loss" is the ratio of quits to layoffs and quits to job openings.[14] When the number of workers quitting far exceeds the number of workers laid off or fired, one can assume that employers have lost a degree of control over workers.

That is exactly what happened during the late sixties and early seventies; the ratio of quits to layoffs reached 2:1, almost twice as high as in the late fifties. And the percentage of workers involved in some strike activity between 1966 and 1973 reached 40 percent. All this despite unemployment creeping up from 4 to 8 percent.[15]

The boom years, plus lots of hard struggle, brought much of American labor unprecedented affluence and power. As the crisis unfolded, working class power was expressed in overt and organized, as well as organic and clandestine, ways. Ford Motor Company claimed that absenteeism in its plants doubled – and in some plants even tripled – during the 1960s. In one factory, workers wrote messages to management on their machinery, such as "Treat Me with Respect and I Will Give You Top Quality with Less Effort."[16] As Michael Perelman points out, the new emphasis on creativity and freedom — plus the cultural chaos and cynicism generated by the war, riots, and police repression — began to express itself on the shop floor as mass insubordination. Increased sabotage, slowdowns, and wildcat strikes became the industrial equivalent of "fragging" officers in Vietnam — where many of the young working class malcontents had no doubt first learned to disobey. Halberstam gives an account of a Ford manager in a plant plagued with absenteeism and sabotage. Among the plant's employees was a young man who consistently skipped work on Fridays or Mondays. When finally confronted by management as to why he worked a four-day week the young man replied: "Because I can't make a living working three days a week."[17] He spoke for a generation; working class power translated into an informal economy-wide slowdown, which meant a measured decline in productivity.

Expressions of working class power were not merely confined to malingering and individual resistance; transportation, mining, and construction industries were routinely brought to their knees by strikes throughout the early seventies. Emblematic of the times was a 1970 laborers' strike in Kansas City which, according to the Builders Association, halted 95 percent of the city's commercial construction projects for over three months. "There are very widespread strikes in construction," commented a perturbed Secretary of Labor George Shultz, "settlements are coming in. They are at extremely high levels. They're higher than last year, which was an extraordinary year . . . This a formula for disaster."[18] That same year grave diggers, school teachers, and sanitation workers struck in numerous American cities; truckers stalled commerce with a series of strikes in thirty-seven cities, while air traffic controllers sowed chaos with a long "sick-out."

Then more than 200,000 of the nation's 740,000 postal workers illegally walked off the job. As local after local joined the wildcat strike, panic set in; the press predicted a national disaster. In desperation Nixon sent in troops to move the mails, telling the nation that the issue was nothing less than "the survival of a government based upon law."[19] But even the onslaught of military scabs was marred by lack of discipline: of the 26,000 National Guard, Army, and Air Force personnel called out, only 16,000 showed, and many of those "got mixed reviews as postal workers," preferring to grab empty mail bags and "disappear for the day." According to *Time*, "The Government's authority was placed in question and the well-being of business, institutions and individuals in jeopardy."[20]

The rail industry was also in constant turmoil. A last-minute act of Congress ended one nationwide strike, but walkouts and "selective strikes" continued. And throughout 1971, 20 to 25 percent of all freight shipments were delayed, causing food spoilage, the emergency slaughter of underfed poultry, and layoffs in numerous other industries.[21] Longshoremen closed both coasts for months at a time, and fishing was also hit by labor action. For much of the summer of 1971 commercial draggers in New Bedford, the fourth largest fishing port in the nation, refused to work.[22] Even workers at Disneyland planned a strike.[23] In fact in 1970 over sixty-six million days of labor time were lost due to work stoppages, the highest yearly loss due to unrest since 1946.[24]

But tight labor markets and over-accumulation were not the only causes of productivity slowdown; poor management and lack of new investment contributed as well. Instead of retraining and retooling, American capital shifted increasingly towards speculation in real estate and stocks. Also clouding the economic outlook were rising fuel prices, which began creeping up even before OPEC's 1973 price shock. Rising oil costs meant rising input costs, as raw materials and transportation became more expensive. Together these components translated into rising *per-unit costs*.[25]

Capitalism had always been prone to cycles of boom and bust, but this time the pattern was different. As the crisis wore on, unemployment began to rise sharply; from below 4 percent in 1969, joblessness pitched up to above 7 percent in 1974.[26] Yet wages and prices did not fall as had been expected. In fact Barry Bosworth, who later worked as an economist for the Carter administration's Council on Wage and Price Stability, noted that "the wage rate increases [during the crisis] had actually accelerated slightly despite the high unemployment."[27] This combination of stagnant growth and rising inflation became known as "stagflation."

The crippling combination of rising consumer prices, rising wages, increasing stagnation, and unemployment continued even after the 1973 oil-shock recession. Nixon tried to discipline labor with a recession in 1971 but was too worried about re-election to really turn the screws. In fact real wages in the US continued to rise, though with diminishing vigor, until 1979.[28]

The historically consistent inverse relationship between wage levels and unemployment is known among economists as the Phillips curve.[29] For the first time in American history the two components of this economic "law" were out of whack. Unemployment was rising yet wages did not fall in reaction.

Also fueling inflation were the government's Keynesian spending habits. Having run the equivalent of a budget surplus in the early 1960s, Johnson began to go into debt with the escalation of the Vietnam war and (to a much lesser extent) the war on poverty; increasingly such projects were paid for by simply printing money.[30] Likewise, Kennedy's tax cuts had increased liquidity during the sixties, which spurred spending and thus inflation.

From the early 1950s through 1965, the annual inflation rate hovered at around 2 percent. Moreover, this average was quite constant, containing neither periods of great price rises nor plunges. But from 1966 onward, inflation rose steadily, peaking at around 6 percent in 1969–70 before it dipped slightly in 1971–72 (when Nixon, his eye on re-election the next year, engineered a quick recession and then imposed across-the-board wage and price controls). Thereafter consumer inflation resumed a steady upward spiral to a peak of almost 12 percent in 1979.[31]

THE PROFIT SQUEEZE

The economic indicator of paramount importance in this story is, of course, the average rate of profit: the *raison d'être* of market economies. The crisis of the late sixties and seventies sent corporate profits into steep decline. Harrison and Bluestone explain: "From a peak of nearly 10 percent in 1965, the average net after-tax profit rate of domestic non-financial corporations plunged to less than 6 percent during the second half of the 1970s – a decline of more than a third."[32] After twenty years of continual expansion during the long postwar recovery, profits began to sag in 1966 and continued to decline steadily until 1974, until they reached an average low of around 4.5 percent.[33] The same pattern of a 30 percent plunge in profits was true from Germany to Japan, as all advanced capitalist countries experienced an after-tax profit decline of between 20 and 30 percent.

This plunge in corporate fortunes had myriad causes and locations other than at the point of production. Taxes and increasing state regulation were particularly bad for profits. Since the New Deal the state had played an increasing role in the economy, but the move towards a bastardized American version of social democracy accelerated considerably during the sixties and seventies. Between 1964 and 1979 the federal government enacted sixty-two health and safety laws which protected workers and consumers, while thirty-two other laws were passed protecting the environment and regulating energy use. Many of these state interventions happened on Nixon's watch. Between 1970 and 1973 Nixon presided over the creation of the Environmental Protection Agency, the Occupational Safety and Health Administration, the Consumer Safety Administration, and the Mine Enforcement and Safety Administration. The direct result of this new regime of regulation was a massive increase in the cost of business.[34]

Though it was Nixon who signed these agencies into law, he did so under duress; massive social movements had forced his hand. Estimates of the added costs to business of these social regulations were enormous. Two Brookings Institution scholars estimated that by 1983 pollution controls alone had cost American firms anywhere from $13 to $38 billion, while the bill on health and human safety was probably between $7 and $17 billion.[35]

At one level the crisis involved a simple contest between the classes. The share of output that went to profits *declined* while the share going to everything else, including the social wage, *increased*. The working class was too powerful and, from the management point of view, needed disciplining. Strangely, many Marxists resist giving the working class its due in respect to the crisis; in fact some even see emphasizing the role of working class power as tantamount to blaming the working class as the cause of the crisis. Robert Brenner, while acknowledging the upward pressure on wages and increased militancy, blames the profit squeeze on international competition and rising state and local taxes. He is correct on the first count but wrong in not seeing increased taxation as the booty of worker and consumer-led class struggle. Regardless of the *exact* etiology of the profit slump, one thing is for sure, *the solution* to the crisis was, as we shall see, to attack labor. Losses by capital, regardless of their origin, can always be recuperated by diminishing labor's share of output. However, an effective business counteroffensive would not come for some time.

CONFRONTATION DELAYED

By the early seventies key elements in the American ruling classes had realized the need for change. First on the list of targets were the new state structures that empowered and, in the eyes of some, spoiled the working class. Health and safety regulations, free higher education, job training, anti-poverty programs, legal aid, humanities grants for trouble makers, and welfare benefits for striking workers![36] All these social democratic reforms were part of the problem, and costing enormous sums. As the Trilateral Commission's 1975 "report on governability" put it, there was a "crisis of democracy" which, though coded, meant that there was *too much* democracy.[37]

The solution, according to New Right theorists like Milton Friedman, Lawrence Mead, and George Gilder, was to cut government. That is, cut taxes on the corporations and the wealthy, deregulate health and safety regulations, and slash state spending on education, welfare, and social programs. And to initiate this the government would have to plunge the economy into a "cold bath recession" so as to scare and discipline labor. But throughout the seventies the Keynesian consensus was too strong: monetarist austerity and a deregulatory war on labor and consumers had to wait until the accession of Ronald Reagan.

REAGANOMICS: THE RIOT OF THE RICH

The crisis of the seventies was finally dealt with in 1979 when Carter appointed Paul Volcker as Chairman of the Federal Reserve; it was the opening salvo of a "new class war." Late in 1979 Volcker dramatically tightened the money supply by boosting interest rates, thus cutting borrowing power and buying power, and diminishing economic activity in general. This monetarist squeeze accelerated when Reagan took office, until interest rates, which had been 7.9 percent in 1979, reached 16.4 percent in 1981. As a direct result, the US economy plunged into its most severe recession since the Great Depression.

In the eyes of Paul Volcker this was a good thing. For the economic stagnation and low profits of the seventies to be vanquished the American people would have to learn how to work harder for less; Reagan's plan was to cut taxes on the rich, gut welfare, and attack labor. As Volcker told the *New York Times*: "The standard of living of the average American has to decline . . . I don't think you can escape that."[38]

In 1981 as the recession was reaching new depths and many in Congress were calling for relief, Volcker again explained the utility of his artificial economic disaster: "in an economy like ours with wages and salaries accounting for two-thirds of all costs, sustaining progress [in price reduction] will need to be reflected in moderation of growth of nominal wages. The general indexes of worker compensation still show relatively little improvement, and prices of many services with high labor content continue to show high rates of increase."[39] The chairman's goal was labor discipline. The recession − though hard on many businesses, particularly small firms − had not yet achieved its purpose: wages were still rising.

Not until the behemoth First Illinois Bank collapsed under the weight of its bad loans and Mexico seriously threatened a default on its $90 billion foreign debt did Volcker relent and open the Fed's spigots, easing interest rates and making credit available throughout the economy, thus stimulating economic activity. But according to Harrison and Bluestone,

> the deep recession did precisely what it was designed to. With more than ten million people unemployed in 1982 it was impossible for organized labor to maintain wage standards let alone raise them. Reductions in wages rippled from one industry to the next and from the center of the country outward. The real average weekly wage fell more than 8 percent between 1979 and 1982, and failed to recover at all in the next five years. Essentially, with wage growth arrested by unemployment, what growth occurred during the Reagan period rebounded mostly to the profits side of the capital–labor ledger.[40]

Before the 1980−82 cold-bath recession, wage freezes and pay cuts in unionized industries had been almost non-existent. Since 1964, and from World War II on, wages had been rising more or less consistently. In 1980 not a single union contract negotiation had ended in a pay freeze or cut. By 1982, 44 percent of new contracts conceded wage freezes or outright cuts.[41] Meanwhile the official unemployment rate, always an under-estimate, reached 10 percent.[42] This was Reagan's monetarist hammer falling on the middle class expectations of organized labor and, by extension, all workers.

Simultaneously, the Reagan administration began looking for a direct confrontation with the American Federation of Labor and Congress of Industrial Organizations (AFL-CIO). A strike by the nation's air traffic controllers in 1981 provided the perfect opportunity.

After pledging his support to the Professional Air Traffic Controllers Organization (PATCO) during the election campaign, Reagan greeted the strike with an executive order firing all 11,000 striking controllers. It was entirely in keeping with the administration's preference for scorched earth foreign policy and apocalyptic rhetoric. This sent a clear signal to management, and labor, that the war was on and that the state would back business to the hilt. University of California labor economist Harley Shaiken, describing the ensuing assault on labor, noted:

> We've always seen aggressive management in many industries. What's different now is that a number of companies who for most of the last 40 years operated on the basis of a certain social contract are redefining the terms of that contract. It isn't just a back alley machine shop with 200 workers going after its union. It's AT&T violating seniority rules. It's Caterpillar threatening to replace its work force . . . Public companies that would have shunned these tactics a decade ago are now using them.[43]

Reagan also began stacking the National Labor Relations Board (NLRB) — the federal body which arbitrates labor disputes — with anti-union activists.

The Reagan administration also sanctioned the use of contingent labor; it even set an example in 1985 by allowing the government to hire temp workers at below union wages. Then in 1986 the Reagan administration legalized homework, a practice many trade unions argued would lead to self-exploitation and child labor, and would undermine established minimum levels of health and safety.[44] And that is exactly what happened. "In 1988 the U.S. Labor Department reported twenty thousand child-labor-law violations, up from thirteen thousand in 1986." New York State noted a 500 percent increase in the number of New York City sweatshops employing children.[45] According to the US Department of Labor, the number of minors illegally employed in sweatshops increased 128 percent in the second half of the 1980s. The United Farm Workers of America estimates that 800,000 children and teenagers work as migrant laborers. The American Academy of Pediatrics estimates that 100,000 children are injured on the job in the United States each year.[46]

Along with the assaults on labor, the Reagan administration did its part to eviscerate social spending. In 1982 alone Reagan cut the real value of welfare by 24 percent, slashed the budget for child nutrition by 34 percent, reduced funding for school milk programs by 78 percent, urban development action grants by 35 percent, and educational block grants by 38 percent.[47]

In 1981 Reagan abolished the Comprehensive Employment and Training Act, throwing 400,000 unemployed on to the job market with the stroke of a pen. Cutbacks in Aid to Families with Dependent Children (AFDC) payments and tighter eligibility rules added another 500,000 unemployed to the job market.[48] These cuts were merely the opening act in the continued demolition of welfare, which only accelerated through the 1990s, with Clinton's creation of Workfare and Temporary Aid to Needy Families (TANF), a scaled-back version of AFDC with a three-year time limit.

Though dressed up as a moral crusade against "the culture of poverty" which hurts the poor (particularly poor Blacks) by encouraging laziness, the Reagan administration's assaults on social spending were really about lowering the costs of doing business. As Piven and Cloward pointed out in *The New Class War*, "Income maintenance programs are coming under assault because they limit profits by enlarging the bargaining power of workers with employers . . . The connection between the income-maintenance programs, the labor market and profits is indirect, but not complicated."[49]

George Gilder, neoconservative theorist and afflatus of the Reagan revolution, put it more simply: "the poor must work hard, and they must work harder than the classes above them."[50]

POWER TO THE RICH!

The wealthy, meanwhile, were enjoying a state-subsidized renaissance. By 1987 Reagan had delivered the richest 1 percent of the population a net tax saving of 25 percent, while the poorest tenth of workers saw 20 percent more of their incomes "swallowed by taxes."[51] The combination of tax cuts, welfare gutting, assaults on labor, and the deregulation of banking and finance created an estimated 2,500 to 5,000 new millionaires and gave "untold added wealth to the nearly 500,000 people who already belonged to that elite circle."[52] Overall, average after-tax profit rates of the 1980s recovered somewhat to an average of 6 percent.[53]

As the state disciplined labor and pampered investors, American corporations began accelerating their international quest for cheap labor. American manufacturing firms had been setting up shop abroad since the mid 1960s;

wage pressures at home drove them offshore while technological innovations in container shipping, jumbo air-transport, and telecommunications facilitated their departure. But deindustrialization really took off during the late 1970s and 1980s. American manufacturers exported jobs by moving entire plants, or entire industries, or subcontracting key parts of industries, to foreign locations where social and environmental regulation was minimal and wages low. For example, in 1972, when the falling rate of profit was beginning to look permanent, the average US worker made $1,220 a month, while Singaporean workers made only $60 a month, South Koreans only $68, and Taiwanese a mere $45 a month.[54]

Between 1965 and 1992 corporations such as GM, Fisher-Price, Trico, Parker-Hannifin, Xerox, Ford, IBM, and GE, moved 1,800 plants, employing 500,000 workers "south of the border." That same year Americans purchased 2.6 million color TV sets. By 1991, Americans were buying twenty-one million sets a year. A year later the last US-based manufacturer of color TV sets, Zenith, departed for Reynosa, Mexico.[55]

As one American CEO put it: "We are able to beat the foreign competition, because we are the foreign competition."[56] Between 1980 and 1985, the Department of Labor estimated that some 2.3 million manufacturing jobs disappeared for good.[57] As industrial jobs disappeared so did attendant retail activity, the local tax base, and municipal employment.

By the mid eighties deindustrialization and the associated decline in local retail, building, and services had dramatically transformed the urban landscape of the Northeast and Midwest. Although for most deindustrialized regions the "hollowing out" of the 1980s was just the dramatic finish to a long slow decline, nonetheless the final calamities appeared as sudden economic implosions.[58]

For example, Detroit, the symbolic center of industrial America, lost half its population during the eighties; as buildings gave way to empty lots, wild game, particularly pheasant and deer, became common hazards on the city's thoroughfares. As in many towns, whites almost completely abandoned the central city; the 1990 census found that Detroit was 80 percent African American and had an official poverty rate of 33 percent.[59] In 1983 depopulation was already so bad and the number of empty buildings and houses so great, that the traditional night of pranks before Halloween became a three-day carnival of arson. At least 800 primarily empty buildings were put to the torch. Over the next five years this practice known as Devil's Night became almost institutionalized, drawing bands of pyromaniacs, journalists, and white suburbanites (some of whom were off-duty fire fighters).[60]

Throughout the country, industrial cities saw a mass exodus of working and middle class residents to the suburbs or Sunbelt. At first the emigrants were predominantly Caucasian, but soon the Black middle class also fled. The result was a massive expansion in the number of urban census tracts that qualify as ghettos (that is, having over 40 percent poverty). Chicago saw its number of ghetto census tracts increase by 61.5 percent between 1980 and 1990. Cities like Cleveland, Philadelphia, and Boston saw similar changes. Overall, the number of African Americans who found themselves living in "ghetto" census tracts due to middle class flight grew by one-third during the eighties, to a total of six million.[61]

As the traditional industrial jobs base of many cities eroded, low wage service work proliferated. But this employment has largely ignored African Americans. Hiring and firing practices in the service sector are more racist than in industrial employment.[62] Sociologists note the "deepening of black–white linguistic opposition" as reasons why white employers avoid African Americans for face-to-face service positions. We might add that two decades of crime-coded racism and fearmongering reportage has certainly fueled racism in the labor market, regardless of speaking styles. In general people of color are 50 percent more likely to be laid off than whites.[63] Municipal austerity has added to the devastation of Black employment; public employment was one of the few realms where affirmative action was enforced with any vigor. Thus public employment, once a bedrock of African American employment, has suffered serious rollback under the ideology of "lean" and "reinvented" government.[64]

William Julius Wilson has noted that, while urban poverty is old, massive joblessness is not. "The consequences of neighborhood joblessness are more devastating than those of high neighborhood poverty."[65] Work is, after all, not just a means to sustenance, it is also a form of social control: it occupies our time, structures our lives, and channels passions. When work disappears, social organization breaks down. The second wave of the criminal justice crackdown is fundamentally about controlling the newly "deregulated" populations created by economic restructuring.

The neoliberal rollback is also a global agenda: Reagan's proxy wars in Latin America, IMF structural adjustment programs, and increased foreign capital penetration of Third World markets have caused massive social and economic disruption. The refugees from war and market expansion first seek haven in the cities of the South, then they head north. This "peripheraliza-tion of the core" helped swell the ranks of the American proletariat and pau-pers (and, as we shall see later, requires a whole policing infrastructure of its own).[66]

Overall, "Reaganomics" increased class and racial polarization, destroyed inner cities, sacked public education and public health services, created epidemic homelessness, increased exploitation of workers, and caused the intensified spatial concentration of a permanently unemployed class. By the mid eighties the contours of this strange new economic geography even extended to the door of Reagan's country redoubt, Rancho del Cielo. In 1985 Santa Barbara's manicured parks and the dry gullies between its mansions hosted an estimated 2,000 "displaced people" in a population of 75,000.[67] By 1987 an estimated two million Americans were homeless.[68] In fact, Reagan created whole new classes of poor and desperate people. It was in response to this social crisis, created by the elite response to the profit crisis, that a new wave of criminal justice crackdown began.

CHAPTER THREE

A WAR FOR ALL SEASONS: THE RETURN OF LAW AND ORDER

> One has to remark that men ought either be
> well treated or crushed . . .
> Nicolo Machiavelli, *The Prince*

Along with great economic transformations, the Reagan revolution kicked off a new round of criminal justice militarization. While the Nixon-era buildup had been a counterrevolutionary war by way of criminal justice and a technocratic reflex to social chaos, the second, ongoing, wave in the crackdown is not so overtly political; it is not about suppressing an American Mau Mau. Rather, it has been about managing and containing the new surplus populations created by neoliberal economic policies, even when these population are not in rebellion.

The quest for renewed profitability in the face of ongoing crises led down the path of brutal, short-term, upward redistribution of wealth. The post-liberal, post-welfare economic equation created more poverty and more opulence. Thus reproducing and governing the social order has required more repression, more segregation, and more criminal justice.

WAR ON DRUGS: POLICING THE "NEW RABBLE"

Years ago criminologist Steven Spritzer described the cast-off populations produced by capitalism as either "social junk" or "social dynamite."[1] A rather blunt and painful nomenclature to be sure, but Spritzer makes useful distinctions. These different segments of the "surplus population" require uniquely tailored strategies of social control.

"Social junk" are those whose spirits and minds are shattered; they are the deinstitutionalized mentally ill, alcoholics, drug addicts, and cast-off impoverished seniors; the lonely, beaten drifters with no expectations of a future and little will to fight. This population – the collateral damage of unchecked market economics – is managed through spatial and social containment. They must be driven away from the beaches, malls, and tony shopping areas of resort towns, financial districts, and the pleasure zones of themepark cities. They are, as Mathiesen put it, "sand in the machine." They pose an ontological threat to market social relations but they rarely coalesce into an organized political threat.

The other segment of the surplus population – "social dynamite" – are those who pose an actual or potential political challenge. They are that population which threatens to explode: the impoverished low-wage working class and unemployed youth who have fallen below the statistical radar, but whose spirits are not broken and whose expectations for a decent life and social inclusion are dangerously alive and well. They are the class that suffers from "relative deprivation."[2] Their poverty is made all the more unjust because it is experienced in contrast to the spectacle of opulence and the myths of social mobility and opportunity. This is the class from which the Black Panthers and the Young Lords arose in the sixties and from which sprang the gangs of the 1980s. In the 1930s this same class provided the brawn for the Communist Party–organized Unemployed Councils that forcibly stopped evictions in New York's Lower East Side.[3]

Thus social dynamite is a threat to the class and racial hierarchies upon which the private enterprise system depends. This group cannot simply be swept aside. Controlling them requires both a defensive policy of containment and an aggressive policy of direct attack and active destabilization. They are contained and crushed, confined to the ghetto, demoralized and pilloried in warehouse public schools, demonized by a lurid media, sent to prison, and at times dispatched by lethal injection or police bullets. This is the class – or more accurately the caste, because they are increasingly people of color – which must be constantly undermined, divided, intimidated, attacked, discredited, and ultimately kept in check with what Fanon called the "language of naked force."

REAGAN'S WAR

As headlines in the the early eighties filled with tales of recession, communist threats, and a new *kulturkampf*, Reagan was quietly ramping up his war on drugs. He boosted the budget for domestic repression, doubling the FBI's funding while the US Bureau of Prisons got a 30 percent increase and the DEA saw moderate budget expansion.[4] At the same time the legal reins of police began to loosen; federal use of wiretaps shot up 22 percent between 1981 and 1982, while the duration of the average tap went from twenty-four hours to twenty-six days.[5] Meanwhile Reagan's Chief of Staff Ed Meese and Attorney General William French Smith started demanding changes in the criminal code. "We must increase the power of the prosecutors," insisted Meese.[6]

As a harbinger of things to come, Reagan launched the massive multi-agency South Florida Task Force, under the leadership of Vice President and former CIA top spook, George Bush. The program became a template for the later and larger Organized Crime Drug Enforcement Task Force Program. By 1984 the OCDETF had created a series of thirteen regionalized federal operations based in "core" cities including New York, San Francisco, Detroit, Baltimore, Houston, San Diego, and Los Angeles. The task forces brought together 200 US attorneys, an army of paralegals and 1,200 agents from the DEA, Customs, FBI, ATF, IRS, and US Marshals service.

At first the Organized Crime Drug Enforcement Task Forces went after traffickers and distribution networks, but soon the Justice Department announced that these elite drug cops were targeting users, because, as one deputy attorney general put it, users are "as much a part of the conspiracy chain as the person who distributes . . ."[7] By mid 1983 OCDETF operations had produced 1,150 indictments.[8]

Meanwhile, governors and attorney generals at the state level launched their own drug war offensives. Most notable, in part because it continues to this day, was California's Campaign Against Marijuana Production (CAMP), an annual paramilitary occupation of northern California's Humboldt and Mendocino Counties by the DEA, California National Guard, Highway Patrol, local sheriffs, and even some volunteer LAPD officers. Beginning in the late summer harvest seasons of 1983, this verdant terrain brought an onslaught of helicopters, checkpoints, warrantless house-to-house searches, and massive operational sweeps by armed drug warriors, in search of remote crops and basement grow rooms. In the skies above, U2 spy planes flew reconnaissance, mapping the forests and hamlets around Eureka and Fort Bragg as if they were the rebel-infested back country of El Salvador's Morazon and Cabañas provinces;[9] Missouri, Florida, and Maine launched similar assaults.[10]

After the 1984 raiding season, California Attorney General and champion of state wiretapping John Van De Camp claimed to have extirpated more than one million pounds of pot – four times the previous year's haul. He described reefer farming as a "violent" $2 billion a year "industry" and boasted that "anytime you make the dopers mad . . . you know that we're doing something right."[11]

While CAMP and the OCDETF were not directly involved with policing the ghetto poor, they nonetheless served the purposes of class and racial containment by building up the state's repressive infrastructure and invoking the legitimizing spectacle of a grave narcotics threat. But, as we shall see, the telos of the drug war was toward increasingly racist and urbanized forms of enforcement.

REAGAN'S COURT

The early eighties also saw a veritable coup in the judiciary, as Reagan stacked the federal bench with mean-spirited, anti-crime, anti-drug zealots, who in turn began handing down law that, as Meese had wished, "empowered the prosecution." From the US Supreme Court came several crucial decisions, among them *Gates vs. Illinois*, which made it easier for police to obtain search warrants based on anonymous tips. No longer would cops have to do tedious investigations in order to get warrants and launch raids; now anonymous tips (and perhaps police-confected tips) would be sufficient. Another key decision was *United States vs. Leon,* which allowed police to use defective warrants (that is, warrants with inadequate probable cause or factual errors) to obtain evidence. More generally, *Leon* gave police a "good-faith" exception to the "exclusionary rule" which requires that courts "suppress" or disregard illegally obtained evidence.

The legal right to suppress tainted evidence keeps police power in check – it is a fundamental safeguard against the slippery slope towards warrantless searches, torturous interrogations, and legal frame-ups – yet Meese decried it as "the bane of law enforcement."[12]

The year of the *Leon* decision, 1984, also brought an election-year spirit of anti-drug jihad. Democratic presidential candidate Walter Mondale campaigned on promises to use the military to fight drugs.[13] At the same time, Meese – who had questioned the existence of hunger in America, deplored legal aid to the poor, and called the American Civil Liberties Union a "criminal lobby" – was fighting for confirmation as US attorney general.[14] The *Washington Post* speculated that if confirmed, Meese (then under investigation by a special prosecutor for taking kickbacks)[15] would "take an activist approach" to criminal justice; it noted that he had been

> a strong behind-the-scenes booster of the Justice Department, lobbying for higher budgets there while other domestic agencies were being cut. He also has lobbied strongly in Congress for broader anti-crime legislation and is believed to have been a major force behind creation of the President's Commission on Organized Crime and the drug task force network now in operation nationwide.[16]

As a young DA in Alameda County, California, Meese had called anti-war protesters "yellow-bellied cowards," prosecuted student leader Mario Savio, and spent his spare time cruising Oakland's ghettos with local cops.

On the campaign trail, president Reagan made it clear that his next four years would bring a renewed anti-crime crackdown. "Permissive attitudes are giving way to a new sense of responsibility," declared Reagan triumphantly.[17] Meese would take this victim-blaming ethos to new heights.

THE 1984 CRIME BILL: THE WILL TO LOOT

The election year brought a new and massive federal onslaught. Thanks to the last-minute chicanery of Republican Congressman Dan Lungren of California, a package of long-developing crime legislation was tacked on to the 1985 appropriations bill. Much of the bill could have become law earlier, in 1982 and 1983, but Reagan vetoed earlier attempts because he opposed creating a cabinet-level drug czar on the grounds that it would have disrupted the chain of command within existing agencies such as the FBI and DEA.[18] But the 1984 package, known as the Comprehensive Crime Control Act (CCCA), dropped the drug czar idea.[19]

The raft of get-tough provisions was described as "the most far reaching anti-crime measures enacted since the 1968 Omnibus Crime Control and Safe Streets Act."[20] Ted Kennedy called it "the most far reaching law-enforcement reform in our history." And the legislation's other main champion, Strom Thurmond, called it the beginning of "a new era."[21] Rudolph Giuliani, then a prosecutor in the newly invigorated Justice Department, explained that "in each area of the bill, there is a slight shift in favor of the Government and away from the criminal defendant."[22]

The bill was indeed the beginning of a new era. Among other things, the act created federal preventive detention so that judges could deny bail to defendants, established mandatory minimum sentences and a "sentencing commission" to devise strict sentencing guidelines, eliminated federal parole, and toughened mandatory minimum sentences for use of firearms in the commission of federal crimes. It also increased the maximum fines leveled in drug cases, scaled back the insanity defense (recently publicized by the straight-shooting John Hinkley), boosted the penalties for political hostage taking and other acts of "terrorism," and, with early incarnations of computer hackers and "phone freaks" like Kevin Mitnick and Kevin Paulsen in mind, made it a federal crime to misuse credit cards or computers.

One of the CCCA's most profound features was the new asset forfeiture statutes, which expanded the government's ability to seize property and cash from convicted – or even accused – drug dealers, in civil or criminal court.[23]

Though first permitted in 1970, with the invention of RICO cases and "continuing criminal enterprises," seizing a defendant's assets was relatively rare.[24] Between 1970 and 1979 the federal government took only $30 million from defendants.[25] Forfeiture laws were again expanded in 1978, allowing the seizure of assets even when connections to drug crimes was quite attenuated. However, police were slow to take advantage of the law. In fact the General Accounting Office issued a 75-page report in 1981 criticizing the federal government for not making "asset forfeiture a widely used law enforcement technique."[26] Reagan's new criminal justice regime took heed, producing a modest increase in seizures. But it was the 1984 crime bill that revolutionized law enforcement's use of forfeitures and sanctioned an insidious police dependency on drug money.[27]

After 1984 state and local police agencies have had the option to try their narcotics cases in federal court and in exchange keep as much as 90 percent of all the "drug tainted" property they can seize. Furthermore, these forfeiture proceedings can be conducted in civil court as an *in rem* procedure *against the property* (as opposed to being tried in criminal court against the owner). This use of civil law in the drug war marked yet another momentous expansion of police power, in part because the burden of proof in civil court is much lower than in criminal court. Civil cases are decided on "a preponderance of the evidence," while in criminal court guilt must be proven "beyond a reasonable doubt." And finally, the law allows seizure of assets in a civil proceeding *regardless of whether or not criminal charges are even filed.*[28]

The new laws also allowed for streamlined, out-of-court "administrative seizure" of assets valuing less than $100,000, without even going to civil court. Instead, the suspect is given thirty days to file a protest, and if he or she fails to do so, the police simply keep all confiscated assets.[29] Needless to say, the new laws created a tremendous incentive for state and local police to collaborate with federal agencies and to try drug cases in federal court (where, by the late eighties, sentences tended to be longer).

Almost immediately local police in law-and-order hot spots like Florida, Georgia, New York, and California formed special assets-seeking narcotics squads and mounted full-scale operations of pillaging and plunder. Nationwide the gross receipts of all seizures shot from about $100 million in 1981 to over $1 billion by fiscal year 1987.[30] By 1990, forty-nine states had created their own forfeiture laws, and a total of between $4 and $5 billion worth of cash and property had been forfeited since the 1984 crime bill.[31]

The drug loot bonanza immediately translated into increased police autonomy from civilian government, diminishing their accountability and insulating law enforcement from popular criticism or challenge. Glendale, California, on the edge of LA, offers a particularly chilling example of how forfeiture laws foster police-state tactics at the grassroots. In pursuit of bandits and booty, the Glendale Police Department (182-strong) created a small "Major Violators Unit" (MVU) in early 1985. This team, and the scores of similar narcotics squads that sprang up simultaneously throughout southern California, were the drug war equivalent of World War II U-boats, quietly roving far and wide in search of easy targets. The more property involved the better. After all, the Glendale PD kept not only 90 percent of any confiscated cash, but hoarded seized weapons, homes, and vehicles as well.

The pursuit of plunder drove the Glendale super-narcs as far south as San Diego and the Mexican border, and as far north as Santa Barbara. During its first three years the MVU made forty major raids outside of its territory. Early trophies included military hardware, cocaine, $8.5 million in cash, and sixteen vehicles, among them a $700,000 Ferrari which the department planned to keep for undercover surveillance.[32]

The 1984 forfeiture laws were prudent enough to prohibit paying police salaries with drug war lucre, but money is fungible. As with "humanitarian aid" to the Nicaraguan Contras (which was also in the news at that time), captured drug cash freed up police budgets and directly or indirectly paid for whatever law enforcement officials deemed necessary. By 1988 the Glendale squad had already pulled in enough swag and cash to pay its annual $330,000 budget two years into the future as well as stock the department with infrared night-vision goggles, cellphones, video surveillance and recording equipment, and a fingerprint reading laser wand. Moreover, they were still waiting for $7.2 million worth of seizures to be approved and forwarded by the overburdened Asset Forfeitures Office of the Department of Justice.[33] Nor was Glendale unique. A dozen or so departments throughout southern California and around the Bay Area established similar squads and were pulling in over $50 million annually, roughly a third of all forfeited assets nationwide.[34] The tidal wave of cash translated into a buying spree: Simi Valley upgraded its SWAT team, outfitted its forces with semiautomatic nine millimeters, and replaced its central computer system; Burbank's wolf-pack funded the department's first chopper; other departments stocked up on dogs, body armor, communication gear, and guns. LA's deputy chief called the forfeiture program "the greatest thing that ever happened to local law enforcement."[35] To aid with the legal work, the federal government supplied additional "cross-over" prosecutors: local district attorneys who are also sworn in as assistant US attorneys.[36]

Given the huge sums of money involved in the forfeiture game, it is easy to assume that police would have started targeting major narco-capitalists, but this was not usually the case. Most forfeiture victims were (and are) non-violent, mom-and-pop pot farmers, or independent, run-of-the-mill dealers.[37]

Take for example the case of Debra V. Hill, who had the misfortune of being a guest in a house raided by police. The usual ransacking turned up a small amount of methamphetamine in a box of clothing that did not belong to Hill. Nonetheless, police confiscated the $550 in Hill's possession. A working class mother, Hill was so desperate for the timely return of her cash that she agreed to forfeit $250 to the prosecutor in return for the remaining $300 if charges were dropped.[38] Or consider the case of Kevin Perry, "a gravel pit laborer from Ossipee, New Hampshire. After he and his wife pleaded guilty to the misdemeanor of growing four marijuana plants, the United States sought to forfeit their mobile home, worth $22,000."[39]

Clearly many of the people targeted by forfeiture laws had indeed accumulated their wealth, however meager, through illicit means. The point is not that all those targeted for forfeitures are innocent but, rather, to show how forfeiture, contrary to its purported goals, does not take the profit out of drug dealing. Instead, the laws merely deals law enforcement into the game.

In fact, forfeiture laws help to put away the mid-level entrepreneurs of the drug trade (the top executives of the drug trade are rarely targeted by law enforcement). The lure of large caches of property, neatly forfeited without a court fight, becomes an incentive for police and prosecutors to broker deals with rich defendants. For example, one New Jersey defendant facing twenty-five years to life on a "drug kingpin" indictment had numerous charges dropped and was given parole eligibility in five years, in exchange for agreeing to forfeit more than $1 million.[40] In Massachusetts, it seems that "in exchange for a dealer turning over drug-related profits of at least $10,000 without a fight in court, prosecutors have been reducing the original criminal charges lodged against the dealer." An investigative series by the *Boston Globe* found that "in nearly three of every four cases in this category, prosecutors revised charges to a lower level of trafficking or eliminated the trafficking charge entirely."[41] Meanwhile Massachusetts prisons fill with small fry, first-time offenders. "[T]he typical drug inmate is doing time based on lower-level drug dealing," reports the *Boston Globe*.[42]

The forfeiture wars also fuel racist policing.[43] Take for example the case of Willie Jones, an African American nurseryman and landscaper, who was off to buy plants and other legitimate landscaping supplies when his $9,600 in cash was seized by cops at Nashville airport because he fitted the "drug courier profile." That is, he was a Black man paying for a round-trip ticket with cash.[44]

In Florida a team of journalists viewed videotapes of approximately one thousand highway stops, and found that police were using traffic violations as a pretext to confiscate "tens of thousands of dollars from motorists." A staggering 85 percent of the targeted travelers were African American, pulled over because they, once again, fitted the nebulous "courier profile."[45] These operations were racist both in application and intent: a 1985 Florida Highway Patrol directive instructed troopers to focus enforcement efforts on "ethnic groups associated with the drug trade."[46]

This tithing of Black, and to a lesser extent Latino, drivers continued throughout the eighties and early nineties. Sheriff Bob Vogel of Volusia County was perhaps the most overtly racist and forfeiture-hungry Florida lawman. Between 1989 and 1992 Vogel's force legally confiscated a total of $8 million in cash from hundreds of motorists: *a staggering 85 percent of whom were African American and 75 percent of whom were never charged with any crime.* "What this data tells me," concluded Vogel, "is that the majority of money being transported for drug activities involves blacks and Hispanics."[47]

To bust cash-laden traffickers and others, Vogel's deputies operated elaborate night-time stings in which they shone lights across the highway so as to ascertain the skin color of passing drivers. Videotapes from the deputies' dashboards revealed scenes that would be comic if they weren't so venomously racist: a bewildered Black man explaining that this is the *seventh* time he has been stopped in one night; another African American shaking his head in frustration as his car is searched for the second time in minutes.[48]

Again, the point is not that all of the victims were innocent: many were indeed headed to buy drugs: I-95 is a major artery for drug trafficking. But it is also a major route for tourists, long-haul truckers, and everyone else. The question becomes who has the right to determine which cash-laden traveler is in pursuit of narcotics and which is merely in pursuit of over-priced escapism at Disney World?

In Oakland, California, police operate under the "impenetrable shield" of the wider society's racism and near total disregard for what goes on in the ghetto; perfect conditions for an over-zealous forfeiture campaign. In 1989 the Oakland Housing Authority Police created its own 24-member special force to see what sort of change and valuables could be shaken from the city's besieged and sprawling public housing projects. Started with federal seed money, the narcotics task force set out to prove to federal founders that it could pull in drugs and assets. The "task force" soon became home for officers too violent to keep their jobs with other forces, and the quest for official forfeiture quickly lapsed into unofficial looting.[49] Task force commander Daniel

Roussard instructed the troops to take "anything and everything on the street corner," and exhorted them to "go out and kick some ass," and to keep arrest numbers high.[50]

FOLK DEVILS AND CRACK-ADDLED CONGRESSMEN: THE 1986 CRIME BILL

As the 1986 elections neared, politicians all over the country were in search of compelling issues that would speak to voters' anxieties — caused in large part by the rising poverty and inequality of the new class war — while avoiding the real cause of those anxieties. Six years of Reaganomics, anti-communist campaigning in Central America, and right-wing cultural backlash had put the country in a foul mood. Sympathetic news stories about "the new poor" had given way to reports on "compassion fatigue" and the pathologies of the homeless and other self-destructive addicts, loafers, and parasites; the ideologically charged notion of "the underclass," a culturally damaged mostly Black and Latino stratum of loafers, was also gaining popularity.[51]

Repeating the mantras of anti-communism helped fund the contras, buy ICBMs, and derail arms talks with the USSR, but it failed to address the obvious social crisis caused by economic restructuring. The crisis at home required a different political vocabulary.

As cities continued to polarize under the dual pressure of real estate speculation and disinvestment, and farms went under in record numbers, politicians searched for the enemy within. Not surprisingly they recycled an old and trusted trope: race spoken through the code of crime and welfare. But this latest iteration was aided by the arrival of a deadly new drug: crack, a cheap smokeable form of rock-cocaine. This election season anti-crack race baiting would be the ticket. The image of ghettos overrun by swarthy baseheads was the perfect lightning rod to absorb the anxieties of a population being economically keelhauled by aggressively pro-business public policy.

Just as the summer legislative session was getting underway, political manna fell from heaven. The promising young Maryland State basketball star Len Bias — recently drafted by the (then mighty) Boston Celtics — dropped dead. Cocaine was the culprit, but crack cocaine was blamed at the time. Shortly thereafter another star athlete, Don Rogers, was also felled by cocaine. The Speaker of the House, Boston Democrat Tip O'Neill, rushed down to Washington to avenge the loss by launching a massive anti-drug initiative. Other lawmakers and President Reagan soon jumped into the fray. Invoking the motifs of martial law and national emergency, Reagan called for a full-scale anti-drug "mobilization" in "what we hope will be the final stage in our national strategy to eradicate drug abuse." Meanwhile, the First Lady called for a "national crusade" and a "new intolerance."[52]

A moral panic of unprecedented proportions had begun. To "set an example" Reagan announced his intention to drug-test federal workers. At once, he and Vice President Bush – on the advice of Nancy Reagan's drug consultant – handed in jars of their urine at Bethesda Naval Hospital to be examined for traces of cocaine, marijuana, amphetamines, barbiturates, heroin, and phencyclidine (PCP or angel dust).[53] Seventy-eight members of Reagan's senior staff were also asked to "volunteer" their urine. "If they don't take [the drug test], they just choose not to take it," explained Deputy Press Secretary Albert R. Brashear. On further prodding he added: "I'm sure that it would be noted that they didn't want to do it . . . probably by their supervisor."[54] After his own test came back clean, Reagan signed Executive Order #12564, mandating that federal employees submit to urine tests. Aspiring politicians throughout state and local governments quickly followed suit, pissing in jars of their own. (Miraculously, the entire district attorney's office in Baton Rouge tested clean.)

Among the few to condemn the pathetic circus was conservative columnist William Safire. "The Reagan administration is undermining three of the most basic rights guaranteed by the Founders: No person shall be required to testify against himself; each of us is protected against unlawful searches; and every person is innocent until proved guilty."[55]

As if such stunts alone would not ignite a wave of hysterical publicity, the DEA launched its own media lobbying campaign. As the head of the DEA's New York office put it: "The media were only too willing to cooperate [in running drug stories] because as far as they were concerned, crack was the hottest combat reporting story to come along since the end of the Vietnam War."[56]

That July all three major TV networks broadcast seventy-four evening news segments about drugs, more than half of them about crack.[57] Likewise, the *New York Times* boosted its drug war coverage from 43 stories in the second half of 1985 to 220 in the second half of 1986. *Newsweek* and *Time* dutifully jumped in line, the latter running three cover stories on crack in as many months. Both called crack the biggest story since Vietnam/Watergate and "the issue of the year."[58] With each week the moral panic grew more intense. Senator Alphonse D'Amato and Assistant US Attorney Rudolph Giuliani went undercover with a hidden TV crew to buy drugs, while the network magazine shows all offered lurid specials on the "epidemic," "plague," and "crisis" that was suddenly gripping the nation – particularly its communities of color.[59] As brutal legislation was taking form on Capitol Hill, Reagan made clear who the enemy was: "Drug users can no longer excuse themselves by blaming society. As individuals, they are responsible. The rest of us must be clear that we will no longer tolerate drug use by anyone."[60]

By October the frenzy had blossomed into some of the broadest, toughest anti-drug legislation yet. Only eighteen lawmakers voted against the catch-all Anti-Drug Abuse Act of 1986, which imposed twenty-nine new mandatory minimum sentences, among them one that set a five-year mandatory minimum for "offenses involving 100 grams of heroin, 500 grams of cocaine or 5 grams of cocaine freebase known as 'crack' . . ."[61] Because African Americans were and are more frequently arrested for crack than powder cocaine this law translated into apartheid sentencing. Furthermore, people convicted under the new laws were to be denied probation or suspended sentences. For federal drug crimes involving physical injures or death, or for "major" second offenses, the mandatory minimum was boosted to twenty years.[62] Thus began in earnest the one-sided race war of the late eighties and nineties.

Consider that in 1980, African Americans made up roughly 12 percent of the nation's population and over *23 percent* of all those arrested on drug charges. Ten years later African Americans were still roughly 12 percent of the total population, but their representation among those busted for narcotics had almost doubled to more than *40 percent*, while over 60 percent of all narcotics convictions were (and are) African Americans.[63]

Putting aside the disparity between crack and cocaine sentences, it is worth noting that the new powder cocaine mandatory minimums were (and are) also severe. In 1984 Roger Clinton, future president Bill Clinton's brother, was busted on federal charges of conspiracy and selling cocaine. He served sixteen months. Had the current laws, enacted in 1986, been in effect, the younger Clinton would have done ten years without parole, emerging from federal prison half-way into his brother's first term as president.[64] By

1987 most states also had their own parallel mandatory minimums operating. As a result state and federal incarceration rates, already on a steep incline, shot up in a nearly vertical pitch. In 1985 roughly 500,000 people were locked away in state and federal prisons; by 1990 that number had doubled; by 1998 that number had reached 1.7 million.[65]

To accommodate the new sentencing laws, the 1986 crime bill provided a massive infusion of cash ($124.5 million) for the Bureau of Prisons, most of it earmarked for new construction. Law enforcement's share was $60 million for the DEA, and $230 million per year for the next three years for state and local law enforcement.[66] With this surge in funds came a new enforcement focus on addicts, users, and petty retail dealers. Users had been targeted all along, but campaigning against the little fish reached unprecedented proportions after 1986.

The new focus on users immediately translated into a massive jump in narcotics arrests. The FBI Uniform Crime Report shows that drug-related arrests soared nationwide during the moral panic of 1986 and the following two years, as local cops, high on federal cash, renewed their assaults on America's ghettos. In 1985 roughly 800,000 people were arrested on drug charges; by 1989 the number of annual narcotics busts had shot up to almost 1.4 million. Then during the early 1990s the annual number of arrests dipped to around one million before slowly climbing again.[67]

THE WAR ON USERS

It was finally open season on "social dynamite" and "social junk," the ranks of which had been fast swelling for six years. On the ground that meant the beginning of a nationwide wave of raids and ghetto sweeps, such as the notorious Operation Hammer in which 14,000 people – mostly young Black men – were arrested and booked in mobile command centers during a massive paramilitary occupation of south LA's deindustrialized ghettos.[68]

In New York City police launched the infamous Operation Pressure Point, described as a series of "large scale attacks" on "drug-plagued neighborhoods," in which officers arrested "large numbers of small-time dealers and buyers."[69] Once a week the NYPD would conduct joint sweeps, stings, and "buy-busts" with federal agents. The prisoners scooped up on these so called "Federal Days" were handed off to US attorneys for prosecution.

Such federally aided municipal police campaigns were always articulated through, and imbricated with, a set of local racial and geographic agendas. For example, the two main targets during Pressure Point were Tompkins Square Park in the East Village and the adjacent Lower East Side – a poor and working class, Eastern European, Puerto Rican, and Dominican barrio.[70] Far from being New York's "worst" copping zones these areas were chosen in part to facilitate advancing gentrification. Both neighborhoods were being targeted by real estate interests for redevelopment and resettlement by "hip" urban professionals: for that to work the local riffraff, junkies, and home-boys had to be pushed out. Part of Pressure Point's strategy involved evict-ing the residents of drug houses and sealing the buildings.[71] Such actions helped pacify rowdy, drug-addled street scenes at the same time that they opened property for redevelopment. (For more on policing and gentrifica-tion, see chapter five.)

In many cities the war on users in fact generated new violence. In Washington, D.C., for instance, law enforcement unleashed Operation Clean Sweep – a year-long offensive against drug use and street sales in the city's Black neighborhoods, a terrain one assistant police chief described as the "drug wastelands."[72] In all, Clean Sweep netted over 28,000 arrests and 313 seized vehicles; among the casualties were almost 1,400 adolescents busted for minor dealing and possession.[73] No doubt D.C. was, and is, wracked by a glut of narcotics and drug-related violence. But there is con-siderable evidence that Clean Sweep's mass arrests and constant police pressure merely fueled violence by stirring rivalries, destabilizing dealers' business networks, hierarchies, and turf arrangements, and setting off bloody power struggles, suspicions, and turf feuds. In 1987 half of all homicides were deemed drug-related, compared with only a third the year before Clean Sweep.[74] Nor was Clean Sweep in any way directed at stemming the supply of drugs, as police preferred to nail hapless users and addicts whom one top police official described as "the financiers of the whole narcotics enterprise." Despite the full-scale assault on the drug trade's customer base, there is no evidence that the level of drug use, addiction, and dealing diminished dur-ing the late eighties.[75]

Miami also reacted to the moral panic of 1986 by attacking low-level users. Operation Sting tallied more than 2,595 such arrests during the sum-mer of anguish and bluster following the Bias death.[76] "To be successful against a mass market, mass arrests are required," explained Chief Clarence

Dickson. Miami tactics involved identifying "hot spots," then using "teams of uniformed patrol officers, traffic enforcement motormen, undercover personnel, and SWAT" forces to clear an area of dealers. Once occupied by police, "undercover officers assumed the role of street dealers," and unsuspecting addicts were scooped up by the dozens.[77] In Orange County, California, a multi-agency task force began Operation Snow Ball, bagging almost thirty "small scale drug dealers" in the first mass raid.[78]

Riding high on the wake of the 1986 crime bill and the Bias-crack hysteria of the same year, Attorney General Edwin Meese descended on the bitter winter streets of north Philly in February 1987 to announce the largest federal-local cooperative drug sweep in American history. It was also the first time federal agents were focusing exclusively on "street level narcotics traffic." The operation's inaugural bust scooped up twenty-six defendants, many of them charged with the brand new crime of selling drugs within 1,000 feet of a school.[79] And so it went throughout the country: open season on urban addicts, economically discarded youth and petty dealers.

CRIME BILLS A·GO·GO: 1988–92

The crackdown of 1986 soon rolled over into the even greater malevolence of the 1988 presidential race. Throughout the campaign GOP candidate George Bush had his Democratic opponent, Massachusetts Governor Michael Dukakis, on the ropes, pounding him as an ineffectual, crime-friendly wimp "lost in the thickets of liberal sociology."[80] The attack reached full frenzy in June with a spate of Hill and Knowlton-produced TV ads, featuring the sordid exploits of William Horton Jr., a convicted murderer who escaped from a Massachusetts Department of Corrections work furlough program and raped a woman in Maryland.[81] Horton, of course, *had to be* African American. The advertisement's function was to invoke the tried and trusted specter of the Black rapist, a threat to white womanhood, white supremacy, and white society. The race-baiting of the Bush campaign shaped not only the presidential race but the election year crime legislation as well.

As Congress began crafting yet another get-tough bill, Bush told the legislators that he would like to see increases in "the certainty and the severity" of punishment, not only for other Willie Hortons but for drug dealers and users as well. He also called for executing drug dealers convicted of murder. "I challenge the Democrats to stand up on this point," he goaded. "You say this is war – then treat it as such. Don't let these killers back on the streets."

From what used to be the left came the Reverend Jesse Jackson, calling for the creation of a "drug czar" and more funding for local police. "We have to convince them [kids] that drug pushers are terrorists," said Jackson.[82] In fact Jackson's bellicose noise was so successful it raised the concern of Health and Human Services Secretary Otis R. Bowen, who warned President Reagan that "one of the remaining candidates for president is getting some of his highest marks for his passionate and creative oratory on the drug epidemic and is poised to steal from our party what has been a traditional Republican issue – law enforcement."[83]

In many ways the Anti-Drug Abuse Act of 1988 marked the new centrality of anti-crime rhetoric and police state policies in American political life. The bill's brutal and authoritarian provisions were so numerous that a complete accounting of them is impossible here. However, one of the most important was the creation of the federal death penalty for persons guilty of participation in a federally defined "continuing criminal enterprise" or any drug-related felony, who intentionally or unintentionally kills another person. The federal death penalty had been proposed and defeated repeatedly throughout the decade, but the fever of the campaign turned capital punishment into the "litmus test" of being "tough on crime."[84]

The bill also created a cabinet-level "drug czar" who would head the Office of National Drug Control Policy and coordinate "anti-drug" policing activities between law enforcement, the military, and intelligence agencies. The Department of Defense received $2 million to train law enforcement and $3.5 million to equip police with military gear. Forfeiture laws were expanded allowing "seizures of convenience" in which the property of small-time users and dealers could be confiscated without going to court. Over $1 billion in additional grant money was ladled out to state and local law enforcement under the Edward Byrne Memorial State and Local Law Enforcement Assistance Program and the Bureau of Justice Assistance (a streamlined reincarnation of the LEAA). The DEA, FBI, US Marshals, Customs, and federal prosecutors all got millions of dollars as well.

Even the National Forest Service began morphing into a militarized wing of the state, as an initial $10 million was allocated to train Forest Service narcotics squads and SWAT teams, which were also given new powers to investigate, pursue, and arrest offenders, on and off federal property. The new bill created another slew of broad, vague, and vicious mandatory minimums: twenty years for drug offenses committed in a federal prison; ten years for endangering human life while manufacturing illegal drugs; and life for third-time federal drug offenders.

Most insidious of all were the statutes grouped under the rubric of "user accountability" that furthered subordination of the state's social service functions to its policing functions. Now public housing tenants who engaged in criminal activity on, or even near, housing projects would be evicted. This law – known as "one strike" – is still much in effect. And while public housing continued its long, slow deterioration from "malign neglect" the Department of Housing and Urban Development was furnished with resources to militarize further the state's urban reservations with security audits, new anti-narcotics enforcement programs, harpoon fencing, resident ID cards, and private security.[85] Whether intentional or not, the effect of such laws further terrorized, undermined, divided, and disoriented impoverished communities of color.

TOO MUCH IS NEVER ENOUGH

As the new drug bill was implemented in 1989, Bush acceded to the White House. Normally, Congress only passed crime bills every two years to coincide with elections, but the Bush administration, particularly its new cabinet-level drug czar, William Bennett, was emphatic and generated extreme media hype. In the interest of intensified prosecution of the drug war, the Bush team had the DEA concoct a crack bust in Lafayette Park, across from the White House. The spoils of that bust showed up a few days later in the hands of the new president during his first major speech. The feckless victim of this setup was a seventeen-year-old high school student named Keith Jackson who could not have found his way to the bust site without assiduous coaxing and explicit directions from DEA undercovers.[86]

The legislative year started with an ambitious package of proposed anti-crime legislation. Though Congress failed to enact all the changes Bush asked for, it did come through with additional money for the (now white-hot) drug war. "Final funding brought total federal anti-narcotics spending for fiscal

1990 to $8.8 billion, up from $5.7 billion the previous year and about $900 million more than Bush had sought."[87]

The next year saw more of the same: Bush again asked for expanded use of the death penalty, limits on *habeas corpus*, and further erosion of the exclusionary rule. All he got was more money: $220 million for the Bureau of Prisons; $900 million for state and local law enforcement grants; and $15 million here and there for the odd propaganda project such as training teachers in the art of "drug-use intervention" and counseling.[88]

The money and legislation of the eighties was certainly having an impact on the ground. Between 1980 and 1987 federal drug convictions jumped by 161 percent, while the number of narcotics offenders sent to prison rose by 177 percent.[89] In New York City narcotics convictions shot from 7,201 in 1980 to 34,366 in 1988, thanks in large part to the busts generated by the NYPD's Tactical Narcotics Teams. Overall, the department estimated that 35 percent of its 1989 budget ($617.1 million) was spent on drug enforcement. The city's total drug war tab, including prosecution, court costs, and corrections, was estimated to be one billion dollars a year.[90] Between 1980 and 1990 California's prison system sucked in an average of 300 new prisoners a week as the total inmate population jumped from 22,000 to 97,309. The state spent $3.3 billion on prison construction, yet ended the decade with its prison system at 180 percent capacity.[91] By 1990 all states except Kansas were operating above capacity or at court-ordered maximums.[92]

Following the American victory over Iraq in 1991, George Bush seemed a shoe-in for re-election. But the economy remained mired in recession after the 1987 stock market crash and before too long, Los Angeles exploded. It seemed that the chickens had finally come home to roost. Into this malaise rode William Jefferson Clinton, who many imagined might launch some sort of updated war on poverty. Instead Clinton carried on with both neoliberal economic restructuring and the criminal justice buildup. With his victory came yet another massive wave in the storm of law-and-order repression.

NEW DEMOCRATS, OLD WAR: THE 1994 CRIME BILL

The nature of criminal justice policy in the Clinton era was first revealed by the candidate's pledge to put 100,000 more police on America's streets. That was followed by Clinton's strategic return to Arkansas, during the height of the New Hampshire primary, to preside over the lethal-injection execution of Ricky Ray Rector, a brain-damaged African American inmate convicted of killing an Arkansas patrolman in 1981.[93] The *Washington Post* reported that hours before his execution, Ricky Ray Rector

> carefully put aside the slice of pecan pie that came with his last meal. Rector always liked to eat his dessert right before bedtime, and he apparently expected to return to his cell for his pie after he had received the lethal injection ordered by Arkansas Gov. Bill Clinton . . . Just hours before he died, Rector told [his attorney] Rosenzweig: "I'm going to vote for Clinton in the fall."[94]

Clinton's first year in office saw no movement on crime legislation, but he did appoint Dade County prosecutor Janet Reno as attorney general. In consummate Clinton fashion, Reno assured all that, despite her personal opposition to capital punishment, she had regularly sought the death penalty during her tenure as Dade County prosecutor and would continue to do so in her new post. This contradiction was enough to alarm even Ohio Democrat Howard Metzenbaum, one of Reno's most avid supporters.[95]

The harbingers of a New Democrat crackdown came to fruition with the election year crime bill of 1994. The legislation began in August 1993 – little more than a year after massive rioting erupted in Los Angeles and scores of other smaller cities throughout the nation – with a Clinton proposal to provide money for 100,000 new police officers, new federal death penalty crimes, and restrictive overhaul of federal appeals in capital cases. Before the bill reached its final form it had acquired a layer of severe election year anti-crime amendments and riders, all fueled by get-tough one-upmanship. Liberal Democrats, unable to mount even a minimal challenge to the bill, attempted to save face by weaving in a few anemic provisions for midnight basketball and expanded park facilities in crime-blighted areas.

The bill, known as HR 666 and by its detractors as "the beast" – another steamroller of fear and disoriented vengeance – was a smashing victory in the state's thirty-year-old, one-sided race war. "This is a historic moment," declared Democrat Charles Schummer of New York, as the new death penalty provisions passed a vote in House. "For the first time, this body is recognizing the anguish on the streets."[96]

THE DETAILS OF DISASTER

The Violent Crime Control and Law Enforcement Act of 1994 was hailed with all the familiar refrains as "an unprecedented federal venture into crime-fighting."[97] And like the crime bills of the Nixon, Reagan, and Bush years, it was. As during the Nixon era, federal involvement in the crackdown took the form of massive federal aid to state and local law enforcement. This largess was delivered through a newly formed $30.2 billion Crime Trust Fund, but the form of local law enforcement was in large part dictated by the conditions upon which federal aid would be given. Among the new law's most important provisions were

- Policing grants totaling $8.8 billion, to be distributed over the following six years, for hiring 100,000 new officers, buying labor-saving equipment and enhancing or initiating community policing programs. The money was to be distributed in the form of federal matching grants which favor states that can make large allocations of their own; the grants diminished over time and terminated altogether after six years. By establishing programs that states would eventually have to fund on their own, the federal policing grants launched local policy-making in a more repressive direction.
- $7.9 billion in grants for state prison building. As with the policing grants, states had to match federal money with funds of their own and were then left to fund the operation of new prisons without aid. The prison grants – in reminiscence of the LEAA state planning agencies and in acknowledgment of the new centrality of incarceration in American politics – required states to develop "comprehensive prison management plans."[98]
- The sentencing commission, established by the 1984 crime bill, was directed to increase penalties in their mandatory guidelines for the manufacture of or dealing of drugs in areas designated as "drug free zones" (usually the areas around schools and playgrounds). People convicted of such crimes would not be eligible for parole.
- Federal capital punishment was expanded to sixteen new crimes, and following the lead of states like Washington, Oregon, and California, a three-strikes provision was enacted. Even in cases where a defendant had two "strikes" in state court and no federal record, the third conviction – if for a violent federal felony, like assaulting a federal officer – could result

in prison for life. Sentences were "enhanced" for federal defendants deemed to be gang members. In special cases, juveniles as young as thirteen could be tried as adults, and the federal government was authorized to help states institute similar laws of their own for sixteen- to seventeen-year-olds.

- The war on immigrants was also bolstered. The Border Patrol received $1.2 billion with which to hire 4,000 new Border Patrol agents (nearly doubling the force) and to buy new vehicles, high-tech surveillance gear, and weapons. Another $1.8 billion was furnished so states could incarcerate, instead of deport, so-called "criminal aliens." One-third of these immigration enforcement funds were set aside for Arizona, California, Florida, Illinois, New Jersey, New York, and Texas. The asylum and deportation process was also streamlined and sped up.
- Other federal law enforcement agencies were given several billion dollars to help cope with the expected increased workloads, upgrade computers, improve record keeping, facilitate communications, update crime labs, and run training and probation surveillance programs.[99]

The buildup of the eighties and nineties was drastic but its effects were felt unevenly; in many respects criminal justice policy develops unevenly and concomitantly with the market system's uneven economic geography. Thus certain spaces and regions have been more heavily impacted or inscribed by the war on drugs, the war on crime, and the war on immigrants. The following chapters depart from a historical narrative and focus more closely on cities, border regions, and prisons, which are the spaces of the new crackdown.

PART II

POLICE

CHAPTER FOUR

DISCIPLINE IN PLAYLAND,
PART I – ZERO TOLERANCE:
THE SCIENCE OF
KICKING ASS

If you peed in the street, you were going to jail. We were
going to fix broken windows and prevent anyone from
breaking them again.
William Bratton, former New York City police commissioner

In Baltimore "rat fishing" is the sport of choice for locals at the Yellow Rose
Saloon. During the annual competition, "ratmen" cast lines with baited glue-
traps deep into the infested alleys. Snagged vermin are reeled in and beaten
to death with bats, a sometimes strenuous task: in 1995 the trophy rodent
weighed in at seven-and-a-half pounds.

That same year two well-heeled animal lovers drove into the badlands to
condemn the destruction of urban fauna. But upon arrival the animal lovers
were disarmed by the intense poverty and dilapidation confronting them.
Particularly disturbing was a rat-infested apartment in which cowered several children. "I never knew people lived like that," said one of the chastened
and retreating do-gooders.[1]

It was a rare moment when opposite ends of the urban universe briefly
overlapped to reveal the Dickensian contradictions of the restructured
American city. To function smoothly, this metropolis of ratmen and animal
lovers requires elaborate, multilayered, mutually re-enforcing systems of social
control, involving political demonization, public and private surveillance,

containment policies, and outright repression. In the race- and class-divided metropolis, policing is paramount; the gendarmes must intervene directly and indirectly to put down rebellion, maintain order, and contain dangerous people, so that commerce, redevelopment, and accumulation may proceed unimpeded.

In the last decade the pressure to police effectively and secure urban space has become all the more important. For centuries "the urban" has been synonymous with filth, lawlessness, and danger, but in recent years cities have also taken on renewed economic and cultural importance as sites of accumulation, speculation, and innovative profit making. For cities to work as such they must be, or at least appear and feel, safe. If the economic restructuring of the eighties and nineties intensified urban poverty, it also created new, gilded spaces that are increasingly *threatened by poverty*. This polarization of urban space and social relations has in turn required a new layer of regulation and exclusion, so as to protect the new hyper-aestheticized, playground quarters of the postmodern metropolis from their flipsides of misery. This contradiction, between the danger of cities and their value, has spawned yet another revolution in American law enforcement: the rise of zero tolerance/quality of life policing.

THE ZERO TOLERANCE REVOLUTION

"Police used to be more passive. Officers rode around waiting to answer 911 calls," explains William Bratton, the former New York City police commissioner who "re-engineered" the NYPD into the Chicago Bulls of law enforcement. Now a jet-setting security consultant, Bratton is still the godfather of innovative policing. "What we do is merely free police to be proactive and fight crime again."[2] Since the early 1990s Bratton has presided over the rise of "zero tolerance" (ZT) or "quality of life" (QOL) policing, which preaches vigorous enforcement of even the most trifling municipal codes in the theory that preventing "disorder" will prevent violence. To understand the rise of this slippery, effective, and dangerous new form of policing it helps to know something about the men who developed and championed ZT, particularly Bratton.

Born and raised in Boston, Bratton began his career as an MP in Vietnam, where he walked the perimeter of an ammo dump with an M-16 and an

Alsastian named Duchess. Upon returning home, he began his mercurial ascent through the ranks of the Boston Transit Police. By the mid eighties, he was commanding the force. After boosting morale and performance and reducing crime on the "T," Bratton moved on to head the Boston Metropolitan Police, and then in 1990 to the New York Transit Police. Finally in 1994 he was crowned urban America's alpha cop: New York police commissioner under mayor Rudolph Giuliani.

Throughout his career, Bratton advanced a theory and practice of aggressive proactive enforcement, with bureaucratic decentralization, and a business-like focus on the "bottom line" of reducing crime rates. In short, he brought post-Fordism to copland. But Bratton did not invent zero tolerance/quality of life policing on his own. A more definitive genealogy of the new siege-craft begins with the policing crisis of the late sixties and the advent of the Police Foundation in 1970, thanks to a $30 million start-up grant from the Ford Foundation. Headed by law enforcement officials and administrators — such as former New York City Commissioner Patrick Murphy and social scientists like James Q. Wilson — the Police Foundation conducted numerous early experiments and studies on police–community relations and "order maintenance." In the face of mass rioting and increasing antagonism between police and communities of color, it was clear that old strategies were inadequate.

From this milieu arose a school of thought exemplified and first popularized by criminologists James Q. Wilson and George Kelling in their 1982 *Atlantic Monthly* article "Broken Windows." Wilson was already a well-known conservative theorist, but Kelling, who ran the Police Foundation's famous Kansas City experiment and Newark foot patrol study only gained fame in the nineties through his close association with zero tolerance enforcement strategies and William Bratton.[3]

The Wilson–Kelling "broken windows" thesis was simple: if police address the small "quality of life" offenses that create "disorder," violent crime will diminish. According to Wilson and Kelling, "disorder and crime are usually inextricably linked, in a kind of developmental sequence." Neighborhoods where behavior is left "untended" become frightening, anonymous, deserted, and "vulnerable to criminal invasion." Police were advised to get out of their squad cars so as better to control "panhandlers, drunks, addicts, rowdy teenagers, prostitutes, loiterers, the mentally disturbed." According to the theory, enforcing laws against public urination, graffiti, and inebriation will create an aura of regulation that helps prevent brutal crimes like rape and murder.[4]

As the broken windows theory gestated on the right-wing margins of urban policy debates, Kelling noticed Bratton's aggressive proactive policing in Boston. By the late eighties the two were in regular communication and collaboration, and in 1990 Kelling recruited Bratton to run the New York City Transit Police. There, in the "electronic sewers" of Gotham with Kelling providing intellectual backup, Bratton began the country's first full-scale implementation of zero tolerance/quality of life policing.

In many ways the story of this new style of law enforcement is quite compelling. At the level of organizational management, reason won out over indifference, habit, and corruption. But at a broader level the story is one of rapidly and insidiously escalating police power; the opening of a new stage in the development of an American-style, democratic police state. The victims of the New York strategy have been people of color, youth, and the poor. The real human cost of this brave new style of enforcement has been enormous. But before addressing those angles, let us continue the story from the cops' point of view.

RETAKING THE SUBWAY

As Bratton saw it, the first step in "retaking" the New York subway system was to capture the attention, passion, and loyalty of the rank-and-file "cave cops." On one of Bratton's first tunnel walkabouts he happened upon a demoralized young cop with a broken radio, assigned to stand guard at a token booth all day. As one might expect, the officer was bored, isolated, and resentful – he saw his mission as dull and pointless. To Bratton it was a microcosm of larger problems plaguing the Transit Police.[5] The subway seemed out of control because the police seemed uninterested in safety. The cops were uninterested in safety because they were given meaningless jobs and inadequate equipment. Morale was abysmal.

To reinvigorate the rank and file Bratton lobbied for more cars, new radios, better uniforms, and most important of all: new Glock nine-millimeter semiautomatic handguns, with fifteen-round clips. The arms gave the much disparaged catacomb cops a new cachet. As with pit bulls and rottweilers, Glocks "got it goin' on." "These kids knew the firearms just by looking at them," wrote Bratton. "It became a big thing on the platforms. 'Hey, Transit's got nines!'"[6]

Along with procuring new paramilitary accessories, Bratton reassigned hundreds of cops guarding token booths to more proactive tasks, such as enforcing minor laws and setting up underground stings. The need to make police work more interesting dovetailed nicely with the broken windows focus on "order maintenance." This was just the sort of "multiple effects" that thrilled Bratton.

"Fare evasion was the biggest broken window in the transit system. We were going to fix that window and see to it that it didn't get broken again."[7] Rank-and-file Transit officers were organized in undercover squads of up to ten and deployed in massive round-up operations against "fare-beaters." No more simple ticketing. People were arrested by the score, handcuffed together, and taken off in long coffles to mobile booking stations. To cut down on paperwork, officers worked in teams processing prisoners in batches of twenty. The paramilitary enforcement style, though focused on a petty crime, nonetheless made many cops feel important; their jobs once again involved action. At the same time Bratton was promulgating a nuts-and-bolts understanding of the broken windows theory to his mid-level brass and underground troops. Thus most cave cops no longer looked down on busting fare evasion as pointless, picayune, or beneath them. As Bratton put it, they "were beginning to understand the linkage between disorder and more serious crimes."[8] No doubt some cops saw the whole campaign as a speed-up: more busts meant more paperwork, more risk, more time in court, and much less drinking coffee and chewing the fat with comrades.

Bratton launched into restructuring the culture of the Transit brass by importing Japanese-inspired management concepts of flattened and decentralized bureaucracies. He forced his commanders to ride trains, visit the tunnels at strange hours, and, most importantly, attend brisk early morning performance evaluation meetings at which district commanders had to explain their strategies to each other. It was a classic case, straight from the pages of Weber – charisma broke open and reinvigorated an ossified bureaucracy. Throughout the underground, "dysfunctional" leaders were demoted, fired, or otherwise sidelined, while those with good ideas and aggressive strategies were rewarded with recognition and encouraged to share their ideas. Meanwhile, ambitious district captains launched muscular, high-profile, mini-crackdowns.

Captain Mike Anbro stood out in this regard. As commander of the underground district sprawling out from the dank entrails of the Hoyt-Schermerhorn station, Anbro set up veritable checkpoints, ordering his troops to stop and search all trains passing through this central Brooklyn hub. As police with dogs swept the trains, conductors would announce: "Your attention, please. The Transit Police are conducting a sweep of the train. There may be a momentary delay while they go through the train and correct conditions. Thank you for your patience."[9] Such sweeps, still in effect from time to time, are simple political semaphore from the state to the people: "We have the guns, we have the dogs, you will obey."

Meanwhile at headquarters, the media team, led by TV-journalist-cum-police-flack John Miller and corporate PR specialist John Linder, concocted a public relations blitzkrieg, plastering the city with pro-cop propaganda boasting 20 percent more cops on the trains, new decoy squads and canine units. The official motto was: "We're taking the subway back – for you."

But who were they taking it from? Among the first and hardest hit were the homeless, who travel, beg, and live in the political and physical basement of the class system: the city's six-story-deep concrete bowels.[10] During the mean, hot summer of 1990, hundreds of these so-called "mole people" were driven from the nooks and crannies of the A and E lines. By August street people and activists were picketing the Metropolitan Transportation Authority's headquarters in protest, charging that the city treated homeless people "like graffiti," an eyesore to be erased.[11] But according to official statistics, crime on the subway – never as bad as imagined – was falling. Between the first quarter of 1990 and the first quarter of 1994 felony crime in the subways dropped 46.3 percent.[12] In the minds of many New Yorkers, these were magical numbers that excused both police brutality and the routine indignities associated with quality of life enforcement.

Bratton's "victory" below ground soon brought a move topside. With the election of former federal prosecutor Rudolph Giuliani to the New York Mayor's Office, the underground super-cop was appointed as Gotham's 38th police commissioner. "We will fight for every house in the city," declared an almost Churchillian Bratton upon accepting the new post. "We will fight for every street. And we will win . . . The best days lie ahead." From the sidelines, law-and-order policy hawks smiled. Chuck Wexler of the Police Executive Research Forum, announced ominously that "what Bill does in New York will have national impact."[13]

Even before the transfer of power, Bratton, with New York Police Foundation funding, started building his leadership team and drawing up a strategy for "retaking" the entire city.[14] The command cadre would include former cave cop Jack Maple; naturalized Irish immigrant and old-school "cops' cop" John Timoney; and John Linder, the focus-group-driven marketing guru who had re-spun the image of the Transit force. Other than Linder, most of Bratton's closest colleagues were ambitious working class men who, like their chief, had risen through the ranks the hard way and emerged from the tunnels into the bright world of the local power elite.

TAKING THE CITY

The year 1994 began with the usual signs of social disintegration and mayhem: the city recorded some of the first cases of cholera and bubonic plague in decades, and on New Year's Eve two cops fell to sniper fire. The casualties provided the perfect opening photo-op for Giuliani's total war on "a city out of control." Jaw set, the angry new mayor went to the hospital bedside of the two wounded cops.[15]

Bratton's overhaul of the NYPD was much like the one he engineered at Transit. His point man was the bulldog and sartorial freak Jack Maple, who dressed like a 1930s gangster in spats and fedora, and who once described taking down suspects as "better than sex."[16] Together Bratton and Maple set about streamlining and decentralizing bureaucracies, "empowering" the seventy-six precinct commanders, and instituting new mechanisms of performance-related accountability, such as the early morning meetings that had worked so well at Transit. On Maple's insistence all precinct captains were ordered to produce weekly crime statistics; previously such numbers were only gathered on a quarterly basis. The early morning hot-seat meetings now involved detailed, computer-aided, spatial and chronological analysis of intricately mapped, real-time crime stats, projected on illuminated wall maps. The process soon acquired the moniker "Comstat" — short for computer statistics.

By the second year of Bratton's tenure, Comstat meetings were being held in the "command center," a mini-auditorium on the eighth floor of the NYPD's fortress-like headquarters at One Police Plaza. The room, with seating for 115, is equipped with eight-by-eight-foot-wide, wall-mounted computer screens – bought with Police Foundation money – that display illuminated icon-filled maps. The commissioner, the chiefs, the deputy chiefs, face rows of precinct commanders and captains in charge of special units, assorted lieutenants and some rank-and-file troops, all in dress uniform. One at a time, beneath the luminous screens, the precinct captains take the stage and report on the situations in their area. Then the interrogation begins: the brass fire off questions and demand answers: "Why so many daytime robberies? Have you contacted Stolen Property? Who exactly are the detectives handling this?" And the local commanders do their best to defend their practices or shift the blame for high crime rates on to other parts of the department, claming lack of cooperation from Narcotics, Vice, or Public Works.

The early Comstat meetings were so rough that *half* of New York's seventy-six precinct captains quit or were transferred from their jobs in the first two years.[17] "When I took over we had a very entrenched command structure. So the meetings tended to be a bit heated and confrontational," says Bratton. "If we see a rash of robberies, we ask the captain what he's doing. Does he have a plan? Is he setting up any stings, has he contacted other precincts to see if the stolen merchandise is in their area? If there's no explanation, and no change in the rate and pattern of offenses, the officer probably won't last," explains Bratton.[18]

More than mere management meetings, Comstat became a sanctimonious, paramilitary, hyper-macho ritual which mesmerized international journalists, policy wonks, and enterprising NYPD officers alike. Comstat was, and still is, high theater as much for external consumption as for constructing a new, more paramilitary, proactive, institutional culture marked by rigor and results-oriented competition. According to police, the Comstat process generates pressure to produce lower crime rates, which in turn helps break down barriers between precincts. Responsibility and focus on "results" gets pushed down the chain of command: captains lean on lieutenants, who lean on sergeants, who lean on beat cops, who, it could be said, lean on civilians. All precinct captains must reduce crime or move on.

"Comstat allows for a transparency that even a walk-around management style can't achieve," says Bratton – who still speaks in the present tense when talking about the NYPD, despite having been fired by Giuliani, who resented the international press garnered by his police commissioner. "You can see who's good and who isn't. You can reach down in the ranks and promote the smart and aggressive leaders or see where the system may be clogged."[19] Bratton also made efforts to break up centralized units like Narcotics, Burglary, and Fraud, so as to redistribute detectives back to the local level. The idea was to turn each precinct into a "mini-police department."

And just as he had done at Transit, Bratton pandered to the vanity and techno-fetishism of his base, bolstering the rank and file with new blue-black uniforms (replacing the "friendly" powder blue shirts that had been introduced in the sixties), Glock 9mms and 2,000 new recruits. But the strategy involved more than just Japanese-style total quality management, decentralized resource allocation, and boosted moral. According to its critics, Comstat and QOL policing have led to massive violations of civil liberties and outright human rights abuses.

THE TERRIFYING QUALITY OF LIFE

The opening shot in the mayor's pacification program – that is to say, in the opening act of his whole approach to governing – was a short, sharp war against "squeegee operators" who, according to Giuliani, had "been harassing and intimidating people for years." Their crime was offering to clean automobile windshields at street corners and at the highway entrances on the west side of the city.[20] Some commuters were no doubt genuinely intimidated by the window washers, but most of these men were simply very poor African Americans doing their best to *invent* work in an otherwise totally hostile economy. Bratton called them "a living symbol of what was wrong with the city," and advised them to "get off their asses" and get jobs.[21]

The squeegee wars were hastened to an end by the vigor of New York's finest, and by the total lack of resistance from their 75 to 100 adversaries. No sooner than this first foe was vanquished than the police set about evicting the ever larger shantytowns from beneath FDR Drive and the Williamsburg and Brooklyn bridges.[22] The plan was clear enough: centrifugal police pressures would extrude Manhattan's poor into outlying boroughs.

Next, the NYPD launched a city-wide round-up of truants: refugee youth escaping New York's hyper-violent and dilapidated public schools. The operations involved a level of fanfare usually reserved for serious narcotics busts. Bratton explained that "if you stop kids who aren't in school, you're probably stopping kids who are no good . . ."[23] Top NYPD planners drew up lists of names and maps of youth hangouts, created seven units to hunt down "at large" truants, and recruited merchants to act as extra anti-truant "eyes and ears." For the renegade bodegas that continued to allow youth to buy beer, smokes, and Philly Blunts (a type of cheap cigar, the wrappings of which are used for rolling joints) the Department of Consumer Affairs stepped up enforcement, leveling fines and yanking licenses.

On the soft side, School Chancellor Ramon Cortines helped legitimize and expand the scope of the operation by sending out a letter to parents and guardians warning of the new offensive and urging cooperation.[24] The NYPD solicited the media for "support," which soon materialized in the form of a TV and print news frenzy featuring the spectacle of teenagers busted in Times Square arcades, holding backpacks high to shield their faces from cameras as they were led out of blue-and-white police vans into special truant detention centers.[25] Meanwhile, the family courts braced for a wave of new cases. It was a masterful orchestration of disparate social forces into a single law-and-order crackdown; multiple layers of public and private social control — from the press to jails — acting in concert to form a totalizing net of surveillance, enforcement, and intimidation. Perhaps archaeologists of a future world will someday read the records of such campaigns as the deranged youth initiation ceremonies they are. What do kids learn from such treatment? How to be cuffed; how to shield one's face when paraded before the press; in short how to act like a criminal. But in 1990s New York, turning police power against children made perfect sense.

The kiddy-sweeps were just an extramural, televised version of what has become the NYPD's routine pedagogical function. Since the early eighties many "third tier" public school students have been offered an unofficial, unacknowledged curriculum on how to be searched, scanned, ID'd, detained, interrogated, and expelled by "school security officers," and the regular police patrolling the halls.[26] This arrangement — the product of long disinvestment, racism, and cynical indifference — has cast the school as semi-carceral training ground, a pre-prison vetting center where students learn to endure, and accept as natural, the police gaze. Under Giuliani the number of cops deployed in schools has tripled. Among their other functions these youth officers act as listening posts on the front lines of the ghetto DMZ, from where they "provide essential information to the Anti-crime and Detective units." The NYPD also created a juvenile database to centralize and disseminate "intelligence" on youth offenders, "their street names, gangs or 'posse' affiliations."[27] The point here is not to deny the reality of youth crime but rather to question the methodology used to address it. Totally absent from NYC's war on kids was any discussion of an educational Marshall Plan or gun control.

Prostitution and pornography were also targeted by the Giuliani quality of life siege. Using both policing and new zoning laws, the legal and illegal wings of the sex trade have been expelled with ever greater vigor to the city's industrial fringe.[28] The tactics available to precinct commanders include impounding cars and publishing the names of johns. While Manhattan cops began to harass sex shops and hookers around 42nd Street, commanders in the 43rd, 45th, and 49th precincts in Bronx launched a full-scale war on prostitution: during a few short weeks in the autumn of 1994 police officers posing as prostitutes busted more than seventy would-be johns and confiscated sixty vehicles in "Operation Losing Proposition."[29] Throughout the city, prostitutes were rounded up by the hundreds; by 1998 the illegal sex trade had been virtually forced off the streets in many areas. As a result, the number of New York City Yellow Pages devoted to escort services jumped from seventeen before the crackdown to forty-eight after.[30]

The Giuliani–Bratton quality-of-life siege was quickly imitated by other cities on the eastern seaboard: Philadelphia started handcuffing truants; Boston made war on street vendors, beggars, and windshield washers.[31] The *Wall Street Journal*'s editorial page cheered them all on and called for the resurrection of reform schools.[32]

Giuliani's war against "disorder" left no stone unturned, nor any publicity stunt unexploited. Pressure from the city even caused the phone company Nynex to set about retrofitting the city's 8,400 street-corner payphones so as to disable incoming calls. Some were even switched from touch-tone back to rotary technology in an attempt to thwart the use of pagers and undermine the retail infrastructure of Gotham's booming drug trade.[33] Whether these changes impacted drug dealing is doubtful, but they certainly telegraphed an ambiance of war to all those whose lives were now inconvenienced. The revamped payphones were another way of militarizing public space and social relations, subtly forcing people to incorporate the motifs of the war on drugs into the script of their daily lives.

One part of the New York zero tolerance regime that is harder to quibble with is "Police Strategy No. 1," which aimed at removing firearms from New York streets. Using new computers, specialized programs, and high-speed links to ATF databases, the NYPD claims to have confiscated over

50,000 guns since 1993; they now take about 2,500 weapons a year.[34] And, quite rationally, these guns are no longer *sold back to the public* at auction, as had been the case.[35]

The Bratton team also unleashed the NYPD's full force on drug dealing. "As of Monday, April 18, 1994, the policy of the New York Police Department will be one of No Tolerance for dealers and buyers at all times," thus read the D-Day-like instructions of "Police Strategy No. 3." Gone were the days of segregating beat cops from narcotics enforcement (a practice designed in the seventies to avoid corruption). Now, any and all police were to pursue dealers, confiscate and trace their guns, confiscate vehicles, close drug houses, and occupy outdoor copping spots. The drug war wasn't just for elite cops anymore, now every precinct commander was responsible for reviewing surveillance and complaints, devising tactics, and initiating joint operations with the Narcotics Division and then *holding* the targeted areas.[36]

Ratcheting up New York's drug war led to immediate action in every borough. For many in drug-plagued communities, the police assault felt like a rescue operation, but for the dealers and non-dealing youth who "fitted the profile," the angry waves of blue were a deadly terror.

THE HIGH PRICE OF ORDER

It was late April 1994, and troops from the 120th precinct were finishing up a three-week sweep in Staten Island's roughneck northeast corner, the natal terrain of hip-hop's Wu Tang Clan.[37] Thirty-six alleged dealers had been busted using tactics straight from the Bratton–Maple play book: if you can't get 'em on felony drug charges bust 'em for drinking in public. As Maple put it: "Your open beer lets me check your ID. Now I can radio the precinct for outstanding warrants or parole violations. Maybe I bump against that bulge in your belt: with probable cause, I can frisk you."[38]

The geographic objective was to take and hold the predominantly African American Park Hill Apartments and a nearby block-long piece of asphalt and "balding earth" known as the Strip, which for lack of parks or recreation facilities served as a makeshift village center. The increased police pressure brought neighborhood tension to a boiling point. The so-called Special Narcotics Emergency Unit had already taken a brick – thrown from an apartment block roof – through the windshield of one of its cruisers. Then, on the evening of the 29th, as a team of officers were frisking prisoners in the street, an M-80 explosive was tossed in their direction. A young Liberian immigrant, Ernest Sayon, aka "Rabbit," allegedly ran from the scene and was tackled by police. Sayon was both a well-liked youth and a known dealer who in recent months had been arrested and shot by rivals. The details of what ensued next are not clear, save for the fact that the unarmed Sayon, beaten by police, arrived at the hospital dead from suffocation.[39]

The killing triggered immediate outrage: more than a hundred protesters converged on the hospital for an angry picket, before moving to the nearby precinct. Throughout the night other groups of protesters – chanting the familiar refrain, "no justice, no peace!" – converged and separated in front of the "one-twenty" and throughout the neighborhood.[40] Black leaders across the city blasted Giuliani and Bratton as bullies and racist thugs. Apparently the potential for popular explosion was alive and well; no matter how depoliticized, crime-terrorized and divided inner-city communities had become, the police task of keeping "surplus populations" contained could still backfire in dramatic ways. In reaction to the familiar dilemmas Kelling once again counseled the need for sophisticated police penetration of inner-city communities. Writing in *Newsday* he urged citizens to trust and collaborate with the state:

> Especially in neighborhoods where the level of trust between police and citizens is low, police must initiate these collaborations. But citizens must respond. Otherwise, the effects of assertive police action will not last, and both citizens' and officers' safety will be jeopardized. Even when a tragedy occurs like the Ernest Sayon death during a police operation on Staten Island, close collaboration between police and citizens can often limit the initial flare-up as well as prevent future conflicts and deterioration of police–citizen relations."[41]

Two years later the same neighborhood again erupted after police beat a woman for interfering with an arrest. Police attacked bystanders who tried to aid her, and in the ensuing melee, cops and civilians were hurt; eight people from the neighborhood were arrested. The battle was followed by another hundred-strong march on the "one-twenty."[42] Similar protest flared in Brooklyn's East Flatbush after undercover officers gunned down Aswon Keshawn Watson, an unarmed 23-year-old African American man. During the following days of protest twenty-two people were arrested.[43] This was followed by the police killings of Anthony Baez and Anthony Rosario; more protests and sit-ins followed, but no major explosions.[44] Then in 1997, Brooklyn's streets filled with enraged supporters of Abner Louima, the Haitian immigrant who was viciously beaten by cops and sodomized with a plunger until his guts ripped. The event precipitating the attack on Louima was the ticketing of a double-parked car, just the sort of minor infraction that would have gone unnoticed in pre-zero-tolerance Gotham.

These episodes of brutality are just the tip of the iceberg beneath which floats the bulk of zero tolerance/quality of life oppressions: the constant hostile gazes from police, the end of sipping beer on stoops, the fear of fines or arrest for playing loud music or riding a bicycle on the sidewalk. Arrest for misdemeanor crimes like jumping turnstiles now means spending a day in the back of a police van waiting for it to fill with other prisoners and then perhaps a night in jail. After all, millions of people in New York City use public space in ways that are technically disorderly: drinking outside, playing music, playing dominos, blocking the sidewalk with lawn chairs, selling trinkets, and throwing footballs in the street (the "offense" for which Anthony Baez was killed).

CRIME RATES AND LEGITIMATING MIGHT

The tremendous expansion of law enforcement's political and social presence in New York was, until recently, only minimally contested. Quiescence was assured by twenty years of fearmongering media, an absence of any political alternatives, and an ideologically sophisticated full-court press by the propaganda machine of the mayor's office and police department. But perhaps even more important has been the tremendous plunge in crime rates, a change that pre-dates Bratton's tenure in New York, but one that accelerated under the regime he established.[45] Left and liberal criminologists have protested politely that police are taking too much credit for recent victories over crime. They attribute the rosy crime stats to a cocktail of forces, including a smaller youth cohort; lower unemployment; the exhaustion and stabilization of crack markets; unusually cold winters; and creative reporting by police, in which robberies are downgraded to lost property, attempted murders to assaults, and unsolved homicides become suicides or accidental deaths.[46] In 1998 press reports surfaced revealing that cops were indeed lying about crime rates. In New York a former chief of the Transit Bureau was forced to retire because a commander under him had fabricated a double-digit crime rate decline in Midtown's transit district one. Likewise, a Bronx commander retired amid charges that he cooked the books in the 41st precinct.[47] In Philadelphia the pressure to produce good numbers was so intense that police fabricated wildly – creating figures that were so distorted that the Bureau of Justice Statistics worried that national aggregate figures had been skewed as a result.[48]

But even after accounting for fraud, creative police reporting, a booming economy, and stabilized crack markets, cohort size, and all other factors, the plunge in crime rates seems quite real and its association with zero tolerance has distilled into political rocket fuel. In New York the numbers are stunning: between 1994 and 1997 misdemeanor arrests shot up by 73 percent, swamping the seventy-seven judges who handle the city's criminal cases, while murder nosedived by over 60 percent.[49] By 1998, the city was looking forward to its lowest murder rate in thirty-three years. And since 1994 overall crime in New York has dropped 43 percent.[50]

During the same period another set of statistics has also emerged. Complaints of police brutality have jumped by 62 percent since Rudolph Giuliani took office in 1994, while in the same period the city has paid out more than $100 million in damages arising from police violence.[51] Brutality complaints increased 46 percent during the first half of 1994 alone.[52] Bratton's response was: "That's too damn bad."[53] Later, when asked about similar complaints in other zero tolerance departments, he explained: "It makes sense that there will be increased confrontation between officers and civilians. We're dealing with anti-social behavior patterns that had been ignored for twenty-five years."

THE MODEL PROLIFERATES

The precipitous decline in crime rates has motivated a wave of New York imitators in other large metropolitan departments. By 1997 police brass from New Orleans, Indianapolis, Minneapolis, and Baltimore had all made the pilgrimage to Gotham or hired Bratton protégés such as John Timoney, John

Linder, and Jack Maple as consultants.[54] All of these departments use versions of the weekly Comstat meetings, at which precinct or district captains go before their entire brass to narrate how the total war on crime is progressing at the grassroots. Likewise, San Francisco has used elements of the philosophy since the early 1990s when former police-chief-turned-mayor Frank Jordan accelerated the ongoing harassment campaign against the homeless. But the SFPD has not adopted the Comstat combination of computerized crime mapping, bureaucratic decentralization, and total quality management.

In Baltimore, the New York–inspired changes led to an immediate increase in reports of police brutality. At first, Police Commissioner Thomas Frazier had called zero tolerance a "buzzword . . . one iota away from discriminatory policing."[55] But political pressure, police union rancor, and renegade campaigns by several "zero tolerance" district commanders have forced Baltimore's brass to copy more and more of the New York methodology.[56] As a result, brutality is on the rise; so is the low-level harassment of Black youths – such as Gregory Schmoke, the mayor's son, who was stopped and hassled without cause.[57]

In New Orleans the switch to zero tolerance has taken place against an almost surreal backdrop of mass police criminality and violence. After decades of festering vice and outright terrorism, fifty NOPD officers were arrested in 1994 on a slew of charges, ranging from rape and drug dealing to robbery and murdering other police officers. A new chief, Richard Pennington, was brought in to deal with the crisis when even the most entrenched of the city's old boys admitted that discipline had completely disintegrated and that the force was out of control. Early in his tenure Pennington even considered firing the entire department, but in the end settled for an aggressive but inadequate purge.

Only a year and a half into its quality of life regime, New Orleans saw a version of the usual results: overly aggressive cops and rising brutality, coupled with declining crime rates in all categories, except homicide. Violent crime in the first quarter of 1997 was down by almost 20 percent compared to the first quarter of 1995. And according to the city's new police commissioner, homicides in the city's public housing fell 31 percent during 1997, while crime overall in the city decreased 24 percent during the same period.[58]

Mary Howell, New Orleans's leading police misconduct attorney, said that in the first three months of implementing zero tolerance, in 1997, she received more complaints of police brutality "than in the last two years combined."[59] Community activists say the Second and the Sixth districts – bitterly impoverished African American communities – have become virtual war zones, with the police on one side and residents on the other. As was to be expected, police enthusiasm for zero tolerance almost provoked a riot. Two notorious officers working the St. Thomas public housing project choked a fourteen-year-old girl after chasing a suspect into her housing project apartment. A young man from a local community group, Black Men United for Change, peacefully intervened by asking what was going on. The officers then turned on him. But as they were stuffing the young man into the back of their patrol car, some three hundred residents from the surrounding projects encircled the scene to, as activists said, "prevent the police from killing this guy."[60]

The litany of zero tolerance abuse goes on: a ten-year-old boy held face down in the dirt, a gun to his head; massive police sweeps in which all Black men encountered are stopped and searched under the auspices of a new "drug loitering" statute.[61] "According to the department's own statistics, citizen complaints against police rose by 27 percent between 1996 and 1997."[62]

Reports from Indianapolis sound like echoes from the Big Easy. The year 1997 brought the introduction of zero tolerance and what the Indianapolis Police Department calls "saturation patrols" against "nuisance crimes and street level dealing." According to the department's spokesperson, the changes weren't simply a matter of ideology: "At first we were too short staffed to do quality of life enforcement." But the new resources provided by Clinton's Community Oriented Policing Services (COPS) program, a legacy of the 1994 crime bill, allowed a law-and-order offensive.[63]

"These campaigns of harassment are relatively new but we're getting lots of calls about them," says Sheila Kennedy of the Indiana Civil Liberties Union. She says the official police statistics on reported abuse by officers are "unrealistic," but her office has definitely noticed an increase in brutality complaints and discriminatory traffic stops involving the African American community. "And in the gay community people feel that the cops are doing some bashing of their own."[64]

As in New Orleans, the Indianapolis version of zero tolerance operates on the minefield left by a long history of police misconduct. In July 1995 the festering social wounds on the city's infamous Northside finally burst into rioting after months of police pressure in which undercovers would conduct "controlled buys" and then call in support from "jump out" squads, paramilitary assault teams trained to swoop and vamp whole street corners in the blink of an eye. The African American neighborhood around 38th and College became ground-zero in this local war on drugs, a violent little vortex where national and local dynamics — from crime bill largess to the personal enmity between specific cops and local youths — converge in explosive ways. As usual it was a typical bust gone bad that started the rioting. Police accosted a 21-year-old African American man named Danny Sales. Though Sales had no drugs, he was in possession of $150 cash, which the police promptly confiscated. Their report on the bust and seizure explained that "Sales could not provide any evidence or explanation of employment." And when the young man protested the seizure of his money, police showered him with baton blows and took him into custody.[65] From there a familiar script began to unfold: more than a hundred infuriated residents picketed the local precinct; cops responded with a massive show of force; as night fell the police attacked with clubs, canine teams, and armored riot vehicles. In response, youth lobbed bricks and looted shops. The next night brought more of the same, plus the eerie clatter of helicopters and fusillades of tear gas.[66]

When the smoke finally cleared thirty-six people had been arrested and eleven others — including one cop and a television cameraman — had been injured by flying rocks, bottles, and police batons. Community activists blamed the chaos on the paramilitary, zero-tolerance-style occupation in which police mistreated dealers and innocents alike.[67] The Justice Department — which since the L.A. riots had been increasingly worried about the destabilizing potential of corruption and brutality among local police — sent in the FBI to investigate the IPD.[68] A year later the IPD's racist esprit de corps was still much in evidence. Almost as a commemoration of the previous summer's riot, a crew of off-duty officers — drunk after watching a baseball game in the mayor's personal skybox — went on a rampage, sexually harassing and groping women and then brutally beating a Black motorist.[69]

From the get-go, Indianapolis's quality of life policing offensive — known as "Project Saturation" — has been imbued with an ethos of racial containment and pacification. But now the IPD's war against Black people is dressed in the pseudo-scientific garb of ZT theory. Playing a role equivalent to that of Kelling and the Police Foundation in New York is the conservative Hudson Institute (momentarily home to that towering intellect, "fellow" Dan

Quayle). To bolster the Hudson-produced studies, Indianapolis also hired Lawrence Sherman, whose work on computer mapping of "hot spots" influenced the formation of Comstat.[70] Sherman and the eggheads from Hudson continue to urge the city's new police chief, Mike Zunk, to "crack down on those low-level types of offenses," so that "law-abiding people will take an interest in their neighborhood."[71]

According to this view, "order" is achieved by "flooding" Black neighborhoods with swarms of cops, including SWAT teams and canine units. It is the strategy of colonial war: peace through superior firepower. In Indianapolis it seems only force is considered a reasonable remedy for dealing with warring sets of Vice Lords and Disciples, the Midwest's equivalents of Crips and Bloods.[72] To whip up public support, official warnings are issued about the spread of crack cocaine outward from its coastal, big-city epicenters into the medium-sized cities of the Midwest, while police call neighborhood watch meetings and go door to door, making their presence felt and spreading the gospel of fear. To complement the front-line muscle, Marion County DA Scott Newman created a squad of front-line deputy prosecutors to work closely with each police district. Under the new regime police "performance is not based on convictions or the number of arrests," but rather on how well they enforce quality of life laws. Among their tools is a new "stay-away order" to control the movement of alleged gangbangers and dealers who are out on bond.[73]

Thus Indianapolis offers another example of overlapping, mutually enforcing systems of control and exclusion, ranging from academic discourse to door knocking, and including the semiotic and physical power of police dogs on the corner.[74]

But so far the IPD's new game plan has not had much of an impact on crime rates.[75] Nor would one expect much different in a city so economically mangled: during the eighties white per-capita income in Indianapolis stayed flat while Black per-capita income dropped 11 percent.[76] Behind the fast-burning desperation of crack dealing and gangbanging "people" and "folks"[77] are much deeper problems, summarized by one of the city's more eloquent columnists:

Deindustrialization crippled the mobility of the Black working class. Suburbanization, the great federal Marshall Plan for the middle class, lacerated African-American communities with freeways and bled them of resources. Downtown revitalization took root in the ruins of homes, schools, churches, corner stores and jazz clubs . . . The [1980s,] decade of sports stadia, office towers, luxury hotels, cultural palaces and tourism also saw Indianapolis lead the nation in the death rate of Black infants. Though scores of millions of dollars from taxes and foundations subsidized glamour projects, money for expanded pre- and post-natal care for poor women came late and grudgingly.[78]

UNDOING THE CONSTITUTION QUIETLY

In Minneapolis the police project a more progressive image. Though openly following the New York model, they emphasize proactive prevention over quality of life busts. "For example we just had a gang shooting," says Chief Robert Olson, a friend of Bratton's and a former commissioner in Yonkers, New York. "So instead of waiting for it to escalate, and then tracking down the culprits, we sent twelve probation officers out with the cops. They tracked down the known gang members, went to their houses, didn't arrest, just talked to 'em. Said: 'Hey we know what's going on. No retaliations.'" The chief claims great success, but unfortunately the city's murder rate has been rising.[79]

Even when such preventive measures work, they can quickly become what criminologist Stan Cohen calls "net widening and mesh thinning."[80] Cohen argues that new "soft" reforms usually fail to displace older, harsher types of repression. Instead, the "soft" controls expand and extend the disciplinary reach of the "harder" ones. For example, the repressive juvenile courts of today were born from the efforts of do-gooders like Jane Addams who wished to "save children" from the adult courts and jails. Intensive probation and parole programs, with their drug testing and electronic bracelets, were developed as alternatives to prison, but now they often come *in addition* to incarceration.[81]

In Anaheim, California, Cohen's thesis has become reality: probation officers, coordinating their efforts with the District Attorney, ride with police, not to preempt gangbanging, but to catch and bust youth who violate the rules of their virtual house-arrest probation. One of the Anaheim prosecutors summed up the policy thus: "If active gang members come out on probation and they sneeze, they're going back to jail."[82] Here too, it is the rhetoric of zero tolerance and quality of life that justifies such heavy-handed control.

And so it is throughout the zero tolerance archipelago: the "broken windows" logic and quality of life lexicon gives pseudo-scientific legitimacy to police state violations of civil liberties. As an NOPD spokesman put it: "Every arrest for a quality of life offense is a potential breakthrough on some other larger case. Every ticket, every bust provides intelligence, on a potential criminal." This logic – first publicly articulated by Maple's "Your open beer lets me check your ID" – turns the struggle for "order" into a Trojan horse for police state tactics.

"People say Z.T. doesn't work because in New York or Baltimore, 80% of the quality of life tickets are never paid and an enormous amount of the misdemeanor court dates are no-shows," says zero tolerance apostle Lt. McLhenny of the Baltimore PD. "But hey, that doesn't matter. Unpaid tickets become [arrest] warrants. What counts is we've got them in the system! We're building a database."[83]

Add to that disturbing admission the fact that zero tolerance is often selectively enforced against people of color and the visibly poor and what emerges is a postmodern version of Jim Crow. Enough unpaid tickets and petty outstanding warrants lead to the criminal labeling of non-deviant populations. But to what end? What interests are served by the quality of life revolution? To answer that question we must dig deeper into the economic and cultural geography of the themepark city.

CHAPTER FIVE

DISCIPLINE IN PLAYLAND, PART II – POLICING THE THEMEPARK CITY

The presence of large numbers of homeless people on our streets
has caused significant damage to our economy . . .
Kent Sims, advisor to the mayor of San Francisco, 1992

It is no coincidence that zero tolerance/quality of life policing developed just
as cities have taken on renewed economic and cultural importance. At the
heart of the new urban security quest lies a vexing contradiction: capitalism
creates and needs poverty, yet is simultaneously threatened by the poor.
Poverty is produced organically by capitalist crisis and deliberately by social
policy. As an abstract political force, poverty is very useful; it scares and dis-
ciplines the working classes, keeps wages down, and provides a platform for
moralizing political circus. But actual groups of poor people in real spaces
can cause great trouble for the business classes. For example, a large hotel
benefits from wages kept low by the threat of poverty, but at the same time
poor people begging or stealing outside such a hotel will hurt business. This
contradiction is all the more pronounced in the current epoch when so much
investment is tied up with consumption and the spaces in which consumption occurs; that is, when profitability is so intimately tied with the fate of
cities.

If the security culture, zero tolerance included, is an integral – even
organic – function of the new metropolis, then a glance back at the history
of the new city is necessary.

BUILDING THE CITADEL

The story of the new security-conscious city is in many ways the flipside narrative of the "jobless ghetto." The natural decline and intentional decimation of manufacturing and transportation as central components in many urban economies have given rise to a business ecology dominated by finance, insurance, and real estate (FIRE), along with high tech, design, cultural production, and tourism. This mix of industries requires and creates both spaces and populations that are particularly threatened by the violence and poverty that wracks much of urban America.

The populations threatened are the new upper-middle classes and the postmodern *rentiers*, those concentrations of highly educated managerial and intellectual labor: engineers, attorneys, designers, accountants, managers, risk analysts, academics, spin doctors, deal makers, and those ubiquitous "project managers." These new burghers require specialized urban work spaces, living quarters, and highly designed, hyper-anesthetized play zones. Thus we get the SoHos, SOMAs, art/technology belts, multimedia "gulches" and "glens" in which entrepreneurs, programmers, financiers, and artists and other "content providers" can "network" and cross-fertilize. The more central parts of the FIRE economy also require specialized spaces: the international airports, super-wired "smart buildings," spectacular corporate towers providing the "signature address," and a retail streetscape of fine restaurants, theaters, convention centers, museums, and promenade neighborhoods.

The flows of professional labor in the FIRE economy overlap with and generate an expanded tourist industry which brings its own spatial imperatives; thus the endless proliferation of even more shopping districts, museums, superstores, restaurants, food courts, urban malls, and yuppie playgrounds like San Francisco's Fisherman's Wharf, Boston's Faneuil Hall, Baltimore's Harbor Place, and Miami's silicone-enhanced South Beach.

Even cities that fall rather low on the international hierarchy of place try to pursue a FIRE/themepark model of redevelopment. Witness the pathetic spectacle of Flint, Michigan, building a convention center; Detroit trying to revitalize its downtown with a phantasmagoric, river-front corporate tower and a luxury housing complex, the "Renaissance Center"; or Camden, New Jersey, building a convention center and $52 million aquarium, yet remaining a bombed out, violent slum battered by unemployment and isolated by white racism. All these schemes have more or less failed, leaving all three cities with little besides massive arrears. To the extent that such projects as Camden's aquarium have succeeded it is due in large part to "boasting of their 'security' from the rest of the city."[1]

The intimate link between security — that is, segregation of poor people of color — and economic value has been an integral part of the FIRE/ themepark city from its earliest evolutionary stages at the end of World War II. As the smoke cleared over Hiroshima and Nagasaki, America emerged as the world's military and economic superpower. Business leaders realized that this new role required rebuilt cities or, more accurately, bigger, modernized central business districts (CBDs) to serve as the managerial cockpits of the global capitalist economy. At the local level this meant building new high-rise central business districts and commuter transportation systems linking these to the white collar labor of the suburbs. From L.A. to Boston, local boosters and "pro-growth coalitions" — involving alliances of labor, big business, and local government — made plans to rebuild America's decrepit central cities as corporate headquarters districts capable of facilitating the global flows of labor, capital, and information. At the same time, Congress passed the Housing Act of 1949, which channeled federal funds to city governments for urban renewal. The stated aim of this program was the alleviation of poverty and the destruction of "blighted" housing, to be replaced by new modern habitation.

The real aim, however, was to clear out the poor and working classes (particularly the darker-skinned poor) who occupied valuable downtown land needed for central business district expansion, and to create "safe" non-Black *cordons sanitaires* around the CBDs. Federal funds were used to raze the "skid rows" and "ghettos" that border most CBDs. As one San Francisco–based Del Monte executive put it: "You certainly can't expect us to erect a 50 million dollar building in an area where dirty old men will be going around exposing themselves to our secretaries."[2]

Critics called the program "Negro removal" because it turned once-vibrant Black neighborhoods into moonscapes. The scope of urban renewal's ruin and displacement is so massive that any study of America's current incarceration binge and police crackdown must recall the era when federal bulldozers laid waste to Black businesses and grassroots economic networks, and forced the refugees into over-crowded public housing. From Philadelphia to San Francisco, vibrant corridors of small businesses, light industry, and fine housing were literally plowed under. With these neighborhoods went some of the jobs, social networks, and transportation links that could have steered many of today's convicts into an alternate, missing, future.

So urban renewal cleared the way for new CBDs and created the *cordons sanitaires*, but also created poverty and social dislocation that later returned as crime and disorder.

GENTRIFICATION: THE KNOCK-ON EFFECT

The corporate rebuilding of America's downtowns created the command-and-control centers needed by transnational business operations, but by the late eighties this process had produced a glut of office space in many cities, including New York, San Francisco, and Chicago,[3] and a shortage of centrally located, up-scale housing. Though there seemed to be endless new subdivisions in the sprawling plastic environs, many of the FIRE and culture professionals – the aesthetic offspring of Jane Jacobs – wanted (and want) the drama of "the urban." Corporate America's happy massification of "bohemian" aesthetics produced a generation of professionals who, like locusts to a delicate crop, instinctively follow artists and students into cities seeking diversity, "authenticity," vibrancy, and the mirage of a non-commodified "lifestyle."

By the late seventies and early eighties, this combination of factors translated into waves of gentrification, in which people in the remaining central-city working class and poor neighborhoods were once again being displaced by the lighter, moneyed classes. This incremental conquest, which seems to reignite with each upswing in the business cycle, involves a strange alchemy between bohemian culture, relatively cheap property, home owner tax credits, and the profit-driven subterfuge of real estate developers.[4] The irony is that in many cases the gentrified playgrounds – Adams Morgan, Cambridge, the Castro, the Village – are communities that had once been slated for demolition by highway construction or urban renewal but were saved by hybrid social movements involving poor people, activists, and middle-class preservationists.

CULTURAL STRATEGIES OF
DEVELOPMENT AND SECURITY

The "organic" advance of gentrification and the exhaustion of the corporate real estate boom of the seventies and eighties rebuild have spurred the rise of what sociologist Sharon Zukin calls "cultural strategies of accumulation."[5] These include city center revitalization based on arts and entertainment, historic preservation (the "heritage industry"), building new parks and waterfront promenades, opening new museums or moving old ones, and building convention centers.[6]

Thus in the early nineties Philadelphia invested $250 million in a convention center and the "Avenue of the Arts," so as to become "the east coast's premier destination city."[7] A panel of Cleveland's "community leaders" – mostly corporate executives like Joseph Gorman, CEO of TRW Inc. – is pushing for $2.7 billion in public and private investment over the next ten years to build a new convention center and an attendant waterfront retail playground. The developers are no doubt buoyed by the smashing success of culture-led revitalization in "the Flats" – a low, post-industrial area on the Cuyahoga River now populated with night clubs, a TGI Fridays, and a much storied Hooters.[8] Meanwhile, Seattle contemplated leveling a neighborhood to build a downtown park; and San Francisco has moved another major museum to its CBD and is subsidizing the construction of an interactive children's fun house, a gigantic multimedia urban themepark to be run by Sony, and yet more expansion at the Moscone Convention Center.[9]

One prime indicator of how widely cultural strategies of accumulation have proliferated is the rate of convention center construction. Since 1977 the number of cities with major convention centers tripled from 100 to 300. In virtually all of these cases municipal and state governments underwrote not only the construction costs but the operating costs as well.[10] This tropism of urban growth coalitions towards the entertainment/culture dollar is part of a general shift away from durable goods consumption towards entertainment. Since 1979 the percentage of all consumer spending (not including medical expenses) devoted to entertainment and recreation has gone from 7.71 percent to 9.43 percent. Since 1991 such spending has increased by 13 percent, and by the mid 1990s Americans spent $340 billion a year entertaining themselves.[11]

Zukin's work has found a wide audience in sociology and geography, while the popular press has focused on the economy of play, but few writers have examined the security imperative that lurks on the dark side of "culture"-based redevelopment strategies. To expose the debt that official "fun" pays to terror necessarily reveals the subtle but ubiquitous role of state repression in everyday life. Again, New York offers a brutally clear illustration of such linkages.

SECURITY, AMBIANCE, AND MONEY-MAKING IN THE BIG APPLE

When Giuliani first became mayor he bad-mouthed public arts funding, lumping it in with welfare and other "unworthy" social services. But even the ghoulish ex-prosecutor, whose only true love seems to be rules and regulations, soon recognized the cash value of culture. "[It] really is the core of a great city," announced the mayor, "to maintain and preserve the arts, certainly as part of the spiritual identity of the city but also because this is an important industry . . . This is vital to our economic renewal."[12] Thus in 1994 – year zero of Giuliani's reign, when the first of the workfare proletariat hit the streets and municipal unions braced for casualties – New York City launched a tourist initiative consisting of publicly subsidized package deals: a hotel stay, restaurant coupons, and opera and sports tickets, with a market value of $345, for only $199.[13]

This demand-side pump-priming soon gave way to wholesale, supply-side subsidies for the culture/entertainment/real estate complex headquartered in the Times Square and 42nd Street area. In partnership with Walt Disney and other major developers the city has poured public money into the conversion of this urban crossroads from porno-Mecca to urban themepark epicenter. "The city and state are jointly chipping in $75 million, mostly to condemn old properties and provide developers with tax incentives." The total development spending for the larger twelve-block Times Square neighborhood is estimated to top $4 billion.[14] As the redevelopment effort got underway and the strip clubs and peep show neon signs blinked out, 42nd Street's theater marquees were momentarily handed over to poets for posting "urban haikus." Meanwhile, at street level a new private security force maintained radio contact with the police, informing the latter of "crimes" ranging "from three-card monte to drug dealing."[15]

As the reconquest of the Times Square Ginza progresses the Big Apple's boosters have become quite candid about the centrality of segregation and repression – that is, zero tolerance policing – to profitable redevelopment. As one representative from the New York City Economic Development Corporation put it, "The reduction in crime has improved New York's quality of life, bolstered job growth and increased investment throughout the city . . . I think the crime decline has been very significant in the city's revival."[16] A Giuliani spokeswoman was even more succinct: "Big business isn't afraid to invest in the city anymore."

By the end of the 1990s tourism in Gotham had set new records, and in August 1998 developers announced plans for a $66 million retail and entertainment complex, this time in Harlem.[17] As the boom of the nineties rolls on, the economic pressure to drive the poor from Manhattan has only intensified.

BIDS, SIDEWALK MERCENARIES, AND "SOCIAL HYGIENE"

To recapitulate: zero tolerance is a central part of the security matrix upon which the FIRE/themepark metropolis depends. But the struggle for order is by no means only a public project. Inside the malls and megastores there is, of course, the ubiquitous store security of hidden microphones and cameras, undercover guards posing as shoppers, electronically tagged merchandise, and the uniformed presence by the door. This private security matrix overflows into the street, where rent-a-cops are imbricated into the larger policing project through a delicate division of labor: private forces control interior spaces, aid the police in holding pacified streetscapes, and even launch offensives against non-violent undesirables.

In a growing number of cities the private components of the security web are controlled by Business Improvement Districts (BIDs): private, self-taxing, urban micro-states that do everything from cleaning streets and guiding tourists to floating bonds and arresting beggars. Like the "burbclaves" and "Franchise-Organized Quasi-National Entities" of Neal Stephenson's cyberpunk classic Snow Crash, BIDs embody all the power and privileges of the state yet bear none of the responsibilities and limitations of democratic government. As one BID-promoting free-marketeer in D.C. put it: "It's up to us to stand up and assert our rights."[18]

Midtown Manhattan, 1994 . . . It's a cold night on the cusp of winter and spring. Two men wearing jackets emblazoned "Outreach Team – Grand Central Partnership" kick a prone figure wrapped in a gray blanket. "Come on, this is private property – you *got* to move!" Standing close by are four activists from the civil rights group Street Watch. Lately, a new private security force known as the Grand Central Partnership (GCP) "Outreach Team" has surpassed the cops as the main violators of street peoples' rights. The sixty maroon-clad GCP outreach workers are themselves homeless and formerly homeless people paid only $1 an hour. Officially, the outreach teams are just "volunteers" receiving a stipend, and legally they are not allowed to order people camped in public to move or leave. But more serious things than legality are at stake here – for example, real estate.

The GCP is one of New York's largest BIDs, controlling roughly fifty blocks around Grand Central Station, with an annual budget of $41 million and managing security contracts stretching from 110th down to Wall Street.[19] Presiding at the apex of this little empire is Daniel Biederman, also the chieftain of the powerful Bryan Park and 34th Street BIDs.

Like all BIDs the GCP's public face is user-friendly tourist information and beautification projects; it improved lighting, cleaned streets, and installed flower planters and new street furniture. But none of these physical investments would "improve business conditions" – as is the outfit's stated goal – if New York's army of paupers was still allowed to bivouac in ATM vestibules and on the granite thresholds of corporate towers. Thus one of the GCP's semi-secret functions is to contract the services of its shabby mercenary force of drug-addled toughs to major landlords wishing to keep their sidewalks riffraff free. Call it free-market social hygiene.

"You're not planning to *physically* remove this guy, are you?" asks Street Watch activist Matt Snyder. "Man, just get the hell out of my face and let me do my job," roars an outreach worker.[20]

Ostensibly, these GCP outreach workers – who in different windbreakers double as the GCP's security force – are merely steering their fellow homeless towards social service programs at the Saint Agnes drop-in center. But the drop-in center, like most homeless shelters, is a filthy social dumping ground, bereft of real services and overrun by disease and vermin. For years licensed only as a drop-in center, Saint Agnes even lacked beds; its four hundred regular clients slept in plastic chairs. (The spot has since become a real shelter, and is run by a GCP spin-off non-profit called the Grand Central

Partnership Social Service Corporation.) The outfit's $125,000-a-year exec-
utive director, Jeff Grunberg, argues that "the business community is too
often excluded from the solution process," and needs to be brought "back
in," adding that a lot of executives "are really decent people." According to
Grunberg, "The homeless should be viewed as customers and social services
as the product." He says his Outreach Team is only guilty of using "a per-
sistent sales pitch."[21]

Inside Saint Agnes the air hangs thick with cigarette smoke and body odor.
Dissident clients describe the drop-in center as an incubator for HIV and
tuberculosis. They allege rampant drug use and unsafe sex. "Our bathrooms
are being renovated," explained Grunberg excitedly, stepping into a small
tiled room. "We found that underneath the urinals there was no drain. For
years this place was flushing into dirt." Not surprisingly, the bathrooms were
constantly flooded with sewage.

Back on the night-time streets, in the forgotten crevasses around the
United Nations Building, the image of BIDs disintegrates further: "They'll
burn your boxes down, they throw gas on you, tear your structures down,
and throw your clothes away," says James Gray, describing the deeds of the
GCP's dollar-an-hour marauders. Gray, who once lived on the streets, spent
two years on both sides of the Midtown battle. For a year and a half in the
early nineties Gray worked for the Grand Central Partnership, first as an outreach worker – for three months – then as a cook at the Saint Agnes drop-
in center. By 1994 Gray had quit and returned to the streets, where he soon
found himself on the receiving end of the GCP's policing efforts.

Despite the late night brutality, the homeless in Midtown are abundant
and stubbornly immobile. The Tudor Towers, a complex of luxury apartments near the United Nations, pays the Grand Central Partnership Social
Service Corporation $2,600 a month to keep its property street-person
free. Despite all "outreach efforts" about ten homeless people still camp in
boxes between the river of traffic on First Avenue and the sheer back face
of the Tudor City high-rises. On this narrow esplanade sits the short, fit, 32-
year-old Frankie. For almost two years Frankie was part of the Saint Agnes
"house gang, the family." Like many New York shelters, Saint Agnes had its
own version of jailhouse culture, where gangs and petty despots called the
shots.

Frankie, however, was down with the crew and was allowed to sleep
upstairs on the floor. To earn his keep he cleared other homeless people out

of the Grand Central area, usually with the offer of services, but when necessary, other means were used. "I seen guys get punched in the face, kicked," says Frankie. "You know it happens. I mean what would you do if you had somebody that's drunk and you got to get them out of an ATM?" Apparently the routine – as Frankie and other outreach workers explain – is to "call for back up and get busy," using what another outreach worker, Chris James, called "strategic force."[22]

Eventually the abuses by midtown BIDs grew so egregious and the constant political pressure from homeless victims and activists so irritating that Andrew Cuomo, then assistant secretary of Housing and Urban Development, withdrew grant money from the GCP.[23] A year later, revelations of possible improprieties at the Grand Central Partnership forced the city to tighten regulation of all BIDs.[24] The GCP was forced to raise its wages, but the use of homeless people as security guards and outreach workers continues.

Eventually, the real threat to the semi-sovereign power of the BIDs came not from the left but from the right. In the summer of 1998, the increasingly paranoid Mayor Giuliani turned on his truckling ally, king of the BIDs Daniel Biederman, accusing him of empire-building. The power and profile of the BIDs was too much; the mayor's staff demanded that the GCP hand over its assets and devolve power. The BIDs vowed to fight it out in court.[25] Giuliani's jealous tantrum aside, New York's private "para-state" enclaves are too well entrenched and too important to business to be dismantled.

A NATION OF BIDs

New York, as always, is extreme but not unusual. BIDs are popping up from coast to coast. In Milwaukee the Downtown BID, established in 1984, deploys guards with radios, to be law enforcement's extra "eyes and ears." They are instructed to give special attention to the "homeless, mentally ill, and inebriates," say city officials. "In other words, they will try to keep the street people in line."[26] Fifty similar BIDs operate throughout Wisconsin; the Milwaukee Downtown BID has the largest annual budget at $1.7 million, with a mix of public and private sector moneys. Philadelphia; Washington, D.C.; Springfield, Massachusetts, and scores of other cities have also chartered BIDs; more than 1,000 exist in forty states around the country.[27]

POLICING OZ: THE CASE OF
SAN FRANCISCO

In New York, because the city's reputation as a whole was so bad, quality of life policing (and its private proxies) have been applied city-wide, though not without some over-emphasis on the center. All crime rates had to go down for Gotham's playground core to be viewed as safe and for Giuliani to mobilize anxious voters for his re-election. San Francisco offers a more instrumentalist version of the broken-windows-inspired crackdown. In this vain city by the bay, security – that is, anti-homeless policing – is openly discussed as economic raw material for the post-industrial themepark economy. Take, for example, a 1989 survey by the Visitors and Convention Bureau that found "street people" were scaring off tourists, damaging the city's number one industry. The survey report, a follow-up of a similar study done six years earlier, noted that:

> Of most concern, however, is that the proportion of visitors concerned about "street people" has increased from 5 percent in 1983 to over 20 percent of all visitors in 1989, and has emerged as the single most disliked aspect about a visit to San Francisco today.[28]

A representative of the Downtown Association, a mini-chamber of commerce, explained the homeless problem as follows:

> Anytime that you have a situation that is perceived as *unsafe* it scares people away. That doesn't mean it is unsafe. But we've heard a lot of comments along the line of: "I don't want to come out of a restaurant late or come out of a theater late." That scares away tourism; be it visitors from other parts of the United States or international tourists. Or, what I call local tourists, visitors from the outlying suburban areas who are not coming into town as much.[29]

The executive director of the Hotel Council of San Francisco, which represents "all the city's major hotels," expressed a similar view. According to this group, homelessness is one of "the top issues of importance" for the city's economy:

You have people on the street who are really aggressive. They congregate at Fisherman's Wharf, Union Square and . . . they intimidate tourists . . . [The San Francisco tourist and hotel industries] are not alone in this world. We have major competition from other cities. And perception is very important. If people perceive an area to be unsafe then they'll stop coming . . . The concern of most travelers today, wherever they go is: number one security, number two cleanliness, and number two, or three, is not being harassed.[30]

The business community wanted a solution. As the Hotel Council's director put it:

I think somewhere along the line someone is going to have to suggest that perhaps there is another area they'd like to go to. I don't think it's proper that when people are paying their taxes and endeavoring to do business that [other] people can just have the right to camp out in front of their place.

The task of retaking the city fell to former police-chief-turned-mayor, Frank Jordan. What ensued was a campaign of quality of life enforcement known as the Matrix program. From 1993 on, the "visibly poor" were herded from one neighborhood to the next by teams of cops citing, arresting, and even jailing thousands of shopping-cart nomads, aged inebriates, and thrown-away youth.

The intellectual author of the program was Kent Sims, director of the mayor's Office of Economic Planning and Development and a former Federal Reserve Bank economist. Sims outlined the social hygiene campaign in a surprisingly candid 1992 white paper. According to that document,

[the] fundamental problem with our City's policy on homelessness has been that it reflects principally the interests of social service agencies and homeless advocates – rather than the needs and concerns of the larger non-homeless community of businesses . . .[31]

From the outset the class and racial priorities of the Matrix program were apparent. Sims pitched anti-homeless repression as a long-term strategy to help the needy:

The presence of large numbers of homeless people [many of whom are African American] on our streets has caused significant damage to our economy. The public's response to the proliferation of homeless people is estimated to cost San Francisco about $173 million annually in taxable sales, and $2.2 million in tax revenues to the General Fund and $1.3 million in tax revenues to the schools and transit – resources we need to serve the homeless and other dependent citizens. In addition to reducing the flow of homeless people into San Francisco, we also must take steps to limit the adverse impact the homeless have on our local economy.[32]

The white paper soon took paramilitary form: on August 6, 1993, Commander Dennis Martel, the SFPD officer in charge of the operation, issued a memorandum outlining the problem:

Some areas of the city suffer from a concentration of individuals who on a regular basis create quality of life problems for neighborhoods by committing nuisance and quality of life criminal offenses (aggressive panhandling, trespassing, obstructing, drunkenness, public urination, lodging, illegal encampments on public and private property, etc.). These conditions have resulted in complaints from residents, merchants and tourists. Common complaints are that residents are frightened and intimidated in their own neighborhoods; residents and tourists will not patronize problematic areas, which results in decreased business, unemployment and neighborhood deterioration.[33]

The theory of an economic/aesthetic threat to the themepark city is clear not only to business elites and planners, but to police brass as well. Commander Martel's memo is almost a seamless continuation of the discursive line developed by San Francisco's downtown business interests.

On the ground, this meant two years of pre-dawn sweeps by mounted cops through Golden Gate Park; endless ticketing in every quarter of the city; mounting charges of human rights violations; news footage of bulldozers leveling hidden homeless shanties and garbage trucks crushing homeless people's shopping carts and worldly possessions. Likewise, activists from the group Food Not Bombs (which gives free food to the homeless and agitates for low-income housing and social services) were being attacked, arrested, jailed, and released in an endless cycle of anti-poor persecution.

By 1995 the political spectacle of homelessness had became an iatrogenic malady. The more Jordan punished the city's nomads, the more amplified their political presence became. The more he pledged to rid the city once and for all of vagabonds, the more people felt that the city really was over-run by beggars and drunks. When Jordan was finally replaced by Willie Brown, the reality of policing the dangerous classes changed little. Quality of life infractions remain a top priority for the SFPD, but now the focus is more pragmatic: maintain order in the downtown citadel, keep most of the visible poor at the themepark's edge; remove the disruptive, psychotic van-guard so that those homeless people who do penetrate the tourist enclaves cause minimal disruption. And most of all, don't draw too much media attention to the intractable nature of the problem.

CLASS WAR IN THE VILLAGE

The security imperative of the FIRE/themepark core also extends to the gen-trifying "near-core" as well. Nor does the voracious advance of the refur-bished, retaken, new central city occur without opposition. Take for example Manhattan's Lower East Side, where a naked class war has raged, off and on, for more than a decade. In the usual pattern, moneyed urban professionals are steadily displacing working class Latinos and low-budget bohemians (usu-ally the first wave white settlers who open the way for redevelopment, but then fall prey to the very process they have helped set in motion). As the neighborhood is converted into a secured playground and urban bedroom community for salaried (as opposed to waged) advertising, entertainment, high-tech, and finance workers, the NYPD has turned its sights on political enemy number one, the post-punk communards of the East Village squat scene.[34]

This war first caught the world's eye during the infamous police riot of August 1988, when officers with tape over their badge numbers and, some say, liquor on their breath went berserk, attacking and pulverizing anti-gentrification demonstrators and bystanders alike in Tompkins Square Park. After years of low-intensity conflict and a more than two-year occupation of the park, large direct confrontations flared up again on May 30, 1995. It began when paramilitary eviction squads from the NYPD launched a huge raid on two East Village tenements, 541 and 545 East 13th Street. Ranks of police decked out with helmets, shields, and batons overwhelmed a "defiant group of squatters" who had been fighting eviction and living under semi-siege for nine months.[35] The raid's logo, the synecdoche of NYPD overkill, was the ubiquitous image of the department's blue-and-white armored personnel carrier.

Propelling the evictions were all the forces one would suspect: the advance of gentrification, real estate speculation, and puritanical hysteria about "freeloading." The first wave bohemians had served their purpose, making the neighborhood appealing to professionals and investors, and now they were being pushed on to homestead the next frontier, just like previous generations of poor white "settlers."

As James Ledbetter described the raids, even mainstream journalists tasted the jackboot:

> John DeSantis, a *New York Times* stringer, was on a nearby roof when the raid broke. A uniformed police officer aimed his gun at DeSantis's face and shouted "Freeze!" DeSantis was then forced to lie on his stomach, as if he were a criminal suspect, and says his arm was scraped as he was dragged off the roof. Three photographers were similarly roughed up; all were wearing police-issued press passes.[36]

The mistreatment of squatters was even worse. After the eviction, East 13th Street between avenues A and B was closed to the public. Police held the perimeter with four officers at each end of the block, others patrolled the middle, while a sergeant staffed a mobile communications center nearby. People who lived or worked in the occupied area had to show ID and cross checkpoints to enter.[37] In this manner forces from the 9th precinct held the street for over a month, without incident.

But under the thunderous cover of official July Fourth pyrotechnics, a crew of tenacious squatters managed to retake 541 East 13th Street. This time the police counterattack was "markedly more violent than during the militarily methodical May 30 eviction . . . Not only squatters but sympathetic protesters, bystanders, and Fourth of July party-goers all say cops beat them." Stanley Cohen, attorney for the housing activists and squatters, said he received more than thirty complaints of police abuse.[38] The scene was so wild WNBC TV felt that footage from the streets warranted interrupting its live coverage of the East River fireworks displays.[39] Again, police battery was indiscriminate. Among the wounded was German journalist Peter Kleeberg, left with a concussion after cops smashed him in the skull with a riot shield and threw him down a flight of stairs.[40]

The next summer brought more of the same.[41] On August 13, 1996, squads of NYPD troops again filled the streets as they moved against barricaded squatters in three city-owned tenements on East 13th Street. Activists from around the city gathered to hold off the attackers. But the NYPD simply rolled through the crowd arresting resisters and scattering the rest into the surrounding streets.[42] More mass evictions followed a few weeks later.[43] As journalist Sarah Ferguson described it, thirty-one people charged with misdemeanor offenses "that ordinarily warrant no more than a desk-appearance ticket" were "strip-searched" and jailed for two days. The New York Civil Liberties Union charged that the NYPD and Giuliani were using park regulations and municipal codes "to undermine protest on the Lower East Side."[44]

This time around, the cops would have to destroy the block to save it. In emulation of the Israeli Army's conquest of the West Bank, the raids were followed up by demolition; the interiors of the five captive tenements were gutted, making them impossible to retake. "We have finally set down the law," said Antonio Pagan, a city councilman whose former base of operations, the non-profit group Lower East Side Coalition Housing Development, was awarded the $4 million contract to redevelop the vanquished squats.[45]

By 1997 squatters were being mysteriously burnt out of their homes, only to have the city bulldoze and tear down the remaining structures.[46] Most poignant of all are the current "enclosures" targeting the lush communal gardens cultivated by Lower East Side residents on the neighborhood's many derelict lots. These collective resources are now desired by the real estate squires with excess capital. And in a replay of the Elizabethan enclosures, the state is using force to facilitate the transfer. Tompkins Square Park as well has emerged from its facelift – it was shut down and rehabbed in the early nineties – as a safe, green enclave, but one that is so militarized, crawling with police cars and scooters, as to be stripped of its civic and politically libertine features. No longer a staging ground for resistance, the park is a sort of bait attraction for the surrounding area, where the rich kids play at slumming in upscale pubs. The whole occupation and pacification of the East Village, from Operation Pressure Point in the 1980s through the current quality of life regime, is an elaborate form of public subsidy to private real estate interests, and one that leaves bare the intimate connection between state repression and the new urban economy of speculation and fun.

BADLANDS

Pacification of the financial and entertainment core and its gentrified buffer zones causes increased immiseration in the urban periphery. In New York facilities serving the poor, such as homeless shelters, free clinics, detox centers, and pieces of the welfare bureaucracy, are being relocated to distant, land-plentiful ghettos. Of New York's thirteen newest shelters, nine are located in peripheral and impoverished parts of Brooklyn and the South Bronx; one is in northern Manhattan. Add to the picture transitional housing for addicts, parolees, mentally ill people, and homeless families, as well as jails, methadone clinics, and the worst of high-rise public housing, and what emerges in cities like New York, Chicago, and Philadelphia are urban reservations, home to populations made redundant, chewed-up, spat-out, and shunted aside by the quest for profit.

These containment zones, as Mike Davis calls them, are increasingly written into the official goals of urban planning. In 1994 New York Mayor Giuliani announced his intention to scrap the failed and hardly noticed policy of "fair share," designed to prevent spaces with low land values from being "overburdened" with social service facilities. Instead the mayor planned to rezone 7 to 10 percent of the city's light industrial areas as "shelter sites" and social services districts. The mayor and his Planning Commission appointee, Joe Rose (coincidentally the scion of a powerful New York real estate family), argued that fair share was "bringing every neighborhood down to the lowest common denominator."[47] And this was bad for "destination appeal."

The Giuliani plan amounted to little more than recognition of *de facto* policy; the vast majority of "burdensome" social service centers are already in remote ghettos, next to bus depots, auto wrecking-yards, incinerators, and public housing projects. But these institutional ghettos, as Jose Vergara describes them, are not the supposedly "wild" zones of a traditional ghetto or a poor neighborhood. Instead,

These "districts" are characterized by their bureaucratic rules, comprehensiveness of form, publicly supported economy and populations marked by the experience of homelessness and addiction. People do not choose to go to these areas: they are sent there, uprooted from neighborhoods and people they know. A small number of downtown officials make the rules that determine who is entitled to reside in most of the housing and use the facilities. Lower-ranking officials select the needy and refer them to these places.[48]

Though Vergara was describing the social service ghetto, his words could just as easily describe the world of public housing.

Finally, there is evidence that pacifying the central city leads to increased concentrations of crime in the urban outlands. In 1993 New York City published maps of its 1,960 homicides: the findings showed that in neighborhoods held by BIDs and the prime tourist zones there were very few murders. Most of midtown Manhattan had no homicides all year. In the quiet precincts crime had fallen 50 percent over three years. But at the end of the train lines and beyond, as well as in Harlem and central Brooklyn, murder rates were rising and concentrating into dense zones of hyper-violence. "In fact killings were so clustered that 12 of the city's 75 police precincts [mostly in the outer boroughs] . . . reported a total of 854 homicides, or 43.6 percent of the total."[49]

IN SEARCH OF A BALCONY, A BUNKER . . . OR JUSTICE

New York is becoming a zero tolerance police state, with Giuliani as its despot. If police nationwide are learning from New York we might do so as well, because Giuliani's increasingly indiscriminate and paranoid bullying may be a harbinger of an over-policed future. Consider the virulent, downward spiral of Giuliani's "civility" campaign: first he came for the squeegee men, then the truants; now it is the street vendors, bus drivers, sex shops, and even protesting construction workers (who fought with cops because the Metropolitan Transit Authority was subcontracting to non-union firms). Giuliani has encouraged residents to photograph people who patronize peep shows and rent skin flicks. He has called on police to report any sloppy moves by the city's 7,000 bus drivers to their superiors and levels fines against them.[50] The police are already ticketing cabbies for violating a list of seventeen new regulations imposed by the mayor, and when they attempt to protest, police shut them down, block their caravans, and threaten them with jail.[51]

Even Manhattan office workers are under the gun for, of all things, jay-walking. To prevent this crime, police have erected metal barricades blocking many midtown crosswalks. When protesters dressed as cows mooed and pressed against the barriers, Giuliani labeled them "anti-car" and set higher fines for jaywalking.[52]

The civility campaign has muffled free speech as well. In typical fashion the clampdown started at the social margins and worked inwards. First to have their ampliphone permit yanked was the loony Harlem-based Israeli Church of Universal Practical Knowledge, a religious group that dresses up in Spartacus outfits and harangues "white devils" in Times Square (in L.A. they can be found at Hollywood and Vine).[53] More troubling is the fact that protest marches by community groups and the left are routinely greeted with an overwhelming police presence. As if that weren't intimidation enough, the Police Community Affairs Office is known to call non-profits and neighborhood organizations to warn them against participation in street demonstrations, citing the possibility of "trouble" and playing up the radical nature of direct action groups like the Lower East Side Collective.[54] In fact, the real repression of dissent in contemporary New York is actually worse than the fictional world of martial law in Brooklyn portrayed in the film *The Siege*. At least in the celluloid version of events, large protests are accompanied by only small police detachments.

The mean-spirited madness took a truly sinister, but almost comic, turn when news broke of Giuliani's plans to build a 46,000-square-foot, multi-million dollar, bomb-proof emergency command center for himself and his high-level functionaries.[55] Even the *New York Times* wondered what dark vision motivated such a scheme. By 1999 the zero tolerance regime had entered a genuine legitimation crisis.

The catalyst was the murder of Amadou Diallo, a 22-year-old Guinea immigrant who worked as a street vendor. Shortly after midnight on the evening of February 5, four officers from the NYPD's elite undercover Street Crimes Unit fired forty-one shots at Diallo, hitting him nineteen times.[56] Diallo was unarmed, hard working, and a practicing non-drinking Muslim. Police later ransacked his home and detained his room-mate in a desperate search for drugs, weapons, or anything that might compromise the dead man and justify the shooting. They came up empty-handed. In short, Diallo was a quintessential New Yorker: a law-abiding, hard working immigrant with his economic bootstraps firmly in hand.

The Street Crimes Unit on the other hand reeked of Jim Crow. Storied for its aggressive tactics, the 380-officer force was more than 95 percent white when they killed Diallo. Police Commissioner Howard Safir – who in 1997 tripled the Street Crimes Unit's force despite objections from the outfit's own commanders – once said he'd like to bottle the SCU's enthusiasm and feed it to other NYPD troops. But in the Bronx neighborhood where Diallo lived, people were less appreciative. Two-thirds of all citizen complaints about illegal police searches were said to involve officers from the SCU – this according to the district manager of Community Board No. 9.[57]

As the PR disaster mounted, the NYPD brass and the Patrolman's Benevolent Association dug in, stalled, and closed ranks behind the accused officers. This standard response merely added fuel to the fire of public outrage. "No justice, no peace" was the refrain as 1,000 people rallied just days after the killing on a snowy street in front of the Bronx building where Diallo met his fate.[58] As the grassroots political movement built, the case began to draw national and international attention. Diallo's mother flew in from Africa to recover her son's body, while Kweisi Mfume – former head of the Congressional Black Caucus, now president of the National Association for the Advancement of Colored People (NAACP) – called for federal involvement in the investigation.[59] A week later the FBI sent agents to examine the bullet-riddled building entrance where Diallo was killed.[60]

Giuliani's response was at best out of touch, at worst blatant provocation: at a news conference with Commissioner Safir the mayor announced that the NYPD would start using hollow-point rounds in their Glock 9mms. This ammunition, illegal according to international rules of warfare, expands upon impact, thus blowing huge holes in human flesh. However, hollow-point rounds ricochet less and don't travel as far or as fast as regular slugs. According to this logic the mayor contended that "hollow-point bullets would actually be safer than the bullets that were being used" the night Diallo was murdered.[61]

The gauntlet had been cast down, and by late March mainstream Black dignitaries were being arrested for blocking the doors at One Police Plaza. Among those led away in cuffs were Congressman Charles Rangel and former mayor David Dinkins. Rallies at City Hall (which is now more fortified than its equivalent in Jerusalem) were regularly drawing lunch-time crowds of thousands.[62] By April over one thousand people had been arrested in acts of civil disobedience.

Even President Clinton was forced to acknowledge the problem. During one of his weekly radio addresses the president said he was "deeply concerned" by reports of questionable shootings and "racial profiling" by police. But his policy proposal was to pledge even more federal money to local cops, only a fraction of which would be earmarked for accountability programs.[63] Nor did the president pledge any money to help the Justice Department start keeping statistics on police brutality.[64] Clinton's comments created a splash of liberal-sounding headlines which gave the appearance of an elite "re-think," but the problem of surplus repression at the local level was, in reality, left unaddressed.

CHAPTER SIX

CARRYING THE BIG STICK: SWAT TEAMS AND PARAMILITARY POLICING

> If you're twenty-one, male, living in one of these
> neighborhoods, been in Fresno for ten years and you're *not* in
> our computer – then there's definitely something wrong.
> Tactical officer, Fresno, California

> Yes, you won the war. We're waging the peace –
> it's much more volatile.
> National Security Agency officer, in *Enemy of the State*

For a sneak preview of a future American police state, travel south from the comfortable illusions of the San Francisco Bay Area on Interstate 99 into the dirty air of California's Central Valley, to Fresno, a sprawling, poorly planned city of 400,000. Pass the forest of pole-perched McDonald's, Best Western, and Motel 6 signs and turn off on one of the city's southern exits into the sprawling ghetto of the southwest side. There, on the pocked streets, among the stucco bungalows and dying railyards, you'll find massive paramilitary police operations underway on almost any night of the week . . .

It's a cold October evening, a helicopter clatters overhead, sweeping its lights across the shabby trees and flat homes. Nearby in the shadows, three squads of ten police officers in combat boots, black fatigues, and body armor lock and load their Heckler and Koch (H&K) MP-54 submachine guns (the same weapons used by the elite Navy SEALs) and fan out through the ghetto. Meet Fresno's Violent Crime Suppression Unit (VCSU), local law enforcement's "special forces" and America's most aggressive SWAT team. Since 1994 these soldier-cops have been conducting the criminal justice equivalent of search and destroy missions in Fresno's "gang-ridden" badlands. "It's a war," explains a police spokesperson.[1]

Paramilitary policing – that is, enforcement using the equipment, training, rhetoric, and group tactics of war – is on the rise nationwide. Fresno's VCSU is only the most extreme example of America's more than 30,000 paramilitary Special Weapons and Tactics (SWAT) teams. First developed by a young LAPD commander named Daryl Gates in 1966 (see chapter one), SWAT teams – also known as "tactical" or paramilitary policing units – were conceived as an urban counterinsurgency bulwark. As one early SWAT officer explained: "Those people out there – the radicals, the revolutionaries, and the cop haters – are damned good at using shotguns, bombs or setting ambushes, so we've got to be better at what we do."[2] Tactical units still treat policing as war, and that is what makes them fundamentally dangerous. If police are soldiers instead of civil servants, and their task is destruction and conquest, then it follows that the civilian community will be the enemy.

Even the etymology of L.A.'s initial tactical unit reveals a bellicose world-view. Gates started with the acronym SWAT – which has both a violent and dehumanizing ring to it – and then filled it in with the name "Special Weapons Attack Team." His superiors saw this candid and robust name as a bit too provocative, so they decided to change it to the more technical sounding "Special Weapons and Tactics." As the crisis of the sixties and early seventies rolled on, most other large metropolitan police departments established their own tactical units with military weaponry, uniforms, and training. Some called themselves SWAT teams, others preferred to be Special Response Team, Emergency Response Team, or Tactical Operations Team.

This first-wave tactical buildup in big cities was followed, during the law-and-order bonanza of the mid and late eighties, by a massive second wave in which new SWAT teams proliferated to *thousands* of small and medium-sized towns. Fueled by the enthusiasm of what sociologist and SWAT scholar Peter Kraska calls "culturally intoxicated young officers" and drug-war pork spending, tactical units have metastasized from urban emergency response specialists into a standard part of everyday policing. Instead of answering four or five calls a year dealing with hostage takings or barricaded suspects, SWAT teams now conduct routine drug raids, serve "administrative" search warrants, and even go after run-of-the-mill parole and probation violators. Overall activity by paramilitary police units – as measured by the total number of "call-outs" – quadrupled between 1980 and 1995.[3] But so far only Fresno uses its SWAT team and its armored vehicles, submachine guns, automatic rifles, attack dogs, and helicopters for routine patrol work, seven days a week.

PAYBACK WITH A TWIST: THE BIRTH OF THE VCSU

Fresno's new super-cops first hit the streets in 1994. Gang violence was wreaking havoc on the Latino and African American south side, where poverty and unemployment are concentrated. A slump in construction, continued mechanization of farming and food processing, along with the departure of agro-processing plants from the surrounding valley, added to the south side's stagnation.[4] In the late 1980s these social conditions were aggravated by a cocaine glut and the city's irrational "growth-at-all-costs" planning policy that gave tax subsidies and abatements for paving over farmland, while schools and social services deteriorated in the name of fiscal rectitude. Added to all this was the recession of the early 1990s, which hit California late but with considerable force. On the south side, unemployment, nihilism, guns, rage, and the relatively late arrival of crack cocaine coalesced into a lethal cocktail of gang-propelled auto-extinction. In the mostly African American southwest parts of town, sets of Crips and Bloods fought each other and feuded among themselves. In the barrios to the southeast, the fratricidal wars involved *norteño* and *sureño* sets from California's prison-based super-gangs *La Nuestra Familia,* the Bull Dogs, and the Mexican Mafia.[5]

By 1994 the violent streets were taking an increasing number of noncombatants, including three children wounded by gunfire in as many months. The second half of the year was particularly bloody: police recorded fifty-five incidents of gunfire resulting in sixty-one casualties, thirteen of them fatal. Fresno's murder rate was already considerably higher than the state average.[6] But what really worried police was a new belligerence towards officers in the field, especially in the African American southwest. That April, an alleged gang member opened fire on cops during a routine traffic stop, then escaped into the night. In May, police units came under fire three different times; often their attackers shot from the cover of the Central Valley's extremely dense winter and spring fog. One assault turned into a full-fledged fire-fight requiring back-up from the heavily armed SWAT team. It was the law enforcement equivalent of calling in a napalm strike on a tree-line. However, the incident that really spooked the PD was the ambush of officer Myrna Loran, who fled in her shot-up cruiser without returning fire or identifying her assailants.[7] To top it all off, an eight-year-old boy named Gary Ramirez took a stray bullet from a drive-by while chasing a puppy.[8]

It would have made poor fiction, but the world of the Fresno PD is already stuck in hyperbolic overdrive and this was just the excuse the department needed: the symbol of innocence cut down by crossfire. Under the cover of this very real crisis of violence, Chief Ed Winchester announced a total war on gangs. With full support from the NAACP and the mainstream leadership of the Black community, Winchester ordered in "the cavalry" – his all-white SWAT team.

Dressed in gray jungle camouflage, military helmets, bulletproof vests, ski masks, goggles, and combat boots, and armed with AR-15s, MP-5s, attack dogs, "flash-bang" stun grenades, smoke bombs, tear gas, pepper spray, metal clubs, and less-than-lethal "blunt trauma ordinances," the SWAT team patrolled the southwest every day until order was restored. Its immediate task was to round up a list of some 200 suspected repeat offenders and veteran gangbangers. The enemy was to be tracked down, busted, and put away for as long as possible. The operation involved raiding homes, stopping cars, interrogating "suspicious persons," and storming an archipelago of "hot spot" corners.

Bringing up the rear was the fawning *Fresno Bee*, dishing out "bang-bang" copy: "[A] special SWAT team armed with machine guns and dogs, slipped into the city's south side Friday night with orders to take dangerous neighborhoods back from drug dealers and gang members."[9] The city councilwoman from the besieged area called the police occupation "long overdue," while the DA asserted that the only difference between the war in Sarajevo and gangbanging in Fresno was the lack of rocket launchers in the latter.[10]

Chief Winchester, enjoying the support and attention generated by his scorched-earth campaign, soon institutionalized the emergency response, and the thirty-member SWAT team became the Violent Crime Suppression Unit. In the name of crisis management the VCSU was free to continue using aggressive and unorthodox tactics that combined old-time thuggery with pernicious high tech. At times that meant cruising in a fleet of cars; at others it meant quietly deploying troops on foot to surround targets and sweep through patches of ghetto.

The street corner raids usually began with officers tossing "flash-bang grenades" (designed to stun and disorient suspects), then swooping in with barking dogs and guns drawn as they bellowed orders to get "the fuck down." Civilian-owned pit bulls, rottweilers and dobermans were shot on sight, while everyone in the targeted area was forced to the ground at gunpoint. As one team of ten VCSU officers established an armed perimeter, another team would train guns on prostrate "bad guys," while a third team would take photos, conduct "field interviews," run warrant checks, note tattoos, scars, clothing, "distinguishing characteristics," and addresses, and add all new intelligence into local, state, and federal databases from the mobile computer terminals in each patrol car.[11] Prisoners were carted out in a huge gray bus with SWAT emblazoned on the side that police likened to a rolling billboard.

Lately VCSU foot sweeps have been less common. The unit now prefers to roam the south side in regular patrol cars, "like a wolf pack" looking for "contact."[12] This is due in large part to declining narco-commerce in Fresno's hot spots. Police and local ethnographers credit the relative calm to the mass internment of a whole generation of OGs (original gangsters) and mid-level players, who are now serving infinities of time in state prison on second- and third-strike charges, or in federal joints under the federal government's mandatory minimum sentencing guidelines.[13] And as the relatively small minority of truly bad-ass semi-organized criminals are buried in human landfills, the VCSU's attention necessarily turns to less and less threatening behavior . . .

It's almost midnight and the Central Valley is getting cold. A typical VCSU operation is underway. The target is a brightly lit gas station known for dealing and surrounded by barren waste ground just outside a rundown suburban ghetto called "the Dog Pound." As the first cruiser approaches, six young African American men on the corner start moving away: that's suspicious behavior, probable cause for a stop. Half the group slips into the dark, three are stopped. More cruisers pull up at high speed, cops pile out and surround the scene, a K-9 team unloads its barking Alsatian. The young men stiffen with fear, hands on their heads, facing the high beams of the police cruisers. Then it's down on the ground, legs out in front, crossed. The field interviews and frisking begin, scars are noted, IDs checked. From a patrol car terminal an officer runs warrant searches through the local Fresno PD database, the California Law Enforcement Teletype System (CLETS), and the FBI's all-encompassing NCIC (see chapter one for the history of the NCIC).

"Bingo," says a crew-cut trooper. One of the youths is wanted; he is cuffed, placed under arrest, his pager and keys taken, and he is stuffed into the back of a squad car.

Next call. A unit has "contact" on the far end of the Dog Pound, and on foot an individual has fled the scene of a traffic stop, entering a nearby house; VCSU cars surge towards the action. While the occupants of the car are dealt with, the VCSU officers with AR-15s and H&K MP-54s surround the area and "holding the perimeter," some look at the house, others look out at the community. A line of five officers rushes the door. Technically they are not in hot pursuit and have no right to storm the building, but they look angry and their guns make it seem serious, so the elderly woman behind the black metal security gate quickly consents to a search. Five big, white cops move into the TV-lit room and grab a Black man named David. "What? Man, I didn't do anything!" he protests. His voice breaks and a tearful grimace momentarily clouds his face.

As police begin searching the small home, with consent from a trembling grandmother, it appears as if the past has suddenly lurched forward and collided with a high-tech future. More than anything else the VCSU robocops resemble the "patrollers" of the old South, the white, slave-catcher militias that spent their nights rousting Black people's shacks in search of contraband, weapons, and signs of escape.

"Are you on parole, probation? What? Huh? Let's go outside, David." The man is cuffed, searched, interrogated, forced to the ground, warrants checked, flashlights continually shone in his face. No drugs found. But David lied, said he wasn't on parole and he is. "That's a violation of parole, David." Another Black man arrested and packed off to jail.

More "contacts" produce three ounces of crack – a huge bust. "He didn't signal, had an air freshener hanging from his rear-view mirror, so we pulled him over. He didn't have ID. So we searched." Boom – the white cops take another Black man to jail. Then the radios crackle: "Code three, at 621 South . . ." An officer needs help. The VCSU's fleet of Crown Victorias race towards the action.

A youth reportedly brandished a gun (not a crime unless there is a victim being threatened) and has sped off to his mother's house. The radios crackle again: "1010, deploy units in the alley." The house is surrounded by the whole VCSU. From behind cars, officers train AR-15s, MP-5s, and the larger MP-54s on the front door and in the windows. Overhead a chopper beats the air, flooding the house with light and scanning the area with Forward Looking Infra-Red (FLIR). Gathering neighbors are kept at bay by detachments of regular Fresno PD officers. A CHP officer and several armed DA investigators arrive on the scene, guns drawn, and crouch dramatically behind vehicles. Because the person who reported the crime was not himself threatened by the gun, the VCSU has no probable cause to enter the house, and so the stand-off continues.

The FPD helicopter overhead runs short on fuel and sweeps back to gas up, as a bigger, louder CHP chopper takes its place pouring down an even brighter klieg light. (In a few months the choppers will have the capacity to send live video and FLIR feed or freeze-frame maps from the air directly to the eleven-inch screens of the VCSU's brand-new in-car "mobile data terminals.")

From the door emerges a Latino teenager, hands in the air, tears streaming down his face. He walks slowly toward the bristling mob of white cops and into the blinding lights. Behind him comes a young woman and two small children, and after them an older woman in slippers and curlers. But the suspect, Juan, stays inside, phone off the hook. Desk jockeys from Probation — until a few years ago, unarmed bureaucrats — are now hovering at the elbow of the VCSU commanding officer. The Probation wannabes are eager for action, wearing jeans, bulletproof vests, and blue windbreakers and toting radios, cuffs, and Smith and Wesson .44 automatics. Juan is on their list so they have the right to storm his home without permission, probable cause, or a warrant. "We can go in. This is the primary [address]. You want to go in? We can do it. You wanna do it?" implore the probation squad. But the VCSU demurs. Like cops generally, VCSU officers are not inclined to follow other agencies.[14] In fact, the VCSU despises other agencies, particularly their rival sibling the Fresno Sheriff's Department, and tonight that includes the weekend warriors from Probation.

After another hour of waiting for Juan, scored to the incessant barking of the Alsatians, the pounding rotors of the CHP chopper, and occasional cajoling from the bull horn, the VCSU is getting bored. Too proud to cooperate with Probation and wanting to keep up a restrained and professional appearance in front of a researcher, they decide to call the siege off and move on to rousting the known hot spots.

Not all VCSU "contacts" end so peacefully. According to members of the unit they average at least one "officer-involved shooting" every three months. The last confirmed kill they had was a former professional football star suffering a psychotic breakdown. Then a few months later they "shot some parolee with a gun," but the sergeant in charge of that operation says he never found out if the guy lived. Between July 1997 and July 1998, Fresno police shot seventeen people, eight of them fatally.[15] But to focus on confirmed kills is to miss the more routine, in many ways more important, forms of everyday non-lethal terror that increasingly define police operations in poor communities. Since the advent of the VCSU the Fresno police have increased their misdemeanor arrests by 48.3 percent.[16] In other words, much of what they do is stop, search, harass, arrest, and brutalize petty offenders, parole violators, and bystanders. With no civilian complaint review board in Fresno, all brutality complaints are handled internally, and statistics on police misconduct, if they exist at all, are difficult to come by.

The VCSU, however, says its searches, field interviews, and house raids are governed by the rules of probable cause. An increasing number of people in the have-not suburbs of Fresno's south side dispute this. Even the NAACP has changed its position. At first the group's criticism was limited to the fact that the VCSU had no African American officers. (As of late 1998 this was still true though not surprising, given that only 38 of Fresno's 655 police are African American.)[17] But the question of representation has slipped off the radar as the more immediate concern of paramilitary occupation in Black and Latino neighborhoods takes precedence.

"We had a whole group of people coming home from church and they were stopped at a gas station, where gangs hang out, and the police made them all get on the ground, lie in the dirt and oil. All of them — in their Sunday best," explains John Nelum, president of the Fresno NAACP, recalling a 1997 incident. Other mainstream African Americans express similar views, and their mood soured even further when the VCSU raided the home of a prominent Black judge. Even the pro-cop *Fresno Bee* has, on occasion, reported that police use violent threats and racist language, and conduct unlawful searches in Black, Latino, and increasingly in Hmong and Laotian neighborhoods.

HIGH-TECH TENTACLES

In many ways this local revolution in policing is the direct result of Clinton's campaign pledge to put 100,000 more cops on the streets. Since 1994, when that malignant promise took the form of the infamous crime bill, the FPD has increased its force from 400 to 655 (on its way to a goal of 800 by 2002), established a plethora of new special units, and introduced new technology into every aspect of policing. Thanks to $28.4 million in federal grants, the FPD will soon have the nation's most advanced "field automation system," complete with electronic notepads which, using cellular phone technology, can communicate with the brand new computers in each patrol car. The computers in turn can communicate with, and search, local, state, and federal databases, thus giving officers in the field nearly instant access to mountains of intelligence ranging from outstanding warrants to DMV records.

Another gadget on the way is a portable electronic fingerprint reader. With this Dick-Tracy-dream-come-true, police can check prints in the field, then automatically and remotely search local, state, and federal databases for matching prints, outstanding warrants, mug shots, and other information. At the strategic level, Fresno will soon be using its own version of the Vietnam-inspired "electronic battlefield" for state-of-the-art, real-time crime mapping and deployment. With this technology, Chief Winchester hopes to begin holding Comtsat-style meetings. This hybrid between Pentagon whiz-bang tech and New York QOL policing is also being adopted by other departments around the country.

While federal largesse paid for much of the start-up costs of Fresno's new fighting force, it is the local city government that will ultimately foot the bill. In Fresno, as throughout the country, federal policing grants may look like windfalls but their long-term effect is to create a new set of fiscal demands. For example, Fresno has hired scores of new cops whose positions are fully funded by Washington for the first two or three years, but when the money from D.C. runs dry the city pays up or explains to suburban voters why the police force is shrinking. Already this burden has forced Fresno to increase its law enforcement spending by about 5 percent annually while all other budget items are frozen or, as in the case of emergency medical care, cut. With a police officer's starting salary, including benefits, at around $56,000 a year, the Police Department consumes up to 45 percent of Fresno's city budget. To appease the FPD's demand for cash the city has even channeled several million dollars from its Housing and Urban Development–sponsored community development block grants into its problem-oriented policing ("POP") teams.[18] The future will no doubt bring more such cannibalization.

GANGING UP ON YOUTH: THE PARAMILITARY PILE-ON

Back on the streets of Fresno, the wonders of a full-time SWAT team are rubbing off on other police agencies. By 1996 the massive funding opportunities provided by the 1994 crime bill's fat federal grant programs and the perceived success of the VCSU (as measured by declining crime rates) had caused a general proliferation of militarized anti-drug and anti-gang law enforcement units in Fresno. Prominent among the new forces is the Sheriff's Department's "Operation Goldstar." A typical Operation Goldstar sweep involves sixty to eighty sheriff's deputies, augmented by DA investigators, probation officers, and liaison agents from DEA, ATF, and FBI. Assembled at staging points and done up in the usual SWAT regalia of combat boots, helmets, jumpsuits, and body armor, and armed with H&K MP-5s, dogs, and battering rams, the Goldstar force sweeps problem corners in Fresno city and its increasingly urbanized unincorporated county environs. The outfit's mission is to search for drugs, guns, and – more often than not – simple "warrant fugitives," that is, people who have failed to show up in court. A typical weekend-long Goldstar sweep will bag between seventy-five and one hundred prisoners a night.[19]

Another prominent new unit is the Multi-Agency Gang Enforcement Consortium (MAGEC). This sixty-strong task force, created to put "vise-like pressure on gangs," combines officers from the Fresno Police and Sheriff's Departments; probation and parole officers; agents from the FBI, DEA, ATF and INS; several armed investigators from the district attorney's office; and even a few agents from the California Department of Corrections' Special Services Unit (SSU), a super-secret police force that operates on and off prison grounds to keep tabs on parolees and other official enemies.[20] Upon christening the new superagency, then-governor Pete Wilson gushed that "California has never seen an army the likes of this."[21]

Formed in mid 1997, this special force is now the dominant police program in Fresno's Latino, Black, and Laotian neighborhoods. Justifying this massive combination and mobilization of repressive powers are the menacing – and absurdly precise – gang figures provided by the Fresno County Sheriff's Department: 236 separate gangs commanding the loyalty of some 7,855 combatants.[22] Because part of MAGEC's mission is "nipping problems before they escalate into violence" by using a large "intelligence unit to gather information and defuse potential gang activity," much of its work necessarily focuses on non-violent offenders.[23] Like the VCSU, the regular PD, the Goldstar sweeps, and the new POP teams, MAGEC uses statutes that prohibit "loitering with intent to sell narcotics" as a justification to stop, interview, search, and run warrant checks on practically anyone occupying public space.

This sort of "intelligence gathering" does not merely "discover" delinquency, but rather by its very nature *produces* criminal identities, and thus justifies ever more layers of aggressive, invasive, and brutal policing. Based on probable cause stops and what police call "consensual contacts," the VCSU, Goldstar, and MAGEC conduct hundreds of field interviews every week, thousands every year. From this surveillance MAGEC alone adds between 300 and 400 *new* names to its gang dossiers and the state database called Cal Gang every quarter.[24]

More than mere inconvenience or humiliation, these interrogations, and the gang databases they feed, create very real liabilities. In a caricature of criminological "labeling theory" the Golden State's "gang enhancement" statute criminalizes membership in a gang. The bombastically titled California Street Terrorism Enforcement and Prevention Act of 1988 states that "any person who actively participates in any criminal street gang" (defined as three or more people involved in criminal activity) can be punished with a year in jail. Thus a person in a gang can be found guilty for crimes committed by his or her associates. When gang members are convicted for other crimes they routinely face two- to three-year "sentencing enhancements" for each separate charge. Thus a person convicted of armed robbery with an illegal weapon will have six years added to his sentence if he is "gang labeled."[25]

How does one earn this dubious distinction? In Fresno, as in most of California, law enforcement uses a standardized list of ten criteria to vet alleged "street terrorists." The determinations include admitting to gang membership; associating with gang members; corresponding with gang members; having one's name appear on a gang document, such as a letter; being identified as a gang member by another police agency; having gang-style tattoos; making gang hand signs; writing gang graffiti; and, most pernicious of all, wearing gang clothing, such as red or blue jackets and baggy pants.[26] If a person meets three of these criteria, he or she is entered into the Cal Gang database as a known gang member. To be deemed an associate, one need meet only two of the standards.[27]

This self-amplifying epistemology generates "offenders" at an exponential rate. Consider the escalating sequence: association with "known gang members" plus baggy pants and *voilà* they open a gang dossier on you. Write a letter to your incarcerated cousin, an alleged gangbanger, and you are moved up the scale a notch from "associate" to "active gang member." Now the people with whom you have frequent contact can be similarly labeled. Thus the more youths labeled "gangbanger," the more people qualified as associates, and so on, in a potentially endless, self-referential cycle.[28] Furthermore, this "paper deviance" – leading to harsh treatment at the hands of the law and time in brutal juvenile prisons – produces *real* criminality. Punishing youth creates damaged people, who create crime and thus "require" more surveillance, more labeling, and yet more damaging punishment.

The building blocks of this labeling-based deviance mill are the ubiquitous police "field interviews" which first suck youth into the criminal justice net. According to activists in Fresno, such as gang-truce organizer Homer Leija of Barrios Unidos, many of the MAGEC, Goldstar, and VCSU interrogations are barely legal. "They stop kids, really young kids, without probable cause and ask to search them and interrogate them and take their photos," says Leija. "And a lot of these youngsters have no idea what the law is and just go along with it because they think they have to, but really they're consenting all the way – all the way to jail."[29]

THE "CIVIL" WAR

Perhaps the most radical legal tool to have developed from the paramilitary war on gangs is the use of *civil injunctions* by *criminal prosecutors*. Using gang dossiers, district attorneys ask judges to grant injunctions – which are essentially restraining orders – that restrict the activities of named, and even *unnamed*, alleged gang members, many of whom have never been convicted of any crime. One injunction prohibited 500 mostly Latino gang members in the San Fernando Valley from gathering in public in combinations of more than two.[30] The original San Jose, California, injunction prohibited gang members from "standing, sitting, walking, driving, gathering, or appearing anywhere in public view" with any suspected gang member. The listed "gangsters" were also barred from carrying "glass bottles, rocks, bricks, chains, tire irons, screwdrivers, hammers, crowbars, bumper jacks, razor blades, razors, slingshots, marbles, [and] ball bearings." And they are enjoined from "approaching vehicles, engaging in conversation or otherwise communicating with the occupants of any vehicle." These unindicted, unconvicted, unsentenced objects of the law are also prohibited from "making, causing, or encouraging others to make loud noise of any kind."[31]

Part of what makes these civil injunctions so disturbing is that the standard of proof in civil court is much lower than in criminal court, the logic being that the consequences in civil cases are of less magnitude.[32] But with the anti-gang injunctions civil courts' lower standard of proof is being smuggled into the high-stakes realm of criminal law. As the injunctions proliferate throughout California, prosecutors in other states, such Texas and Illinois, have adopted the tactic.[33]

Another weapon used by the Fresno Police and Sheriff's Departments is the county-wide 10 p.m. curfew for youth under eighteen. As one probation officer put it, the curfew "gives police a tool to contact kids they suspect are likely to engage in anti-social behavior." According to a recent study by the Justice Policy Institute, Fresno police arrested 733 youth for curfew violations in 1997, making their "curfew arrest rate more than twice the state average." Moreover, Fresno's curfew is applied in a racist fashion: Fresno County Latinos are five times more likely than whites to be arrested for curfew violation; while African Americans in the county are three times more likely than whites to be arrested for such violations.[34]

SWAT NATION

As goes California, so goes the nation. Fresno is just one example of a national movement towards paramilitary law enforcement. The routine use of tactical units for everyday policing is common coast to coast. And once established these expensive attack teams become their own justification: big budget outlays compel police departments to show "good use" – that is, to deploy their SWAT teams whenever possible. In other words, to demonstrate that the training junkets, trips to regional and national "SWAT competitions," and the monthly paint-ball exercises – which consume the attention of many a tactical unit – are in fact necessary and cost-effective, SWAT teams must stay busy in the field. Thus paramilitary police units are increasingly called out to execute petty warrants, conduct traffic stops, and round up non-violent suspects. On occasion we even see SWAT teams doing crowd control at official parades in place of regular cops or, more commonly, conducting raids in place of detectives doing investigations.[35]

Take for example a recent tactical assault in Tacoma, Washington. After a shooting deemed to be Vietnamese-gang-related, police SWAT teams launched pre-dawn raids on nine homes, dragging people from their beds and one naked woman from the shower. In all about forty Southeast Asians were detained all day and interrogated for hours at a time. Almost all the detainees were released for lack of evidence. "It was horrible," said one female prisoner. "We didn't get to use the restrooms, eat or anything until almost 1 p.m. I felt sick when I went home."[36] By all accounts this raid was not the dramatic culmination of careful police work, but was a substitute for lengthy police investigation. Instead of sending detectives to do interviews and follow up leads, the police sent SWAT teams to round up any and all involved parties, most of whom turned out to be innocent.

One of the most infamous SWAT "fishing expeditions" was Operation Ready-Rock, launched in November 1990 by the Chapel Hill police. In response to drug dealing in North Carolina's college-town version of Sodom, the guardians of order received a "blanket" warrant allowing them to search every person and vehicle on the 100 block of Graham Street. The sweep was aimed at what law enforcement viewed as a criminal space. The warrant request explained that

During the past 10 months, in our personal observations during surveillance, controlled buys and undercover buys, we believe that there are no "innocent" people at this place . . . Only drug sellers and drug buyers are on the described premises.[37]

To execute the warrant the CHPD assembled a force of forty-five tactical officers from four different agencies, including the State Bureau of Investigation's elite Special Response Team. The assault force – dressed in combat boots, green camo' battle dress uniforms, body armor, hoods, masks, goggles, and kevlar helmets – armed itself with the usual array of "tactical" gadgetry: less-than-lethal "blunt trauma impact ordinances," chemical sprays, and H&K MP-5s, MP-54s, and Colt AR-15s. For maximum results, the operation was launched on a Friday night with teams of officers storming the block from all directions, cutting off every path of escape and then combing the area with drug-sniffing dogs. Even amidst the military frenzy the courtesy of the old South prevailed: whites were allowed to leave the area, while more than a hundred African Americans were searched. The warrant also included the search of a pool hall called the Village Connection. In typically "proactive" fashion SWAT commandos made a "dynamic entrance," smashing in the front door and forcing the occupants to the floor at gunpoint. While the captives were searched and interrogated, the bar was ransacked for contraband. The commotion left one elderly man trembling on the floor in a pool of his own urine.[38]

The stunt, costing thousands of dollars in public money, netted thirteen arrests for minor cocaine and methamphetamine possession. The innocent victims of the raid, who spent the evening being berated and humiliated by cops, later filed a mildly successful class action suit. But no police officers were ever reprimanded or punished, nor were new guidelines for drug raids adopted. Some months later, one of the involved units, the State Bureau of Investigation's SRT, shot a cleaning lady as she fled from a bank where she had been held hostage by would-be thieves.[39]

Elsewhere in North Carolina the popularity of paramilitary police grows vigorously. The most twisted encapsulation of what this means surfaced in Greensboro, where the public library's bus-sized "bookmobile" was, for lack of funds, retired – along with its card catalog, 2,000 volumes, and two librarians. Shortly thereafter, the bookmobile, with plenty of mileage left in it, was converted into a mobile command-and-control center for the Greensboro police department's elite twenty-three member tactical SRT. "It's a great piece of equipment," said a police spokesman. "It's really so much better than what we had before." In the previous van one of the SRT officers, a six-foot-five-inch-tall hulk, had trouble standing up.[40]

Throughout the country most large-scale tactical sweeps do not even make the local papers. One that did was D-Day, or Operation Jump Start, a full-scale assault on the rough edges of Meredith, Connecticut, a working class city of 75,000. Launched on June 6, 1997 (hence the D-Day reference), the operation involved the New Britain SWAT team, two tactical units from the state police, and scores of back-up units from surrounding jurisdictions. A state police Cessna provided air reconnaissance, while armored personnel carriers and various police trucks ferried the mobile force to and fro as it stormed a slew of locations in search of *Los Solidos* street gang members. The tactical swarm arrested forty-nine people but many hundreds saw the display of force, were interrogated, searched, and otherwise subjected to the will of the paramilitary invaders.[41]

When police treat whole communities as the enemy the results can be grim. For example, on October 30, 1998, a masked and fatigue-clad tactical force of ninety police officers and state agents launched a violent pre-dawn raid on the Martin Luther King and Marcus Garvey resident-owned housing cooperative in San Francisco in search of a drug gang called the Knock Out Posse. During the raid, police commandos blew open doors with special "shock-lock" shotgun rounds, cleared rooms with flash-bang grenades, and took the entire community hostage for several hours.

At a police commission meeting following the operation, a train of furious and sobbing African American victims recounted in scabrous detail how police officers slapped and kicked them, stepped on their necks, and pressed pistol and shotgun muzzles to their heads as other officers ransacked their homes, up-turning beds and ripping open closets. Among those held at gunpoint were city employees and grandmothers; scores of people with no charges against them and clear records were "flex cuffed," including weeping and terrified children as young as six, some of whom urinated in their pajamas as they were separated from their parents. Police Chief Fred Lau explained this last touch — cuffing the kids — was to keep them from "running around." One woman was hospitalized after a fit of seizures, while other people were so distraught they stayed home from work for days. For dramatic effect, a pit bull named Bosco — which many residents described as well liked and friendly — was shot inside an apartment, dragged outside and shot again. A straight-faced deputy police chief, Richard Holder, told commissioners that according to police "intelligence" gathered during "covert operations," the dog was "known for its jumping ability and was shot in mid-air."[42]

All in all, the raid netted eleven arrests, a pound of "high grade" marijuana, less than four ounces of rock cocaine, seven pistols, and $4,000 in cash – 80 percent of which the SFPD may get to keep and spend, thanks to state and federal asset forfeiture laws. Residents said the money wasn't drug lucre – rather, it had been collected from a circle of friends to help pay for the funeral of the recently deceased resident Germain Brown.[43]

SWAT TO KILL

The aggressive nature of SWAT operations leads to greater use of violence by both police and their surprised targets. As tactical units proliferate and increase their call-outs, they end up killing more people. A CBS News survey of SWAT encounters showed a 34 percent increase in the use of deadly force between 1995 and 1998.[44]

The most egregious case of a violent SWAT mishap involved commandos from the super-elite 2,000 member Navy SEALs who were illegally "training" with a paramilitary police unit in Albuquerque, New Mexico. The target of the raid was a young alleged drug dealer named Manual Ramirez. To capture their prey the raiding party attached a tow truck cable to Ramirez's front door. As one team smashed in the back windows – without announcing that they were police – the tow truck ripped the door out of its frame, and masked, helmeted goons swarmed in. Ramirez, asleep on the couch, awoke to the sound of glass breaking and his female cousin screaming about robbers. As he reached for an unloaded pistol the commandos pouring through the gaping front door shot him dead. The ensuing search turned up a brace of "marijuana cigarettes" and a small quantity of crystal methamphetamine.[45]

In 1992 during a tactical raid in Everett, Washington, a sheriff's SWAT-team member shot and killed 28-year-old Robin Pratt as she ran to shield her infant daughter. Pratt was not a suspect in the case.[46] A similar moment of confusion lead to a Greensboro SWAT team killing 56-year-old Charles Irwin Potts during an over-zealous narcotics raid. As masked commandos kicked in his front door, Potts jumped up from his card game and caught a blast of automatic fire. Officers say Potts was reaching for a gun; two civilian witnesses dispute that claim. No drugs were found in the search.[47] In 1998, in nearby Greensville, South Carolina, SWAT officers shot and killed a unarmed "drug suspect" after an informant gave them bad intelligence.[48]

In relatively sleepy Bethelhem, Pennsylvania, SWAT officers not only killed a suspect while raiding an alleged drugs house, but in the process inadvertently set the building on fire and burnt it down, perhaps due to a faulty flash-bang grenade or tear gas igniting.[49] In Dinuba, California – population 15,269 – the brand new SWAT team, apparently still unclear on how to read street maps and thinking they were at the lair of serious drug dealers, burst into the bedroom of 64-year-old Carman Gallado. When the retired farmworker reached for a pocket knife the Dinuba SWAT team shot him fifteen times. Gallado's widow later received a massive settlement.[50] Few victims are so lucky.

In December 1996, the Albuquerque SWAT team – so well trained by the Navy SEALs – shot and killed 69-year-old Ralph Garrison as they served a search warrant on two buildings adjoining Garrison's property. Hearing a commotion, Garrison went outside to investigate, and was greeted by armed officers, ensconced in darkness, ordering him back inside. After calling 911 to report suspicious activity and retrieving his handgun, Garrison went back outside, whereupon SWAT offices dispatched the senior with eleven rounds from their submachine guns.[51] The bereaved widow Garrison set about demanding answers from the tightlipped APD, but the stress and grief soon leveled her by way of a massive stroke. No officers were prosecuted.[52]

Mistaking police raids for robberies is a common theme in SWAT killings. Tactical officers often fail to follow the law and properly identify themselves during raids. This is in part because SWAT units maintain that *how* they bust suspects (that is, with overwhelming force so as to psychologically demoralize) is just as important as *that* they bust suspects. For example, the Miami tactical unit (once featured in a nauseatingly uncritical Discovery Channel documentary) raided the home of a senior citizen "drug dealer," who pulled a gun. The police commandos responded with seventy-five lethal rounds from their MP-5s. The victim's fifteen-year-old great-granddaughter, who survived the raid by hiding in the bathroom, said that as police kicked in the door her great-grandfather told her to call 911 because they were being robbed.[53]

Mistaken identity also leads to the accidental death and wounding of tactical officers. This was the case as recently as the fall of 1998, when a deputy in Pierce County, Washington, was shot and killed by Brian Eggleston, a small-time Tacoma pot dealer who, quite credibly, swore he opened fire only because he thought his assailants were burglars.[54]

One group that tends to fare poorly at the hands of pugnacious and heavily armed paramilitary units is the mentally ill. In quiet Canton, Connecticut, a tactical squad known as the North Central Emergency Services Team was sent to bring in a paranoid schizophrenic named Neil Cretney. But Cretney, who had twice been manhandled by the local constabulary because of his strange behavior, was barricaded in his room with what police said was an ax. After only two hours of negotiation the team stormed Cretney's hideout with bulletproof shields, less-than-lethal bean-bag guns, pepper spray, stun grenades, and tear gas, then used firearms to blow their man to kingdom come.[55] Cretney's relatives say he had long suffered from a "paranoid" premonition that uniformed agents of the state would kill him.[56]

Often the murder of the mentally ill is simply written off as "suicide by cop." To be sure, there are indeed many cases when police are faced with furious adversaries who can and will kill if the officers fail to fire first. And there are also people who do genuinely want to die in a hail of police bullets. But "suicide by cop" is also becoming a facile excuse for killing off the mad. This becomes obvious when one considers the level of threat posed by many of these suicidal adversaries. For example, in 1998 the above-mentioned Miami SWAT team shot a sickly 76-year-old man who suffered from advanced emphysema, claiming that he lunged with two kitchen knives so as to provoke their fire.[57] It is hard to believe that a team of huge, armored, shielded cops, with all the time in the world and all the pepper spray and bean-bag rounds they could ever need, *had to* slay a frail and addled senior citizen.

FRIENDLY AND NOT-SO-FRIENDLY FIRE

Sometimes overly aggressive SWAT officers become their own worst enemies. For example, in late 1998 a tactical officer was shot and wounded by a fellow SWAT member during a botched Dallas raid. He was the third Dallas officer wounded or killed by friendly fire in the last seven years.[58] That same year a San Bernadino, California, SWAT team exchanged fire with itself after using a flash-bang grenade to raid an empty house. Amidst the smoke and confusion one tactical officer mistook his comrade for a "bad guy" and opened fire, hitting his fellow cop in the leg; the wounded officer returned fire as he went down.[59] A year and a half earlier, the Oxnard, California, SWAT team had similar problems while serving a search warrant on a two-story townhouse that turned out to be empty. "During the operation, officer James Jensen threw a flash grenade onto a second floor landing. The explosion sent smoke into surrounding rooms. Jensen and other SWAT team members, including Sgt. Daniel Christian, stormed the second floor, and in the turmoil Christian mistook Jensen for a gun-wielding criminal" and blasted his colleague with three rounds of double-naught buckshot from his 12-gauge. The direct hits killed Jensen on the spot.[60] After this "tragic mishap" much soul-searching ensued, as did a multi-million-dollar lawsuit, filed by Jensen's devastated widow. But less than a year later the Oxnard SWAT team blundered again. This time the crew was responding to a domestic disturbance call from an eight-year-old who said his parents were arguing. The SWAT team surrounded the house and demanded that the suspect surrender. But as the belligerent and unarmed husband, Larry Panky, emerged, senior officer Scott Hebert lost his cool and opened fire, killing Panky. A DA investigation later exonerated Officer Hebert on the grounds that he mistook shots from his comrades' less-than-lethal weapons as an exchange of gunfire between Panky and the police.[61]

When SWAT officers *are* shot by suspects the responding wrath is awesome. Consider for example the case of Visalia, California, SWAT officer James Rapozo, who was caught by a slug in the armpit as his team crashed into the home of sixteen-year-old Alfonso Hernandez. In response to Rapozo falling his SWAT brothers opened up with a fusillade of lead that literally ground Hernandez's corpse to a ragged mess, riddled with thirty-nine fragmenting rounds. SWAT slugs also pierced the walls into adjacent apartments, forcing people to dive for cover, and in one case almost hitting an occupied baby crib. Another man inside at the time, nineteen-year-old Emiliano Trevino, took cover in a corner as the shooting started and was hit five times.[62]

Even more ghastly were the recent actions of the Portland, Oregon, Special Emergency Reaction Team. Just before midnight on January 27, 1998, a black clad team of SERT raiders besieged a house occupied by a lone gunman dressed in body armor and equipped with a stockpile of assault rifles and ammunition. As TV choppers beat overhead, SERT commandos shot it out with the suspect, loading the house with tear gas and moving in under the cover of an APC. By the time the siege ended two cops had been wounded and a third was dead. Officers, described by observers as "frenzied," finally stormed the bullet-riddled building and dragged out the wounded suspect. Once on the lawn officers stripped and searched their captive, then lashed him to the tailgate of an armored SWAT van and paraded the bloodied perp' like a dead buck as the van made its way to the hospital.[63]

SNOUTS IN THE FEDERAL TROUGH

As tactical raids and paramilitary sweeps become more common, the common police take on more paramilitary attributes. In other words, paramilitary policing units militarize the regular police by osmosis as the weaponry, training, and tactics of the police special forces are gradually passed on to the regular police. In that vein, numerous departments are starting to equip their *regular* officers with semiautomatic and fully automatic assault rifles. Leading the way is the LADP. The catalyst there was the much storied North Hollywood shoot-out – in which two heavily armed gangsters re-enacted the spectacular shoot-out scene from the film *Heat* by coolly blasting away at the LAPD after a botched bank heist. The bank robbers had chosen to go out in paramilitary style: along with black jumpsuits, ski masks, and body armor they carried a cache of high-powered military assault rifles and hundreds of rounds of ammunition. Much of the action was caught on video by news helicopters and is now *endlessly* recycled by "docudrama" TV shows like *Cops*. The media-savvy LAPD, making the most of the fact that its officers were momentarily outgunned – they commandeered weapons from a nearby gun store – promptly ordered 600 M-16s from the Defense Department.[64] With that the race was on.

Following the bloody Portland raid of 1998, Chief Charles Moose followed suit by giving his troops AR-15s, at a cost of $310,000. So far the new military rifles have provoked very little political complaint, from either the Black community (which will, no doubt, end up facing this new arsenal) or from Portland's overly abundant lifestyle-liberals. When the police received shotguns in 1975, there was at least some public acrimony accompanying the escalation.[65]

Numerous departments in Florida are also buying AR-15s and M-16s for their regular beat officers, the Orlando Police Department being one of the largest. The Orange County Sheriff's Office also bought a shipment of 261

M-16s, while the Sheriff's Office in Fort Lauderdale ordered a cache of Ruger
Mini 14 semiautomatics (the weapon of choice among many prison guards).[66]
And, as the big cities rearm, so too must the small town constabulary, who
fancy themselves as miniature versions of "the real thing." For example,
police in Apopka, Florida, worried about "well-armed criminals" and incap-
able of imagining local gun control, is spending federal grant money to buy
ten AR-15 semiautomatic rifles for its ten sergeants. This despite the fact
that Apopka's seventy-five officers have only fired their weapons in the line
of duty six times in the last thirty years.[67] In Pinole, California, it was revealed
that police were using MP-5s during routine patrols when they shot a man
during a domestic dispute.[68]

Facilitating the transfer of surplus military weapons and gear to the police
are a number of federal agencies, foremost among them the Law
Enforcement Support Office (LESO) in Fort Belvoir, Virginia, a branch of
the Defense Logistics Agency. As journalist Peter Cassidy found out, "In 1997
alone law enforcement agencies obtained 1.2 million pieces of military hardware. During the 1995–97 fiscal years, the Department of Defense distributed to civilian departments more than 3,800 M-16s, 2,185 M-14s, 73 M-79
grenade launchers, and 112 armored personnel carriers."[69] (One outfit calls
its APC "mother," while another in east Texas calls theirs "bubba one" and
"bubba two."[70]) Overall, more than 11,000 police agencies have received
such equipment for free, paying only transportation or shipping costs. Among
the recipients are cops in twenty-three states who received 6,400 bayonets
during 1996–97. One bayonet-equipped agency assured the press that the
long knives would only be used for cutting down pot plants.[71]

"Basically, you go in and take the stuff you want," said an Air Force officer
in charge of coordinating a Midwestern branch of the LESO. "For example,
if you have a small police department, and funds are limited, you can contact us and we can get you a police car for nothing."[72]

Surveying public reaction to this proliferation of military-style organization and firepower, it seems that Americans have once again mistaken quantity for quality. The simple theorem seems to run as follows: the more gear,
the more effective the force; the higher the caliber, the better the weapon;
the more violence, the better the policing. This false equivalence between
the capacity for state violence and public safety is hard to shake, especially
when the whole discourse of law enforcement takes place within a larger
context of increasingly racist, anti-poor demagogy. Victim-blaming is the

currency of mainstream politics. And the discourse of victim-blaming quickly turns into one of enemy-making and from there into a discourse of war. As economic contradictions deepen, the racialized class Other – the immigrant, the urban mendicant, the cheats, the dark-skinned, the "thieves," and "predators" – looms ever larger in the minds of the economically besieged middle and working classes. As politicians face the fact that the corporate system *will not* and *cannot* profitably accommodate the needs of the poor and working majority, they necessarily turn to crime-baiting and racially coded demonology as a way of inciting, mobilizing, and diverting legitimate political anxieties towards irrelevant enemies.

THE CULTURE OF MILITARISM

In reality, military technology and training do not make people safer. Military gear brings embedded in it a set of militaristic social relations. Aggressive group tactics, automatic weapons, and infrared scopes all displace and preclude the social skills, forbearance, and individual discretion essential to accountable and effective civilian policing. The metaphor of war also implies the possibility of victory in which one side vanquishes another. Thus one impact of the new paramilitary police technology is a "culture of militarism" that gestates in the world of tactical policing. Peter Kraska, the pre-eminent sociologist of SWAT, argues that young officers find the military regalia of SWAT "culturally intoxicating." In part this is because "the elite self-perception and status granted these police units stems from the high status military special operations groups have in military culture."[73]

But the military world-view is not confined to the ranks of SWAT. Tactical units, having close relations with the armed forces, act as ideological transmission-belts between the military and the regular police. As we saw above, the use of automatic weapons is already spreading from the military to SWAT teams, and from there to regular cops. Promulgating the gospel of war and "special ops" is even written into the mission of many tactical units. Fresno's VCSU, like the L.A. and Miami SWAT teams, spends much of its time training regular rank-and-file police in the special arts of what increasingly looks like low-intensity conflict, or counterinsurgency warfare.

The culture of militarism is also fostered by the weapons industry, professional associations of tactical officers (which are organized at a state, regional, and national level), and a slew of magazines, books, and videos aimed at cops and gun freaks. Foremost among these "cultural mediators" is the National Tactical Officers Association (the largest SWAT officers association) and its publication *Tactical Edge,* which is marketed exclusively to police; civilians are prohibited from subscribing. *Tactical Edge* is best described as "news you can use" for SWAT officers. Articles cover new law enforcement technology (long exegeses on ammunition testing are common), tactics, conferences, and the politics of managing SWAT teams in what the authors usually perceive as a misinformed and hostile political environment. Many of the writers have impressive backgrounds in policing, spooking, and law enforcement planning. And most of what appears in *Tactical Edge* has a pragmatic, clinical tone. For example:

> The sniper team is most often considered to have primary responsibility for delivering "real time" intelligence information during the course of an operation. Don't forget, however, that the officers manning the inner perimeter are in excellent positions to complement and expand upon a sniper's efforts in this area. By virtue of their location, inner perimeter team members are often in better positions to detect both visual and audible indicators of activity that can be crucial to identifying a suspect's location and anticipating his actions.[74]

Less secretive and very widely read is the magazine *SWAT,* subtitled "Special Weapons and Tactics for the Prepared American." Published by Larry Flint, of *Hustler* fame, *SWAT*'s ammunition and weapons reviews are peppered with lines like "tactical officers and home owners will be glad to know . . ." These panegyrics generally read like pornography for gun nuts and over-eager cops. For example:

> During penetration, the prestressed Quick Shok projectile expands rapidly and then splits into three even sections. These segments or fragments penetrate in separate directions in an ever-widening pattern inside a soft target. Fragmentation is the main cause of tissue disruption.[75]

Like *Tactical Edge, SWAT* is replete with articles analyzing new hollow-point shells, fragmenting rounds, bean-bag rounds, H&K weapons, training opportunities, etc. But *SWAT* also indulges in easy-reading profiles of tactical squads and special operations groups from around the world. Dozens of similar cop-oriented publications and scores of books and videos also promulgate the paramilitary, technophilic police culture. Woven into this discourse is a right-wing political world-view in which impending chaos is held back only by the besieged, misunderstood men and women of law enforcement who, despite the efforts of pernicious liberals, endeavor to protect the public and face up to the ever greater challenge of "better armed criminals . . . bigger and more violent street gangs . . . increased numbers of extremists [and] increased violent crime."[76]

CONCLUSION: THE SPECTACLE OF TERROR

If there is a parable to be drawn from the story of paramilitary policing in the US, it is that the political theatrics of terror are by no means dead. Physical terror and spectacular displays of violence are still central to the state's control of the dangerous classes. The helicopters, guns, and constantly barking dogs of the American tactical army are a blunt semaphore to the lumpen classes and working poor. So too are the frequent gang sweeps, field interviews, and curfew busts. In all cases the message is clear: "They wouldn't do this in north Fresno," is the constant refrain from that city's working class African Americans and Latinos.[77] The VCSU, like many SWAT teams, even brags about the "deterrent" effect of its high-profile ruthlessness. The point is that *ritualized displays of terror are built into American policing. Spectacle is a fundamental part of how the state controls poor people.* As one VCSU sergeant put it: "They see our big gray SWAT bus, and the weapons, and they know we mean business."[78]

If violent theatrics help insinuate the power of the state into the every-day life of the ghetto, then Michel Foucault's thesis – that power is in-creasingly exercised through relatively invisible, increasingly medicalized discursive means, such as psychiatry, psychology, medicine, and social sciences – seems in need of revision.

In *Discipline and Punish*, Foucault argues that the history of punishment and social control in Europe (or more particularly France) involves a shift from punishing the body directly to controlling subjectivity, the soul, or the human interior, thus making bodies docile and useful. Foucault focuses on the spectacular public torture rituals of the ancien régime, in which the sovereign re-established power by taking revenge upon the body of the criminal. Foucault then traces the ruptures that lead to modern "disciplinary" forms of control; forms of power that act upon human consciousness and subjectivity, and thus enlist us in the useful, productive regulation of ourselves and our bodies. Thus he writes, "[t]he soul is the effect and instrument of a political anatomy: the soul is the prison of the body."[79]

For Foucault this shift is not a history of improved human rights or moral progress, but rather one of increasingly effective, totalizing, and pernicious mechanisms of social regulation. While public executions may at first glance seem rather a muscular expression of legal power, they were, as Foucault argues, dangerously inefficient, wasteful, and almost haphazard affairs. Foremost among public torture's inefficiencies was the role of the crowd, to which far too much power was distributed. The spectators, a central part of the ritual of public torture and execution, sometimes rebelled and rioted, attacking the scaffold to free or kill the prisoners and in other ways disrupt the power of the sovereign. As a result punishment was increasingly hidden and professionalized, its effects made more constant and continuous. The ancient art of torture and confession transmogrified into the modern methods of investigation and interrogation by which judicial truth and the inner workings of the modern delinquent are known. And thus was born the criminal subject, with free will, a sense of morality, and a "soul."

This progression, away from sovereign power towards "disciplinary power" or "bio-power" is, for Foucault, linked to the development of capitalism and industrial society's need for more constant and totalizing exploitation of bodies. "Thus discipline produces subjected and practiced, 'docile' bodies. Discipline increases the force of the body (in economic terms of utility) and diminished these same forces of the body (in political terms of obedience) . . ."[80]

From the vantage point of the late sixties, the height of the therapeutic, rehabilitation era, the age of "full employment" in many European economies, this argument made sense. The increasing embourgeoisement of the European and American working classes, the medicalization of social problems like poverty, and the totalizing modernist faith in rational and technical solutions to all human problems, gave resonance to the continued progression of Foucault's thesis. In the name of science and increased humanity, social control was achieved less and less through the semiotics of physical terror and increasingly through scientific explanations and thera-peutic interventions that turned the deviant into his or her own regulator, thus producing useful and docile bodies.

But as the class terrain of advanced capitalist society began to bifurcate in response to the profit crisis of the early seventies and its neoliberal solu-tions, so too has social control. The middle classes still immerse themselves in the discursive prisons of "self-help" and self-actualization; their deviance is "sickness" (addictions, compulsions, and other maladies); their cure is an attempt to function better, realize their "full potential," maximum health, find spiritual "wholeness," achieve "proper time management," business suc-cess, etc. But on the other side of the class divide, amidst the social and eco-nomic wreckage of the down-sized American dream, the energy of bodies and minds is not so needed. Here deviance is no longer seen as individual sickness, as it was during rehabilitation's heyday. Rather, the surplus classes are simply bad people made so by a corrosive "culture of poverty" or, in the Charles Murray school of thought, by crypto-racist, "genetic" deficiencies. Thus the "super-predators" – as neoconservative criminologist Di Iulio calls the impoverished pre-teens of America – and "lost generations" of the ghet-to cannot be saved, or used efficiently. And so we see state power once again manifest in an increasingly violent, ritualized politics of terror. As "actuari-al" crime control becomes the name of the criminological game, whole com-munities become the target of social control.

After all, paramilitary sweeps, like the public executions of the ancien régime, "make everyone aware, through the body of the criminal, of the unrestrained presence of the sovereign [or in this case, the modern state and its police]. The public execution [like a paramilitary police sweep] did not re-establish justice; it reactivated power."[81] Nor are SWAT operations in public space the only site of such ritualized displays: the courts, the jail house visiting room, the cell block, and the endless – seemingly looped – real-life action footage of shows like Cops, LAPD, and True Stories of the Highway Patrol all serve to distribute terror into the everyday lives of the poor. This class-biased shift away from reform toward an updated discourse of evil makes sense: many bodies – particularly those of young working class and lumpen men of color – are superfluous to capital's valorization. A growing stratum of "surplus people" is not being efficiently used by the economy. So instead they must be controlled and contained and, in a very limited way, rendered economically useful as raw material for a growing corrections complex.

Perhaps this explains why social control, in the broadest sense, has bifurcated in ways Foucault never fully examined and why the seemingly soft, scientific discourses of "deviance" and "rehabilitation" have given way to a new, more cynical, rhetoric of war, law enforcement armies, lost generations, and "bad guys."

CHAPTER SEVEN

REPATRIATING *LA MIGRA'S* WAR: THE MILITARIZED BORDER COMES HOME

We are under full-scale invasion by those who have
no right to be here.
Republican Rep. Elton Gallegly, California, 1997

California and Arizona
I make all your crops
Then it's north up to Oregon
to gather your hops
    dig the beets from your ground
    cut the grapes from your vine
to set on your table
your light sparkling wine
Woody Guthrie, "Pastures of Plenty," circa 1935

July 27, 1997: thirty cops and six Border Patrol agents in mixed teams begin a massive immigration "round-up" in Chandler, Arizona. Sweeping through the barrios of this desert city, some 120 miles north of the US–Mexico border, the combined force stops Latino drivers and pedestrians at random, conducting warrantless searches, harassing and, in a few cases, beating their victims. For five days the early morning hours are shattered by tactical, house-to-house searches in which bellowing police roust whole families with blinding flashlights and big guns. As the sweep unfolds, cops and INS officers humiliate Latinos on public highways and interrogate children on their way to school. All in all, authorities deport 432 undocumented migrants and two US citizens, some wearing nothing more than underwear.[1]

Following the raid eighteen Latinos who were victimized in the sweeps file a $35 million class action lawsuit alleging violations of their Fourth Amendment rights. The Arizona attorney general soon condemns the raid, finding that searches were in fact conducted without warrants. Transcripts of police and Border Patrol radio communications reveal that officers from both agencies had cavalierly dispensed with the usual fig leaf of probable cause. In a typical call to a back-up car, a bike officer says: ". . . to any [police] motor, there's a red Intrepid leaving from the property, no probable cause."[2] It seemed that the only criterion at work was skin color. Police and INS arrest reports were equally bald-faced in their racism and constitutional violations. One Border Patrol agent justified a bust by noting that he "immediately noticed the lack of personal hygiene displayed by the subject, and a strong body odor common to illegal aliens."[3] Even more disturbing are the accounts given by the shaken Latino residents of Chandler who told the attorney general that their children were left too scared to venture outdoors, that they had been "made to feel like cockroaches," and that relations between Latinos and Anglos seem irrevocably strained. Among those stopped and harassed were Arizona's top-ranked amateur golfer and people whose families had resided in California and Arizona for the last 150 to 200 years. One pregnant woman was so traumatized she stayed hidden in her house for weeks.

"They really went too far, entering homes, detaining all the Mexican looking kids," says Alberto Esparza, vice-president of the newly formed Chandler Coalition for Civil and Human Rights. "They even beat a few people up. This one seventeen-year-old kid ran and when they caught him they beat him real bad." The youth was a US citizen.[4] The Border Patrol, in crisp military fashion, investigated itself and found no wrongdoing – while the good ol' boys of the Chandler PD cut straight to demanding an apology from their critics.[5]

THE MIGHTY INS COMES HOME

Welcome to what the INS calls "Integrated Interior Enforcement." With an annual budget of $4 billion, most urban sectors of the border thoroughly militarized, and 24,000 armed INS enforcement personnel working in inspections, investigations, intelligence, Border Patrol, and detention, the INS has opened a second front in its war on immigrants.[6] "We're finally getting the same interior buildup that we've had on the border," explains an enthusiastic Virginia Kice, INS western regional spokeswoman.

The combined police-Border Patrol raid in Chandler was just one example of a growing trend toward increased cooperation and "cross-deputation" between law enforcement and immigration authorities. Since the late nineties, militarized immigration enforcement – which first developed in the no-man's land of the US–Mexico border in the name of fighting drug smuggling and illegal immigration – has been repatriated, piece by piece, to the US interior. From the pumpkin fields of Washington State to the poultry plants of the Midwest to the barrios of urban California, the INS is teaming up with local police, the FBI, the DEA, and even the military to implement the most aggressive and totalizing police surveillance and enforcement regime the country has ever seen. Often these multi-agency interior enforcement operations involve heavily armed tactical raiding parties backed up by helicopters and dogs.

The primary product of this campaign is increased fear and anxiety among America's immigrant working class, particularly among the Latino communities of the Southwest. As interior enforcement takes hold, the number of deportations has risen dramatically, from 69,226 in fiscal 1996 to 113,790 in fiscal 1997.[7] Nationwide, the number of people held by the INS has increased by 70 percent since 1996.[8] At any one time, the INS holds up to 20,000 people in its vast archipelago of public and private detention facilities. Many of these prisons are nothing more than run-down motels, surrounded by barbed wire and infamous for their wretched conditions, overcrowding, and violence.[9]

The crackdown on immigrants crossing the US–Mexico border and on immigrants living in the US is best understood as a state response to global economic restructuring. Both increased immigration and mounting repression of immigrant communities in the US have their roots in the business system's efforts to resolve its recurring crisis of profitability. Since the early seventies transnational corporations in search of new markets and cheap labor have exported capital with renewed vigor to peripheral and semiperipheral regions of the world. The flipside of American deindustrialization has been increased industrialization in parts of the Third World. Such foreign investment causes the destruction of traditional economies, the enclosure of traditional lands, the privatization of national industries, and, as a result, the deracination of whole populations.

As Saskia Sassen has shown, these macro-economic changes propel urbanization (that is migration from the countryside to cities) and in turn "push" would-be immigrants from the cities of the south to the economic core regions of the north. Meanwhile, restructuring in the core economies like the US "pulls" immigrants north. In North America the booming low-wage service sector and the downgraded, post-unionized industrial sector must slake their thirst for cheap labor with imports. California's fields, Iowa's abattoirs, the restaurants of New York, all need immigrants who will work hard at dangerous and dirty jobs for little remuneration. Likewise, the newly enriched burghers of America's salaried class need ever more domestic servants, nannies, and gardeners.

These labor markets actively recruit from the south, as well as rely on the continued momentum of previously established cross-border "migration chains."[10] While all of these patterns pre-date the profits crisis of the seventies, that crisis and its ensuing restructuring initiated a new and massive wave of global immigration. Thus the story of policing the immigrant "other" is connected to the story of post-seventies political-economic restructuring that underpins the other arguments in this book. The shrill xenophobic rhetoric and ruthless policies of the 1990s immigration wars are, like crime bills, zero tolerance, and the rise of SWAT teams, part of "policing the crisis."

Politically, the repressive anti-immigrant impulse is both an organic expression of nativist hostility and a very useful, rational system of elite-inspired class control. For example, the virulent California ballot initiative Proposition 227, which ended bilingual education, was sponsored by the bigoted plutocrat Ronald Unz, and embraced by a frightened and confused white middle class. Likewise, Proposition 187, which cut state benefits to legal immigrants, received massive support from the then California governor Pete Wilson, who was quite obviously trying to make immigrants a scapegoat for middle-class political and economic anxieties.

THE NEW WAR

Interior enforcement, *la Migra*'s second front, involves three central features: the first is a raft of new draconian federal laws that mandate the arrest, detention, and deportation of all non-naturalized immigrants who have *ever committed a felony or broken an immigration law*. The second is increased inter-agency co-operation between immigration officials and the police. The third feature is intensified computerized surveillance and increased networking between law enforcement intelligence systems.

IIRIRA, the legal vise

The first tine of the interior enforcement trident is the Illegal Immigration Reform and Immigrant Responsibility Act (IIRIRA) of 1996 and a few supporting provisions in the Anti-Terrorism and Effective Death Penalty Act (AEDPA) of 1996.[11] Under these audacious and inflexible new laws, "developing interior enforcement" means that even *legal* residents with prior felony convictions (including twenty-year-old drunk driving convictions) can and are being deported. While immigrants have always lived with the risk of deportation, IIRIRA and AEDPA ushered in three significant changes: the number of crimes that could lead to deportation was expanded, the laws became retroactive, and "aggravated felons" could no longer contest their deportation in any way.[12] Perhaps the most socially destructive feature of all this is that IIRIRA can be applied retroactively.

Consider the case of Scott Shelly, a white, middle-class Canadian married to an American and once an instructor of physics at Portland Community College. In the spring of 1998 Shelly was arrested, shackled, and summarily deported without a hearing because he had failed to fill out a two-page immigration form upon returning to the US from one of his frequent visits to Canada.[13] More egregious is the case of Luis Gabriel Gurrea, a "soft-spoken office supervisor with no criminal record," who overstayed his temporary visa. For this crime his home was raided and Gurrea was deported to his native Argentina. In the wake of Gurrea's expulsion his wife, the mother of his infant daughter, was raped. "I need my husband home," said Mireya Gurrea to an immigration judge. Meanwhile, Luis sobbed into the telephone from Buenos Aires, describing his woes to an *L.A. Times* reporter: "They never let me explain anything . . . I'm not a criminal. I paid my taxes every year. I just want to be back with my wife and daughter."[14]

The IIRIRA's zero tolerance retroactivity also scrambled the life of Catherine Caza, born in Ontario, Canada, but raised from age three in the US. Eighteen years ago Caza was arrested for selling twenty-one Quaalude pills to her beau, who turned out to be an undercover narcotics agent. Caza pleaded guilty and was sentenced to five years' probation. But in 1998 her case was dredged up and she was expelled in the name of American safety.[15] Aberrant over-reactions by the INS? It would seem not.

In September 1998 Texas INS agents drew up a list of immigrants with convictions for "aggravated felonies" and launched a series of massive predawn raids. Dubbed Operation Last Call, the state-wide assault hit hundreds of homes, rounding up 116 immigrants in El Paso, 101 in Harlingen, and over 500 more across Texas. All were guilty of three or more drunken driving convictions.[16] The prisoners included a few hardened criminals but there were just as many "model non-citizens" – for example, the clean and sober Isaias Jauregui, "a construction subcontractor in Mesquite, Texas, whose last DUI conviction was six years old." After six months in jail for that conviction Jauregui entered a rehabilitation program, then Alcoholics Anonymous, completed his five years' probation and at the time of his capture was sober and working on a college degree.[17]

David Balderama was another "model immigrant." Born in Mexico, Balderama moved to the US as a child; once grown, he raised four children, bought a home and was a hard-working, tax-and-union-dues-paying steel worker finally approaching retirement. But over the years Balderama had racked up three DUIs, and was permanently deported as part of Operation Last Call. Activists charged that INS teams had smashed into homes without permission, without warrants, and roughed up innocents in the process.[18]

Extending the long arm: inter-agency collaboration

Traditionally, police agencies operated within strict legal and geographic compartmentalization, which served to check their repressive powers. But in the name of fighting drugs and undocumented immigration at the US–Mexican border, many of these "firewalls" are being wiped away. For example, in 1980 the INS was "tasked" with policing immigration *and only immigration*. By 1990 the INS/Border Patrol had been empowered – under Titles 19 and 21 of the U.S. Code – to enforce both contraband and narcotics laws; that is, to act in the capacity of DEA and Customs agents. As one senior official told a 1990 Senate hearing, this "enables those agencies to conduct warrantless border searches which are valuable in the border communities and inland areas vulnerable to air smuggling."[19]

When this sort of legal cross-fertilization is not possible for administrative reasons, it often occurs in a *de facto* form. This is most obvious in border regions where Border Patrol agents and the local police regularly ride together. In downtown El Paso, six Border Patrol agents participate in joint bike patrols with local police.[20] Thus when a joint INS-police patrol makes contact with a "subject," the police officers and Border Patrol agents can simply pass the person back and forth, from the enforcer of state criminal codes to the enforcer of federal immigration and contraband laws. If the subject has papers, the local police can search for drugs or run a warrant check. If the person comes up clean they can be checked for immigration status and any record of illegal re-entries. Likewise, if the police have no probable cause the Border Patrol agent might just find some to initiate an immigration stop.[21] Thus Latinos who run stop signs can be checked for immigration papers and undocumented jaywalkers now live under the threat of deportation.

The same obtains in Tucson, Arizona, and throughout California's Imperial Valley, where dual-agency teams travel in cars and Broncos. In Fresno, INS and Border Patrol agents are part of that anti-gang flotilla known as MAGEC (see chapter six), and have even taken their war into the halls of the public schools. On April 2, 1998, Border Patrol agents stormed Roosevelt High School, and arrested and deported three Latino youths for fighting. The next day students walked out in protest and managed to get one of the youths brought back from Mexico.[22]

In San Diego, the INS has substations throughout the county, including one in the downtown police headquarters. With 2,500 Border Patrol agents stationed in the San Diego area, and new agents arriving all the time, the INS has taken to setting up checkpoints throughout California's southern counties. Frequently targeted are Greyhound buses, the long distance arks of the poor, which in the Southwest are usually packed with Mexican and Central American immigrants.[23] Between its highway checkpoints the Border Patrol prowls the barrios, some as far as an hour and a half from the frontier, conducting stops, searches, and interrogations.

And, lest one get a Manichean image of khaki-clad crackers rousting and hounding *la Raza,* it is worth noting that many Border Patrol agents in the Southwest are Latino. Like the rest of law enforcement, working for the INS is a common path of upward mobility, and so it attracts working class Mexican Americans, African Americans, and many women. Like the prison guards of California, *la Migra*'s troops are a diverse lot. Moreover, while the mission of the Border Patrol may be racist, that does not mean the agents of that policy themselves hold racist attitudes; they merely execute a racist task.

INS and police collaboration further racializes law enforcement by extending the Border Patrol's race-based standards for stops and searches. In this regard, the nightmare of the Chandler raid was just an extreme expression of normal procedure.[24] In reality skin color is often the only criterion the INS/Border Patrol uses to make stops. But according to the law, the agency is supposed to have "reasonable suspicion" before pulling over a car or stopping a pedestrian for questioning. Typically the INS covers "reasonable suspicion" with descriptions such as "heavily laden car, traveling near the border, with a Latino driver who wouldn't make eye contact."[25]

Further away from the border the hunt for the undocumented is less likely to involve INS patrols. In the big cities of the North *la Migra* prefers to piggyback on regular police operations. Facilitating this tactic is the INS Violent Gang Task Force (VGTF), which has units in sixteen of the nation's largest cities. In L.A. the VGTF – involving roughly eighteen INS agents and a varying number of LAPD gang specialists – operates as a special anti-*cholo* dragnet within the LAPD, which allows both agencies to share information and street-level support.

"Often the PD will have known gang members with long rap sheets, from [the] 18th Street [gang] or whatever, but can't get them on anything," explained Michael Flynn, assistant director for investigations in the INS's Western Region. "If guys like that are deportable, we're called in to make an arrest."[26] In other words, the police draw up hit lists, which the INS uses to conduct hundreds of residential raids every year. And when such activity lulls, INS officers play a supporting role in hundreds more LAPD gang raids. "When it's a PD operation we set up a command center, and process the criminal aliens. At other times we take the lead," explained another INS official.[27]

In Los Angeles all of this cooperation takes place despite the common assumption among immigrants' rights activists and liberal Angelenos that the LAPD had been forced into a position of non-cooperation with the INS. After vigorous community mobilization in the seventies the LAPD was indeed compelled to issue Special Order Number 40, prohibiting officers from actively helping the INS. But the directive says only that "officers shall not initiate police action with the objective of discovering the alien status of a person."[28] All other forms of collaboration are permissible.

In Newark, New Jersey, the VGTF has eight INS agents working with police as part of a state-wide effort to track down and deport immigrants with criminal records; they arrest and expel about twenty people a month.[29] In Washington, D.C., the Violent Gang Task Force targets legal immigrants with past convictions even if they live by the law.[30] A much larger force roams Chicago and its edge cities, deporting hundreds every year. Lisa Palumbo, counsel with the Legal Assistance Foundation of Chicago, described the unit's effect thus: "It sends a chill within the entire community . . . we receive calls from people who say they're afraid to go out."[31] The metaphor of immobility is apt, as interior enforcement keeps immigrants "in their place," physically and politically.

Increased INS involvement in the domestic law enforcement's anti-drug jihad means that even more Latino, Caribbean, and Asian non-combatants become collateral damage. For example, in 1997, the Portland, Oregon, suburb of Tigard was surprised to find one of its impoverished pockets, the rundown Tiffiny Court housing complex, under military-style occupation by a tactical force of sixty police officers and federal agents. With the usual overkill the lawmen rounded up more than a hundred undocumented immigrants, along with a handful of suspected drug dealers, and deported the lot.[32]

The INS is also establishing substations in county jails. From these innocuous little nodes at the front end of the legal system INS agents can siphon off huge numbers of undocumented immigrants and legal residents who have previous felony convictions. In Los Angeles, where some of the earliest substations were established, seventy-five immigration cops work in round-the-clock shifts. That force, plus a powerful new computer system, can catch up to 90 percent of the deportable foreign-born people passing through the jail. The INS estimates that of the 25,000 prisoners in L.A. county jails, 18 percent are deportable "criminal aliens."[33]

These high-tech INS jailhouse substations are set to vault from pilot program to national norm. A 1997 law, sponsored by Congressman Elton Gallegly (Republican, Simi Valley), mandates that within four years the nation's hundred largest jail systems be thus equipped.

Dossier society for them

The third component of the interior enforcement regime is *la Migra*'s state-of-the-art computerized surveillance system, which has exponentially expanded law enforcement's control over immigrant populations. At the heart of this brave new techo-dragnet is a massive "biometrics" computer system called IDENT. Developed in partnership with EDS (the firm that made Ross Perot rich), IDENT digitally photographs and fingerprints captured immigrants and stores this intelligence in the system's vast central database.

Unlike the NCIC and most state law enforcement systems, IDENT does not rely on matching names or identification numbers to find files. Instead this fully "biometric" system can automatically compare millions of digital images – be they fingerprints, hand prints, or mugshots. Thus when former deportees are recaptured and forced to give their prints to the scanning pad of an IDENT terminal, their biometric files are retrieved, regardless of what name, Social Security number, or date of birth the captive provides.[34] After only two years online, IDENT's "electronic curtain" already had 227 terminals around the country, contained the fingerprints and photos of nearly two million people, and was adding more files every day.[35]

It is no coincidence that IDENT – the most powerful and advanced computer surveillance system in the country – was developed for use on impoverished, disenfranchised immigrants. As sociologist David Lyon points out, the introduction of new social-control-and-surveillance technologies always starts by targeting society's weakest and most marginalized groups. From these social margins the strategies and technologies spread in toward the mainstream.[36] Consider fingerprinting, once reserved for identifying only violent criminals; the practice is now a common prerequisite for receiving a driver's license and even cashing checks. Another example is the role of Social Security numbers, at first a simple tag for managing state benefits; they are now the equivalent of national personal identification numbers.

A different, but equally powerful computer system – called the Law Enforcement Support Center (LESC) – also facilitates the expansion of inter-agency information flows required by "integrated interior enforcement." The LESC is a massive INS computer database and interchange. Located in Burlington, Vermont, the system functions as the cyber hub of a vast national network linking state and local files with thousands of high-speed direct "dedicated lines," and has nearly unfathomable computing and storage capacity. The LESC, only a few years old, will soon tie INS files directly into the intelligence systems of most of the nation's police departments. So far only Arizona, Iowa, and California are participating: other states are set to come online by the century's end.[37]

Linking local police terminals and arrest files with the databases of the mighty INS is profound in and of itself, but the LESC will be further enhanced. Communication between the various nodes on the national LESC network takes place *automatically* and at lightning speed. The system operates in the following manner: when police in Tucson or L.A. book a foreign-born person – be they legal resident, undocumented, or naturalized citizens – the booking computer is triggered to send the suspect's information to the LESC in Burlington. There, incoming data is processed and matched against existing dossiers; any information on the suspect is then automatically bounced back to the local police, all within minutes. As the LESC system improves and expands, police in the field will be able to check a person's immigration status from their patrol car terminals, "even when the crime or infraction isn't worth taking the person into custody . . . like, on running a red-light," as one INS spokesperson put it.[38]

Law enforcement boosters love LESC's "resource multiplier effect" and because it is automatic, they claim it avoids all "human error."[39] But error – that great liberal shibboleth – is a minor issue. So too, at a certain level, is the question of individual personal privacy. More sinister are the LESC's and IDENT's *intended* uses as broad tools of social control. Properly operated, both are mechanisms for tracking, controlling, and intimidating whole populations. Both will have a deleterious impact on immigrants, achieving the subjective changes of Bentham's panopticon: making the effects of power constant, even while its application is intermittent. In other words, immigrants will fear the law more intensely knowing that INS/police intelligence systems are automatic, infallible, and instantaneous. The electronic dragnet will force internalization of the INS gaze, causing immigrants to keep to themselves, stay out of sight, and steer clear of politics. And the INS optics will work even when – perhaps best when – one's hand is not on the high-tech fingerprint pad; the IDENT/LESC files will reside not just in digital vaults but in the minds of millions of migrants, forced to live as virtual outlaws.

THE LOGIC OF REPRESSION: POSTMODERN PALMER RAIDS

For many Americans, invoking the specter of class rebellion and state repression sounds either romantic or paranoid. The official images we receive of ourselves consistently omit struggle, rebellion, and resistance. America, it is assumed, has been a politically tranquil country since the sixties. But in truth, class struggle in America is quite real and continues even in the quietest of times. Only when viewed in this context can we fully understand the many political meanings of "interior enforcement."

Despite a myriad of causes and effects the immigrant crackdown is at one level simply a repressive service performed by the state for the employer class. For example, it is common knowledge in California that some growers who hire immigrant labor covertly call the INS "on themselves" to intimidate and drive away restive workers. Indirectly, all INS raids serve this end: keeping the immigrant working class disorganized, intimidated, and obedient.

Consider the following: in September 1998, INS agents raided a Staten Island laundry service five days after workers there filed a complaint against the owner, who had kept over $159,000 in back wages. Ten Mexican nationals were deported without their unpaid earnings. Activists suspected self-reporting by the boss.[40] Another example involves a video reproduction firm called Mediacopy in the San Francisco Bay Area. This bottom rung of the information economy witnessed a massive INS raid just as its Latino labor force was about to vote for union ratification. *La Migra*'s forces arrested, shackled, and deported ninety-nine workers in what were described as filthy and fetid buses. Managers at Mediacopy admitted they knew the INS was planning a raid. Following the bust, managers launched aggressive anti-union mop-up operations that included intimidating leaflets and videos that cast unionization as an invitation for more raids. To top it all off, the company withheld news of a follow-up INS "verification" visit until the last minute, sparking a new wave of panic among the employees.[41]

In Portland, Oregon, day laborers started an independent organizing drive only to find themselves victimized by a spate of violent INS raids. Organizing was destabilized and the effort momentarily defeated. In a huge apple warehouse in eastern Washington a Teamsters' unionization drive came under assault from an employer-retained union-busting firm that made constant and explicit reference to the vulnerability of immigrant workers and, in typical fashion, cast unions as anti-immigrant, claiming that organized labor benefited from high worker turnover, and thus from frequent INS raids and deportations.[42]

In the Midwest immigrant labor is becoming ever more essential to that region's massive and wretched meatpacking industry. According to a report by the General Accounting Office, up to 25 percent of Nebraska and Iowa meatpacking workers are undocumented. In a trade where 22.7 percent of all workers were injured during 1995, and where arthritis, repetitive strain injuries, and poverty are the consolation prizes for survivors, labor discipline is paramount. With world and national markets already saturated by an overproduction of cheap food, it is imperative that employers keep their wage bill as low as possible. An eruption of wildcat strikes or vigorous organizing could amputate corporate profits. Thus undocumented laborers, kept compliant by INS raids and surveillance, are increasingly the preferred employees.[43]

Toward that end, the meatpacking industry has entered an unholy alliance with the immigration police so as to manage labor better. The program, dubbed Operation Prime Beef, will, the INS says, involve "building a partnership with top managers in the meat packing/processing industry and giving them the tools they need to ensure a legal work force."[44] The emphasis is on "legal," but in reality the program is designed to ensure a steady, but thoroughly intimidated, supply of labor. Prime Beef will give employers advanced warning about raids, which will help businessmen to incorporate INS operations into their own local labor control agendas. The program will also empower employers to conduct their *own* immigration inspections – that is, use federal law as they see fit, to intimidate who they want when they want.[45] This upper-echelon cooperation is nothing new; employers have long colluded with the INS. In 1995, 125 workers were arrested in an immigration raid at a meatpacking plant in Schuyler, Nebraska. Excel Corporation, which owned the plant, bragged about working "more than a month with the INS to plan the raid."[46] The next cohort of Mexican meatcutters to hit Schuyler no doubt watched their step.

In southern California organizers with the American Friends Service Committee report that an INS campaign called Operation Clean Sheets, in which the INS raids San Diego's large hotels, is having a very direct and negative impact on labor organizing. "We go into the hotels, on behalf of the unions, to tell people their legal rights and hardly anyone shows up," says Roberto Martinez of the American Friends Service Committee. "At one meeting we had zero – literally no one showed up. People are very frightened right now." Martinez points out that it has always been difficult to organize undocumented migrants. But he says that since 1994, the fear among immigrants – and even Chicanos – has grown tremendously. "The raids and the [INS] checkpoints keep people immobilized in every sense."[47]

This anti-immigrant fear-generating policy, like the spectacular inner-city tactical raids discussed earlier, operates in part through a theatrics of terror, and the blunt semaphore of sudden unexpected violence. Perhaps one of the most semiotically charged raids ever occurred during 1996, in Jackson Hole, Wyoming. With no apparent warning a large mobile force of local sheriff's deputies and Border Patrol agents swept through town, snatching Latino workers from the kitchens of twenty-five restaurants, rousting them from their homes, and literally grabbing them as they rode by on bicycles. The 153 captives were rounded up, cuffed, searched, and corralled into a yard where police wrote large identification numbers on their forearms in thick black ink. Almost fifty of the prisoners were legal residents or US citizens, and were eventually released after their friends and families furnished the appropriate papers. However, the undocumented were transported off to detention in a manure-strewn cattle truck.[48] The jumble of tropes at work in this real life allegory are as obvious as they are grotesque: mass arrests, numbered forearms, cattle cars . . .

THE CONTRADICTIONS OF EMPLOYER INTERESTS

Interior enforcement's control of the new immigrant working class is not without contradictions, nor are the agendas of the INS and employers always coterminous, or coordinated. Very often the interests of *employers in general* are served by damaging the interests of *particular employers*. For example the Jackson Hole raid left many businesses reeling. Taco Bell lost 75 percent of its workforce and the president of the local chamber of commerce was forced to work three days, virtually without rest, to keep his industrial laundry service operating.

In both cases native and naturalized employees refused to work overtime, nor were documented and US-born job-seekers willing to take such arduous employment for the standard five dollars an hour that is the going rate for "back of the house" service work in posh Jackson Hole. But if undocumented immigrants did not live in fear of surprise INS raids, would they be willing to toil for such meager remuneration?

In Salt Lake City a Latino-owned tortilla factory was raided by a tactical force of seventy-five heavily armed agents from six different local, state, and federal police agencies, including the INS and DEA. As SWAT officers blew open a utility closet door and a K-9 team searched the attic, workers and eighty-two customers were thrown to the floor, cuffed, and brutalized. In the wake of this onslaught the tortilla factory's business plummeted by two-thirds and its owner, Rafael Gomez, who was physically attacked during the operation, was almost ruined. But *employers in general* benefited from the new pulse of fear that shot through the social networks of Latino immigrants.

Likewise, in Genesee County, New York, armed INS agents raided a dozen vegetable farms, where they smacked, shoved, and jabbed Latino workers, regardless of their documentation. On one farm an INS agent even fired at fleeing laborers, then lied about it to investigators, and finally explained that he was aiming for their legs.[49] The effect of all this on workers in the area was horrific. Latinos throughout the mostly white up-state farm belt told reporters that they curtailed their movements, kept their children under closer watch, and generally tried to stay out of public view. But the repercussions for many farm owners were also negative. Torrey Farms, for example, had its entire workforce deported or run off; the losses to its crops included 3,000 tons of unpacked cabbage and 40 acres of butternut squash. Such farm owners, who suffered the ruinous economic effects of being raided, clearly had their immediate self-interest damaged by the INS.[50]

But the growers' more general, long-term interests *as a class* were most definitely helped by the raid. What, after all, keeps agricultural labor so amazingly inexpensive, unorganized, and efficient, if not a pervasive culture of fear among immigrant laborers? To the extent that raids "reproduce" a supply of poorly remunerated agricultural labor, then the economic damages suffered by *individual employers* are simply the diseconomies and political externalities of maintaining the interests of *employers in general.*

It is axiomatic that owners of capital need labor to be inexpensive relative to the price of labor's product if profits are to remain healthy, and that impoverished people, driven by desperation, will generally labor for lower wages than people with some degree of social power and wealth. But some-times poverty is not enough. In many dangerous and dirty low-wage labor markets — such as food processing, agriculture, and apparel manufacturing — employers seem to prefer not just poor workers, but *criminalized* workers. A labor supply of undocumented, ideologically demonized, and literally hunted immigrants is to American capitalists what drugs are to America's consumers: an essential import.

The usefulness, if not necessity, of criminalizing immigrant labor became apparent in the wake of the 1986 Immigration Reform and Control Act (IRCA), which gave green cards to 1.2 million undocumented farm workers. As soon as these laborers received this slightest of legal protections, the vast majority of them evacuated the fields in search of better employment.[51] As soon as these migrant laborers were "legal" they had a degree of upward mobility; poverty alone was not enough to "keep them down on the farm." Only police terror can assure that. To remain passively trapped at the very bottom rung of the labor market, immigrants must be legally and ideologically constructed as *criminals*.

But anti-immigrant police terror is not merely instrumental to labor control: lest the arguments here seem too functionalist it is important to point out that immigrant bashing is also a racist crusade with an *autonomous* ideological life. Bigotry becomes its own end, and reproduces with a virus-like self-propagation. Irish and Russian immigrants, though often working and residing in the US long after their papers expire, are not subject to the same sort of abuse and commando-style raids suffered by Latino, Asian, Caribbean, and African immigrant communities. White European immigrants are seen as "belonging" because they are white, while people with darker skin can still be seen as foreign even after several generations of assimilation and acculturation.[52] And immigrant bashing is a politically and psychological cathartic practice for beguiling politicians and frustrated white people, regardless of its economic impacts.

BORDER LINE POLITICS

Though interior enforcement is a project with its own momentum its immediate roots lie in the militarization of the US–Mexico border. This thin 2,000-mile-long police state is still the ultimate testing ground for law enforcement power and technology. The geographic frontier is also the political frontier where systems of militarized social control undergo constant refinement and expansion. At the border immigrants have even fewer rights than in the interior, few connections, usually very little money, and usually less access to the "official" language.

DOMESTIC DMZ

From the dark US wastelands overlooking Tijuana's eastern slums, Border Patrol agent Albert Barrajas watches the pitch black night on the small screen of his army surplus infrared night-vision scope. Below him ghostly figures shift restlessly: "Aliens on the fence line." Three pale shapes hoist themselves over the cold, dark background of a metal wall. Radios crackle, and Barrajas directs his team of Bronco-driving agents down toward the "echo four section of the fence." The would-be migrants scatter: two dash into a drainpipe leading back to Mexico, while the third runs panicked along the cold metal fence.

"Bronco on the E two, there's a single moving east," mumbles Barrajas into his radio. On the scope, "the single" is frantic for an opening or low point in the recently installed fence – surplus metal landing mats, donated by the National Guard, and so sharp in spots they can sever fingers. Even on the strange little infrared screen the immigrant's terror is palpable.[53]

Here on the US–Mexico border law enforcement sees through military eyes. Since the early 1980s the massive paramilitary buildup here has involved new equipment, expanded police powers, and unprecedented inter-agency cooperation. Urban sectors of the border now seethe with guard towers, motion sensors, night scopes, impassable 18-foot-high concrete "bollard fencing," and swarms of Border Patrol agents – 7,000 of them to be exact, about 80 percent more than in 1994.[54] And according to a September 1997 report in *Helicopter News,* the Border Patrol received forty-five state-of-the-art Black Hawk choppers to augment its fleet of over fifty Vietnam-era Hueys.[55] Meanwhile, on the ground agents have at their disposal ever more army surplus night-vision goggles, infrared TV cameras, hypersensitive microphones, thousands of high-tech motion sensors, and scores of new mobile klieg "stadium style" floodlights.

GI Joe on the border

Despite the murder of the eighteen-year-old shepherd Esequiel Hernandez in August 1997 by a secret reconnaissance squad of armed US Marines in Redford, Texas, thousands of soldiers are still heavily involved in border policing.[56] The army builds roads and provides aerial reconnaissance, while National Guard units search vehicles, staff border checkpoints, and conduct both air and ground surveillance missions.[57] In 1995 the Department of Defense valued the military hardware on the border at $260 million.[58]

Facilitating this trend are the military's Joint Task Force-Six (JTF-6) and a consortium of federal, state, and local law enforcement agencies called Operation Alliance. Set up in 1989 to help fight drugs on the US–Mexico border, JTF-6 was initially restricted to aiding the DEA. Later, with the increasing conflation of immigration and drugs, the INS/Border Patrol was brought in.[59]

Technically none of this imbrication between the military and domestic law enforcement violates the Posse Comitatus Act of 1878, which made it illegal for soldiers to be deputized or arrest US citizens. Officials at JTF-6 describe their mission as training and support, not actual law enforcement. But as the ever expanding role of the JTF-6 shows, the line between training and doing can be blurry. "For example," says JTF-6 Lieutenant Colonel Bill Riechret, "We can't do real-time [intelligence] link analysis, but we did translate 11,670 pages of surveillance transcripts for law enforcement in FY '97."[60] Or consider the fact that local law enforcement personnel conducting anti-narcotics surveillance and raids are often ferried around the border region in Army or National Guard choppers.[61] And, if the example of the Navy SEALs who killed a man in Albuquerque (see chapter six) is anything to go by, there are probably many other joint military–law enforcement operations underway that never receive public scrutiny.

But even in the military there are pockets of discomfort with its growing involvement in policing. One military expert described the dilemmas surrounding the armed forces' counter-drugs operations thus: "This is not 'go out, find them and shoot them'. That's really important, because if you ask the military to go do a task . . . that's what the military does. We are designed to go out and win the nation's wars."[62] Another military officer, also discussing the issue of military involvement in policing, explained that soldiers are good at "killing people and breaking things." Still another noted how the "Clausewitzian concept of war [as] annihilation is deeply embedded in the army psyche."[63]

One of the more surreal, but widely read, examples of military discomfort with its growing involvement in domestic policing is the fictional short story called "The Origins of the American Military Coup of 2012." Written by an active duty officer, awarded a prize by General Colin Powell, and published in *Parameters,* the academic journal of the Army War College, this story takes place against the sinister, if somewhat silly, backdrop of a future America run by General Thomas E. T. Brutus (get it?). As "Commander-in-Chief of the Unified Armed Forces of the United States," Brutus resides at the White House, as "permanent Military Plenipotentiary." The story takes the form of a letter – written by an anonymous future military officer who, like many others, is imprisoned and awaiting execution – in which the narrator explains the origins of the coup starting in 1992. Contributing trends included "the massive diversion of military forces to civilian uses, the monolithic unification of the armed forces, and the insularity of the military community." The doomed narrator goes on:

> The military's anti-drug activities were a big part of the problem. Oh sure, I remember the facile claims of exponents of the military's counter-narcotics involvement as to what "valuable" training it provided . . . Did they seriously imagine that troops enhanced combat skills by looking for marijuana under car seats? . . .
>
> The devastation of the military's martial spirit was exemplified by its involvement in police activities . . . If military forces are inculcated with the same spirit of restraint [that law enforcement should have], combat performance is threatened. Moreover, law enforcement is also not just a form of low-intensity conflict. In low-intensity conflict, the military aim is to win the will of the people, a virtually impossible task with criminals motivated by money, not ideology.[64]

As one might expect, the "Coup of 2012" does not demonize the military as a dangerous institution to be kept in check. Rather, the author, Lt. Charles Dunlap, sees the root of the problem as the corrosive and enfeebling nature of police work and humanitarian missions. Dunlap's coup scenario runs as follows: due to its watered down post–Cold War mission, the military finds itself unable to fight off 10,000 Iranian zealots during "the second Persian Gulf War of 2011." In the wake of that ignominious defeat the military only seems capable of policing the home front. Added to this crisis is domestic "frustration" with democracy, which can't seem to deal with either foreign wars or domestic troubles. The final straw is the untimely death of a president. Then, with a few legal acrobatics, the military takes power through constitutional means and starts rounding up dissidents for execution.

Despite such warnings from within the armed forces, collaboration between soldiers and cops is increasing. And the pages of *Parameters* are more likely to offer uncritical articles about the military's need to prepare for post–Cold War "operations other than war," such as counter-narcotics work, than they are to warn against such new tasks. Dunlap's dark premonition is, despite its popular reception, not indicative of the general thrust of military thinking.

And more important than the doctrinal debates of military planners are facts on the ground. A mere ten years after the birth of JTF-6 – which some call the first real breach of the Posse Comitatus Act – the military is in the business of training police in the use of night-vision scopes, canine teams, data analysis, aerial surveillance, "mission planning," marksmanship, and interrogation. As one JTF-6 officer explained: "You'd be surprised how little some heartland police know about interviewing and interrogation . . . We also teach 'survival Spanish.' Like: 'law enforcement – get down!'"[65]

More ominous still are the military's courses such as "Close Quarter Battle" and "Advanced Military Operations on Urbanized Terrain." Such curriculum includes lots of storming apartments, kicking in doors, rappelling down walls, and mock shoot-outs. Among the more unexpected agencies to request such training in 1995 and 1996 were law enforcement outfits from Atlantic City, New Jersey; Burlington, Vermont; Columbus, Ohio; and Niagara Falls, and Rochester, New York, along with cities like Philadelphia and Seattle. JTF-6 has also built training complexes for elite cops in San Diego and Hillsboro, Florida, near Tampa. The first INS units to receive such instruction were the elite air-mobile Border Patrol Tactical Teams (BORTACs), which were later deployed in Los Angeles during the Rodney King riots.[66] During the L.A. riots of May 1992 the military set up JTF-LA, a miniature version of JFT-6, which oversaw military deployment and co-operation with law enforcement during and after the conflagration.[67]

Military involvement in domestic policing and anti-narcotics and immigration enforcement is largely restricted to specially designated regions called High Intensity Drug Trafficking Areas (HIDTAs). The first of these was established, not surprisingly, on the border. In 1989, all counties within 150 miles of the US–Mexico frontier were declared a single HIDTA. At first the JTF-6 and Operation Alliance, both created around the same time, were limited to this area. But as critics predicted, HIDTAs soon proliferated, and with them the military's involvement with law enforcement. The nation is now graced with seventeen of these federal hot spots, encompassing major metropolitan areas – like New York-New Jersey, the San Francisco Bay Area, greater Chicago, L.A., and San Diego – as well as the marijuana-growing wilds of the rural Northwest and Appalachia.[68]

APARTHEID BY OTHER MEANS

The sum total of the new zero tolerance immigration laws, the militarized border, the massively expanded system of electronic surveillance, and increasing collusion between police and the INS is the *de facto* criminalization and political marginalization of documented and undocumented immigrants alike.

Whether by design or default, the state's increasingly hostile stance towards immigrants is politically useful because it bolsters racial and class hierarchies. Also, border militarization and interior enforcement, like so much of the post-sixties criminal justice buildup, serve as pre-emptive counterinsurgency. As was shown above, terrorizing migrant workers keeps wages low and that boosts profits. Terrorizing undocumented Latinos at the new border DMZ and with interior campaigns, helps to break cross-border family ties and demoralizes Latino communities in the US. As Roberto Martinez of the American Friends Service Committee put it, "People aren't just scared of going north, thanks to these road blocks boxing in San Diego County, they're scared to go anywhere, especially back south . . . We get calls all the time from the barrios that women are too scared to leave their homes. I'm serious – this is a real crisis."[69]

Particularly hard hit by this xenophobic regime are the social networks of women. The INS does not target women more than men; rather, women are more likely to cross back and forth across the border to attend to family obligations. And they are more likely to have immigrated with dependent relatives or children. Thus a young mother's deportation is more likely to have reverberations beyond her immediate fate than would that of a single man. Likewise, women in all communities tend to be more involved in friendship networks and to be more politically and socially active as community organizers, engaged church members, or care-givers. Despite the image of the dashing male leader and the bearded guerrilla, female social networks have more often than not been the bedrock of social movements. By targeting undocumented Latinas in particular, the new border regime serves to disrupt and generally undermine Latino communities in the US. Because many of these social networks are, like the social bandits described by Eric Hobsbawm, "pre-political" formations, damaging them damages the future of political mobilization and the crucial preconditions for political organizing and thus becomes pre-emptive counterinsurgency.

More generally, there is *de facto* apartheid emerging in the Southwest; working class Latinos live under a fundamentally different set of laws than Anglos. And as INS surveillance and enforcement raiding continues in Ohio, Washington, New York, and other interior states, the same legal pattern is emerging nationwide.

Close to the border the new regime is even insinuating itself into the lives of those with nothing to fear from *la Migra*. San Diego's Interstate 5 now offers a "Pre-enrolled Access lane" (PAL) where those with proper clearance – registered fingerprints and photos, a barcode on their car – can speed through Customs on their way back from Mexico. "Be a PAL," urge the official bumper stickers.[70] Likewise, it is common for Latino hotel workers in San Diego to wear name tags (presumably designed to put guests at ease) which identify the wearer by name and geographic origin. Thus most tags read something like "Juana, Morales, Mexico," or "Guillermo, Vera Cruz, Mexico." These seemingly innocuous IDs, like the PAL stickers, invoke the border and inscribe people with insider or outsider status. And so it is that the entire social landscape of the border region is being remolded by the politics of the militarized frontier. The anxious right-wing voters and home owners of Southwest suburbia – the ones who in the early 1990s organized vigilante border actions, such as shining their headlights at the ranks of would-be migrants waiting across the border – get their federally subsidized, political theater; politicians get easy scapegoats; employers get docile labor; and the national security state gets a bulwark against the slow-motion social and economic implosion of Latin America.

As for new immigration flows, those who must cross the frontier will continue to do so; pushed by continued enclosures, disruptive direct foreign investment, civil war, structural adjustment, and natural disasters such as Hurricane Mitch. Only now, with a militarized border and an incipient police state greeting them here, the price of a ticket north or across an ocean will be higher in both financial and human terms.

PART III

PRISON

CHAPTER EIGHT

THE RISE OF BIG HOUSE NATION: FROM REFORM TO REVENGE

> The point of view of the institutional staff is treatment . . .
> Actually, the hopes of the prison employees resemble yours for
> the well-being of your loved-one while he is in prison and for his
> welfare and happiness later on when paroled.
> Dr. Norman Fenton (assistant to the director, California
> Department of Corrections), *Treatment in Prison: How the Family
> Can Help*, circa 1960

> We want a prisoner to look like a prisoner, to smell like a
> prisoner. When you see one of these boogers a-loose, you'll say,
> "I didn't know we had zebras in Mississippi."
> Democratic Rep. Mack McInnis, Mississippi,
> circa 1997

The law-and-order buildup of the late sixties and early seventies did not immediately translate into higher incarceration rates. In fact, it was not until the early eighties that imprisonment and prison construction surged. For most of the century the nation's incarceration rate hovered between 100 and 120 per 100,000 citizens. In 1975 and 1976, as relative calm returned to America's previously riotous cities, the rate of imprisonment began to increase. It then plateaued until the accession of Ronald Reagan to the presidency and Fed Chairman Paul Volcker's vicious 1981 recession.[1] Since that time, the US has been on a frenzied and brutal lockup binge.

ONCE UPON A REFORM

The official "crim-think" of the 1970s did not place prison on a pedestal: the utility of jailing "bad" people was often viewed with skepticism. Of the more than $800 million dispensed by the LEAA in both 1973 and again in 1974, only $113 million went towards incarceration, and much of that was channeled into "community corrections" schemes that funded drug treatment, pre-release centers, prison clinics, work furlough programs, and intensive parole and probation.[2] At the time, such programs were often attacked from the left as mere extensions of the criminal justice net under the pseudo-medical guise of "rehabilitation." This critique was correct: the new reforms usually came *in addition* to the old institutions, extending, not displacing, the power of prisons. They were, as Stan Cohen and others put it, examples of criminal justice "net widening and mesh thinning."[3] This critique aside, it is worth noting that, despite a massive expansion in the state's repressive power, prison populations were, in general, not expanding.[4] Instead, the seventies was the era of penal rationalization and modernization.

In the sixties most prisons were overcrowded, dilapidated, and highly volatile. The warm weather gulags of the South were in particularly desperate need of modernization. Like Jim Crow generally, the barbarism of Southern prisons was an international scandal which undermined the moral authority of the American political system in its battle against "international communism." On plantation prisons like Angola, Cummins Farm, and Parchment, conditions remained fixed in a terrible social amber, mostly unchanged since the post-Reconstruction boom years of Southern corrections. Violent and nonviolent offenders alike were housed in huge dormitories, fed slop, and given little medical care. Armed prisoners – called "trusty shooters" – served as guards, earned pardons by killing escapees, and were free to abuse and use their fellow captives in every imaginable way. Male and female inmates slaved in cotton fields, washrooms, and on public roadsides ten hours a day, six days a week, in broiling sun and freezing rain; bullwhips, sweat boxes, shotguns, and electrode torture kept them moving; death and escape rates were astronomical. In Mississippi and Texas, versions of this system lasted until 1974 and 1980, respectively.[5]

In the North, many prisons were cramped, vermin-infested century-old fortresses, which undermined the legitimacy of incarceration. In 1973 the LEAA released the findings of its newly hatched National Advisory

Commission on Criminal Justice Standards and Goals. The commission's message was simple: "*Corrections must commence reform now.*" Among the recommendations were many that by today's standards sound downright radical: clarify and protect prisoners' rights, a ten-year moratorium on prison construction, increased pay and professionalism of prison guards and administrators, and recruitment of corrections personnel from "minority groups" and – believe it or not – "among ex-offenders."[6]

What caused this sudden fit of liberal morality? The seismic shocks of Vietnam, urban riots, political bombings, and the mass mobilization of poor people also shook the bowels of America's prison system. Throughout the country, prisoners were organizing and demanding their rights. In California, official "bibliotherapy" gave way to the novels, memoirs, and writ writing of death row savant Caryl Chessman. This milieu in turn produced Chicano self-help groups like EMPELO and the study groups of the Black Muslims, the mercurial and mesmerizing screeds of Eldridge Cleaver, and then the radical reading groups and organizing cells of the Black Panther Party and Black Guerrilla Family. From this magma of political inspiration and rage emerged the revolutionary movements in support of the Soledad Brothers (including George Jackson) and the more reformist California Prisoners' Union. Such pressure forced a series of major reforms which improved prison conditions and were formalized in a Prisoners' Bill of Rights.[7]

The South, too, saw mass rebellion. In the land time forgot, trusty shooters came under attack as militant African Americans formed secret, and not so secret, chapters of the Black Panther Party. In Angola the struggle was led by Ronald Ailsworth, Albert Woodfox, and Herman Wallace. As civil rights activists overturned *de jure* segregation, their sights soon focused on the abominations of Southern penitentiaries. On the inside a generation of autodidact writ writers started blasting away at the legality of prison conditions, and, thanks to a smattering of liberal federal judges, many of these suits resulted in muscular federal consent decrees.[8]

In Walla Walla penitentiary in Washington, political prisoners of the George Jackson Brigade and politicized social inmates joined forces and won the right to wear civilian clothes, ride motorcycles around the yard on weekends, and receive radical literature in the mail. Gay and bisexual inmates, led by Ed Mead, organized Men Against Sexism, a group of "tough fags" who used violence to protect weaker inmates against rape and physically punished sexual predators.[9]

Animating much of this struggle and reform was the specter of the 1971 Attica prison rebellion, in which 1,300 convicts took control of a prison yard and held about a dozen hostages for four days. The self-organized prisoners' society of "D-Yard Nation" sent a shock wave of humiliation and terror throughout New York's elite that was best captured by Governor Nelson Rockefeller's description of Attica as a "step in an ominous world trend."[10] Far from being an isolated incident, the prison rebellion was seen as the expression of a communist fifth column at work in the system's entrails.

Though the uprising ended in carnage, it was not a simple victory for the state. First of all, Attica was in part a reaction to the murder of George Jackson and thus indicated a nationwide political consciousness emerging among convicts. Attica also involved "problem" inmates who had been stirring up political trouble elsewhere in the system. Second, the slaughter by guards – in which thirty-nine prisoners and nine hostages were killed – was a ham-fisted affair that unveiled the state as brutal, desperate, and unprepared. Recall that there were no tactical squads on the scene with infrared scopes and blunt trauma ordinances; instead the assault force was composed of New York state troopers and vengeful COs from Ossining using deer rifles brought from home. Nor did this assault force of vengeful rednecks have a plan or unified command structure. As they blasted away into clouds of tear gas, killing their hostage colleagues, the international press corps watched in horror.[11] For America's forward-looking political elites and rational criminal justice planners at the LEAA, Attica was at best a sordid humiliation, at worst, a terrible harbinger of future conflagrations.

All of this prison-centered, legal, literary, and violent struggle produced a momentary, but very real, crisis of legitimacy for American criminal justice. Mainstream policymakers temporarily soured on the idea of prison as a secure dumping ground for capitalism's social wreckage and social dynamite.

Amidst this crisis, prisoners' quality of life improved slightly. Life inside remained hellish, but prisoners won the right to law libraries, and the armed trusty system was eliminated, while rules around grooming, attire, visitation, correspondence, organizing, and reading were loosened in most states.[12] In short, much of what is chalked up to rehabilitation-era enlightenment was really just the political booty of class war. "The Man" gave a little to keep a lot.

THE CURRENT CRISIS

Today the nation's prisons and jails brim with 1.8 million people, and few observers seem much bothered. Another three million are "doing time" outside, as satellites of the court system, subject to unannounced visits from parole and probation officers, mandatory urine tests, home detention, or the invisible leash of electronic shackles. Millions more are connected to punishment from the other end, making their living directly or indirectly from the Keynesian stimulus of the nation's lockup costs. And since the early eighties incarceration has changed in both quantitative and qualitative terms: there are more prisons, more captives, and conditions inside are in many respects worse and more restrictive than ever.

So who goes to prison? "Super-predators" and psychos? In 1994, only 29 percent of all prison admissions were for "violent offenses" such as rape, murder, kidnaping, robbery, and assault; while 31 percent of all entrants were jailed for "property offenses" such as fraud, burglary, auto theft, and larceny; 30 percent were "admitted" for "drug offenses" including possession and trafficking; and almost 9 percent were imprisoned for "public order offenses" such as weapons possession and drunk driving.[13]

What are the causes of this lockup binge? First and foremost the transformation of the class and occupational structure of American society. But remember that the first part of the criminal justice crackdown began in the late sixties as counterinsurgency by other means; the police were ill-prepared for the task of a multifaceted rebellion, and thus federal aid focused on policing and other "front end" forms of criminal justice.

The second round of anti-crime repression, which began in the early and mid eighties, was a reaction to a different set of contradictions. With the onslaught of Reaganomic restructuring, rebellion *was not* a pressing political issue: there were no riots, no Black Panther Party, etc. Instead, increased poverty and the social dislocations of deindustrialization were threats to order. In a broad sense the social breakdown, disorder, and floating populations created by neoliberal economic restructuring had to be managed with something other than social democratic reform. The liberal, ameliorative social control strategies of the war on poverty era (discussed in chapter two) inadvertently empowered working people. This had a deleterious effect on capital's efforts to boost sagging profit margins by gouging workers. In short, redistributive reforms helped throw the Phillips curve out of wake.

Reproducing the business system, and the American social order generally, required containing the poor. Policing and the war on drugs are part of
this political triage. But police repression requires a carceral component. Cops
alone cannot manage the cast-off classes. And the police need more than
firepower to animate their orders; the threat of prison is a crucial part of
their arsenal. Prison also mops up huge numbers of poor African American,
Latino, and Native American people, particularly men. Thus the criminal
justice buildup is a bulwark against the new dangerous classes because it
absorbs and controls them and extends its threat onto the street.

But the criminal justice buildup was not necessarily designed with class
and racial containment as its sole aim. In many ways the incarceration binge
is simply the *policy by-product* of right-wing electoral rhetoric. As economic
restructuring created a social crisis for blue-collar America, politicians found
it necessary and useful to speak to domestic anxieties; they had to articulate
the trouble their constituents were facing, but in politically acceptable forms
which would avoid blaming corporate greed and capitalist restructuring. This
required scapegoats, a role usually filled by new immigrants, the poor, and
people of color, particularly African Americans. And so it was in the 1980s
that people of color and the poor (usually conflated as one category) came
under renewed ideological assault. Charles Murray's *Losing Ground*, George
Gilder's *Wealth and Poverty*, and Lawrence Mead's *The New Poverty* relaunched
the age-old poor-bashing that lurks within all Protestant cultures and gave it
a neo-racist twist. The "underclass" became shorthand for the swarthy urban
loafers.[14] People of color were cast as parasites, and violent predators pil-
fering middle-class (read white) America by means of such Great Society
programs as AFDC and Head Start.[15] And the most potent anti-poor symbol – the one that always surpasses the welfare mother and the mendicant
addict – is the young dark criminal, the untamed urban buck, running free
threatening order, property, and (white) personal safety.

For writers like Mead, "the solution must lie in public authority. Low-
wage work apparently must be mandated, just as a draft has sometimes been
necessary to staff the military. Authority achieves compliance more efficiently than benefits, at least from society's viewpoint. Government need not
make the desired behaviour worthwhile to people. It simply threatens
punishment . . ."[16]

Amidst this climate of racialized class hatred, crime baiting emerged as
a form of super-potent political fuel. The modern origins of this electoral

strategy were, as discussed in chapter one, the ravings of Barry Goldwater. The recent nadir, which made anti-crime fearmongering requisite for all aspiring politicians, was of course the Willie Horton coup by George Bush.[17] And winning elections by invoking the phantom menace of the psychotic Black rapist eventually escalates into actual policymaking, such as the federal crime bills discussed earlier, or the more than 1,000 new criminal justice statutes created by the California state legislature in the late eighties and early nineties.[18] Such new laws, mandating stiff prison sentences, led to rapidly increasing rates of incarceration. In fact the federal government has gone as far as to punish states that do not choose the gulag path. The 1994 federal crime bill – the Violent Offender Incarceration and Truth-in-Sentencing Law of 1994 – authorized $7.9 billion for prison construction grants, but *only* states with "truth-in-sentencing" requirements, which mandate that violent offenders serve 85 percent of their sentences, will be eligible for the money.[19]

Thus, I am arguing that incarceration is at one level a rational strategy for managing the contradictions of a restructured American capitalism. But at another level, the big lockup is merely the useful policy *by-product* of electoral strategies in which right-wing politicians *use* the theme of crime and punishment to get elected, while masking their all-important pro-business agenda. Finally, in the following chapters, I will argue that, regardless of what politicians say or believe, prison's main function is to terrorize the poor, warehouse social dynamite and social wreckage, and, as Foucault argued, reproduce apolitical forms of criminal "deviance." Such social pathology is useful because it justifies state repression and the militarization of public space, sews fear, and leaves poor communities – which might have organized for social justice – in disarray, occupied by police and thus docile.

CHAPTER NINE

PRISON AS ABATTOIR:
OFFICIAL TERROR

It must be acknowledged that the penitentiary system in America is severe. While society in the United States gives the example of most extended liberty, the prisons of the same country offer the spectacle of the most complete despotism.

Gustave de Beaumont and Alexis de Tocqeville, *On the Penitentiary System in the United States and Its Application in France*

There is a paradox at the core of penology, and from it derives the thousand ills and afflictions of the prison system. It is that not only the worst of the young are sent to prison but the best – that is the proudest, the bravest, the most daring, the most enterprising, and the most undefeated of the poor. There starts the horror.

Norman Mailer, introduction to *In the Belly of the Beast*

Corcoran state prison is a landlocked slaveship stuck on the middle passage to nowhere. Surrounded by cotton fields and a huge dusty sky, the prison's concrctc buildings look like an isolated set of warehouses, ringed by miles of coiled razor wire, security lights, and a lethal electric fence. Here California's Black and Latino "super-bad" are buried in the Security Housing Unit (SHU) – a prison within the prison – denied fresh food, adequate air, and sunlight. They spend twenty-three hours a day in tiny cells, with no work, no educational programs, and often in total isolation. Psychologists say such environments lead to rapid psychological decomposition among inmates, but the insanity infects corrections staff as well.[1]

On April 2, 1994, Corcoran SHU inmate Preston Tate was taken from his five-by-nine-foot cell by corrections officers (COs) to a small triangular concrete exercise yard. What followed next was captured on silent, grainy black-and-white video by prison surveillance cameras. The young African American, Tate, looks around him nervously and talks to his "cellie." Then two Latino prisoners enter the scene. The Black and Latino prisoners lunge towards each other with explosive energy. After several seconds of pounding, swinging, and grappling, guards in the gun booth above the yard and behind the camera fire wooden baton rounds into the tangle of convicts. The battle in the yard continues a few seconds more until a guard fires a single 9mm, fragmenting "Glazer safety round" from an H&K mini-14 assault rifle, blowing open Tate's skull. On the video Tate goes limp and the other inmates roll away from his corpse.[2]

The killing, though tragic and sordid, was not unique. Tate was just one of the 175 inmates shot with live rounds by California prison guards between 1989 and 1994, twenty-seven of whom died. Hundreds more were hit with less-than-lethal wooden block baton rounds. Nor would Tate be the last to die for fighting. From 1994 through the first half of 1998, twelve more inmates were shot dead by corrections officers and another thirty-two were seriously wounded.[3] Only one of these inmates was armed with a weapon. Out of all these shootings only a handful were investigated and only two guards were punished, with 180-day suspensions.[4]

The unofficial prison-yard executions once again put California in the vanguard of bad policy. In all other states *combined*, only six inmates were shot by guards between 1994 and 1998. In every one of these cases the victims were trying to escape. Even Texas — where corrections administrators pride themselves on running a very tight ship – only one inmate, an escapee, was shot and killed during those four years. In fact, only California allows the use of deadly force to break up prisoner fist fights.[5]

The carnage in the Golden State's prison yards has two driving causes: the California Department of Corrections' (CDC's) "integrated yard policy" (in which rival inmates are deliberately placed within each other's reach) and the unofficial practice among thuggish COs of staging and betting on "gladiator fights" between convicts from rival gangs or ethnicities. While horrifying in their own right, the Corcoran set-up fights and murders also illustrate how independent social actors can work concomitantly at different levels to achieve a shared, if unspoken, goal.

At the micro-level, COs (also known as "screws" or "bulls"), were staging fights as a form of sadistic diversion, even videotaping the fights for later viewing, and gathering to watch the contests from gun towers. But this local practice, which occurred in other prisons as well, was given a veil of legitimacy by the CDC's integrated yard policy, which mandates the mixing of rival gangs and races in the name of teaching tolerance and testing prisoners' "ability to get along in a controlled setting."[6] Not surprisingly, fist fights and stabbings were, and still are, epidemic throughout the system.[7] *Norteños* associated with *La Nuestra Familia* fight *sureños*, the soldiers of the "Eme" or Mexican Mafia. *Sureños* in turn go after African American convicts who run with the prison gang called the Black Guerrilla Family, or any of the various prison-stranded sets of Crips and Bloods. They, in turn, make war on the "white trash" and bikers who populate the ranks of the Aryan Brotherhood and the baggy-pants-clad Nazi Lowriders. The white convicts in turn make war on Blacks and *norteños*.[8]

The integrated yard was a sure recipe for racial pyrotechnics, but its supporters extended all the way to the apex of the CDC. In 1992, a handful of disgusted, courageous Corcoran COs augmented the "shoot to maim" policy by sending in armor-clad, shield-wielding "special response teams" to break up fights. "No one got hurt and we resolved the conflict without discharging a firearm," explained whistle-blower and former Corcoran lieutenant Steve Rigg. But the paper-pushers in Sacramento would have none of it. Word came down from the director that no line officers were to put themselves in jeopardy. The policy was simple: "let the guns rule the yard."[9] According to Rigg: "That became a turning point. The Corcoran way of quelling violence – shooting first and then asking questions – became the state's way."[10]

There was yet a third layer to this nefarious and informal conspiracy. The product of the CO sadism and bureaucratic over-reaction – that is, the ultraviolence in the yards – became statistical fodder for CDC budget building. CDC Director James H. Gomez routinely dispatched ominous missives to the legislature in which he cited the crisis of rising violence as yet another reason for spending more money. The statistical expression of manufactured mayhem also showed up in CDC five-year master plans, in which the revenue-hungry Gomez menaced lawmakers with evidence of mounting inmate violence, as the supposed harbinger of a system on the verge of detonation.[11] On August 30, 1995, for example, the director wrote:

Violence rates in the prison system, which originally declined with the opening of the first new prisons in 1984, have recently been increasing, as evidenced by a 30 percent increase in the rate of assaults on staff. The lack of prison capacity will exacerbate these conditions and further endanger the safety of the men and women who staff these prisons.[12]

This organically evolving strategy – of packing prisons, fomenting violence, then using the bloody statistics to leverage more tax money for the CDC – worked flawlessly. By 1995 the CDC's budget, at almost $4 billion, finally eclipsed California's spending on higher education, and the state's thirty-three massive prisons housed more than 150,000 convicts.[13] But starting in 1994 the semiautonomous, mutually reinforcing layers of this bureaucratic empire building began to unravel.

The first breach occurred at Corcoran, the bloodiest of the CDC's joints. Even before the Tate family filed its lawsuit, three guards, disturbed by the increasingly out-of-control violence of their colleagues and frustrated by their superiors' active disinterest, had gone to the FBI.[14] With the political embers of the L.A. riots still glowing, the Justice Department had started taking seriously charges of official brutality. In dozens of cities around the country, it had become apparent that the legitimacy and smooth functioning of criminal justice and, by extension, the whole state was being undermined by the "surplus repression" of renegade cops at the local level. And so, just as Feds had investigated the police in New York, Philadelphia, and Detroit, they began looking into the habits of Corcoran's killer COs.

Perhaps the most dramatic moment in this FBI investigation came on October 7, 1994, when agents from the CDC's Special Services Unit – a combined gang intelligence/internal affairs unit – chased CO whistle-blower, Richard Caruso, for forty-five miles at high speed while he raced to deliver stolen documents to FBI headquarters in Fresno.[15]

Soon thereafter, the *Orange County Register* published a serialized exposé after a Corcoran inmate was shot dead *inside* his cell.[16] The reports found that COs reported 185 incidents involving "shots fired" and thirty-eight inmates wounded in 1990 alone. In 1991, there were 205 shootings, with seventeen inmates wounded.[17] And by 1994 any semblance of accountability among prison guards had broken down: it was open season on convicts. By 1995, the FBI was well into its probe, the Tate family had filed suit, while ham-fisted CDC bureaucrats scrambled to concoct a cover-up.[18] But the brutality continued unabated. During the summer of 1995 — even as FBI agents were gathering evidence from Corcoran's files — a gang of guards beat and tortured a busload of thirty-six newly arrived African American prisoners, some of whom had been charged with assaulting guards in other facilities.[19] Eventually, eight Corcoran staff were fired for their participation in the assault.[20] Around the same time a federal judge — handling a civil rights suit filed by the brilliant writ-writing prisoner Steven Castillo — released a ruling packed with gory, almost unbelievable, details about the routine sadism at Pelican Bay State Prison. It seemed that psychotic prisoners were being beaten, tortured, and left chained in their own excrement for days. In one case a prisoner who had gone mad in solitary confinement was submerged in a vat of boiling water until his skin dissolved. On better days "therapy" for the mentally ill prisoners consisted of watching cartoons from inside a phone-booth-sized cage.[21]

Two years later one of the worst of the Corcoran COs had turned state's evidence. Roscoe Pondexter, a six-foot-seven-inch former bench-warmer for the Boston Celtics, enjoyed his life as a "fish cop." His specialty had been strangling inmates while other guards crushed and yanked the victims' testicles. "We called it Deep Six. It's like taking a dive underwater and not coming up. You give the prisoner only enough air to hear your message . . . It wasn't in the manual. It wasn't part of the official training. It was grandfathered to me by my sergeant and the sergeant before him," explained a contrite Pondexter.[22] As the body count mounted, even Corcoran Warden George Smith had to acknowledge the barbarism: "I'll admit that some of my staff have gone crazy."[23]

ROLLBACK IN THE BIG HOUSE

The violence in California's maximum security prisons is in many ways just an extreme expression of the nationwide campaign to degrade and abuse convicts. According to the rhetoric of many politicians, going to prison is no longer punishment enough. Thus we see a wave of sadistic political fads: from chain gangs and striped uniforms to the stunning evisceration of prisoners' legal rights. This bureaucratic abuse of incarcerated people gives rank-and-file COs license to bend the rules — that is, torture and kill their captives. Driving these mean-spirited policies is the feedback loop of hatred and fear that flows between pandering politicians and a paranoid, profoundly confused public. In the fantasy world of the revanchist middle classes, prison is a country club where convicted killers and rapists do laps in Olympic-sized swimming pools. Take for example this letter to the law-and-order obsessed *Fresno Bee*:

> A schoolmate of mine was viciously murdered in his home while his wife was forced to watch, then beaten and left for dead herself. After serving a 10-year sentence, the perpetrator has fathered two children through conjugal visits, completed his college degree, received his veterans benefits, and every two years he is reviewed for parole.[24]

Such vitriol both fuels, and is fueled by, political demagoguery. To create and appease such voters, politicians confect anti-crime nostrums with ever more vicious ingenuity. In the name of just deserts and facing down enemies, many states now deliberately deny or restrict inmates' access to coffee, orange juice, exercise equipment, telephones, air conditioning, heat, adequate clothing, counseling, and music.[25]

One very important prison "privilege" that is fast disappearing is conjugal visits. These overnight contact visits help maintain ties between prisoners and their families. Mainstream criminology has long shown that without intact families and social networks parolees are more likely to re-offend. But, as in the case of welfare debates, the specter of the dangerous classes enjoying sexual pleasures elicits paroxysms of rage from the right wing. In 1995, California – one of only eight states with conjugal visits – banned the practice for sex offenders, lifers, and those deemed to have disciplinary problems. The governor proclaimed that "for far too long, inmates have seemingly had more rights than their victims. We must make clear to those who commit crimes that prison is a place for punishment."[26]

Another politically symbolic issue is prison weightlifting. In 1994 Wisconsin's hawkish governor Tommy Thompson ordered all free weights removed from prison gyms, and soon followed that up with a ban on movies and pornography. Georgia too went after the iron, confiscating 150 tons of equipment. Ohio, South Carolina, Arizona, Mississippi, and California have also yanked the weights from their medium- and high-security lockups. And, by congressional order, federal joints will let their weight piles "wither away" by not replacing broken equipment. Numerous other states are scaling back and restricting weightlifting, and have eliminated martial arts training.[27]

Leading the charge against the evils of "driving iron" is Andrew LeFevre of the Law Enforcement Alliance of America, his claque of crime victims, and a bevy of paid political hacks in state legislatures. To make their case the anti-iron forces frequently invoke low-intensity conflict's logic of total war at the grassroots: "Too many criminals spend their time in prison becoming even more violent, criminal machines," explained anti-weight crusader Ohio Republican Rep. Steve Chabot. Another politician wants to "keep federal prisoners from engaging in activities that could increase their strength or fighting ability." Weights were also cited as crucial weapons in Ohio's 1993 Lucasville riot, and during Rikers Island jail riots inmates attacked and injured sixteen guards with weights and exercise benches.[28] Thus the weight piles stopped being sink holes for prisoner frustration and low-cost management tools and became super-charged political props.

A similar logic explains other assaults on convicts' living conditions. For example, California is ending quarterly care packages from home, plans to institute random drug testing, and is switching from a variety of civilian-style denim uniforms to white jumpsuits emblazoned with "CDC Inmate."[29] The state is also imposing – through administrative means only – military-style "grooming standards" that outlaw dreadlocks, ponytails, beards, handlebar mustaches, and (for men) lipstick, mascara, and earrings. To give the new grooming standards an added air of utility the CDC has launched an "everyone wins" scheme called Locks of Love in which long-haired convicts can donate their locks to "sick children who need wigs."[30]

Meanwhile, Arizona has banned electric hot-pots, hotplates, and pornographic magazines. Grinning prison bureaucrats explained the changes in purely pragmatic terms: it costs nearly $2 million a year to keep electric hot-pots and hotplates fired up.[31] Chain gangs are also on the rise. From Indiana and Washington to Alabama and Arizona, chain gangs are back; both state prisons and county jails are putting prisoners in chains and distinctive uniforms and forcing them to clear trash from roadways and cut weeds.[32] In Wisconsin the chain gangs have to wear 50,000-volt stun belts.[33] These experiments in public torment – often initiated at the county level where elected, publicity-seeking sheriffs control the jail systems – are cheap political theater. The actual amount of work performed by chain gangs is of minimal economic value. But the normalization of the chain gang spectacle inflates a symbolic economy of revenge. If voters become inured to coffles of convicts and conditioned to enjoy the pillorying of official enemies, all other forms of repression will seem natural: just part of the inmate-manicured landscape.

THE PRISON LITIGATION REFORM ACT: LEGAL GARROTE

In 1996, hell got a little bit hotter when Republicans dropped another of their legislative neutron bombs, the Prison Litigation Reform Act (PLRA), which overhauled inmate access to the civil courts. This sedulously crafted piece of legal language is so vicious, detailed, and sweeping that it has baffled journalists and academics into near-total silence. The legislation effectively locks prisoners out of court, cuts them off from their professional allies on the outside, and draws a legal veil over official practices of physical and psychological torture. The PLRA's provisions are too numerous and detailed to fully explain in this book, but here are some of the law's most important aspects.

Central to the PLRA is a course of baroque bureaucratic hurdles. Previously, prisoners were free, or rather able, to file civil rights suits under Title 42, United States Code, section 1983 whenever they saw fit. But now convicts must first exhaust all "administrative remedies," which involves long forms, review by distant panels, appeals, counterappeals, and applications for hearings before special panels. Besides being time-consuming and futile, this caricature of administrative remedy requires that convicts appeal to their abusers. For example, if a prisoner wants to sue guards for raping her, she must first file complaints, outlining her case, with those very guards.[34]

Once administrative remedies have been exhausted and a convict is still willing to go to court, he or she faces another set of hurdles. The Prison Litigation Reform Act states that "no federal, civil action may be brought by a prisoner . . . without a prior showing of physical injury."[35] In other words, fear and psychological trauma are still grounds for a suit, but only if one can also show physical injury. If that can be done, the inmate faces the next difficulty: a $120 court filing fee.

Since 1915 the poor have had the right to file suits without paying filing fees; until 1996 this *in forma pauperis* statute applied to convicts as well. After all, most prisoners are from poor families, thus receive little or no money from home, and earn between five and fifty cents an hour if they work in prison industries. In the post-PLRA world, indigent prisoners must first submit an affidavit declaring all their assets and income, and a certified copy of the previous six months of their prison trust account records. Only in cases where a prisoner has absolutely no income from prison labor, and no donations to a commissary or trust account from family or friends, and no reasonable prospects for such income in the future, will they be granted *in forma pauperis* standing. Most often this exhaustive bureaucratic struggle – conducted from behind bars, through handwritten forms, delivered by less-than-enthusiastic corrections officers – will end in defeat.[36] In such cases "the court shall assess, and when funds exist, collect . . . an initial filing fee" of 20 percent of the required $120 fee. From then on the inmate will have 20 percent of their monthly income raided by the courts until the full filing fee is paid.[37] If a prisoner should have two suits or should file an appeal they are, in many jurisdictions, required to pay yet another $120 filing fee, thus doubling their monthly payments.[38] (Most states already levy a 10 to 30 percent tax on commissary accounts.)

Given these torments one might ask why prisoners file suits at all. The obvious answer is that very often their lives literally depend on it. Less obvious is the fact that no one else will do it for them. Even during the height of liberal courts and government-subsidized legal aid to the poor, most attorneys were wary of taking on poorly paid and difficult inmate lawsuits in which the state has all the advantages and limitless resources. The PLRA has compounded this situation further by actively discouraging lawyers from taking inmate-filed cases. Previously attorneys who won prison lawsuits were awarded fees to be paid by the defendants (that is the prison, its administrators, the individual guards, or the Department of Corrections). Such fees were calibrated to the going market rate, attorney skill, hours, and expense of the case, etc. Attorneys' fees were *not* extracted from the prisoners' damage award.

Now, in rare cases of victory, attorneys' fees are taken directly out of the prisoner's award and cannot exceed more than 25 percent of the total payout. That may sound fair but remember that prisoners, who do not command huge incomes, often have difficulty showing how being shot, raped, beaten, or tortured has caused them material loss. Thus their damage awards are always small in comparison to most victorious civil suits on the outside.

Take for example a recent case in which a federal inmate who labored in a prison factory, for pennies an hour, lost his hand on the job and received only $928.[39] In that case, attorney's fees would not even cover the cost of xeroxing and collect calls. In short, handling suits for inmates is not only a thankless, arduous task requiring a legalistic war of attrition against behemoth, secretive, advisories; it now *costs* attorneys money even when they win.[40]

So prisoners are left to their own devices. But this avenue of struggle is considerably constricted. Thanks to the PLRA's "three strikes" provision, many inmates are losing access to the courts completely. The provision states that any inmate who has three lawsuits dismissed as "frivolous" or "malicious" will be *permanently barred from ever filing another case*. This statute is all the more extreme when considering that inmates often enter prison illiterate and totally unfamiliar with the treacherous minutiae of the law. Subsequently, many a novice writ writer has poorly constructed, confused cases thrown out as "frivolous" for purely technical reasons.

The wrecking ball of the PLRA also swings against the power of federal judges who might find against prisons and their administrators. For example, federal courts can no longer impose indefinite consent decrees (these are binding court orders to change conditions). Now all federal action against prisons ends after two years. Lest that seems like a technical point, there are roughly 450 jails and penitentiaries currently under consent decree. Had the federal courts been similarly defanged during the seventies we might still have "trusty shooters" manning the perimeter at Angola. Likewise, "preliminary injunctions" and "temporary restraining orders" pertaining to prison conditions – once indefinite forms of federal intervention – now automatically expire after ninety days.

Also undermined are the powers of "special masters," outside expert investigators who monitor prison conditions. In what Paul Wright calls "a classic piece of micro-management," the PLRA cuts the pay for special masters from unspecified highs to $40 an hour. Judges and lawyers qualified to be a special master will not move to the boondocks to oversee reform at renegade prisons unless they receive better remuneration. Already, special masters in a few high-profile cases are deserting their posts for lack of adequate pay.[41] The sum total of these changes is that federal judges – never great friends of convicts to begin with – are now rendered effectively impotent in the rare cases when they do rule for convict plaintiffs.

FAHRENHEIT 451 COMES TO LOCKDOWN

Taking a cue from the PLRA's depredations is a movement among states to abolish prison law libraries. Far from being a mere convenience, access to law books is fundamental to prisoner safety, quality of life, and the integrity of the legal system as a whole. Arizona was the first state to destroy its jailhouse law books. The initial justification for shuttering the thirty-four libraries and dumping the books, typewriters, and office furniture was, as usual, thrift: an estimated $500,000 to $800,000 would be saved.[42] But achieving economies was not the real goal, as the state soon farmed out the task of facilitating inmate access to the courts by hiring three paralegal firms at $800,000 a year. One group of pettifoggers was soon exposed as straight-up con artists, complete with rap sheets and bogus degrees.[43]

The real function of the book banning was soon apparent. "The contract paralegal system is what our worst fears said it would be – and more! The program is set up to operate to be an obstacle to court, not a stepping stone," explained an anonymous Arizona inmate.[44] California, not to be outdone, soon decided to stop maintaining and updating its law libraries starting in early 1998. The CDC says this will save $700,000 annually.[45] Idaho has also stripped its prisons of law books. As the order towards that end cleared its final legal hurdles, Idaho prison officials began pilfering the books, desks, typewriters, and office supplies, all of which prisoners had purchased with their own money. "The worst part of this whole ordeal," explained one Idaho convict writing to *Prison Legal News*, "is that I have noticed the gulag mentality of the IDOC officials slip even further toward the 'go ahead, sue us' state of mind, as now they are well aware of the difficulties that Idaho prisoners will face in attempting to vindicate their rights and seek redress in the courts."[46] Georgia has also pillaged its law libraries and replaced them with a team of private contractors who were soon exposed as nothing more than legal saboteurs, giving prisoners blatantly destructive and incorrect advice.[47]

For those on death row the legal situation is compounded further by the Anti-Terrorism and Effective Death Penalty Act of 1996, which limits the condemned to only one federal *habeas corpus* appeal and requires that it be filed within six months of the denial of one's last state appeal. Mounting an investigation and preparing a federal *habeas* case in six months can be nearly impossible, especially when crucial exculpatory evidence may take years to surface.[48]

The assault goes on . . . In 1994 federal Pell grants were wiped out by an amendment to the massive 1994 crime bill. With the loss of that money, degree-granting programs in thirty-two prison systems simply ended.[49] By 1998 only eight states still offered limited degree-granting programs, all of which run on volunteer labor.[50] This evisceration of higher education in prison flies in the face of both common sense and the best available research. Though not a cure-all, education does have powerful salutary effects; several high-profile studies have shown that the more education an inmate receives while incarcerated, the lower his or her chance of recidivism will be.[51]

Despite the ever tighter squeeze of the bureaucratic straitjacket, one "luxury" will never desert the big house, that psychic meat grinder television. As R. B. "Bucky" Rives, executive director of the Louisiana Sheriffs' Association, explained to the press, TV is good because it keeps inmates docile and dumb. "It's cheap to put a TV set in front of 33 guys and let it baby-sit them," said another jailer.[52] Convict journalist Adrian Lomax, who has singlehandedly waged war on the idiot box for years, summed it up best: "In 18 years of incarceration, I've never seen a prison day room that didn't have a television. Inmates in Wisconsin, like most states, are also allowed to have their own TVs. In fact, having your own TV is not permitted, it's encouraged . . . Prisoners who can't buy their own TVs can borrow the state-owned sets at no cost . . . The dominant treatment program in American prisons, the one imposed every day, is TV therapy."[53] And while the mass media marinates the brains of American convicts, the counterdirectional flow of information – from prisoners to the media – is being constricted. So far California, Pennsylvania, and Virginia have completely outlawed media interviews with incarcerated people. Far from parochial mean-spirited theater, the press bans make perfect sense. After all, the barbarism of the new gulag could be too much for even mainstream America were it to be fully and routinely exposed.[54]

CHAPTER TEN

BALKANS IN A BOX: RAPE, RACE WAR, AND OTHER FORMS OF MANAGEMENT

I was even told by the pigs who transported me to prison that I
was being sent there to be reduced to a punk, to be shorn of my
manhood. They felt I would be less arrogant once I had been
turned into a cocksucker . . . Before I was twenty-one years old
I had killed one of the prisoners and wounded another. I never
did get out of prison. I never was a punk.
Jack Henry Abbott, *In the Belly of the Beast*

Racial violence permeated the prison system like the stench of a
decaying dead body.
Johnny Spain, former prisoner and Black Panther

Dad was quite correct in believing that he was no longer looking
at the well-behaved, polite, loving son he had raised. What he
saw was a walking time bomb, ready to explode. It took the
county of Los Angeles about four months to construct me,
behind the walls surrounding that munitions-manufacturing plant
they call juvenile hall.
Dwight Edgar Abbot, *I Cried, You Didn't Listen*

Wayne Robertson, aka the "Booty Bandit," lives in the padlocked world of
the Corcoran Security Housing Unit. For a time his calling was to beat, tor-

ture, and sodomize fellow inmates. Far from being a "threat to institutional security" and packed away in solitary confinement, this psychopathic serial rapist was used by guards as a latter-day "trusty shooter." Though correctional officers never gave Robertson a shotgun or horse to ride through the cotton fields, or offered the possibility of a pardon if he killed an escapee, Robertson was nonetheless the Man's enforcer. He specialized in "checking" abrasive young street toughs. If the COs found a prisoner particularly annoying, restive, or obnoxious they would just transfer the offender for a stay with the towering and bulky Mr. Robertson, who would discipline his young charge by battering his head, smashing his nose, tearing open his rectum and then abusing and ridiculing him for days until the victim was reduced to the status of a psychologically broken, politically servile "punk," the lowest form of life in the prison argot. For his services, the COs gave their monster tennis shoes and extra food.[1]

The case that finally exposed this semi-official use of rape as a disciplinary tool was brought by Eddie Dillard, a 23-year-old former gang member from L.A. serving time for assault with a deadly weapon. While in Calipatria State Prison, Dillard made the mistake of kicking a female guard; for his sins Dillard was promoted to the top of the COs' shit list. First he was transferred to the Corcoran SHU, where Preston Tate and so many others had been dispatched by exploding bullets and where countless new arrivals, mostly young Black or Latino men, were beaten by racist guards. After a period in the hot claustrophobic pods of the SHU, Dillard was transferred – by order of Sergeant Alan Decker – to be housed with the Booty Bandit. Dillard immediately protested the transfer, pointing out that Robertson was a known predator. The official reply was unambiguous: "Since you like hitting women, we've got somebody for you."[2]

For the next several days Robertson beat, raped, tortured, and humiliated Dillard, while guards and other inmates listened to the echoes of the young man screaming, begging for mercy, and calling for help. Finally when the cell door opened Dillard rushed on to the tier and refused to go back inside.[3]

Released from prison and back in L.A., Dillard recounted the trauma he still suffers: "They took something from me that I can never replace. I've tried so many nights to forget about it, but the feeling just doesn't go away. Every time I'm with my wife, it comes back what he did to me. I want a close to the story. I want some salvation. But it keeps going on and on."[4]

Had it not been for the attention of activists, journalists, and investigations by the FBI and later California State Assembly hearings, Dillard's case would have gone unnoticed; he would have been just another hapless "punk" reduced to jailhouse chattel, to be sodomized, traded, and sold as a slave. In the fatalistic logic of the big house such horrors are explained away with resort to a sort of macho karma: "he must have wanted it or he would have fought it off." Thus is the fate of a punk.

PUNK FACTORY

Rape is both absolutely central to, and yet largely invisible within, the politics of incarceration. Hundreds of thousands of men and women alike suffer this most horrible of physical and emotional tortures as an unwritten part of their sentences. And unlike most rape on the outside, rape in prison is usually not a one-time event; instead the victim is often forced to live with and serve their tormentor for years on end. In that respect prison rape is more akin to child sexual abuse or slavery. Women, as we will see below, are routinely raped by male guards, while male prisoners are generally raped by other convicts.

In male prisons sexual slavery most often starts in two ways. A younger inmate might be taken under the wing of an older inmate; once debt and dependence are established the older inmate will rape and "turn out" the young prisoner. The other method is simple gang rape in which a weaker inmate is attacked with overwhelming numbers and "punked" by a crew of prisoners, who then announce their control to the general population, which in turn cements the deal through their tacit or active approval of the victim's new status. Once "turned out," a punk is vulnerable to assault from all sides as the prison grapevine informs everyone of his subordinate status. In the interest of survival, a newly minted punk will usually choose one inmate as his "Man," "daddy," or "husband." In exchange for usufruct of the punk, the Man offers protection against other aggressors. Although the "wolves" and "booty bandits" have sex with other men, they are, in the hyper-macho cosmology of prison, not homosexual because they are not sexually penetrated. The cult of "Manhood" – and the struggle to defend, defile, and define it – is the axis around which the prison sex system turns.

The subordinate "gender" in male prisons includes the so-called "punks," straight or gay men forced into a submissive sexual role, as well as "queens,"

gay men and transsexuals who may embrace homosexual sex and their gendered role as the sexual submissive. Queens may suffer as sexual slaves and
rape victims, but very often they use their sexual powers to play stronger
inmates off against one another or to find a husband of their own liking.
Punks and queens, like women in the straight world, are forced into roles
that range from nurturing, mothering wife to denigrated, over-worked
"whore."[5]

The scale and horror of jailhouse buggery is difficult to measure, let alone
really fathom for those on the outside. One academic study in a Midwestern
prison, relying on anonymous self-reporting by prisoners and therefore liable
to underestimate the problem, found that 22 percent of male respondents
had been raped or forced into sex while incarcerated. Only 29 percent of
that number said they had reported their attacks to prison authorities.[6]
Another study conducted in 1982 at a California state prison surveyed hundreds of inmates and found that 14 percent had been "pressured into having
sex against their will."[7] Extrapolating from these and other studies, a conservative estimate is that roughly 200,000 male inmates in America are raped
every year, and many of them are raped daily. The group Stop Prisoner Rape
estimates the real figure to be closer to 290,000, noting that most investigations into the scope of sexual terror in prisons and jails do not count
inmates who have sex after pairing off for protection, and usually ignore the
much higher rates of rape at juvenile facilities.[8] Robert Dumond, a mental
health clinician with the Massachusetts Department of Corrections, writing
in the *International Journal of the Sociology of Law*, and citing evidence from
prison officials, argues that a young prisoner's chances of avoiding rape in an
adult facility are "almost zero . . . He'll get raped within the first 24 or 48
hours That's almost standard."[9]

What then is the role of rape in the daily ordering of prison life? So much
sexual depredation is actively ignored by officials, and even sanctioned by
them, that rape almost seems like a central part of prison management.
Corrections bureaucrats deny this, and even deny that rape occurs. But it is
obvious that the rape epidemic in prison bolsters the power of guards and
administrators. Thus it is important to excavate the rare instances in which
administrators and guards do tip their hand, revealing the extent of their con-
nivance with the sex-chattel system.

For example, the *Boston Globe* reported that guards in Massachusetts'
prisons use "booty bandits" much like their brethren in California. "Several

prisoners at Shirley [State Prison] said that Slade [a notorious prison rapist] has had a long history of attacks there, but that he is typically reshuffled by the guards into cells with 'fresh fish,' or new inmates."[10] In the age of AIDS, prison rape is also a form of Russian roulette, which makes it an all-the-more terrifying weapon. As one HIV-positive prison rape survivor put it, "Nowhere in the book of rules was it written that I got to be here to get raped, that I have to have them destroy my mind, that I am supposed to get AIDS." This same inmate went to the guards for protection but said their reply was, "Welcome to Shirley. Toughen up, punk."[11]

When asked to comment on the low-intensity rape and AIDS-driven death camps being run by the Massachusetts Department of Corrections, spokesman Anthony Carnevale said: "Well, that's prison . . . I don't know what to tell you."[12]

The trope of prison rape as "just deserts" circulates even in the genteel upper echelons of the criminal justice system. For example, an assistant United States attorney, seeking the extradition of three Canadians accused of fraud, warned that if any one of them resisted extradition they would face a long, hard prison term as "the boyfriend of a very bad man." The presiding Canadian judge didn't find this amusing and temporarily blocked extradition.[13]

More often, prison satraps belie the centrality of rape to their management strategies by their absolute and total denial that prison rape even occurs. For example, Utah prison officials, seeking accreditation of their system's medical facilities, denied that there had *ever* been a single rape in any Utah prison, a claim that was no doubt difficult even for caffeine-free Mormons to believe. The emphatic denial was made all the more absurd by ample documentation to the contrary, including a trial transcript in which one inmate was convicted and sentenced to fifteen extra years for raping a fellow prisoner.[14] In Massachusetts, following a *Boston Globe* exposé on prison rape, corrections bureaucrats still felt free to deny the reality of a high-profile rape case even as the victim was in the hospital undergoing rectal surgery.[15] Nor is it uncommon for prison officials to "accidentally" lose crucial evidence and "forget" to conduct medical exams when rapes are reported.[16]

Such denials are perfectly rational: to admit that inmates rape each other is to invite lawsuits. In 1994 the Supreme Court ruled in *Farmer vs. Brennan* that penitentiary officials *are* responsible for protecting prisoners from sexual predation. The case was launched by a transgender person – serving twenty years for credit card fraud – who was housed with violent male prisoners and, to no one's surprise, was viciously gang-raped.[17] Since then, several other inmates have tried to sue for damages after contracting HIV during their tenure as jailhouse sex slaves. One such case involved a 28-year-old married man used as a prostitute by a prison gang which peddled him from cell to cell in full view of guards. In at least two cases COs even brought customers to the victim's cell or escorted him down the tier to other cells where customers raped him and then paid the inmate pimps with cigarettes, drugs, and candy. Despite the precedent of *Farmer*, this young man was not awarded damages.[18]

James Dunn, who had been turned out as a young inmate in Angola, Louisiana's maximum security plantation prison, described to Wilbert Rideau, the doyen of jailhouse journalists, how officials actively supported the prison's slaveocracy:

> Everything and everybody in here worked to keep you a whore – even the prison. If a whore went to the authorities, all they'd do is tell you that since you already a whore, they couldn't do nothing for you, and for you to go back to the dorm and settle down and be a good old lady. Hell, they'd even call the whore's old man up and tell him to take you back down and keep you quiet . . . the most you'd get out of complaining is some marriage counseling, with them talking to you and your old man to iron out your difficulties.[19]

A veteran corrections officer, also from Louisiana, described a similar situation:

> There are prison administrators who use inmate gangs to help manage the prison. Sex and human bodies become the coin of the realm. Is inmate "X" writing letters to the editor of the local newspaper and filing lawsuits? Or perhaps he threw urine or feces on an employee? "Well, Joe, you and Willie and Hank work him over, but be sure you don't break any bones and send him to the hospital. If you do a good job, I'll see that you get the blondest boy in the next shipment."[20]

Lee Bowker, in his now somewhat dated book, devoted a whole chapter to documenting direct involvement by penitentiary staff and administrators in setting up, watching, and profiting from the rape of prisoners.[21]

FORGING PRISON'S SECOND SEX

Rape in male prisons is not only about indirect rule and subcontracting terror to latter-day trusty shooters, it is also the process by which the "normality" of a sexist world is reproduced in an all-male purgatory. In the big house, layers of collective, individual, and institutional violence act in concert to culturally manufacture prison's "second sex" and thus reproduce the binary gendered world of the outside. The ritual of gang rape, by which a prisoner is turned out; the jailhouse culture of fear and aggression which mandates that the strong shun and attack the weak; and the official tolerance and encouragement which facilitates this terrorism, all act together in a mutually reinforcing fashion to reproduce a sexist culture of "gender" in prison.

There are of course some transgender people in the joint, but the demand for a "weaker" gender often outstrips this possible "supply."[22] So the sexualized "other" is manufactured with almost Fordist regularity, on the conveyor belt of absolute sadism and homicidal violence. Thus, jailhouse rape is more than sadistic thrills: it creates a gender and, therefore, a division of labor and a set of class relations. Sex-slaves are used as prostitutes, domestics, and "wives." They are forced to provide all the sexual, manual, and emotional services that men in a sexist society normally extract from women. Along with "giving up ass" the punk must make beds, clean cells, shine shoes, pass messages, do laundry, run errands, write letters, shop, smuggle contraband, and listen to endless confessions, threats, soliloquies, and bombast from his "Man." As one punk wrote: "It is not uncommon for a Man to develop a genuine concern and affection for his punk and passionate love affairs are common in prison. Some couples even go through imitation marriage ceremonies . . . The one difference that stands out is that most men feel comfortable letting other men have access to their sexual partners . . .," so punks are loaned, traded, pimped, and outright *sold* as property.[23]

This gendered slave class is integral to the everyday micro-politics of order in the prison society: they provide a financial and psychological subsidy to the dominant criminal class. By keeping inmates content and divided, the prison slavocracy defuses political troubles. Donald Tucker — a survivor of numerous jailhouse gang rapes and self-described "punk" (who himself turned out a punk of his own) — summed it up best when he described the function of prison rape and why officials collude with the rapist class:

Rape exists and will continue to exist in confinement institutions because it serves the interests of too many powerful elements of jail and prison societies, including the administration. Officials use it to divert prison aggression, destroy potential leaders, and intimidate prisoners into becoming informers (as before the [1980] New Mexico prison riot); the Men at the top of the prisoner power structure benefit sexually, psychologically, and financially from the Punks who are turned out by this process or the fear of it; and the rapists, initiators, and followers themselves who come in for a share of the action.[24]

One point worth emphasizing is that the rape factory is politically docile: if inmates fear, hate, kill, and rape one another, the chance of a Spartacus arising from their ranks is almost nil. Politicized prisoners in the seventies knew this and therefore put the fight against sexual terror at the forefront of their organizing agendas. According to Herman "Hooks" Wallace who was a founding member of the Angola Penitentiary's chapter of the Black Panther Party and is still in prison fighting trumped-up charges – a precursor to radicalizing and mobilizing Black convicts was a heroic struggle against rape:

The biggest challenge [in organizing] came from the inmates who felt they were living comfortably. They had stables of men who they had forced to play the role of women. They prostituted them and had them taking care of all their sexual and financial needs . . .

Our primary objective was to stop the men from raping and exploiting other weaker men. We stood in the way of everyone when the "fresh fish" would make their appearance and gave them the protection they needed until they felt they no longer needed our protection. One man, a brother named Ervin Braux, was killed while trying to defend another prisoner from being raped.

Many of the guys who possessed the so-called "slaves" began to back away as they understood what we were doing. It was working![25]

Wallace's victory against rape also reveals the absolute indispensability of rape for those who wish to control and contain overcrowded, miserable prisons. Wallace and his comrades were framed for the murder of a white guard and were confined to solitary on death row.

OPEN SEASON ON WOMEN

Inmate-on-inmate rape also occurs in women's prisons and jails, but a far greater problem for female convicts is the sexual depravity and aggression of their male (and sometimes female) keepers. From coast to coast, guards routinely rape women prisoners with near-total impunity.[26]

Cut to the jail in Washington, D.C., on a June evening. The air is thick, humid, and hot; in contravention of the institution's rules, all cells are open, and soul music bounces off the sticky concrete walls and steel bars. At one end of the tier the officer in charge, Yvonne Walker, is dancing with inmates. Before long one prisoner is half-naked, undulating on a table. Soon, Walker is disrobing while another inmate performs a Bangkok sex trick with a lit cigarette. Guards and prisoners alike cheer wildly.

Welcome to the everyday madness of the Washington, D.C., City Jail for Women.

Down the tier one inmate remains alone in her cell, and then it starts. "Sunday is a dancer, too," shouts someone, referring to Sunday Daskalea, the inmate lying in her open cell and one of the few non–African American prisoners. The guards and prisoners call for Daskalea, demanding that she come dance. When she does not appear a guard dispatches a posse of three inmates to retrieve her. What ensued next was a hybrid sexual assault involving inmates and staff. Daskalea is forced to strip and dance, and other prisoners rub her down with oil as the male and female guards cheer them on. It was the fourth time that month that guards had coerced prisoners into stripping and performing sex acts.[27] But that was in many ways the least of what went on in the D.C. jail. In fact, the place seemed to *run* on sex and rape: even job assignments were contingent upon providing sexual services to the guards.[28]

This abusive sex carnival was stumbled upon quite by accident during a legal service clinic in 1991. "We had been running a pregnancy educational program focusing on rehabilitation and life skills," recalls attorney Brenda Smith of the Women's National Law Center, "and more and more women were showing up pregnant." According to Smith, scores of women become pregnant each year in D.C.'s prisons and many of the expecting inmates had been in for longer than nine months. On top of that, corrections officers were strongly and quietly "encouraging abortions." That left only one explanation: the pregnancies were the byproduct of epidemic rape.

When investigative journalist Christopher D. Cook asked D.C. prison officials why there was so much coerced sex in the D.C. system, spokesman Jimmie Williams said, "I don't think anyone can answer that question. It happens in prisons all across America . . . sex is a normal part of prison life." He added, "People are locked up and forced to live a celibate life . . . I guess those desires get out of hand. It's not proper, but it happens. I don't think anyone [on the outside] really knows what goes on inside of those cell blocks . . . They've got their own set of rules."[29] And in D.C. the rules are that female prisoners "put out" for guards or pay the price. According to a prisoner-filed lawsuit, inmates are either forced into sex with violence or threatened with loss of "privileges," such as access to soap, visits, etc.

Although the rape camps operated by the District of Columbia seem particularly egregious, a raft of recent lawsuits reveals that sexual abuse of female prisoners by guards is rampant all over the country. In Arizona, rape was so prevalent that the US Justice Department filed suit in March 1997, charging that state Department of Corrections officials were "consciously aware of, but deliberately indifferent to" a pattern of sexual abuse and misconduct. Nearly a dozen female inmates testified that they had been forced to have sexual encounters with male prison employees.[30]

Male guards have even been known to pimp female prisoners to male inmates. In March 1998, a federal judge awarded $500,000 to three women prisoners who had been housed in a male wing of the federal prison in Dublin, California, and then sold by COs as sex slaves to male inmates in the solitary confinement unit. Women who complained about or reported the 1995 rapes were further punished with beatings and more rape. One woman resisted her attacker, who explained that he would get "his $50 worth of pussy, ass, or ass whupping." Eight prison officials, including the former western region director for the Federal Bureau of Prisons, were forced to quit as a result of the case.[31] In D.C., guards also gave male inmates access to female prisoners, in Lorton jail's library and in other secluded areas.

Often the rape of women begins as soon as they are captured and booked into police stations. Over thirteen months in 1996–97, authorities arrested eight Metro-Atlanta cops and charged them with raping female captives.[32]

In America's booming private for-profit dungeons, the rape crisis is even worse, because officials and COs are less accountable to prisoners or the public. Inmates in corporate penitentiaries are often sent far from their home state and thus have few (if any) local contacts to help them expose abuse.

When Barrilee Banister and seventy-seven other female Oregon prisoners were shipped off to a Corrections Corporation of America (CCA) facility in Florence, Arizona, they found that guards expected them to perform strip shows and sexual favors.[33] According to Banister, COs pressured Oregon prisoners into "oral sex and sexual intercourse . . . We were in fear that if we refused to submit to the COs' requests that our safety and well-being would be in jeopardy." When the prisoners complained to public officials in Oregon, CCA goons tried to mollify the captives with cash.[34]

These accounts are in no way unique. Most of the COs holding the keys at the nation's 170 state prisons for women are still men (since the Civil Rights Act of 1964 it has been deemed discriminatory to female guards for prison administrators to segregate their staff by gender: thus the cross-gender guarding). By profession COs are trained to physically and psychologically dominate prisoners. In a world where sex is often infused with motifs of domination, it is no wonder that the combination of male keepers and female charges translates into rape on a mass scale. And while intercourse behind bars is usually a forced, ugly affair, it can quite often appear "consensual" because of the tremendous power imbalance between women prisoners and their armed male keepers. The lack of overt violence in many such jailhouse liaisons merely reveals the extent of institutionalized violence that inscribes the details of everyday life in women's prisons. In the ladies' lockdown bare necessities such as cigarettes, library access, or adequate supplies of soap become "perks" to be doled out by lecherous predators in uniform. Women who refuse guards' advances, or dare to complain, face not only poverty and discomfort during confinement, but beatings and solitary confinement.[35]

Unfortunately, an accounting such as this, of women prisoners raped by armed officers of the state, could go on indefinitely. A 1996 report on the subject by Human Rights Watch covers the crisis in only five states yet runs to almost 350 pages, each one replete with horrible accounts of male COs sexually exploiting female prisoners.

Immediately, two culprits emerge: a misogynist culture and the war on drugs. With the advent of mandatory minimums, special narcotics squads, and now with the rise of zero tolerance policing, arrests for prostitution, possession, and drug sales have skyrocketed; so too have female rates of incarceration. Between 1980 and 1994, the female prison population surged by nearly 500 percent (compared with 300 percent for men).[36] Only 16 percent of women sent to prison annually are sentenced for violent crimes; the rest have been convicted of crimes against property, such as stealing and fraud, or for narcotics and public order offenses like selling drugs or prostitution.[37]

The relative invisibility of the rape crisis in women's prisons correlates directly to the racist and misogynist contempt conditioning most mainstream coverage of the "fallen" female addict, sex worker, thief, or convict.

PRISON GANGS: THE INDISPENSABLE ENEMY

While guards wield the power to kill and rape, they do not rule supreme. The fault lines of power in the big house are notoriously murky. Sociologists long ago noted that guards do not unilaterally control prisoners but, rather, broker control with inmates. As the prison population grows, average sentences become longer, and mega-prisons of 5,000 inmates become the norm, paramilitary prison gangs – the secret, racialized, micro-governments of the inmates' world – become all the more central to how penitentiaries function. In analyzing this form of jailhouse deviance it behoves us to recall Foucault's early thesis about the political uses of crime. Prison gangs organize much of the prostitution, drug dealing, rape, extortion, and general *sub rosa* business activity that goes on inside. Thus prison gangs organize and regulate huge swaths of everyday life behind bars and also create violence and social pathologies which, while apparently disruptive, render penitentiaries governable and justify increased repression, surveillance, and control. Thus gangsterism and interpersonal violence in prison, as on the street, are forms of auto-oppression and should be treated as such.

But the role of prison gangs is not without contradictions: they are politically useful to prison administrators in keeping inmates divided, yet they also pose a threat to staff. Any form of autonomous convict organizing, including prison gangs, has the potential to get out of control, become politicized, and fuel rebellion. Also prison gangs assault and kill staff and generally promulgate an anti-authority ethos. The official war on prison gangs is best seen as a management strategy designed to contain, shape, and direct violence, rather than eliminate it.

By the mid eighties most state prison systems had reported some sort of gang activity. But the largest systems – California, Texas, Florida, Illinois, and New York – have the oldest and most organized gangs. The gang scene is different in every state, and within states it changes from prison to prison, thus a thorough accounting of prison gangs is impossible. The stories below focus on California because, as is the case with so many corrosive social trends, the Golden State leads the way in this field, too.

The California Department of Corrections says that 7,000 of its nearly 160,000 prisoners are "validated" prison gang members. It estimates that many thousands more are "gang associates." To validate a prisoner, CDC gang investigators must have three or more pieces of evidence indicating gang affiliation, such as a confiscated gang constitution or communications; self-admission; the testimony of a "confidential informant"; or gang tattoos, also known as "tacts" or "blocas." In reality these criteria are rather arbitrary and are frequently used against prison activists and jailhouse lawyers who are not gang affiliated.

According to inmates and administrators alike, everyday life in California's high security "level three" and "level four" lockups is heavily influenced by a myriad of large and small prison gangs, many of which are just the incarcerated extensions of large street gangs. Traditionally there have been four underground prison gang superpowers, divided into two allied forces. The Mexican Mafia and the Aryan Brotherhood cooperated in a jail-house war against *La Nuestra Familia* and the Black Guerrilla Family. All of these gangs tried (not always successfully) to organize themselves in strict vertical command structures, with "generals," "central committees," or "councils" giving direct, sometimes written, orders down the line to "captains," "lieutenants," and "soldiers." Membership is said to be "blood in, blood out," meaning that an inductee has to kill or commit some significant act of violence to become a full-fledged member. Likewise, death is said to be the only exit, though in reality people often leave these gangs without consequence once they are out of prison.

With this microcosmic gang version of the Cold War in mind, law enforcement officials, most notably Daryl Gates, have cast California prison gangs as vast, all-powerful organized crime structures that can kill anyone, anywhere, at any time.[38] But even at the height of their power, the paramilitary "big four" never matched up to this fantasy. In the last decade, as prison populations have soared and the state has built sixteen new penitentiaries, the old gang structures have transmogrified and fractured. Even during simpler times, it was questionable how well convict gangsters really maintained strict paramilitary structures, or how large and coherent these formations were. But in the ultra-treacherous world of California's ever expanding gulag, gangs have broken down into a complex jumble of sets, sub-sets, and crisscrossing alliances that vary from joint to joint, yard to yard, and even tier to tier. Many inmates, rather than being solders in mega-gangs, are more informally associated with "cars," racial and geographic cliques and sub-cliques that band together for self-defense, mutual support, and business.[39]

However, big prison gangs, whether organized vertically (as organized crime structures) or horizontally (as social, cultural, and martial networks), do exist and they exert considerable influence. Their primary impact is to promulgate racism, fear, and hatred among prisoners. In that respect gangs, like rape, are an indispensable part of ruling America's captive populations: this is true whether the vastly outnumbered COs know it or not.

Prison journalist Willie Wisely best captured the climate of gulag California's slow-motion race war when recounting his time in Corcoran's maximum security labyrinth: "In California, racial politics require you to go to yard in segregation or SHU. It's mandatory. It doesn't matter if you're scared or don't want to go. You go, or you're marked as a coward and subject to assault or stabbing. So when the door opened for yard I went."[40]

Another convict commented: "I thought segregation was dead, but there it was, as vivid as an Alabama lunch counter in the '50s."[41] And when violence flares between the races, everyone is expected to pitch in; those who do not can expect to be dealt with harshly or even killed by their racial "brothers." Even peace-oriented, politicized people – such as the former Crip and gang truce leader Dewayne Holmes, who was framed and served several years in the mid nineties – have to "put in work" during racial brawls, even when that means fighting childhood friends. The war inside stops for no one.[42]

But inmate racism is not simply the natural product of cellblock wars, nor just a hangover from outside, it is also nurtured by prison's overtly racist official structures. In some California joints, weightlifting equipment (when it existed) was segregated: labeled "B" for Black, "W" for white, or "L" for Latino. Also, haircuts and other activities are often scheduled by race. In one respect this official segregation is merely a reaction to the "organic" race hatred among inmates. But the racial gangs and war among prisoners can also be seen as a *de facto* perpetuation of the *de jure* segregation which, in most prisons, lasted until the 1960s.[43]

THE CONSTELLATION OF FORCES

But what of the structure and history of prison gangs? The two predominantly Chicano gangs, the Mexican Mafia (or "Eme" – Spanish for the letter "M") and *La Nuestra Familia* (also known as *La Familia*, or NF) are reported to be the largest and most organized gangs in California prisons. Both are said to exert considerable power on the streets through their relationships with the many semiautonomous *norteño* and *sureño* "sets" such as White Fence, Maravilla, the Bulldogs, 18th Street, and F-Troop in Santa Ana.

Like so much of America's new paramilitary culture, current prison gangs have their roots in the social and economic upheaval of the 1960s. According to gang legend, studies by the Department of Justice, the CDC, the California legislature, and a few progressive sociologists, the current constellation of gangs began when "la Eme" first emerged in 1956–57 among a small group of "state-raised" Chicano youth from L.A. who were locked up in the Deuel Vocational Institution at Tracy. Early on this clique extorted and robbed Black and white inmates, but soon started preying on Chicanos from Fresno, Sacramento, and other northern and rural parts of California and whom the Eme ridiculed as "farmers." To break up the emerging Eme, authorities scattered its cadre to Soledad, Folsom, and San Quentin, aka "la pinta." This Eme diaspora soon set about recruiting new members and ripping off new populations of inmates.

By the late sixties a group of Chicano convicts from rural areas and cities north of Bakersfield had formed a gang, first called the "Blooming Flower," then *La Familia Mexicana* and finally *La Nuestra Familia*. The now infamous thirty-year-old war between *norteño* and *sureño* street gangs is said to have begun when some Eme soldiers (*sureños*) robbed a *Nuestra Familia* member (a *norteño*) and wore his shoes on the San Quentin yard: the NF rose up in response. Shortly thereafter, an Eme peace emissary was "shanked" to death by *Familia* soldiers in the California Institution for Men at Chino. By the mid seventies the CDC was attempting to impose total segregation between Eme and NF forces, "even sending them in separate waves to the pre-release center."[44]

According to California prison officials and federal researchers, *La Nuestra Familia* and its newer allied spin-off, the Northern Structure, are the most vertically organized prison gangs in the state. Officials have confiscated what they claim to be the by-laws of *La Nuestra Familia*, which lay out in great detail a paramilitary structure bound up with an elaborate code of honor.[45] In the seventies the NF ran extensive education programs that taught its *soldados* the skills needed to survive as gang warriors in the dungeons of California: enemy identification, how to conduct and survive interrogations, as well as basic literacy and gang history.[46] According to confiscated documents, full-fledged "made members" of the NF are under orders to set up "regiments" when they return to the streets, but it is unclear if such regiments, under the direct control of "shot callers" in prison, really exist. There are, however, less formal links between Latino street gangs and prison superpowers. Both deploy the same rhetoric and iconography: *sureños* and la Eme wear blue and claim the number 13, which corresponds to the letter M, while *norteños* and *la Familia* wear red, and claim 14. And indeed, some street sets even "pay taxes" to *veteraños* inside. But this sort of horizontal and ideological affiliation does not equal the vertical integration that law enforcement often claims. Furthermore, there is almost always fierce internecine warfare between *norteño* sets, just as there is among *sureños* and among the largely African American sets of Crips and Bloods.

Nonetheless, "la Eme" and *La Nuestra Familia* do have power outside prison. A high profile example of this emerged when three former Eme cadre served as consultants to the Edward James Olmos film *American Me,* about the rise of the Mexican Mafia. Unfortunately for the consultants, the flick portrayed one Eme founder as having been raped as a youth. In retribution, the three consultants – traitors in the eyes of the gang   were machine-gunned to death in their homes by Eme hit squads and Olmos was forced into a gilded Hollywood version of armed hiding. In the aftermath, more than a dozen alleged Mexican Mafia soldiers were busted and sent to prison.[47]

A more positive example of la Eme's influence emerged during the days of the nationwide post–Rodney King gang truce movement. In September 1993 la Eme ordered an end to drive-by shootings in East L.A. on the grounds that too many "civilians" were getting caught in the crossfire. Violators of the new rule were threatened with death. The edict was delivered throughout the autumn of 1993 at a series of tightly guarded meetings, such as one that drew more than 1,000 homeboys to Elysian Park, near Dodger Stadium. The new rules of engagement between warring *sureño* sets were explained by one young *soldado* as follows: "If you have to take care of business, they were saying, at least do it with respect, do it with honor and dignity."[48] In other words, do not shoot regular folks.

The Eme order and, more importantly, street-level organizing by truce-building gangbangers, led to a precipitous decline in east L.A.'s homicide rate during 1993 and 1994.[49]

The gang estimated to be numerically strongest in California prisons is the Northern Structure, a gen X spin-off started by *La Nuestra Familia* in the mid eighties. The catalysts for this new formation are said to have been a major RICO case which sent a bunch of NF veterans to federal prison and the CDC's campaign to isolate other "shot callers" in its new generation of super maximum security prisons. In recent years, the Northern Structure has clashed with the old guard NF; in one case the quarrel even spilled out into the streets of San Jose.[50] Though claiming the same color, and officially allied, NF and Northern Structure sets are, in some prisons, at war with each other.[51]

Among California's African American convicts, the old school prison gang is the Black Guerrilla Family. Originally formed as a revolutionary movement of Black nationalist and Marxist convicts, the BGF has since disintegrated into an organized crime structure, though it still retains some Black power rhetoric and symbols, and many of its veterans are politicized and principled. The earliest cadre of the BGF were Panthers, or Panther associates who had been purged by the increasingly moderate Huey P. Newton or had defected in protest at the new electoral line. Many BGF soldiers had been associated with George Jackson's "Black Family." They hooked up with some of the dissident followers of Eldridge Cleaver, who called themselves the Black Liberation Army and may, or may not, have had relations with the BLA faction which split from the Panthers and operated outside prison on the East Coast. The BGF took form and began to grow in the wake of George Jackson's 1971 assassination, and the left/right, East Coast/West Coast splits in the Black Panther Party outside.

Early on, the group stuck close to its revolutionary program, focusing on organizing and educating inmates. BGF reading covered everything from Jackson's *Prison Letters* and the works of Mao to *The Anarchist Cook Book*. Former convict Dorsey Nunn, now a prominent prison activist, explained the BGF's positive impacts:

I learned to read from the BGF . . . We swallowed up Malcolm. We swallowed up George. We swallowed up Huey. We read some Eldridge, Mao Zedong, Ho Chi Minh. And if you didn't know a word you ask your homeboy, your comrade, and say "Hey man! What is this word, what does it mean?" And it was rewarding to have a homeboy who started out after you come and ask you and be blessed and privileged enough to teach him.[52]

The BGF also took offensive action against COs and white convicts, stabbing (among others) the future convict writer Dwight Edgar Abbot, who at that time was an angry young racist.[53] But by 1973 and 1974, the BGF, with no more than an estimated two hundred or three hundred members, was degenerating into simple gangsterism, while other African American prisoners carried on with real politics.[54] The BGF even carried out some "hits" on the street, usually against other quasi-political gangsters, but the one that received the most attention was the shooting of George Jackson's former attorney, Fay Stender, who was left paralyzed and a year later took her own life.[55]

As late as 1978 a Board of Corrections briefing paper discussing the BGF reported that "There is a consensus that a desire for revolution remains, with various reasons being offered for lack of activity . . . Some criminal conduct is viewed as a means of obtaining the resources for action."[56] This same paper, and later accounts as well, indicate that during the late seventies a BGF faction in southern California associated with James "Doc" Holiday steered the group down the path of full-blown criminality, leapfrogging from robbing drug dealers to being drug dealers. In 1979 Holiday was busted on cocaine charges and is, deservedly or not, frequently cast as a major BGF capo,[57] But politics, or at least revolutionary iconography and mythology, were still "causing much internal dissension in the organization [during the mid eighties], due to a split in the group between the 'thugs' who want to make big money, and the diehard revolutionaries who still think of themselves as political prisoners . . ."[58] Around the same time the BGF was occasionally attacking guards. In one famous confirmed kill they skewered a CO's heart with a jailhouse spear (such weapons are usually fashioned with scrap metal blades and a shaft of tightly rolled newspapers).[59]

The symbolic link between the BGF and the politics of the Panthers was displayed on the public stage for one final and sordid act in 1989, when 25-

year-old Tyrone Demetrius Robinson, a BGF foot soldier, was released from the Corcoran SHU after several years in prison. In the pre-dawn hours of August 22, Robinson encountered Huey P. Newton on Center Street in West Oakland. A few weeks earlier Newton had allegedly robbed Robinson of 14 vials of crack cocaine and $160. This time the penitentiary-fresh child of the streets was armed and the fallen revolutionary hero turned base-head was not. According to a witness Robinson pistol-whipped Newton and then shot him in the head three times. Robinson, who confessed to the killing, had allegedly bragged to several people that he would "make rank" in the BGF for his deed. Many others speculated that he would more likely make the grave for being a reckless loudmouth.[60]

Since that tragic night Robinson — who as a toddler ate at the Panther's free community breakfast program and now lives in the Pelican Bay SHU — has read the works of Newton and become, in his own way, a political devotee to the man he helped martyr.[61]

Today the BGF remains the gang for African American lifers; most Black prisoners, though, like prisoners generally, try and stay out of gangs altogether and "do their own time." But youth who were in gangs on the street generally affiliate with the ever shifting constellations of prison-stranded Crips and Bloods. According to the book *Monster* — the autobiography of Sanyika Shakur, aka Kodey Scott — the mid eighties saw some Crips with long terms form the Consolidated Crip Organization (CCO), while some convict Bloods combined into the United Blood Nation. Much like the early BGF these groups, which reportedly still exist in some form,[62] fit the mold of pre-political formations: deploying nationalist tropes, studying Swahili and occasional Marxist texts, and adopting a paramilitary structure to ensure group security. But ultimately they did little more than perpetuate the traditional race war against *norteño*-affiliated Latinos and Ayran Brotherhood–affiliated whites. According to Shakur, the CCO began to fall apart in the late eighties as war broke out with the new, less political Blue Note Crip Organization.[63]

The late sixties also spurred a gang formation among white inmates known as the Aryan Brotherhood; in higher security level three and four prisons, this racist gang once dominated the social space among white prisoners. The rise of the AB – like California prison gangs generally – is best understood through the context of demographic transformations of the postwar era. World War II increased the demand for labor in the fields, steel mills, and shipyards of California and thus created a massive influx of African American and Latino laborers. But as automation, deindustrialization, and racist hiring practices took their toll, Latino and African American communities found themselves increasingly ghettoized and unemployed. This, coupled with the age-old tradition of racist policing and biased courts, meant that Black and Latino people found themselves immediately over-represented in California's jails and prisons. (This racist pattern goes all the way back to the gold rush, when it was the Chinese who were most heavily targeted by the white institutions of the law.) By 1951, 20 percent of California's prison inmates were Black, while only comprising 4.4 percent of the state population. By the late sixties the racial composition of California's historically segregated and white-dominated prisons had been radically transformed. Blacks and Latinos began to outnumber whites and as a result dominated the politics of the yard. As white convicts slipped into minority status, or parity, their gang formations took on increasingly political and overtly racist forms. In 1968 the remnants of the "Bluebirds," a white San Quentin gang, were reborn as the Aryan Brotherhood.[64]

Getting an accurate count of current AB numbers is impossible, but the CDC says it has about 220 validated AB cadre locked in the Corcoran and Pelican Bay SHUs. That number does not give any indication of the number of AB members "on the main line." As one former AB associate put it: "They never really come out in front and say, 'Yeah, I'm A.B.,' 'cause they're afraid they're going to be segregated. They're afraid people will think they're in there to carry out a contract."[65]

Tattooed with swastikas and SS lightning bolts, AB soldiers exude the image of the hardcore racist, and many of them are. But AB racism can be tempered by a criminal pragmatism. The gang is first and foremost concerned with controlling its share of prison yard drug dealing, extortion, and prostitution scams. Racial warfare comes second to business. Towards that end the AB has been in alliance with the Eme for more than two decades. Corrections officials report that the AB has conducted assassination "hits" on behalf of Eme shot-callers and in other ways has cooperated in the Eme's war against *La Nuestra Familia*. There is also evidence that the AB–Eme partnership extends to the streets. Their most famous outside operation was the 1976 heist of Lloyds Bank of California, in which a posse of AB and Eme marauders boosted $111,500. While most of the band were later busted, the loot was never recovered.[66]

Criminal solidarity aside, racism and segregation are still all-important to hardcore AB soldiers. "It's all politics in here," explains a white prisoner in California's Pelican Bay State Prison, who though saying he's not a racist, adds that he does not associate with African Americans. "You're not allowed to take a cigarette from a Black or share a candy bar with one." The first time he made that mistake an AB heavy gave him a clear warning not to cross the color line.[67] Another reputed AB member locked away in the Pelican Bay SHU points to the visiting booth next door, where an alleged member of the Black Guerrilla Family, who is also the younger sibling of a famous Black Panther martyr, sits: "I've known this guy, for jeez, seventeen years," he says. "There's nothing personal between us, he's a fine individual. We might nod hello, but we don't talk to each other. In terms of group interest we're just on opposing sides."[68]

Like all infamous old prison gangs, the AB has spawned franchises around the country. Though bearing the same name, the many AB gangs in other states operate as independent entities and in fact are often incredibly hostile to each other. The Arizona AB, for example, is said to view the less political, more pragmatically criminal California AB as sellouts.[69]

As the AB proliferates and its old guard leadership becomes increasingly isolated, the white gang scene becomes more variegated. For example, law enforcement specialists in Florida report that in many states young AB recruits are shifting away from Hitlerian and Nazi symbolism towards a white supremacist ideology that harks back to Celtic and Norse mythology. Younger AB soldiers often work runes, clovers, and traditional Irish knotwork, along with swastikas, into their tattoos and artwork. Intercepted AB communications reveal the increasing use of Gaelic phrases and codes. Interestingly, this recuperation of a nationalist language is a direct imitation of Black convicts' practice of speaking and writing Swahili so as to circumvent prison surveillance. Likewise Chicano inmates use the indigenous Mexican language Nahuatl in the same way. Gaelic imagery aside, white prison gangs are still dominated by extreme racists: in the South, prison-based factions of the Ku Klux Klan, the American Nazi Party, and the Dirty White Boys make race war on the yard.[70]

Despite being relatively small in numbers the AB makes up for it in ferocity. Perhaps their most audacious actions in California, which also marked them as prime targets for neutralization, were a series of coordinated assaults on staff in 1987. The actions were planned as revenge for the shooting of an

AB inmate who had stabbed a Black prisoner in a brawl. The first assault happened on July 7, when an alleged AB member, smuggling a knife in his rectum, produced it during a strip search and jammed it into the neck of rookie CO, Carl Kropp. A few hours later, an off-duty guard was wounded when two ABs pulled up next to his vehicle and unloaded a shotgun into the driver's side window. Later investigation revealed that nineteen-year-old Judith Box – an employee of the State Franchise Tax Board and the moll of reputed AB heavy Philip "Wildman" Fortman – had been furnishing the "white brothers" intelligence that included the home addresses of eight Folsom COs and the warden, Robert Borg. Around the same time, a major AB member almost escaped during transportation when he produced a two-shot derringer that he had stored in his rectum and tried to kill his guards.[71]

As repression and transfer to super-isolation units takes its toll on the old guard AB, a new gang calling itself the Nazi Lowriders (NLR) has emerged among young white prisoners. CDC gang investigators believe that the NLR started in the California Youth Authority in the mid seventies. After a long dormancy, the gang was revived in the late eighties with the help of some AB veterans. Estimated to be 1,000 strong, the Nazi Lowriders – named thus because they are racists and wear their baggy pants, in classic Cali-style, sagging low – are described by one CDC investigator as "the gang on the horizon. An extremely violent bunch of disenfranchised white guys who cause lots of problems for staff and inmates." Said to be less paramilitary than the AB and more racist (despite having a few Latino and Native American members), the NLR is a horizontally organized gang with various warring factions, some of which are close to the AB and Eme, others operating alone.[72]

Most prisoners are not formally "tipped up" with prison gangs. Instead they bide their own time and usually hook up with a "car" of homeboys of the same racial group or from the same neighborhood, city, or county. These small geographic cliques may in times of crisis hook up and relate through the rubric of *norteño*, Crip, or white affiliation. For example, Black prisoners from the Bay Area are often called "415s" (after the region's former area code). This loose affiliation is not a formal paramilitary gang, but the Four-Fifteens look out for each other, fend off the more numerous down-state Crips and Bloods, and also run dope, pimp, fight, and (in some joints) control specific job assignments and other perks.[73] The many loosely associated sets, cars, and tips of the new overcrowded prison may form symbolic alliances with each other, as between the Northern Structure and other *norteños* – or they might be "beefing" amongst themselves given the balance of forces and local details of yard politics.

LET THEM EAT EACH OTHER: THE BOUNTIFUL RACE WAR

All of the gangs discussed above engage in the same set of activities: smuggling drugs, extorting weaker inmates, turning out punks, pimping, and launching self-destructive, super-violent wars against one another. Prison gangs are both a survival strategy for convicts and the organized expression of the predatory and parasitic class of prisoners. That may disturb some readers on the romantic left, but the facts are fairly straightforward: prisoners who embrace fratricidal warfare do much to keep themselves down. One African American prisoner – serving double life in California's High Desert prison, a joint known for its racist staff and heavy NLR presence – summed up the situation as follows: "Let a white boy on the yard with me and it's on . . . I don't trust him and he don't trust me. I'm afraid of him and he's afraid of me. Draw a barrier line and he knows where he's supposed to be and I know where I'm supposed to be. It's the same like you got with that no-fly zone in Iraq."

Given sentiments like that it's no wonder the days of the militant con are gone. Nor can the demise of a left-wing prison culture simply be blamed on COINTELPRO-style repression. The self-oppressing systems of racialized hatred that convicts create – with help from the Man: recall the arranged fights at Corcoran – are the ultimate form of social control. What makes such insanity so difficult to break is that participation in fratricidal gang warfare, when viewed from the immediate survival interests of an individual prisoner, is rational behavior. You "put in work" or pay the price. The totalizing, scripted nightmare of "yard politics" is too massive for any single individual to buck. But viewed from the macro-level of collective long-term interests, prison gangs are political suicide. They are a form of organic, decentralized, self-fueling social control, a cultural system of indirect rule that simultaneously oppresses from the inside while justifying repression from the outside.[74]

Of course all of the tyrannies discussed earlier – loss of weights, restricted visiting, curtailed library access, bureaucratic hurdles blocking the way to court, official terror, the rape system – fuel the boredom, fear, anger, and hopelessness that are the raw material of the dungeon race war. "They were teaching us not to get along and telling us it was OK not to get along," recalls former prisoner Marc Madow. "I watched men come in who were racially neutral but who left walking the walk and talking the talk of hatred and fanaticism."[75]

Prisoners – the unacknowledged experts on the politics of the cage – see a logic behind this strategy: "Inmates dramatically outnumber guards, so [the prison] has a vested interest in keeping the inmate population divided against itself rather than [against] them. Guards need to channel any kind of unrest away from themselves and onto another group."[76] Former prisoner Johnny Spain agrees: "When blacks and whites fought, guards turned the other way – or worse, provided the white inmates with weapons. I realized that prisoners killing prisoners only made life easier for the guards."[77] San Francisco County Deputy Sheriff Michael Marcum, a former prisoner who, quite amazingly, is now a jail warden, tells the same story about the utility of prison gangs:

> It's important to understand that prisons are fearful, dangerous places even for staff. So a staff can – if you're an officer and you've gotta supervise 200 people on a tier, it's a lot easier for you if that tier is split up into five bickering factions rather than having 200 people all looking at you as, "Gee, why should we comply with the rules and regulations he's putting out?" So there is also that sort of staff encouragement of this kind of thing in many institutions.[78]

Along with the gladiator fights at Corcoran further evidence of a *sub rosa* divide and conquer strategy is emerging in recent court cases. For example, a jury awarded $8,000 to a member of the Northern Structure after it was proven that guards had knowingly placed him, handcuffed, in a cell with an Eme rival who gave the *norteño* a vicious beating.[79]

The prison race war is by no means quarantined to the yards: the hate factory discharges 90 percent of its product back to the streets. And as Mike Davis has pointed out, that means the race war inside is being exported to the neighborhoods. Perhaps the clearest case of this is the current conflict between Latinos and African Americans in Venice, Santa Monica, and Culver City, in which over a dozen people have been killed, and many more wounded. As part of this feud, three African American families in the Mar Vista Gardens housing project have had their homes firebombed. Many activists believe that the new racial vendettas are a direct extension of the madness bred by the CDC and L.A. County Jail.[80]

WAR AMONG THE KEEPERS

Prison's racial poison is by no means confined to the ranks of convicts: the other side of the gunrail is also infected. Just as the captives clique together, so too do the keepers. The ranks of the CDC are rife with sexism and racism, despite the agency having led the state in affirmative action hiring, with 47 percent of its staff being white women or people of color.

At Corcoran the COs who administered mass beatings to the busloads of new prisoners were called "the Sharks." Some members of this CO gang even came to work on their days off just to get in on the action. Another gang of screws at the California Institution for Men at Chino called itself SPONGE, a disgusting acronym for the equally disgusting name, "Society for the Prevention of Niggers Getting Everything." Less overtly racist than these secret guard crews is the "European American Officers Association." The guard who started this hundred-strong outfit decries the power of "special interest groups" which "have direct lines of communications with the director." Despite a CO culture of silence, other signs of "racism in the ranks" have emerged: a white guard carved a swastika in the wooden stock of his rifle; another had complaints filed against him by colleagues for fraternizing with AB prisoners; another proudly showed off his Ku Klux Klan membership card; female guards complain of harassment; a Jewish guard was handcuffed to a fence by fellow COs, who happened to be neo-Nazi skinheads; a Black guard had his new truck vandalized and was forced to request a transfer out of his highly coveted supervisory position. Racism among the screws has even led to segregated institutions: Wasco, Tehachapi, and High Desert are predominantly staffed by whites, while Lancaster is largely Black.[81] Within institutions guards segregate themselves by work shift and unit. Prisoners in the Corcoran HIV yard report that white and "militaristic

Latinos" share shifts and force Black officers into isolation on all-Black shifts of their own.[82]

THE SHU – SNITCH FACTORY, LOONY BIN, AND MEAT GRINDER

In the name of combating prison gangs, the CDC has developed a ferocious internal war-machine complete with special investigators, secret informants, kangaroo courts, and isolation units. The center of this strategy in California, as in the federal system and many other states, is the Security Housing Unit. These previously discussed super-maximum prisons within prisons are where inmates live one or two in a cell for twenty-three hours a day. They eat, sleep, and defecate behind solid metal doors. Their contact with the world is through a "tray slot" where guards pass them meals and through which their hands are cuffed and uncuffed before and after going to the exercise yard or their bi-weekly shower. The prisoners usually get no more than an hour or two a week in the SHU's meager law libraries. They have no jobs, no educational programs, limited access to telephones, and can only visit their families through bulletproof glass, using bugged and tinny intercoms. Thus smothered, the prisoners are watched twenty-four hours a day by closed-circuit TV, for years on end.[83]

Subsequently, life in the nation's SHUs is marked by "extraordinary social isolation [and] unremitting idleness," interrupted only by occasional episodes of intense and sudden violence when cellmates attack each other, yard fights break out (or are set up), or when guards perform "cell extractions." Cell extractions involve teams of six to ten guards in body armor, helmets, gloves, and gas-masks, injecting tear gas or pepper spray into a prisoner's cell, then popping open the door and charging in, beating, and manacling the prisoner.[84]

The ultimate measure of the architectural, social, and physical violence of the SHUs is the intensity and prevalence of the insanity they create. "The psychotic inmates are – unequivocally – *the* most disturbed people I've ever seen," says Dr. Terry Kupers, a veteran psychiatrist and one of the few independent medical experts to have toured SHUs in California, Indiana, and Pennsylvania. "They scream and throw feces all over their cells. In a mental hospital you'd never see anything like that! Patients would be sedated or stabilized with drugs. Their psychosis would be interrupted."[85]

The roots of the SHU are as old as prison itself, reaching back to the great Quaker prison "reformers" like John Howard and Benjamin Rush who, in the eighteenth century, advocated work, silence, and isolation as salubrious responses to crime and disorder.[86] A more recent angle on the phenomenon is that SHUs are just updated versions of "the hole" – that section of any prison where incorrigibles are punished with stints of total isolation. But a more precise genesis of the SHU starts, like the rest of our story, amidst the tumult of the 1960s. By that point, internal exile to "the hole" was often permanent and was euphemistically called "administrative segregation." At San Quentin, the place for such punishment was the "Adjustment Center." With the rise of militant prisoners and jailhouse writ writers the AC was soon filled with a cohort of "incorrigible" nationalists, communists, and self-styled POWs. George Jackson penned *Blood in My Eye* from the dank confines of the AC. In fact, the "ad seg" tiers became Black Bolshevik hotbeds teeming with smuggled books and covert study groups. The more radicalized the prisoners became, the more control and isolation the state imposed.[87]

The need for new maximum security units was even articulated by the unctuous Governor Reagan. By the late eighties California was realizing the New Right's vision with a massive lockup construction boom. Most new prisons included high-tech maximum security units. But the ultimate end of the line emerged when the concrete dried on more than 2,000 SHU cells in Corcoran and Pelican Bay; the latter even has "walk alone" yards in which prisoners exercise in isolation.[88]

Placement in the SHU can be "determinate" and based on some disciplinary infraction, such as possession of weapons or drugs, or it can be "indeterminate" when based on gang affiliation. For prisoners sentenced to the SHU as "validated" gang members there are only three paths of exit: snitch, parole, or die.[89]

To snitch, a prisoner must "debrief": that is, name names and undergo extensive interrogations by Special Services Unit (SSU) investigators. Such capitulation to the Man is the ultimate violation of the convict code and is tantamount to signing one's own death warrant, as any known snitch will be beaten, raped, and/or knifed once returned to general population. Nor does psychological surrender to the SSU necessarily lead to freedom. The human rights group California Prison Focus has documented several cases of prisoners who, facing life sentences in the SHU and justifiably unable to handle the thought of never touching their relatives again, chose to debrief only to remain locked in the SHU, without explanation.

The other two options require eons of patience. A prisoner can wait until he has served his entire prison sentence and get paroled from both prison and the SHU. Or he can wait for death, whichever comes first.

The high-tech hell of the SHU is justified by invoking the threat of gangs and psychotic rebels, but the brutal little boxes are also used for controlling political and proto-political inmates, namely activists, jailhouse lawyers and, increasingly, a new breed of organic intellectual, the jailhouse doctors. With the rise of the prison AIDS crisis, HIV-positive prisoners have been forced to study medicine on their own, demand their right to do so, and fight for the proper treatment when poorly trained and unmotivated prison medical staff ignore or haphazardly poison them.[90]

These leaders and thinkers often play a crucial role in bringing convicts together. For example, before being locked down in the SHU the increasingly famous jailhouse lawyer Steven Castillo was not only filing high-caliber suits against the CDC, he was also helping to organize peace between warring *norteños* and *sureños*.[91] Removing such positive influences is crucial to brewing that special prison alchemy of orderly chaos.

Even as regards gang violence, the "debrief or die" policy's wholesale manufacture of snitches has not brought peace to the yards. Rather the CDC might as well have spiked prison water supplies with paranoia-inducing psychotropic drugs. The SSU's in-house war merely destabilizes old gang structures, sets off lethal purges against real and imagined "rats," and has left power vacuums on the mainline. These in turn trigger violent leadership struggles between younger gangsters and even the formation of new gangs such as the NLR, which arose in the wake of old guard ABs being buried in the SHUs. Recently, Pelican Bay alone witnessed a half-dozen snitch-driven murders in which AB cellies have been killing each other off in the name of purging the organization of sellouts and traitors.[92]

But all these predictable failures, like many law enforcement defeats, serve the bureaucracy of control better than victory ever could. As seen throughout this chapter, mayhem in prison is parlayed into empire building.[93] The more "deviance" the big house excretes, the more the guards and administrators need new prisons, new SHUs, more gang investigators, further expansion into outside communities, closer cooperation with other agencies, better computers, more dossiers, new tracking software, better guns, more tear gas, more body armor, more tactical Special Reaction Teams, and so on. Thus corrections bureaucracies grow, like most others.

As in the pages of Max Weber, the corrections "officialdom" becomes a parasitic interest group that expands and strengthens the bureaucracy upon which it feeds. This dynamic converts the purported ends ("public safety") into means for the bureaucrats' self-perpetuation. In California, the CDC prospers in an ecology of endless crisis: there must always be the threat of riot, perennial violence, overcrowding, and other public safety "needs" to which more guards, more prisons, and more resources are the only answer. And so, this chapter ends near where it began, at the nexus of bureaucratic economic interest and the bountiful race war on the wedge-shaped yards of the Corcoran SHU, where chaos brings manna from Sacramento — $4 billion a year, to be exact.[94]

CHAPTER ELEVEN

BIG BUCKS FROM THE BIG HOUSE: THE PRISON INDUSTRIAL COMPLEX AND BEYOND

What business enterprise could conceivably succeed with
the rate of recall of its products that we see in the "products"
of our prisons?
Chief Justice Warren E. Burger, 1985

I admit that I have a serious drug problem and am no angel –
but I am *not* an animal that needs to be locked up for the
rest of his life!
John J., serving life for burglary

It's like a hotel with a guaranteed occupancy.
Ron Garzini, private prison booster

In 1964 a tsunami swept over Crescent City, California, completely destroy-
ing the downtown. Only nine people died but the town – nestled just below
the Oregon border – never recovered. It was rebuilt as a shabby imitation
of southern California's worst planning examples; empty parking spaces and
box-like buildings dominate the landscape.

In 1989 another tsunami hit – and this time the tidal wave was political. The California Department of Corrections rolled in, and with little

opposition built the sprawling $277.5 million Pelican Bay State Prison, one of the newest, meanest super-max lockups in the system. Pelican Bay, an international model of sensory deprivation and isolation, deems half its inmates incorrigible and locks them away in the SHU, twenty-three hours a day. The prison is also Crescent City and Del Norte County's largest employer – and in many ways the region's new colonial master.

The new prison's political and economic clout is all-the-more exaggerated due to Crescent City's extreme isolation and poverty. Only four of the area's seventeen sawmills are still in operation, commercial salmon fishing is dead, and during the mid eighties 164 businesses went under. By the time the CDC came scouting for a new prison site, unemployment had breached 20 percent. Del Norte County, with Crescent City at its heart, was in a seemingly terminal economic torpor. Prison was its only hope.

To clinch a deal with the CDC local boosters found a piece of cheap unincorporated land, fed water, sewer, and power lines to it, and otherwise soothed local anxieties about hosting several thousand criminals. Today in Crescent City the emerging American police state means economic survival; Pelican Bay provides 1,500 jobs, an annual payroll of $50 million, and a budget of over $90 million. Indirectly, the prison has created work in everything from construction and pumping gas to domestic violence counseling. Just the contract for hauling away the prison's garbage is worth $130,000 a year – big money in California's poorest county. Following the employment boom came almost 6,000 new residents: Del Norte's population (including 4,000 prisoners) is now 28,000. In the last ten years the average rate of housing starts has doubled, as has the value of local real estate.[1]

Also cashing in on the action is a huge Ace Hardware, a private hospital, and a 90,000-square-foot K-mart, selling everything from toothpaste to Spice Girl paraphernalia. Across from K-mart is an equally mammoth Safeway. "In 1986 the county collected $73 million in sales tax; last year it was $142 million," says County Assessor Jerry Cochran.

On top of that, local government is saving money by using low-security "level one" prisoners in place of public works crews. Between January 1990 and December 1996, Pelican Bay inmates worked almost 150,000 hours on everything from school grounds to public buildings. According to one report, the prison labor, billed at the meager sum of $7 per hour, would have cost the county at least $766,300. "Without the prison we wouldn't exist," says Cochran.

THE PRISON INDUSTRIAL COMPLEX

Little town and big prison: it is a marriage that has been replicated scores of times in recent years. From Bowling Green, Missouri, to rural Florida, economically battered towns are rolling over for new prisons. Nationally, the tab for building penitentiaries has averaged about $7 billion annually over the last decade; in 1996 alone contractors broke ground on twenty-six federal and ninety-six state prisons. Estimates for the yearly expenses of incarceration run between $20 and $35 billion annually, and one report has more than 523,000 full-time employees working in American corrections – more than in any *Fortune* 500 company except General Motors.[2] In the American countryside punishment is such a big industry that, according to the National Criminal Justice Commission, 5 percent of the growth in rural population between 1980 and 1990 was accounted for by prisoners, captured in cities and exiled to the new carceral arcadia.[3]

Is prison building the current delivery system for Keynesian stimulus in a post–Cold War, demilitarized America? Is the emerging prison industrial complex replacing or augmenting that behemoth constellation of civilian government, military power, and private capital that Eisenhower dubbed the "military industrial complex" and which for two generations has been America's *de facto* industrial policy? This is the line argued by a few on the left and, to some extent, by writers in the *Wall Street Journal* and *Atlantic Monthly*. But this analysis begs several questions. First, is the military industrial complex – driven by the Pentagon budget – withering and being transformed piece by piece into a domestic war machine? A glance at the facts suggests not. The 1999 Pentagon budget topped $297 billion, the greatest in real terms ever, and six to ten times the total annual tab for incarceration. So while Heckler and Koch and other arms dealers may be pushing their wares on America's cops and fomenting a paramilitary culture, and Wackenhut sinks more capital into private prisons, these expansions are not *forced* by a peace-driven Pentagon downswing.

Nonetheless, we might ask: are *specific* corporate interests *driving* criminal justice policy, as is often the case with military policy? This "prison as Pentagon" argument generally cites three ways in which incarceration bolsters capitalism: broad Keynesian stimulus (as in the case of Crescent City), the privatization of prisons and prison-related services, and the exploitation of prison labor by private firms. All of these features of the prison industrial complex are important, but none of them — alone or together — explains *why* we are headed for what Jerome Miller calls a "gulag state."[4]

The rest of this chapter will explore each of the crucial points on the prison–business nexus, and then turn to another explanation for the lockdown economy, one based not on *direct* and *specific* corporate interests, but rather on an analysis of punishment and terror as class struggle from above.

CARCERAL KEYNESIANISM?

As with Pelican Bay and Crescent City, new prisons seem to gravitate towards the terrain of economic devastation. For example in 1994, Rome, New York, lost 5,000 jobs when Griffiss Air Force Base shut down. Exacerbating the crisis was Lockheed Martin's slow withdrawal of almost 1,000 well-paid jobs from nearby Utica. Chicago Pneumatic Tool Company also decamped to the sunny non-union climes of North Carolina, taking 430 more well-paid manufacturing jobs. But as this industrial base slipped away, new prospects emerged on the economic horizon: some of the best jobs in the region belonged to the 2,612 people employed at four nearby state prisons. And so the local boosters at the Rome Chamber of Commerce started lobbying for new dungeons in the hope of capturing a few more of those $36,000-a-year jobs.[5] In this case, prison was clearly a local solution to military and defense contractor restructuring; other areas of the country offer similar examples.

Victorville, in southern California's dry "Inland Empire," spent most of the nineties in an economic tailspin after George Air Force Base was shuttered in 1992, taking more than 5,000 military and civilian jobs with it. By late 1998 town leaders were aggressively courting the Federal Bureau of Prisons in an attempt to win the right to host a new 1,900-bed, $60 million prison just outside town. The new lockup promised to deliver anywhere from 250 to 800 jobs and a $1 to $2 million annual payroll.[6]

Not far from Victorville is the hamlet of Blythe, the victim of nearly two decades under the yoke of the chronically low price of its agricultural produce. Blythe's first move toward economic resuscitation was the 1988 arrival of a big new penitentiary. Civic boosters liked the first joint so much they won themselves a second in 1995.[7] Other agricultural areas are also trying to make the switch from produce to prison. For example, South Bay, Florida, "the town that lettuce built," is prime incarceration country. Less than sixty miles from moneyed and manicured Palm Beach, South Bay is nestled on the southern edge of Lake Okeechobee. Economically speaking the town is light years away from Florida's tourist simulacrum: with 3,500 residents, South Bay is the land of trailer parks, cane fields, and unemployment. When there was talk of building a $32 million prison in the area, the town fathers jumped. Even before South Bay Growers, one of the nation's largest producers of winter vegetables, fired 1,336 workers and switched from labor-intensive row crops to highly automated sugarcane production, the surrounding area had an unemployment rate of 22 percent. The planned South Bay Correctional Facility – a piece of Wackenhut's transnational private prison empire – promised up to 400 jobs and an $11 million annual payroll. To cement the deal the Palm Beach County Commission donated a plot of land worth $300,000. "This is one of those win–win propositions . . . We're determined to see that bad people stay in prison a lot longer," reassured the economically practical Governor Lawton Chiles.[8] While the multiplier effect of prison salaries will staunch some of the economic damage in and around South Bay, it will not create prosperity.

One of the saddest attempts at prison-based growth was a case in northern Missouri, where local boosters offered to retrofit the defunct Tarkio College into a minimum security pen. Such schemes to convert bases, factories, or schools rarely come to fruition because contractors prefer building from scratch.[9] After all, most prison builders can get land for free from desperate local governments. In 1989, Florence, Colorado, bought 600 acres of ranch land for $100,000 and gave it to the Bureau of Prisons, which proceeded to build four major lockups there.[10] In the early nineties this sort of prison-courting by way-of-subsidy reached absurd proportions. In 1991, recession-ravaged Appleton, Minnesota, population 1,552, sold $28.5 million in municipal bonds and built a city-owned, state-of-the-art, medium-security prison on a fallow soybean field. "The world has written us off," explained a city bureaucrat. "It's up to us and us alone. Nobody is going to help bail us out."[11] Fueled by desperate optimism and little else, the Appleton prison found itself unable to fill a single cell nor meet its debt obligation until mid 1993.[12]

Even in the best of situations prison stimulus is often overestimated. In Florence, Colorado, home of those four Bureau of Prisons penitentiaries, the economic payback and linkages have been less than expected. About 30 percent of the prison's employees live outside the county, commute huge distances, and end up spending and paying taxes elsewhere. While a local firm has the garbage contract, most prison purchasing is done on a regional and national level, thus bypassing local retailers. To top it all off the pens pay no property taxes.[13]

Prison stimulus can also mean economic distortion. In oil-busted Fort Stockton, Texas, two big prisons meant an influx of relatively well-paid construction workers and then guards, all of which triggered a mini real estate bubble and skyrocketing rents. Crescent City, California, suffered a similar housing crunch. In Fort Stockton, even the optimists saw the town's new economic function as bringing only a short-term reprieve: "Growth," said one, "will probably continue for the next two to three years."[14] In the southern end of California's Central Valley, near the prisons of Avenal, Corcoran, North Kern, Pleasant Valley, and Wasco, the incarceration industry has put such a strain on the local schools, sewers, roads, and medical services that the state was recently forced to dole out $2 million in mitigation funds.[15]

And what of prison building's spin-off effects? After all, the economic magic of military Keynesianism is worked not through the wages of soldiers as much as it is through bomb building's concatenated forms of technological and industrial spin-off. Cold War pork spending and government incubation of defense industries has helped develop the US interstate highway system, state universities, commercial jets, most of telecommunications including the Internet, the microprocessor, fiber optics, and laser surgery. All of these institutions and technologies were hatched with government money in government-subsidized universities; and all were directly, or indirectly, part of the technological race against Soviet socialism. In short, the American high-tech sector is a byproduct of Pentagon spending. No such economic linkages can be attributed to the prison boom. Rather, the best it can offer is the occasional example, such the growth at Pueblo Community College: thanks to the high number of penitentiaries located in the Pueblo to Cañon City corridor, the college's criminal justice program has gone from several dozen students in 1985 to a current enrollment of about 600.[16] In fact, criminal justice and justice administration programs are on the rise nationwide.[17] But this cottage industry, in what amounts to vocational training in the arts of repression and file keeping, hardly compares to the Cold War–inspired high-tech revolution.

Besides the quantitative question of growth, prison stimulus has disturbing qualitative implications. Like prison itself, the incarceration business often advances racist agendas. In the prison economy, people of color are the fodder: two-thirds of all prison admissions are Black or Latino people. Meanwhile, downwardly mobile white working class men are most often the keepers. In most states well over half of all guards are white men. As the guarding profession grows, the demographics of public employment tend to skew towards the profile of the white male turnkey. Due to the rise of rural prisons, white men in Illinois still get more than half of all newly created public sector jobs, while the percentage of white women and people of color employed by the state has declined throughout the 1990s. Former Illinois governor Jim Edgar explained the increasingly pallid complexion of public employment thus: "One of the few areas we've hired people in the last two years has been for prisons in down-state Illinois and, unfortunately, that isn't where you necessarily recruit a lot of minorities."[18] Thus cleavages of race, class, and geography are enlisted to reproduce and manage an unfair economic system.

In conclusion, it is safe to say that incarceration is a small-scale form of Keynesian, public-works-style stimulus. New penitentiaries can revive economically moribund regions and, acting as anchor industries, can bring in other employers such as medical services and retail chains. But these pockets of pork-driven prosperity remain tiny islands in a vast sea of stagnant agriculture, deindustrialization, and what we might call post-organized, downgraded manufacturing. The gulag provides opportunities for localized growth but it does not and will not assume the mantle of *de facto* industrial policy, because it cannot and will not replace the economic role of military and aerospace spending.

PRIVATE PRISONS

Another player in the matrix of interests referred to as the prison industrial complex is the fast-growing and powerful private prison industry. Through assiduous cultivation of state officials the private prison industry is increasingly active in shaping criminal justice policy, but its partnership with the state also faces problems: recent events have unveiled private jailers as cheats, liars, and liabilities.

For-profit lockups currently control some 5 percent of all US prison beds; they make huge profits and spend amply to sway politicians and public opinion. The current round of private incarceration began with a Reagan-sponsored experiment to house INS detainees at private detention centers in Houston and Laredo, Texas. The architect of the plan was Attorney General Meese (who now works at a for-profit, pro-privatization think-tank). In response to the federal government's broad invitation to capital, a pair of Tennessee entrepreneurs, using money from Kentucky Fried Chicken and the know-how of several public sector corrections veterans, set up the first private prison company, Corrections Corporation of America. At the apex of this fast-growing empire is a troika of well-connected good old boys: Doctor Crants, CCA's president and visionary; his old West Point room-mate, CCA co-founder Tom Beasley, who quite conveniently served a stint as chairman of the Tennessee Republican Party; and finally, providing the technical expertise, is T. Don Hutto, former commissioner of the Virginia and Arkansas Departments of Corrections.[19] Others board members include corrections veterans such as Michael Quinlan, former director of the Federal Bureau of Prisons.

For most of the eighties and early nineties, CCA, like its competitors, concerned itself with cherry-picking: seeking easy-to-handle contracts for minimum security prisons. This was a prudent attempt to prove that private capital could handle society's cast-off populations without any major explosions. But CCA and the others soon set out for bigger prizes. Fifteen years after the first "experimental" incarceration of immigrants, corporate jailers now control roughly 100,000 prison beds nationwide in over a hundred different facilities in twenty-seven different states.[20] CCA's market share is approximately 52 percent of all privatized American prison beds.[21] Globally, its empire includes seventy-eight prisons holding more than 63,000 beds in twenty-five states, the District of Columbia, Puerto Rico, Australia, and the United Kingdom. However, the company's political and geographic strong-hold remains Tennessee, where it dumps inmates from Wisconsin, Hawaii, Montana, the District of Columbia, and Puerto Rico into a sprawling, barely regulated private prison system.

Financially CCA has performed handsomely. One investment firm dubbed it "a theme stock for the nineties."[22] In 1995 the company went pub-lic at $8 a share: by the year's end the price had soared 462.5 percent to $37. However, recent scandals and increasing disenchantment among state legislators have brought CCA stock down to roughly half its peak value. But the company, capitalized at $3.5 billion, is still a "secure" investment and growth remains strong.[23] To maintain market dominance CCA does things the old fashioned way: giving generously to politicians and buttering up the press. In recent years Doctor Crants has distributed more campaign money to Tennessee politicians than any other individual.[24] The company also operates a robust lobbying operation in D.C. and in several states where it has investments.[25]

The next largest private jailer is Wackenhut Corrections, with about 17,000 beds at twenty-four facilities. Named after its founder, former FBI agent George Wackenhut, the firm is a subsidiary of Wackenhut's private security service, which made it big more than forty years ago by scooping up contracts to guard America's nuclear waste dumps and testing installations. Wackenhut also did some freelance spooking: by the late sixties the corporation had dossiers on three million American "potential subversives." This was the largest collection of private surveillance files in American history and was later handed over to the FBI. By the 1970s and 1980s the company had expanded into strike-breaking and guarding US embassies. George Wackenhut still runs the business from his castle-like mansion in Florida and from the deck of his yacht, *Top Secret*. Since going public in 1994, Wackenhut's stock price has soared 800 percent and split once.[26] The company's board of directors is, like CCA's, a juice-laden den of far-right political muckety-mucks, including Frank Carlucci, former NSA advisor to President Reagan; Bobby Inman, formerly deputy director of the CIA; and for a long time, the now deceased Jorge Mas Conosa of the Miami-Cuban lunatic fringe and the Clinton inner circle.

Behind CCA and Wackenhut is a hungry pack of some sixteen other firms that run local jails, private prisons, and INS detention centers. Underwriting the growth of both public and private prisons are a battery of mainstream financial houses. It is estimated that giant Wall Street firms such as Goldman Sachs, and Merrill Lynch write between $2 and 3 billion in prison construction bonds every year.[27] And like any self-preserving "industrial complex," the private prison sector is cultivating a coterie of paid opinion makers. Most notable is the Private Prisons Project at the University of Florida, Gainesville, which receives over $60,000 in grants every year from private jailers. The project's staff of researchers focuses on tutoring journalists and churning out predigested policy briefs which are spoon-fed to state and federal lawmakers. The center's director, Charles W. Thomas, has been quoted literally hundreds of times as a non-partisan expert, despite the fact that he personally owns stock in CCA, Wackenhut, and a slew of other for-profit dungeons. Private prison firms have also flown journalists to plush overseas hotels with limousines on call.[28] Swimming alongside the big fish of incarceration are schools of for-profit caterers, prison HMOs, private transport companies, architecture firms, and other subcontractors that feed at the margins of the prison industrial complex.

So clearly we have the formation of an "industrial complex" in the original sense of the word, a government-backed juggernaut of mutually reinforcing corporate interests. These companies are led by people – powerfully connected men – with sophisticated political agendas and who are positioning for long-term growth and political influence.

A MORE EFFICIENT GULAG?

But what of the great savings so loudly and frequently proclaimed by the private jailers' academic and journalistic claque?[29] The most definitive test of such assumptions was a broad 1996 study by the General Accounting Office, which reviewed and compared all the major studies of private prisons' cost and quality conducted since 1991. The GAO was less than enthusiastic in its appraisal of private lockups: "These studies do not offer substantial evidence that savings have occurred."[30]

Generally, the GAO found that public and private prisons cost taxpayers roughly the same. For example, a study from Louisiana found that "average inmate costs per day for the two private facilities studied were $23.75 and $23.34, respectively, and the comparable daily operational costs for the public facility studied were $23.55 per inmate." Most studies reviewed by the GAO did not address quality of service, as calculated by rate of assault, injury, or inmate and staff satisfaction. The two studies that did address such criteria reported "equivocal findings."[31]

To the extent that private prisons do save on expenses, most of the surplus goes not to the state but, rather, takes the form of corporate *profit*. That is after all the private jailers' raison d'être. And the drive towards lower costs – that is, the drive toward greater profit – engenders various other problems. Private prisons make money by cutting corners, which means skimping on food, staffing, medicine, education, and other services for convicts. It also means fielding poorly trained, ill-equipped, non-unionized, and often brutal guards. Exploitation of staff leads to high turnover rates, while the drive to keep overhead low means that many open positions remain vacant for months on end. One private prison in Florida, according to state audits, had an annual staff turnover rate of 200 percent.[32]

Private prisons also achieve economies by eliminating labor through specially designed, automated "hands-off" prisons. Eric Bates describes what happens at new private prisons when the panopticon meets the bottom line:

> The design of the "control room" will enable a guard to simultaneously watch three "pods" of 250 prisoners each. Windows in the elevated room afford an unobstructed view of each cell block below, and "vision blocks" in the floor are positioned over each entranceway so guards can visually identify anyone being admitted. The high-tech panel at the center of the room can open any door at the flick of a switch.[33]

Such futuristic profit pens are built to function with no more than five guards controlling 750 inmates, or at least that is the plan. "It was bizarre," explained a former guard from one such joint. "One time I was working central control and there were 200 to 300 inmates wandering the halls."[34]

PRIVATE HELL

Private prisons produce a unique set of "externalities." The first political rumbling from within the bowels of the CCA empire came borne on clouds of pepper spray and smoke in the summer of 1995. Prisoners from North Carolina – homesick, ill-treated, and packed into a Tennessee house of corrections – trashed and burnt two of their dorms. The riot lasted several hours and was only put down when CCA's overwhelmed guards finally handed over operations to local SWAT commandos.[35] Another dent in the image of for-profit prisons was the riot at an INS detention facility run by Esmore Correctional Services, which housed non-criminal, would-be migrants awaiting immigration hearings. The "facility" in question was actually nothing more than a Motel 6, retrofitted with bars, bunks, and fences. Packed into tiny rooms with no access to exercise or other activities, the detainees endured months on end of stultifying boredom, bad food, smelly toilets, and humiliation at the hands of Esmore rent-a-cops. On June 18, 1995, desperation peaked; the three hundred detainees finally exploded, trashing their rooms, smashing up toilets and burning mattresses. After the riot was suppressed, twenty-five immigrants were transferred to the Union County jail, where guards administered methodical punishment beatings.[36]

Since these first conflagrations, private prisons have become known for their lack of services, brutality, frequent escapes, and inmate violence. But the industry's reputation reached a new nadir on July 25, 1998, when six Washington, D.C., prisoners busted out of the CCA-owned Northeast Ohio Correctional Center in Youngstown, Ohio. Built to house 1,700 medium security prisoners from D.C. and other jurisdictions the Youngstown joint (Ohio's only private dungeon) was plagued with problems from the moment it opened in May 1997. Poorly constructed, understaffed, and immediately filled to capacity with both medium *and* maximum security convicts, the CCA prison became a chaotic gladiator's pit where nonviolent burglars and crack addicts were haphazardly thrust into cells with seasoned rapists, habitual killers, and other high-security predators. The fifteen months of operations preceding the escapes saw forty-four assaults, sixteen stabbings (including one guard), and two murders. When state inspectors finally did arrive, they were turned away at the gate.[37]

But it was the news that six very angry young men from Washington, D.C., had cut open CCA's chain-link fence, crossed an electrified barrier, plowed through yards of razor wire and were now at large among the good people of Youngstown that really sent shock waves of fear throughout Ohio, and, for different reasons, throughout the ranks of CCA investors.[38] For almost a week regular police, tactical squads, canine teams, and helicopters combed an ever widening circle around the prison in search of the runaways. One by one cops busted the desperate, exhausted escapees, some of whom had been badly wounded by the razor wire. The last escaped inmate, Vincent Smith, was finally taken down in the backyard of Susie Ford's house. A 54-year-old grandmother of three living on the outskirts of Youngstown, Ms. Ford got the news live – when her frantic sister telephoned telling her to turn on the television: "That's our building! That's our building!" Indeed it was. And the Ford sisters watched their screens in amazement as police swarmed through the shrubs out back.[39]

The next months brought a cascade of revelations and inquiries. It seemed CCA's rent-a-cop security force was not only ill-equipped and poorly trained but battered by employer racism and reckless penny-pinching. The new prison was so unsafe, staff were soon deserting in droves. "I stopped counting at seventy," said Victoria Wheeler, a former CCA guard. Another former CO, Linda Carnahan, recalled how she was sent, completely untrained in the use of firearms, to patrol the perimeter with a shotgun. "I told my captain that if we had an escape, I didn't know how to pick up a gun and shoot it. He said go out there anyway." CCA had deliberately passed on firearms training because state certification costs up to $3,000 per person.[40]

A later report by the GAO found, among other things, that 80 percent of the CCA guards had no corrections experience; many of the guards were only eighteen or nineteen years old; prison medical records went unaccounted for while more than 200 chronically ill inmates were left untreated in general population; and almost no effort was made to separate violent psychos from peaceful convicts. Later inmate civil rights suits alleged that guards violated regulations by using tear gas inside; that prison tactical teams dragged inmates naked and shackled across floors; and that during cell searches convicts were forced to strip, kneel, and were shocked with stun guns if they moved. One female clerical worker – made to inventory inmate processions during such a cell raid – summed it up thus: "I told my roommate that the guards here are like people who got beat up in high school and this was their way of getting back at the world."[41]

The ongoing pandemonium in the Youngstown joint was a product of CCA's greed. So eager were the boys in Tennessee to start counting ducats that they rushed to fill the new prison by importing 150 convicts per day until the prison was full. Normal procedure in opening a new penitentiary is to process only 80 to 100 inmates *per week*, so as to check for security flaws.[42] But CCA was reimbursed per day, per inmate. Adding insult to injury, CAA had won handsome concessions from Youngstown just for building the penitentiary. Ravaged by deindustrialization, with an official unemployment rate of over 10 percent, the city had supplicated CCA in the usual fashion: fawning civic boosters gave CCA a hundred acres of prime real estate (much of it aggressively annexed from a smaller town) and an $11 million tax break.[43] Coincidentally, the tax abatement was directly proportional to that year's Youngstown City School District budget deficit. In fact the city's public schools – which had just eliminated 149 jobs and *closed* six schools – were in such horrible condition that Ohio State Auditor Jim Petro declared a fiscal emergency.[44]

Even before CCA inmates had "hit the fence," local police and democratic lawmakers were having second thoughts about the efficacy of hosting scam artists from Tennessee and their captives from the District of Columbia. For one thing, neither the city nor the state had any regulatory control over CCA, in part because none of the convicts was from Ohio. When a state legislative bill designed to impose limited control on CCA was set to become law, the company's president David L. Myers killed it with a lobbying blitzkrieg that included personally calling lawmakers at home with threats to abandon the Youngstown prison and take its 400 jobs elsewhere.[45] Nonetheless the breakout caused a change of heart among legislators, and all further moves to expand private prisons in Ohio were blocked. In response to this and other political heat, CCA began experimenting with PR retailing in the form of "fuzzy" TV commercials intoning, "CCA. Quietly going about the business of public safety."[46]

The Youngstown debacle was not particularly unique, just well publicized. And despite the fact that for-profit jailers try to keep their captives away from the press (in Youngstown CCA put a gag order on prisoners), the bad publicity is mounting. For example, at Brazoria County Detention Center in Angleton, Texas (a Capital Correctional Resources Incorporated facility), guards made a "training video" of themselves beating, stun-gunning, and siccing dogs on naked prisoners from Missouri. Injured inmates were dragged, face down back to their cells. After the screws' rampage, cell block telephones were cut off, preventing the Missouri captives from calling home.[47] The video was later obtained by lawyers and broadcast nationally. On it a guard taunts: "Gentlemen, you might not like it here, but this is the way it is. Do what you're told."[48]

The sadism of Brazoria was the hybrid result of power-tripping guards and institutional greed: CCRI paid its bulls only $8 an hour, gave them little training, and hired convicted felons. One of the video's star performers, the CO Wilton David Wallace, had served six months in federal prison in 1984, for abusing inmates while employed as a Texas state prison guard. The CCRI-leased jail/prison was also abusing its charges in less dramatic ways: a typical menu revealed endless lunches of black-eyed peas, corn bread, and water. The punishment diet was peanut butter sandwiches and water.[49] In 1996, fourteen convicts and two guards were injured at a CCA prison in

Texas when convicts rioted to protest at poor food, inadequate recreation, and other problems.[50]

At a Wackenhut facility in New Mexico, a supervisor ordered his subordinates to beat a verbally belligerent prisoner. According to a state investigation, inmate Tommy McManaway was restrained and repeatedly kicked in the groin while lying face down on the floor. When the assault was exposed the supervisor told two lieutenants and a sergeant to "stick to their stories and he would back them up."[51] Most of the time, abuse in private pens is kept hidden by just this method.

Not long ago, more bad news emerged from a CCA joint in Tennessee which housed exiles from Wisconsin. The trouble began when a CCA screw was attacked, beaten, and left in a coma. The following "investigation" took a brutal and arbitrary form. A seven-member "SORT" team – these are CCA tactical units, based outside the prisons and called in to do the heavy lifting – tortured between fifteen and twenty prisoners with beatings and electric shock.[52] At first both CCA and Wisconsin officials dismissed inmate complaints and suits, but as evidence mounted, and family members protested, the cover-up collapsed. Wisconsin State officials and the FBI began investigating and several CCA staff were canned.[53] Overall, Tennessee officials say the rate of serious incidents at CCA prisons is sometimes as much as 28 percent higher than in state prisons.[54]

Private juvenile facilities have also been exposed as abusive. One such outfit in Colorado, operated by Rebound Corporation and housing 184 teenage felons, was shut down because it overused restraints, allowed sex between staff and inmates, and in other ways physically abused its wards – all of which culminated in the preventable suicide of a thirteen-year-old boy. In 1998, South Carolina canceled a juvenile contract with CCA after numerous escapes, allegations of excessive force, and documentation of torture by claustrophobia in which as many as eighteen boys were packed into a one-person cell with only cups for toilets.[55]

News of such abuse and growing opposition from organized labor has begun to hamper the expansion of private prisons. Even Tennessee Governor Don Sundquist, an ardent supporter of for-profit incarceration, was moved to propose a ban on private prisons that release out-of-state inmates in Tennessee or house out-of-state sex offenders and habitual escapees. He also called for private prisons to reimburse the state for the costs of post-escape manhunts and riot suppression.[56]

SCREWS, BULLS, AND COMPLICATED AGENDAS

Interestingly, the most important check on the private gulag's expansion is the growing political muscle of unionized prison guards. As incarceration in general booms, so too do the ranks, assets, and raw power of organized COs. In recent years guards have taken tentative steps to check the expansion of for-profit jailers. The union that set the model and still leads the fight against privatization is the California Correctional Peace Officers Association (CCPOA).

Originally little more than a moribund social club, the CCPOA has become one of the most fearsome political machines in Californian history. Since 1983, the number of COs in California has ballooned from 1,600 to more than 28,000 and their real salaries have more than doubled to an average of $41,000. The CCPOA now commands a budget of $17 million, an assault force of twenty-two in-house lawyers, and a huge political war chest. In just the first half of 1998 the guards doled out over $1 million in political contributions.[57]

The CCPOA's chieftain is the fedora-wearing, savvy and pugnacious Don Novey, who cut his teeth as a rank-and-file bull, walking the tiers in Folsom from 1971 through 1986. Fluent in Polish and German – thanks to stints at the Defense Language Institute and the Counter Intelligence Institute in Washington, D.C. and service with the Army's 503rd Counter Intelligence Division in Europe from 1969 to 1971 – Novey took control of the union presidency through a contested election in 1980. It was the eve of the great incarceration boom, and through serendipity, hard work, and prudent public relations, the CCPOA was set to expand apace. Priority number one was remolding the turnkeys' public image: Novey started cultivating friends in the press corps, sent guards (whom he insists on calling corrections officers) to give toys to hospitalized children, and dubbed the COs' mission inside "the toughest beat in the state."[58] He also increased guard training, improved their uniforms and weaponry, and established a formidable legal machine to defend the rank and file against suits and disciplinary hearings. Most important of all, Novey bought politicians.

While the CCPOA has lavished lawmakers with cash, giving former California governor Pete Wilson almost $1 million to win the election in 1990, its power is disproportionately larger than its war chest. The California

Teachers Association gives almost as much as the CCPOA and its membership outnumbers the CCPOA's ten to one, but the teachers get very little for their cash.[59] Along with money and organization the CCPOA has commanded the ideological high ground issue of the 1990s: crime. Being tough on crime has become a right-wing litmus test. The issue of crime, unlike education, has a visceral power rivaled only by the once mighty anti-communist hysteria. The CCPOA has assiduously courted this public fear and pandered to desires for strong and simple solutions.

No strategy illustrates this better than CCPOA involvement with the victims' rights movement, a right-wing form of political "astro-turf" – that is, a bought and paid for pseudo "grassroots" activism. More than fourteen crime victims' groups – at least five of them formed since the election/riot year of 1992 – are active in legislative politics. Novey's CCPOA fertilizes much of this law-and-order populism by channeling funds – about $60,000 a year – to the movement through a CCPOA-controlled political action committee called Crime Victims United. Like the guards' other lobbyists, the CVU pushed hard for passage of California's "three strikes" legislation. Another group, the Three Strikes You're Out Committee, used more than $100,000 of CCPOA money to launch the infamous sentencing law in 1994. Such spending also pays off in the form of political appointments: Republicans funded by the CCPOA have given luminaries in the victims' rights lobby crucial policy appointments. These appointees in turn pressure to keep sentences long, cut down on parole, and recommend the creation of new criminal statutes.[60] A so-called "victims' rights day" even serves as the CCPOA's annual political gala. There, surrounded by empty coffins symbolizing the multitude of murder victims, Novey bequeathes the CCPOA's official favor upon that season's political darling. For a long time that was Republican Attorney General Dan Lungeren, but in 1998 he was snubbed for the Democratic governor-to-be Gray Davis.[61]

OPPOSING PRIVATIZATION

Despite being a solidly right-wing organization that would cannibalize most social spending to advance the cause of prison building, the CCPOA still represents workers – even if they are salaried, paramilitary, state functionaries. Thus it viciously opposes privatization. "We call them dungeons for dollars because their allegiance is to stockholders, not to the public," says CCPOA spokesman, Lance Corcoran. The CCPOA even draws on left-liberal sources in its fight against Wackenhut, CCA, and the rest. For example, its magazine *Peacekeeper* reprinted an article with an anti-privatization spin from the *Village Voice* by the well-known progressive journalist Jennifer Gonnerman.

But while the might of the CCPOA has kept private prisons at bay for a decade and a half (there are private jails, federal prisons, and half-way houses in California), it is not clear how much longer that situation will prevail.[62] In what lobbyist Jeff Thompson called "our Gettysburg," a CCA hireling and Democratic state senator, Richard Polanco, has pushed through legislation to build a 2,000-inmate private prison in California City, a dusty hamlet in the Mojave desert. "Build and they will come," says Polanco, echoing the standard refrain from CCA flacks. As yet it is not clear whether the inmates to fill the CCA foothold will be from California or elsewhere.[63] Despite this setback, other guards around the country are finally beginning to follow the CCPOA example.

In most states the COs' road to political power leads through the American Federation of State, County, and Municipal Employees (AFSCME), whose Corrections United subdivision represents 100,000 publicly employed prison guards. Calling private prisons "a threat to public safety" and "a taxpayer rip-off," AFSCME president Gerald McEntee has stepped into the fray, producing a sixteen-page report and a video on problems associated with private pens.[64] But the more interesting AFSCME actions against the for-profit jailers are happening on the ground, at the local level. In Pennsylvania, for example, three hundred guards marched outside the Pennsylvania Department of Corrections shouting "Death to privatization." This, and intensive lobbying, forced free-market-loving Governor Tom Ridge to kill plans for leasing the state's newest lockup to a private company.[65] In Wisconsin, the State Employees Union, led by Green Bay prison guard Gary Lonzo, has effectively blocked privatization. "These privateers come in, and they're only in it for one reason," says Lonzo. "They're not going to build a prison in Wisconsin unless they make money. And to make money, they have to pay generally substandard wages, [and provide] less training and less programming."[66] Privatization in Virginia, with one for-profit dungeon, has also run into opposition from angry AFSCME guards. And when Nebraska guards flexed, state legislators shut the door on Wackenhut, which had been trying to grab a piece of that state's prison system. Privatizers in Iowa are also facing well-organized COs who decry privatization as a "prescription for disaster" and use their weight with the Board of Corrections to shut out for-profit jailers. "This isn't for rent-a-cops," explained prison guard Wade Erickson.[67] Even before the Youngtown escape, four hundred Ohio guards protesting any further privatization converged on the statehouse. "The next thing you know, they're going to want to privatize another, then another one, then another," said a guard in a skunk-skin hat which, as he explained, signified the odor of CCA.[68]

Perhaps the most dramatic campaign against prison privatization occurred in Tennessee, CCA's own gently rolling Siberia. In 1997 the company launched plans to take over the state's *entire* prison system. For a moment, CCA-drafted legislation was teetering on the brink of passage; it even seemed that the company had won the consent of union leadership. But a counteroffensive, involving churches, student groups, and the 2,000 rank-and-file prison guards of the Tennessee State Employees Association tipped the scales. Using the Internet to link forces and disseminate information (much of it leaked by CCA prisoners and disgruntled employees), the coalition forced the pro-privatization politicians and waffling union leaders to back down. By October 1998 there was another attempt at total privatization, which triggered a protest by some 2,000 guards at the governor's office and the nearby CCA world headquarters. As political backdrop the COs had the spectacle of yet another big escape: four inmates had just busted out of CCA's South Central Correctional Facility in Clifton, Tennessee, and were still at large.[69]

The politics of guard unionism are wrought with contradictions: they have been instrumental in creating and shaping the prison industrial complex by bolstering hawkish anti-crime politicians and lobbying for get-tough legislation like three strikes. And the CO unions, in California and elsewhere, have protected their rank-and-file members against any and all disciplinary procedures. However, in their fight against privatization the guards defend not only their own interests but inadvertently the larger agenda of public accountability and democratic control over state functions. As bad as public prisons are, private one are worse, both in fact and in principle.

PRISON LABOR: SAVIOR, DEMON, OR DUD?

Another important piece of the prison industrial complex is the exploitation of prison labor by private and state-owned companies. Convict labor, seen as efficient economics and moral just deserts, has developed many powerful champions in recent years, among them Senator Phil Gramm, who said he wants "to turn every federal prison in this country into a mini industrial park." Edwin Meese, former US attorney general and architect of the Reagan-era war on drugs, has also taken up the cause, editorializing in the *Wall Street Journal* that "the time is ripe to reduce the cost of incarceration by expand-ing inmate work programs." As early as the 1970s, the conservative Supreme Court Justice Warren Burger was calling for prisons to become "factories with fences." Are we poised for a mass expansion in convict labor? Is prison labor driving the big round-up?

Already American convicts toil for private firms making copper faucets, blue jeans, circuit boards for nuclear power plants, and stretch limousines. In San Diego prisoners working for CMT Blues were employed tearing "made in Honduras" labels off T-shirts and replacing them with labels reading "made in USA." Other convicts take reservations for TWA, work at telemarketing and data entry, and slaughter ostriches for export to Europe. In Washington State, *Prison Legal News*'s Paul Wright uncovered evidence that a company called Exmark uses a "flexible" pool of prison laborers to package everything from Microsoft Windows 95 to Starbucks Coffee products to JanSport gear and undertakes "literature assembly" for telecommunications giant US WEST. Subcontractors for Eddie Bauer and Victoria's Secret have also used inmate workers. Meanwhile, in Louisiana CCA has teamed up with the work-clothes manufacturer Company Apparel Safety Items (CASI) in the nation's first part-nership between a private prison and a private manufacturer.[70]

This current wave of prison labor began with the Federal Prison Industries Enhancement (PIE) Act of 1979, which allowed private corporations to enter "joint ventures" with state prisons for the first time since the New Deal. During the 1930s, labor militancy and the moral scandal of Southern con-vict leasing inspired Congress to pass the Hawes–Cooper Act and then the more stringent Ashworth–Summers Act, which imposed local regulation on convict leasing and made it a felony to transport or sell prison-made goods across state lines. But in the two decades since the advent of the PIE program, over fifty different joint ventures have begun in thirty-two states.[71] According to PIE rules, a joint venture must consult local unions before starting up, pay "prevailing wages" (which in practice usually means minimum wage), and must not displace existing employment. Most work in prison pays only pennies per hour, but even in PIE joint ventures 80 percent of the convict's remuneration is taken by the state in the form of taxes, room and board, victim restitution, court fines, and mandatory savings or family support payments. So while PIE inmate workers are "paid" minimum wage they usually only receive between 65 cents and $1.50 an hour.

More numerous than these PIE joint ventures are the state-owned "prison industries" which make everything from furniture and clothing, to food, road signs, and computers. Unlike the public–private joint ventures, the state-owned prison industries can only sell to other government agencies. Some state-owned firms, unable to sell to the private domestic market, can pitch their products internationally: one of the few that does is Oregon's UniGroup which sells convict-made jeans called "Prison Blues" in Japan and Italy.[72]

The largest single employer of prison labor – with 18,000 convicts making 150 different products – is Federal Prison Industries, also known as Unicor. The company is state-owned and can sell only to other federal agencies, but those markets are guaranteed, carved out for Unicor by law. Currently Unicor makes everything from safety goggles and wiring for Air Force fighter jets to body armor for the Border Patrol and road signs for the Park Service; in 1998 the firm produced $512 million in goods and services.[73]

Given all this hard work going on in the big house it would appear that America's 1.8 million prisoners are becoming a Third World within, a cheap and bountiful labor reservoir already being tapped by big business and Uncle Sam alike. Some observers even imply that the corporate desire to harness prison labor is driving prison expansion. But closer examination complicates this picture.

As of March 1998, after almost twenty years in operation, all of the nation's PIE joint ventures combined still had only 2,539 convicts working for private firms. Adding in Unicor workers and all the inmates who work in state-owned industries and local jail industries, and the total number of working inmates swells to 72,000. That is a big number, but it is still less than 5 percent of the entire incarcerated population; and proportionally fewer inmates work today than in 1980.[74] In other words, prison labor, while expanding, is not keeping pace with booming incarceration rates. Thus it is not driving the lockup binge. Add together the small number of inmates working and the wide array of products they make, plus the massive amount of press the subject receives (the Internet is filled with hundreds if not thousands of stories about "the new slavery"), and the prison labor boom appears to be a mile wide and only an inch deep.

This is not to suggest that prison labor is unimportant; politically and ideologically it is quite pernicious. And for the inmates who do the work, issues of fairness and safety are absolutely paramount. But in terms of explaining *why* the state, at every level and in every place, is so eager to plow people into prison, prison labor is a sideshow. Nor is prison labor a great source of profit. For example, in the state sector most prison industries end up *costing* the government money, or at best break even. This is suprising considering that public prison industries usually pay wages as low as 15 cents to $1.12 per hour. Despite these Third World wages penitentiary work programs – from Unicor to the California Prison Industry Authority (PIA) – almost always require hidden state subsidies and elaborate protections like guaranteed contracts and preferential bidding rules. For example, Unicor's contract "set asides" with federal agencies ensure it up to 50 percent of the market for federal office furniture. In this respect and others, Unicor operates under *ideal* business conditions; it is guaranteed a labor supply at absurdly low wages, is given direct subsidies, and has a guaranteed market. Yet Unicor is an economic basket case. If forced to compete with the private sector, it would collapse in a mater of months. Unicor products provided to the Department of Defense, on average, cost 13 percent more than the same goods supplied by private firms.[75] Navy officials say that, compared to the open market, Unicor's "product is inferior, costs more and takes longer to procure." The federal prison monopoly delivers 42 percent of its orders late, compared to an industry-wide average delinquency rate of only 6 percent. A 1993 report found that Unicor wire sold to the military failed at nearly *twice* the rate of the military's next worst supplier. "The stuff was poor quality," said Derek Vander Schaaf, the Pentagon's deputy inspector general, adding: "If you can't compete at 50 cents an hour for labor, guys, come on."[76]

At the state level, 25 percent of correctional industries reported net losses in 1994.[77] But this unflattering number is actually unrealistically low, because many industries that boast of profits in their annual reports fail to disclose the massive subsidies they receive. For example, California's PIA claims to be in the black, but state auditors tell a different story. In 1998 the PIA employed 7,000 of the state's 155,000 prisoners in everything from dairy farming to computer refurbishing, and operated with the usual pampering of guaranteed markets and obscenely low wages; and like Unicor, the PIA was unable to meet its costs. In fact the PIA is kept on life support, with operating subsidies and handsome capital outlay funding from the state worth more than $90 million.

Nor can the PIA offer savings to other state agencies. The California Legislative Analyst Office found that "state agencies could save $12 million annually if they were free to make purchases from other sources instead of the PIA."[78] Virginia's prison industries, which have become PIE-certified but cannot maintain many contracts, have also been blasted by state auditors for inefficiency and corruption. The financial hemorrhaging of Virginia Corrections Enterprises reaches mind-boggling proportions. VCE made pants at an average of $28.19 per pair, but was contracted to sell them to a private firm for $2.50 each. VCE made similar losses on numerous other products.[79] The company that purchases the finished pants did quite well but in this case it was taxation, not convict labor, that provided the subsidy.

Even in Texas — where all prisoners must work *and none gets paid a cent* — subsidies are the name of the game: the Texas Corrections Industries, with 8,000 convict laborers, is unable to pull its own weight and depends on financial reinforcement from the state. Nor can state prison industries which have sidestepped the PIE program lure in many private partners.[80] In short, prison industries are inefficient.

Such schemes can make money for the private firms that dare to venture inside but returns are rarely generous enough for many businesses to want to stick around. It remains easier and more profitable to do business on the outside. At first this seems puzzling. Decried as slavery by the left, boosted as super-efficient tough love by the right, and exaggerated in scale by both, prison labor is actually a small, not very profitable, part of the American gulag.

There are several concrete reasons why capital avoids the penitentiary. The first is lack of space. In many states day rooms and gymnasiums are filled with bunks, while the yards are full of prefab-dorms, so finding space for business workshops is difficult. Another hurdle is the morally tainted nature of prison-made products. For large corporations with retail profiles, the economies that might be gained in using prison labor are outweighed by the risk of generating bad publicity. Montgomery Ward, for example, has a company charter prohibiting the use of child, slave, or prison labor. Thus most firms that do exploit prison labor are small startups or subcontractors. But even these little fish find that the stigma of using captives as labor can blow up in their faces. One example of this was the short-lived, poorly conceived apparel company "Inkarcerated," which tried to market prison-made sportswear bearing the slogan "fitness is a life sentence." Unfortunately for Inkarcerated, few retailers cared to be associated with convict labor. The only business to sell the prison-besmirched merchandise was 24 Hour Fitness, the West Coast McDonald's of exercise salons. Eventually, Inkarcerated collapsed due to disinterest in its "controversial product."[81]

Fear of lawsuits also keeps business away from prisons; inmates are seen as aggressive and vexatious litigants. Another obstacle blocking capital's path into the big house is the CO. In California, business lobbies and the CCPOA often find themselves on the same side of the legislative battlefield. But at the level of specific businesses conducting day-to-day operations in actual prisons, this unity breaks down. Entrepreneurs with manufacturing and telemarketing operations in prison – especially small firms in emerging industries – need flexibility, mobility, and speed. They must move materials and equipment quickly without being searched. Likewise, laborers need to operate in a flexible yet punctual fashion. Prison provides none of this. Instead, it offers the exact opposite: a world where bureaucracy, hierarchy, delay, snafus, scarches and more searches, and the surly centralization of power define every detail of daily life. Guards are in large part responsible for this culture: they want total control of everything, all the time. As one CCPOA representative put it: "We want to help defray costs and keep inmates busy, but it's our backs that get stuck with the homemade knives when things get out of control."[82]

Thus work in prison is punctuated by frequent pat-down frisks, strip searches, long delays for "count," and arbitrary periods of lockdown in which inmates are confined to their cells for days or weeks at a time. Forget overtime shifts running until midnight; the screws have a schedule all their own.

There are other safety-oriented problems getting in the way. In California, for example, many prisons have at least two gates, but CO-supported rules prevent both gates from ever opening simultaneously. This means firms doing business in prisons can never ship products or materials in long tractor trailer trucks, and instead must use smaller delivery trucks. This automatically drives up production costs. Location is also a factor. Many new prisons are in isolated rural areas far from metropolitan markets and transportation hubs. Doing business in such a place means higher transportation costs and greater difficulty providing oversight. Even the weather can be a crisis in prison. In California, when it rains hard, drowning out sound, or thick fog rolls in, obscuring vision, all activity on prison grounds halts.

Many of these picayune and invasive rules are standard prison procedure, but they are exacerbated by the guards' security obsession. And the prison culture of control can become self-amplifying: control for safety's sake soon breeds control for its own sake. For example, a San Francisco firm called DPAS, after a long and arduous cooperation with the CDC, finally abandoned its data processing and "literature assembly" operations in San Quentin State Prison when COs refused to allow the convict workers to collate slightly pornographic material.

And if such overbearing and puritanical interventions were not enough, there is simply too much cheap, militarily disciplined labor on the outside to make the hassles and irrationalities of doing business in prison worthwhile. With wages as low as 40 cents an hour in Honduras, and generous tax breaks to boot, why open a sweatshop inside some bureaucratic hellhole where you have to pay minimum wage?[83]

The final nail in the coffin of profitable prison work is the poor quality of slave labor. Or conceived another way: the high price of convict resistance on the shop floor. True, many joint ventures can skim the demographic cream and get highly motivated, skilled workers inside prison, but there are just as many malingerers and saboteurs who aren't impressed by 15 cents to $1.50 an hour and who, with some justification, waste their time, steal materials, break equipment, and occupy themselves with their own little side projects on company time. This is particularly true in the state sector, where wages and job site safety are abysmal. On the outside we only catch glimpses of convict dissatisfaction in the form of suits for minimum wage, strikes, and criminal scams run over business phones.[84]

OUTSIDE OPPOSITION

Prison labor also faces challenges from outside the walls. Some of the very business people who could be using convict labor instead find themselves literally walking picket lines with union members to protest economic encroachment by state-owned prison industries. "How often can labor and management be on the same side?" asked Tom Tabaska, a manager at John Deere & Co., as he marched with unionized machinists to condemn Unicor's plans to make lawn mowers. "No way was I going to pass up this."[85]

Furniture manufacturers organized in the Business and Institutional Furniture Manufacturers Association (BIFMA) are also going after Unicor's "monopoly."[86] In the realm of apparel the Federal Glove Contractors Coalition and the Union of Needle Trades, Industrial and Textile Employees (UNITE) have teamed up to target Unicor's dominance of the military glove market.[87] Such struggles have even brought together the likes of conservative Representatives Peter Hoekstra and liberal Democrat Barney Frank, to craft legislation that would end the federal government's "mandatory purchasing" agreement with Unicor. The anti-Unicor bill had the ardent support of both the AFL-CIO and the US Chamber of Commerce. At the same time the conservative crime hawk Congressman Bill McCollum proposed a bill that would have left intact Unicor's privileges and would have allowed federal prison industries to sell on the open market. Both these bills, and others proposing the elimination of minimum wages for joint venture inmates, have so far gone nowhere. But in the last instance, it seems likely that the combined muscle of business and organized labor will keep the new convict leasing to a minimum.[88]

It is important to note that business and unions find themselves on the same side for different reasons. Unions oppose expansion of prison labor because workers don't want to compete against slaves. Business is split over the issue; a few firms, generally low-margin subcontractors, are drawn to the joint ventures because they promise subsidies, low wages, and the illusion of a steady work force. But businesses with substantial fixed capital in the free world are threatened by the idea of facing state-subsidized competitors. Nor are big businesses attracted by the prospect of entangling their operations in the treacherous ganglia of correctional bureaucracies. The government may be a generous, docile, bovine-like partner when it comes to buying new bombers and paying for endless R&D on missile defense systems and other boondoggles, but involving this same beast in the actual production process is a capitalist's nightmare.

THE SEMIOTICS OF CONVICT LABOR

What, then, is the function of prison labor? The state would save money by closing most prison industries, private capital does not seem eager to jump inside prison walls, and prisoners, though desperate for money, do not appreciate being exploited. What interests are served by convict labor?

The real service of prison labor is ideological. Working convicts make prison look efficient, moral, and useful. The right wing loves the trope of the toiling convict; it is the perfect hybrid between moral revenge and economic efficiency. Let the imagination drift rightward: the bad, lazy, evil, racially "otherized" convict busting ass under the gunsights of a good-old-boy CO, so as to pay taxes, victim restitution, rent, and family support while simultaneously turning a profit for some well-meaning, innovative entrepreneur. And if that is not enough we can pretend that prison labor rehabilitates. Thus convict labor becomes the ultimate conservative revenge fantasy.

A particularly good example of the ideologically freighted nature of convict labor is the PIE program, which in a fantastical way attempts to please every possible constituency (the state, victims, the feds). With so many symbolic causes getting a piece of the convict-produced surplus-value, none ends up getting much at all. Between 1979 and 1996 all PIE-employed prisoners were paid a total of $75 million, from which $5.5 million was paid for victim restitution, $16 million went for room and board, $4.4 million for "family support," and $8.9 million for federal, state, and local taxes.[89]

Political symbolism also causes the left to fixate on prison labor. In a weird symbiosis the left hates prison labor for the very same reason the right loves it: both *use* prison labor as a political symbol in the same way, but for diametrically opposed ends. The flipside of the right-wing fantasy sketched above is the left-wing nightmare of the gulag state providing Black and Latino bodies for exploitation by corporations. This vision, glimpsed in the new convict leasing, is the ultimate condemnation of the business system and links it directly to the history of American chattel slavery.

Prison labor programs can also be seen as the institutional artifacts of the bygone era of rehabilitation. From its radical Protestant-inspired birth onward, work has been central to prison's modernist/Calvinist project of reforming and remaking the criminal. The Dutch Rasphus, the Quaker treadmills, the Auburn system, and the Southern chain gangs all traded on the idea of labor's spiritual, political, and culturally salubrious effects. Likewise, Unicor and the state prison industries – arriving at the present, after a sojourn in the rehabilitation era – are propelled by the American cult of work as panacea; work as socio-cultural medicine for the slothful classes. This ancient sentiment is still played on by prison labor's biggest boosters. Senator Phil Gramm explained the moral function of convict labor thus: "If we can get some value out of it, I view that as God's work."[90]

CRISIS AND CONTROL

Much of the current critique of the prison industrial complex relies on showing the *direct involvement* of *specific economic interests*.[91] This "interest group model," the preferred style of muckraking journalists, borrows heavily from the accurate left critique of how the arms lobby created the military industrial complex. Making direct causal links and finding proverbial "smoking guns" is a powerful path of argument. But interest groups go only so far. Ultimately the whole of capitalist society is greater than the sum of its corporate and non-corporate parts. To really understand America's incarceration binge and criminal justice crackdown, we need to move from a narrow interest-group-based model to a more holistic class analysis that looks at the needs of the class system and class society in general.[92]

Even if prison building created no Keynesian stimulus, and there were no private prisons to profit from locking up the poor, and if prison labor were abolished – in other words, if all directly interested parties were removed from the equation – American capitalism would still, without major economic reforms, have to manage and contain its surplus populations and poorest classes with paramilitary forms of segregation, containment, and repression. At the heart of the matter lies the contradiction discussed earlier: capitalism needs the poor and creates poverty, intentionally through policy and organically through crisis. Yet capitalism is also directly and indirectly threatened by the poor. Capitalism always creates surplus populations, needs surplus populations, yet faces the threat of political, aesthetic, or cultural disruption from those populations. Prison and criminal justice are about managing these irreconcilable contradictions.

Consider once more the numbers: while it is true that the recovery of the late nineties drove down official African American male jobless rates precipitously (from 13.6 percent in 1992 to 8.5 percent in 1997) there remains a barely concealed stratum of suffering below this green statistical turf. After all, "official statistics exclude from the labor force millions of people who don't have jobs, say they want jobs, but are not actively searching for work (according to the government's definition of searching). And if they are not part of the labor force, they are not considered unemployed."[93] When "discouraged workers" who have given up the quest for employment and the incarcerated are added to the equation, the real unemployment rate for African American men emerges as a brutal 25.2 percent.[94] Among Black youth during the mid nineties unemployment was twice as high as among white youth.[95] And overall African American and Latino *poverty* rates are even higher. These two major American ethnic groups together make up 22.8 percent of the US population "but account for 47.8 percent of Americans living in poverty."[96] Overall, 35.6 million Americans – 40 percent of whom are children – are impoverished. Despite a momentary buoyancy in the economy, Black and brown poverty has been increasing steadily since the mid seventies.[97] The trend towards immiseration and isolation accelerated during the eighties and throughout much of the nineties.

Now compare this statistical sketch of the "surplus population" to the numbers on incarceration. According to the Sentencing Project, nearly one-third of all African American men between the ages of twenty and twenty-nine are "under criminal justice supervision on any given day." In other words they are in prison or jail or on probation or parole. Drug "offenders" make up the bulk of this jailed and semi jailed population. And while African Americans constitute only 13 percent of all monthly drug users, they represent 35 percent of all drug arrests, 55 percent of all drug convictions, and a staggering 74 percent of drug prisoners. While Black women are not incarcerated at the same rate as Black men, their rate of incarceration on drug charges is accelerating exponentially: the number of Black women in prison rose by 828 percent from 1986 to 1991.[98]

To reiterate how this buildup occurred, recall that politicians in the age of restructuring face a populus racked by economic and social anxiety. The political classes must speak to and harness this anxiety, but they cannot blame the US class structure. So they invent scapegoats: the Black/Latino criminal, the immigrant, the welfare cheat, crackheads, super-predators, and so on. These political myths are deployed, first and foremost, to win elections. But the eventual *policy byproducts* of this racialized anti-crime discourse are laws like three strikes and mandatory minimums. Most important, of course, are the drug laws. Drug offenders constituted more than a third (36 percent) of the increase in state prison populations between 1985 and 1994; in the federal system drug offenders make up more than two-thirds (71 percent) of the prison population.[99]

The question still remains: if capitalism always creates a surplus population, why did it not use criminal justice to absorb, contain, and isolate these groups in the past? To some extent it did. But in each epoch and place capitalist societies have developed specific and unique combinations of co-optation, amelioration, and repression to reproduce the class structure and deal with the contradictions of inevitable poverty. In the nineteenth century in the US, westward expansion offered a way of harnessing and alleviating the social pressure of poverty; racism directed other pressures, and whatever class struggle was left over was managed with bayonets. Early in the post-war era, profits were high enough to afford an ameliorative compromise: capital bought relative peace with labor in the form of an incipient welfare state and cooperation with organized labor. And in Europe, working class power, democratic political structures, and a cultural ethos of reform have maintained many strong welfare states. But in the US, the international crisis of over-production, declining profits, and the domestic challenge of racial and class rebellion required a move away from a politics of the carrot towards a politics of the stick.

To restore sagging profit margins capital launched a multifaceted domestic and international campaign of restructuring. Though the cause of the profit plunge was multifaceted – the rising organic composition of capital, and general over-production and saturation of global markets – *class struggle was also a key part of the equation.* Some on the left wish not to "blame" labor for the profit crisis. But the distribution of surplus-value is, at a certain level, a zero-sum game. And by the 1960s popular forces had exacted heavy concessions from capital in the form of an expanded social wage and increased regulation on business. Regardless of the real etiology of the crisis, capital's solution has focused heavily on redisciplining labor: that is, on assaulting the living standards and general power of working people.

In the US this has meant that older forms of absorbing and co-opting the poor and working classes with welfare and employer concessions had to go. These forms of social democratic and Keynesian intervention – while keeping class struggle contained, providing stimulus, and legitimizing the market system – had the unfortunate side-effect of *empowering* the laboring classes in ways that were destructive for business profits. Recall Juliet Schor's "cost of job loss" discussed in the second chapter of this book. With strong unions, inexpensive higher education, and ample welfare, the classes that sell their labor had less reason to take poorly paid, dangerous, or dirty work. To truly discipline labor, *all* alternative avenues of sustenance had to be closed. Thus we had the Reagan-Bush-Clinton welfare enclosures, the assaults on environmental regulation, the rights of labor, consumers, and the poor; in short, the near total evisceration of all New Deal and Great Society forms of downward redistribution.

The great business counteroffensive of the eighties and nineties has helped restore profits, but it has also invigorated the perennial problem of how to manage the surplus, excluded, and cast-off classes. This then is the mission of the emerging anti-crime police state. As the class structure polarizes in the interests of restored profitability, the state must step in to deploy and justify police terror, increase surveillance, and overuse incarceration. This politics of punishment works in two ways: it contains and controls those who violate the class-biased laws of our society, but prison also produces a predator class that, when returned to the street, frightens and disorganizes communities, effectively driving poor and working people into the arms of the state, seeking protection. Thus both crime control and crime itself keep people down.

This emerging anti-crime police state, or criminal justice industrial complex, though not necessarily planned as such, is the form of class control currently preferred by elites because it does not entail the dangerous side-effects of empowerment associated with the co-optative welfare model. The criminal justice crackdown, and its attendant culture of fear, absorbs the dangerous classes without politically or economically empowering them. The war on poverty and the raft of social democratic reforms associated with it also absorbed surplus populations, but this model of social control ran the risk of subsidizing political rebellion, or at least economic disobedience in the form of proletariat "slacking." Recall the case of the young Ford worker discussed in chapter two who refused to work a full week because he did not need to. Or consider the radical welfare rights movement of the early seventies. Problems like those cause business profits to decline, especially when part of a general crisis of over-production.

Criminal justice also reproduces racism in a coded and thus ideologically palatable fashion: this updated version of hate has massive retail appeal. In a system of haves and have-nots, divisive infighting among society's lower ranks is preferable to clearly defined struggle between the major classes.

RECOMMENDATIONS

Most books on criminal justice end with a coda earnestly enumerating what new and better things those in charge might do. My recommendations, as regards criminal justice, are quite simple: we need less. Less policing, less incarceration, shorter sentences, less surveillance, fewer laws governing individual behaviors, and less obsessive discussion of every lurid crime, less prohibition, and less puritanical concern with "freaks" and "deviants." Two-thirds of all people entering prison are sentenced for non-violent offenses, which means there are literally hundreds of thousands of people in prison who pose no major threat to public safety. These minor credit card fraudsters, joyriders, pot farmers, speed freaks, prostitutes, and shoplifters should not rot in prison at taxpayers' expense.

There are other reasons we need to demand "less": There is already an overabundance of good ideas on how to handle troubled youth, drug addicts, impoverished streetwalkers, and wife beaters. Some of these alternatives to incarceration have proven expensive failures, but many are quite inexpensive and effective. Academic criminology is replete with studies of what works and what does not, the best and latest iteration being Elliot Currie's excellent *Crime and Punishment America: Why the Solutions to America's Most Stubborn Social Crisis Have Not Worked — and What Will.* Currie, with typical patience and precision, exposes the so-called "commonsense" theories about the deterrent effect of repression, and then methodically enumerates alternative programs that will help reduce violence. We need not retrace that same terrain here.

Rehearsal of the workable alternatives to jailing ever more people of color and poor whites can become a self-deluding project. The discourse of the liberal policy wonk operates on the assumption that rational plans will displace irrational ones. But in reality any soft form of control can easily be grafted on to the most repressive police state. One could conceive of a regime that routinely uses capital punishment, genetic fingerprinting, militarized police *and,* for the barely deviant, ladles out endless hours of anger management, therapeutic probation, public shaming, and elaborate forms of restitution. Therapy and the gas chamber are by no means mutually exclusive. Newer, softer, more rational forms of control do not automatically displace repression, surveillance, and terror. Until there is a real move towards *decarceration*, any accretion of humane forms of intervention will not displace the criminal justice crackdown and prison industrial complex. We need a commitment to limiting incarceration and then a policy of "harm reduction" in which we could decriminalize drugs, give junkies their dope, decriminalize sex work, and subsidize prostitute organizing efforts; we could cut off the retail supply of cheap guns and tax other firearms at 500 percent, while at the same time eliminating draconian gun penalties like "sentencing enhancements," which mete out excessive punishment for firearms possession and use. And since the need for work is at the heart of any real war on crime, we could create jobs that pay a living wage and meet human needs.

To achieve anything like this we need more popular resistance and more economic justice. This book has been short on tales of protest and long on the story of repression, but there is opposition to the emerging anti-crime police state in many quarters. Even in the level four HIV unit of Corcoran State Prison, inmates are filing joint grievances against abusive staff, building alliances with outside activists, and, when they can't stand the torment any longer, attacking COs. Across the country there is an incipient police accountability movement, struggling to subordinate police departments to civilian oversight and keep violent officers in check. The murder of Amadou Diallo has sparked a broad-based and committed movement for police accountability in New York City. In D.C., and many state capitals as well, the tenacious lobbyists and grassroots activists of Families Against Mandatory Minimums (FAMM) and similar groups toil on because they must. Meanwhile, from Chicago to St. Louis to Watts and East L.A., veteran gangbangers like Dewayne Holmes labor without recognition and despite police sabotage to maintain the truce movement that started in the wake of the Rodney King riots. In Texas and California, Latino youth, shaken awake by the immigrant bashing of the mid nineties, are organizing walkouts and protests to demand more school funding and less policing. All over the country there are small pockets of dedicated activists fighting against tremendous odds and the deafening silence of the mainstream press. These are the people pointing the way out, the way forward, away from the waste, terror, and abuse of America's criminal justice lockdown.

NOTES

1 NIXON'S SPLENDID LITTLE WAR: SOCIAL CRISIS AND CONTAINMENT

1   In Detroit half the apprehended snipers were poor white "hillbilly" transplants from Kentucky, Tennessee, and Southern Ohio. For more details, see Dan Georgakas and Marvin Surkin, *Detroit, I Do Mind Dying: A Study in Urban Revolution* (Boston: South End Press, 1998).

2   Richard Boyle, *Flower of the Dragon: The Breakdown of the US Army in Vietnam* (San Francisco: Ramparts Press, 1972), chapter 4.

3   See John Irwin James Austin, *It's About Time: America's Imprisonment Binge*, second edition (Belmont, CA: Wadsworth Publishing, 1997), p. 143.

4   Ford, quoted in "Johnson's crime message," *New Republic*, January 18, 1967, p. 10.

5   "Goldwater's acceptance speech to GOP convention," *New York Times*, July 17, 1964.

6   Richard Nixon, "If mob rule takes hold in the US: a warning from Richard Nixon," *U.S. News and World Report*, August 15, 1966.

7   Quoted in Katherine Beckett, *Making Crime Pay: Law and Order in Contemporary American Politics* (Oxford: Oxford University Press, 1997), p. 28.

8   Quoted in Dan Baum, *Smoke and Mirrors: The War on Drugs and the Politics of Failure* (Boston: Back Bay Books, 1996), p. 11. Baum provides countless other such nuggets in his detailed account of this period. My analysis is indebted to and predicated upon his excellent work.

9   James Reston, "Political pollution: myths about the candidates," *New York Times*, August 18, 1968.

10 Thomas Cronin, Tiana Cronin, and Michael Milakovich, *The U.S. versus Crime in the Streets* (Bloomington: Indiana University Press, 1981), p. 68.

11 Baum, *Smoke and Mirrors*, p. 11.

12 Quoted in Arnold S. Trebach, *The Heroin Solution* (New Haven, CT: Yale University Press, 1982), p. 231.

13 It is important to note that many powerful interests welcomed, encouraged, and guided the cultural revolution of the 1960s; see Thomas Frank, *The Conquest of Cool* (Chicago: University of Chicago, 1997). But other factions of the ruling classes conflated lifestyle rebellion against "mass society" with real political militancy.

14 "Text of Nixon message on plan to attack drugs abuse," *Congressional Quarterly Almanac*, vol. 24, 1969, p. 57A.

15   On inflating addiction rates, see Baum, *Smoke and Mirrors.*

16   "Comprehensive drug control bill cleared by Congress," *Congressional Quarterly Almanac*, vol. 26, 1971, pp. 534, 535.

17   "Congress enacts no new programs for crime control," *Congressional Quarterly Almanac*, vol. 25, 1970, p. 687.

18   "Comprehensive drug control bill cleared by Congress," p. 540.

19   All quotes on pot and My Lai from "Military drug abuse," *Congressional Quarterly Almanac*, vol. 26, 1971, pp. 539–41.

20   "Massive federal aid authorized to fight crime," *Congressional Quarterly Almanac*, vol. 26, 1971, p. 557.

21   Ibid., p. 557; "Congress clears 1970 organized crime control bill," *Congressional Quarterly Almanac*, vol. 26, 1971.

22   Margaret Ratner and Michael Ratner, "Grand jury: from shield to sword to Starr Chamber," unpublished paper, Center for Constitutional Rights, no date.

23   H. R. Haldeman, *The Haldeman Diaries: Inside the Nixon White House* (New York: P. G. Putman's Sons, 1994), p. 53, quoted in Baum, *Smoke and Mirrors.*

24   Head of ODALE Myles Ambrose, quoted in "Law enforcement: the Collinsville reich," *Newsweek*, May 14, 1973; "In the name of the law," *Time*, May 14, 1973.

25   "Police terror," *New York Times*, July 2, 1973.

26   "Law enforcement: the Collinsville reich," *Newsweek*, May 14, 1973; "In the name of the law," *Time*, May 14, 1973.

27   "Law enforcement: $3.25 billion through FY 1976," *Congressional Quarterly Almanac*, vol. 29, 1974, pp. 359–81.

28   See Edward Jay Epstein, *Agency of Fear: Opiates and Political Power in America* (Verso: London, 1990), p. 214.

29   Quoted in "Criticisms of LEAA," *Congressional Quarterly Almanac*, vol. 29, 1974, p. 361.

30   Quoted from V. I. Lenin, *State and Revolution* (New York: International Publishers, 1932), pp. 10 and 18.

31   For a rather uncritical but comprehensive account of the endless struggle for police reform, see Robert M. Fogelson, *Big City Police* (Cambridge, MA: Harvard University Press, 1977).

32   National Advisory Commission on Criminal Justice Standards and Goals, *A National Strategy to Reduce Crime* (Washington, DC: Government Printing Office, 1973), p. 83; also for similar concerns, see Norman C. Kassoff, "State laws: police training," *The Police Chief*, August 1966; "A model police standards council act," *The Police Chief*, August 1967; "The police need help," *Time*, October 4, 1968; the illiterate sheriff story comes from a conversation with Dave Smith, former grant administrator for the State Planning Agency of Missouri and then the LEAA liaison for the San Francisco Police Department from 1976 to 1978. Clearly rural Missouri was not a politically important piece of geography in the early seventies but this story is nonetheless illustrative of a larger problem.

33   The President's Commission on Law Enforcement and Justice Administration, *The Challenge of Crime in a Free Society* (Washington, DC: Government Printing Office, 1967), p. 12.

34   Col. E. Wilson Purdy, "Riot control – a local responsibility," *FBI Law Enforcement Bulletin*, June 1965.

35   Quinn Tamm, "Is police protection at the breaking point?" *The Police Chief*, March 1966.

36   Daryl Gates, "Control of civil disorders," *The Police Chief*, May 1968.

37   *The Iron Fist and the Velvet Glove: An Analysis of the U.S. Police*, second edition (Berkeley, CA: Center for Research and Criminal Justice, 1975).

38   Clark MacGregor, "Criminal justice: priorities and programs for the seventies," in S. I. Cohn and W. B. McMahon, eds., *Law Enforcement, Science and Technology II, Proceedings of the Third*

National Symposium on Law Enforcement Science and Technology (Chicago: IIT Research Institute, 1970), p. 8.

39   President's Crime Commission, *Task Force on Police* (Washington, DC: Government Printing Office, 1968), p. 44.

40   Allen T. Osborne, "The management development program of the Los Angeles Police Department," in Cohn and McMahon, *Law Enforcement*, pp. 293, 296.

41   Oliver Welch and Charles Cory, "A mandate for state planning: upgrading law enforcement," *The Police Chief*, February 1970.

42   US Department of Justice, *Sixth Annual Report of LEAA* (Washington, DC: Government Printing Office, 1974), p. 119.

43   Robert Clark Stone, "A revolution in police training," *FBI Law Enforcement Bulletin*, July 1973.

44   LAPD Chief Thomas Reddin, quoted in "Law enforcement faces grave challenges," *FBI Law Enforcement Bulletin*, January 1968.

45   "Trends in urban guerrilla tactics," *FBI Law Enforcement Bulletin*, July 1973.

46   J. Edgar Hoover, "Law enforcement faces the revolutionary-guerrilla criminal," *FBI Law Enforcement Bulletin*, December 1970.

47   "Police killings in 1973 – a record year," *FBI Law Enforcement Bulletin*, April 1974.

48   "Snipers in ambush: police under the gun," *Time*, September 14, 1970.

49   Colonel Nicholas D. Rudziak, "Police-military relations in a revolutionary environment," *The Police Chief*, September 1966.

50   US Department of Justice, *Sixth Annual Report of the LEAA* (Washington, DC: Government Printing Office, 1974), p. 73.

51   *The Iron Fist*; "The national crime information center: a special report," *FBI Law Enforcement Bulletin*, January 1968.

52   Lt. Jack W. Baker, "Computer applications in law enforcement," *FBI Law Enforcement Bulletin*, June 1968, pp. 3–4.

53   Ibid.

54   For a detailed history of the NCIC and a critique of electronic surveillance and record keeping, see Diana R. Gordon, *The Justice Juggernaut: Fighting Street Crime, Controlling Citizens* (New Brunswick, NJ: Rutgers University Press, 1991).

55   George O'Tool, "America's secret police network," *Penthouse*, December 2, 1976, p. 204, quoted in *The Iron Fist and the Velvet Glove*.

56   "The National Crime Information Center: a special report," *FBI Law Enforcement Bulletin*, January 1968.

57   Otto Rhoades, "Illinois State Police emergency radio network," *FBI Law Enforcement Bulletin*, October 1967.

58   See Gerald Horne, *Fire This Time: The Watts Uprising and the 1960s* (New York: Da Capo, 1997), pp. 56–7; also Daryl Gates with Diane K. Shah, *Chief: My Life in the LAPD* (New York: Bantam Books, 1992).

59   Sheriff Peter J. Pitchess and C. Roberts Guthrie, "Project Sky Knight: a demonstration in aerial surveillance and crime control," LEAA dissemination document prepared for the Office of Law Enforcement Assistance, US Department of Justice, May 1968, p. 114.

60   Ibid., p. 11.

61   Richard F. Coburn, "Police units expands helicopter operations," *Aviation Week & Space Technology*, January 1969.

62   *The Iron Fist*, chapter 9; Commander G. N. Beck, "SWAT – The Los Angeles police special weapons and tactics teams," *FBI Law Enforcement Bulletin*, April 1972.

63   *Report of the National Advisory Commission on Civil Disorders* (New York: New York Times Company, 1968), p. 206.

64 "Training for the future," *FBI Law Enforcement Bulletin*, March 1974, p. 23.

65 James Q. Wilson, "Crime and law enforcement," in Kermit Gordan, ed., *Agenda for the Nation* (Washington, DC: Brookings Institution, 1969), p. 204.

66 For a review of these early experiments written close to the time, see Lawrence Sherman *et al.*, *Team Policing* (Washington, DC: The Police Foundation, 1975); also see James Q. Wilson, *Thinking about Crime*, revised edition (New York: Vintage, 1985, 1974), for an overview of these early trials.

67 Quoted in *The Iron Fist*, p. 135.

68 Ibid., chapter 13.

69 Alvin A. Rosenfeld, "The friendly fuzz," *The Nation*, April 21, 1968.

70 "Citizens' war on crime: spreading across U.S." *U.S. News & World Report*, March 23, 1970.

71 *The Iron Fist*, chapter 13.

72 "Crime and judiciary," *Congressional Quarterly Almanac*, vol. 30, 1975, p. 271.

73 Polls cited in ibid., p. 272.

74 "Congress repeals 'no-knock' laws," *Congressional Quarterly Almanac*, vol. 30, 1975, p. 273.

75 *Federal Drug Strategy: Drug Abuse Prevention*, Strategy Council on Drug Abuse, November 1976, quoted in Baum, *Smoke and Mirrors*.

76 "Drug law revision" (text of President's message to Congress), *Congressional Quarterly Almanac*, vol. 32, 1977, p. 273.

77 Anita Frankel, "'New Panthers' face old problems," *Seven Days*, Febuary 24, 1978.

2 FROM CRISIS TO ROLLBACK

1 Quoted in Richard Brooks, "Maggie's man: we were wrong, *Observer*, June 21, 1992.

2 Thomas Frank, *The Conquest of Cool* (Chicago: University of Chicago Press, 1997), p. 1.

3 Philip Armstrong, Andrew Glyn, and John Harrison, *Capitalism since 1945* (Oxford: Basil Blackwell, 1991), p. 23, put the figure at 50 percent. Mike Davis argues that capacity doubled, "The political economy of late-imperial America," *New Left Review*, no. 143, 1984, p. 8.

4 William Ashworth, *A Short History of the International Economy since 1850*, second edition (London: Longmans, Green, 1962), p. 259.

5 Armstrong *et al.*, *Capitalism since 1945*, p. 155.

6 For the quintessential story of state-led capitalist development, see Alice Amsden, *Asia's Next Giant: South Korea and Late Industrialization* (Oxford: Oxford University Press, 1992).

7 Armstrong *et al.*, *Capitalism since 1945*, p. 155.

8 Ibid., p. 157.

9 Barry Bluestone and Bennett Harrison, *The Deindustrialization of America: Plant Closings, Community Abandonment, and the Dismantling of Basic Industry* (New York: Basic Books, 1982), p. 14.

10 Juliet B. Schor, *The Overworked America: The Unexpected Decline of Leisure* (New York: Basic Books, 1992), p. 111.

11 Charles Sable, quoted in Bluestone and Harrison, *The Deindustrialization of America*, p. 10.

12 On excess capacity or over-accumulation, see Armstrong *et al.*, *Capitalism since 1945*, especially chapter 11.

13 Samuel Bowles, David Gordon, and Thomas Weisskopf, *After the Waste Land: A Democratic Economics for the Year 2000* (Armonk, NY: M. E. Sharpe, 1990), p. 83. It is important to note that during the late sixties and early seventies acute unemployment did increase but,

from the capitalist's point of view the beneficial effects of unemployment did not. We will address this point in more detail later on.

14 Juliet B. Schor, "Wage flexibility, social welfare expenditures and monetary restrictiveness," in M. Jarsulic, *Money and Macro Policy* (Boston: Kluwer-Nijhoff, 1985); Juliet B. Schor and Samuel Bowles, "Employment rents and the incidence of strikes," *Review of Economics and Statistics*, vol. 62, no. 4, 1987, pp. 584–92.

15 Bowles *et al.*, *After the Waste Land*, pp. 72 and 37.

16 Michael Perelman, *The Pathology of the U.S. Economy: The Costs of a Low-Wage System* (London: Macmillan, 1993), pp. 32–5.

17 David Halberstam, *The Reckoning* (New York: William Morrow, 1986), p. 488, cited in Perelman, ibid.

18 Quoted in "More trouble for builders – strikes go on, pay keeps rising," *U.S. News and World Report*, June 29, 1970, p. 50.

19 "Labor turmoil: truce and new threats," *Time*, April 6, 1970, p. 8.

20 Ibid.

21 "Rail strikes begin to hurt everywhere," *Business Week*, July 31, 1971.

22 "When New Bedford stops its fishing," *Business Week*, August 18, 1973.

23 "New wonder at Disneyland," *Newsweek*, September 21, 1970.

24 See Table 37, *Monthly Labor Review*, vol. 99, no. 6, June 1976, p. 111.

25 This assumes that existing capital stock is continually being paid for, or that every firm has some debt, which is usually the case.

26 See Bowles *et al.*, *After the Wasteland*, table on p. 37.

27 Quoted in Richard Cloward and Frances Fox-Piven, "A class analysis of welfare," *Monthly Review*, vol. 44, no. 9, February 1993, p. 28.

28 See Bluestone and Harrison, *The Deindustrialization of America*, footnote 12, p. 11.

29 For a more mathematical and technical definition, see David W. Pearce, ed., *Macmillan Dictionary of Modern Economics*, fourth edition (London: Macmillan, 1992), p. 330; also see Robert Haveman, "Unemployment in western Europe and the United States: a problem of demand, structure, or measurement," *American Economic Review*, vol. 71, no. 4, December 1977, pp. 44–50 for proof of the historical accuracy of the Phillips curve. This same relationship was noted by Karl Marx when he wrote about the "industrial reserve army of labor." Marx argued that the unemployed were functional for capitalism, because they served as a cudgel with which to psychologically and at times physically menace the working class. An ample pool of desperate hands helped to quiet proletarian demands for redistribution. Also the most desperate of the unemployed, or unemployable, the "*déclassé* rabble" or "lumpen proletariat," could also serve as capital's shock troops and strike breakers. Marx saw the "production of a relative surplus population" as "a necessary condition of modern industry." See Karl Marx, *Capital* (New York: Random House, 1906), vol. 1, chapter 25, p. 695.

30 Bowles *et al.*, *After the Waste Land*, p. 44.

31 Graph from ibid., p. 37, also statistics, p. 36.

32 Bennett Harrison and Barry Bluestone, *The Great U-Turn: Corporate Restructuring and the Polarization of America* (New York: Basic Books, 1988), p. 7; also Norman Glickman, "Cities and the international division of labor," in Peter Michael Smith, ed., *The Capitalist City* (Oxford: Blackwell, 1987), p. 71.

33 Bowles *et al.*, *After the Waste Land*, p. 45. See Figure 4.4, "Declining profitability after the mid sixties"; Andrew Glyn, Alan Hughes, Alan Lipietz, and Ajit Singh, "The rise and fall of the golden age," in Stephen A. Marglin and Juliet B. Schor, eds., *The Golden Age of Capitalism: Reinterpreting the Post-war Experience* (Oxford: Clarendon Press, 1990), p. 77, Figure 2.10.

34 Ibid.
35 David Vogel, "The 'new' social regulation in historic and comparative perspective," in Thomas K. McCraw, ed., *Regulation in Perspective* (Cambridge, MA: Harvard University Press, 1981), p. 162.
36 For examples of business class consternation about "subsidizing strikes," see "Should strikers get public aid?" *Business Week*, March, 24, 1973; "Feeding the hand that bites you," *Forbes*, February 1, 1973.
37 Michel J. Crozier, Samuel P. Huntington, and Joji Watanuki, *The Crisis of Democracy: Report on the Governability of Democracies to the Trilateral Commission* (New York: New York University Press, 1975).
38 Volcker, quoted by Steven Rattner, "Volcker asserts U.S. must trim living standards," *New York Times*, October 18, 1979, p. A1.
39 Quoted in Michael Perelman, *Pathology of the U.S. Economy: The Cost of a Low-Wage System* (London: Macmillan, 1993), p. 43.
40 Harrison and Bluestone, *The Great U-Turn*, p. 92.
41 "Who says concessions are a thing of the past?" *Labor Notes*, June 1986.
42 Armstrong *et al.*, *Capitalism since 1945*, p. 243, Figure 14.5.
43 Quoted in Kevin Philips, *Boiling Point: Democrats, Republicans and the Decline of Middle-Class Prosperity* (New York: Random House, 1993), pp. 173–4.
44 Robert Pear, "Temporary hiring by US is pushed under new policy," *New York Times*, January 2, 1985, p. 1; Nancy L. Ross, "Can a man's castle become his sweatshop?" *Washington Post National Weekly Edition*, September 1, 1986, p. 20.
45 Kevin Philips, *The Politics of Rich and Poor: Wealth and the American Electorate in the Reagan Aftermath* (New York: Random House, 1990), p. 219.
46 Richard Barnet and John Cavanagh, *Global Dreams: Imperial Corporations and the New World Order* (New York: Simon and Schuster, 1994), p. 333.
47 Richard Nathan and Fred C. Doolittle, *Reagan and the States* (Princeton, NJ: Princeton University Press, 1987), Table 3.2.
48 Frances Fox-Piven and Richard Cloward, *The New Class War: Reagan's Attack on the Welfare State and its Consequences* (New York: Pantheon Books, 1985), pp. 33–4.
49 Ibid., p. 19.
50 George Gilder, *Wealth and Poverty* (New York: Basic Books, 1981), p. 82.
51 George J. Church, "Are you better off? For much of the middle class, the answer is no – yet it isn't hurting Bush," *Time*, October 10, 1988.
52 Janice Castro, "What, no pool in the foyer? Keeping up with the Joneses, 1987 style," *Time*, September 21, 1987.
53 See Table 10.2, Bowles *et al.*, *After the Waste Land*, p. 159.
54 Armstrong *et al.*, *Capitalism since 1945*, p. 88.
55 Donald L. Barlett and James B. Steel, *America: What Went Wrong?* (Kansas City: Andrews and McMeel, 1992), p. 35.
56 Quoted in Richard Barnet and Ronald Miller, *Global Reach* (New York: Simon and Schuster, 1974), p. 305.
57 Cited in Joyce Kolko, *Restructuring the World Economy* (New York: Pantheon Books, 1988), p. 309.
58 For an example of long-term planning and intentional deindustrialization, see Robert Fitch, *The Assassination of New York* (New York: Verso, 1995).
59 "A man, a plan," *The Economist*, March 12, 1994, p. 33.
60 Ze'ev Chafets, *Devil's Night, and Other True Tales of Detroit* (New York: Vintage Books, 1990).

61 William Julius Wilson, *When Work Disappears: The World of the New Urban Poor* (New York: Random House, 1996), p. 14.

62 Tony Duster, "Crime, youth unemployment and the underclass," *Crime and Social Justice*, vol. 33, no. 2, April 1987.

63 Leslie Innis and Joe R. Feagin, "The black 'underclass' ideology in race relations analysis," *Social Justice*, vol. 16, no. 4, winter 1989.

64 See Mike Davis, "Who killed Los Angeles?" *New Left Review*, no. 197, January–February, 1993.

65 William Julius Wilson, *When Work Disappears: The World of the New Urban Poor* (New York: Vintage, 1997), p. xiii.

66 Sakia Sassen, *Mobility of Labor and Capital* (Cambridge: Cambridge University Press, 1990).

67 "A hobo jungle with class; Santa Barbara, Reagan's neighbor, wrestles with 2,000 homeless," *Time*, March 31, 1986.

68 Evan Thomas, "Coming in from the cold; a deep freeze exposes the plight of up to 2 million homeless," *Time*, February 4, 1985.

3 A WAR FOR ALL SEASONS: THE RETURN OF LAW AND ORDER

1 Steven Spitzer, "Toward a Marxist theory of deviance," *Social Problems*, no. 22, 1975.

2 Relative deprivation is a concept originating with sociologist S. A. Stouffer and developed by Robert K. Merton. This concept proposes that people experience material deprivation in relation to the position of others and in relation to stories, myths, or ideologies of success. Thus crime and the breakdown of social norms often occurs not when poverty increases but when poverty is increasingly seen as unfair, unnatural, or as failure. Likewise, political rebellion occurs not when immiseration is greatest, but when immiseration and inequality are seen as unjust, unnatural, and vulnerable to change. Political rebellion occurs when a class, race, or gender sees its current lot in relation to potential justice and the privilege of others. See Robert K. Merton, *Social Theory and Social Structure* (New York: The Free Press, 1957).

3 Francis Fox Piven and Richard Cloward, *Poor People's Movements: The Functions of Public Welfare* (New York: Vintage Books, 1971); see also Jeremy Brecher, *Strike!* (San Francisco: Arrow Books, 1972) and Richard O. Boyer and Herbert M. Marais, *Labor's Untold Story* (New York: United Electrical, Radio and Machine Workers of America, 1977).

4 Kathleen Maguire and Ann Pastore, in US Department of Justice, Bureau of Justice Statistics, *Sources Book of Criminal Justice Statistics, 1990* (Washington, DC: US Government Printing Office, 1991).

5 Francis J. Flaherty, "Silent intruders: open season on privacy," *The Progressive*, April 1984.

6 Quoted in Dan Baum, *Smoke and Mirrors: The War on Drugs and the Politics of Failure* (Boston: Back Bay Books), p. 138.

7 "Tougher stance toward users weighed in war on drugs," *San Diego Union Tribune*, April 2, 1985.

8 Steven Wisotsky, *Beyond the War on Drugs: Overcoming a Failed Public Policy* (Buffalo, NY: Prometheus Books, 1990), pp. 99–101; also Robert E. Taylor and Gary Cohn, "Dealing with drugs – the drug trade: war against narcotics by U.S. government isn't slowing influx," *Wall Street Journal*, November 27, 1984.

9   "Q&A: John Van de Kamp, California Attorney General," *San Diego Union-Tribune*, September 1, 1985.

10   Baum, *Smoke and Mirrors.*

11   Joe Hughes, "State destroys record pot crop," *San Diego Union-Tribune*, October 27, 1984.

12   Ibid.

13   "Mondale plan to use military in anti-drug fight misguided," editorial, *Omaha World Herald*, October 8, 1984.

14   Mary Thornton, "Meese may have surprises for both supporters and foes," *Washington Post*, February 28, 1984.

15   "Meese says he hopes courts will drop exclusionary rule," *San Diego Union-Tribune*, October 24, 1984.

16   Mary Thornton, "Meese seen taking an activist approach," *Washington Post*, January 23, 1984.

17   Quoted in Alan L. Otten, "Dealing with drugs – the drug trade: experts in the field of narcotics debate ways to curb abuse – one side touts legalization, other wants crackdown; probably neither is right," *Wall Street Journal*, November 29, 1984.

18   "Reagan vetoes package of anti-crime bills," *Congressional Quarterly Almanac*, vol. 38, 1982; "Anti-crime package stalls in Senate again," *Congressional Quarterly Almanac*, vol. 39, 1983.

19   "Major crime package cleared by Congress," *Congressional Quarterly Almanac*, vol. 40, 1984.

20   Ibid., p. 215.

21   Quoted in "Impact of Uncle Sam's new crime law," *U.S. News and World Report*, October 22, 1984, p. 50.

22   Quoted in Richard Stengel, "More muscle for crime fighters," *Time*, October 29, 1984, p. 74.

23   "Major crime package cleared by Congress," *Congressional Quarterly Almanac*, vol. 40, 1984.

24   The specific acts which created modern forfeiture were the Organized Crime Control Act of 1970 and the Comprehensive Drug Abuse and Control Act of 1970.

25   Eric L. Jensen and Jurg Gerber, "The civil forfeiture of assets and the war on drugs: expanding criminal sanctions while reducing due process protections," *Crime and Delinquency*, vol. 42, no. 3, July 1996, pp. 412–34.

26   "Asset forfeiture – a seldom used tool in combating drug trafficking," Comptroller General to the Honorable Joseph R. Biden (Washington, DC: General Accounting Office, 1981).

27   By 1983 a few states had drawn up their own seizure laws which allowed local police to keep portions of seized cash. For example, in California local police agencies were permitted to keep as much as 65 percent of seized assets. The remainder went to the state Department of Mental Health, while vehicles had to be handed over for auction. See Stephanie O'Neil, "Police departments enjoy a boom from their drug busts: roving narcotics squads capture cash, cars, homes with traffickers," *Los Angeles Times*, October 23, 1988.

28   Eric Blumeson and Eva Nilsen, "Policing for profit: the drug war's hidden economic agenda," *University of Chicago Law Review*, winter 1998, pp. 36–112.

29   Bob Rowald, "Scizure of traffickers' assets is effective tool in drug fight," *San Diego Union-Tribune*, November 19, 1987.

30   Gordon Witkins, "Hitting kingpins in their assets," *U.S. News and World Report*, December 5, 1988.

31   Jensen and Gerber, "The civil forfeiture of assets," p. 3.

32   Stephanie O'Neil, "Funded by the crooks: police hail bonanza in out of town drug battle," *Los Angeles Times*, May 5, 1988.

33   Ibid.

34   Ibid.; "SF police share seized drug assets," *San Francisco Chronicle*, June 27, 1986.

35   Witkins, "Hitting kingpins in their assets."

36   Pearl Stewart, "Oakland drug war adding prosecutors, football players," *San Francisco Chronicle*, January 29, 1985.

37   "Pot growers in danger of losing homes," *Seattle Times*, April 28, 1985.

38   See statement of Mark J. Kappelhoff, Legislative Counsel on behalf of the American Civil Liberties Union, Monday, July 22, 1996, Congressional testimony copyright 1996 by Federal Document Clearing House, Inc.

39   Ibid.; *USA Today*, May 18, 1992.

40   Jensen and Gerber, "The civil forfeiture of assets."

41   Dick Lehr and Bruce Butterfield, "Small-timers get hard time: some major dealers evade stiff sentences others can't escape," *Boston Globe*, September 24, 1995.

42   Ibid.

43   Statement of Mark J. Kappelhoff, Legislative Counsel on behalf of the American Civil Liberties Union, Monday, July 22, 1996, Congressional testimony copyright 1996 by Federal Document Clearing House, Inc.

44   Andrew Schneider and Mary P. Flaherty, "Drug agents far more likely to stop minorities," *Pittsburgh Press*, August 12, 1991; also see Steve Berry and Jeff Brazil, "Tainted cash or easy money?," *Orlando Sentinel*, June 14, 1992; 60 Minutes: "You're under arrest" (CBS television broadcast, April 5, 1992).

45   Jeff Brazil and Steven Berry, "Color of driver is key to stops in I-95 videos," *Orlando Sentinel Tribune*, August 23, 1992.

46   *Common Characteristics of Drug Couriers*, Florida Department of Highway Safety and Motor Vehicles, Office of General Counsel, May 8, 1985, sec. I.A.4, cited in Wisotsky, *Beyond the War on Drugs*, p. 127.

47   Jeff Brazil and Steven Berry, "Blacks, Hispanics, big losers in cash seizures," *Orlando Sentinel Tribune*, June 15, 1992; Jeff Brazil, "Congress tackles forfeiture abuses," *Orlando Sentinel Tribune*, October 1, 1992; Brazil and Berry, "Color of driver is key."

48   Brazil and Berry, "Color of Driver is Key."

49   Harry Harris, Paul Grabowicz, and Michael Collier, "Six OHA officers indicted," *Oakland Tribune*, August 25, 1990; Brian Johns, "Two more 8-year prison terms for ex-OHA cops," July 13, 1991.

50   Blumeson and Nilsen, "Policing for profit," p. 12.

51   Barbara Jaeger, "A rocky year for charity in 1986, only one concert fund-raiser was an unqualified success," *The Record, Northern New Jersey*, December 21, 1986.

52   Reagan, quoted in "Congress clears massive anti-drug measure," *Congressional Quarterly Almanac*, vol. 42, 1986, p. 92.

53   William Safire, "The 'Jar Wars' in Washington," *San Francisco Chronicle*, August 12, 1986.

54   Merrill Hartson, "Reagan, Bush to take drug tests Monday to set examples," *Associated Press*, August 7, 1986.

55   Safire, "The 'Jar Wars.'"

56   Robert Stutman, *Dead on Delivery: Inside the Drug Wars, Straight from the Street* (Boston: Little, Brown, 1992), p. 217.

57   Craig Reinarman and Harry G. Levine, "The crack attack," in Craig Reinarman and Harry G. Levine, eds., *Crack in America: Drugs and Social Justice* (Berkeley: University of California Press, 1997), p. 20.

58   Ibid.

59   Ibid.; Abbie Hoffman, *Steal this Urine Test* (New York: Viking, 1987), p. 113.

60   Quoted in Katherine Beckett, *Making Crime Pay: Law and Order in Contemporary American Politics* (Oxford: Oxford University Press, 1997), p. 57.

61 "Congress clears massive anti-drug measure," *Congressional Quarterly Almanac*, vol. 42, 1986, p. 98.

62 Ibid.

63 Table 4.7, *Sourcebook of Criminal Justice Statistics, 1982*, Bureau of Justice Statistics (Washington, DC: Government Printing Office, 1983), p. 400; Table 4.7, *Sourcebook of Criminal Justice Statistics, 1991*, Bureau of Justice Statistics (Washington, DC: Government Printing Office, 1992), p. 444.

64 Lamar James, "Roger Clinton receives 2-year sentence in cocaine case; terms given 2 others," *Arkansas Gazette*, January 29, 1985; David B. Kopel, "Sentencing policies endanger public safety," *USA Today Magazine*, November 1, 1995. This article miscalculated Clinton's sentence under mandatory minimums as five years, because they forget to calculate his suspended sentence for conspiracy.

65 Calculated from Figure 6.1 in *Sourcebook of Criminal Justice Statistics, 1995*, Bureau of Justice Statistics (Washington, DC: Government Printing Office, 1996), p. 555.

66 "Congress clears massive anti-drug measure," *Congressional Quarterly Almanac*, vol. 42, 1986, p. 99.

67 See Table 24, *FBI Uniform Crime Reports 1985* (Washington, DC: Government Printing Office, 1985), p. 164; Table 24, *FBI Uniform Crime Reports 1989* (Washington, DC: Government Printing Office, 1989), p. 172; Table 24, *FBI Uniform Crime Reports 1990* (Washington, DC: Government Printing Office, 1990), p. 174; Table 29, *FBI Uniform Crime Reports 1996* (Washington, DC: Government Printing Office, 1996), p. 214.

68 See Mike Davis, "The hammer and the rock," in *City of Quartz: Excavating the Future in Los Angeles* (London: Verso, 1990).

69 Peter Kerr, "Police turn focus to small-time drug dealers" (New York Times News Service), *Dallas Morning News*, April 13, 1987.

70 Captain Patrick Carroll, "Operation Pressure Point, an urban enforcement strategy," *FBI Law Enforcement Bulletin*, April 1989.

71 See chapter three for a full discussion of gentrification.

72 This quote and official quoted below, from Elsa Walsh, "D.C. police will enlarge PCP sales areas," *Washington Post*, September 17, 1986.

73 Kerr, "Police turn focus"; "Jails filled, but drugs still problem," *Washington Post*, December 17, 1987; Victoria Churchville, "District drug sweep snares children drawn into dealing," *Washington Post*, August 13, 1987.

74 Victoria Churchville, "Drug-linked D.C. Killings Rise Sharply," *Washington Post*, June 16, 1987.

75 "Jails filled," *Washington Post*.

76 "Hundreds in Miami feel 'sting' of cocaine, pot raids," *Los Angeles Times*, October 26, 1986.

77 Clarence Dickson, "Drug stings in Miami," *FBI Law Enforcement Bulletin*, January 1988.

78 Mark Pinsky, "South County drug raids nets nearly 30," *Los Angeles Times*, June 7, 1986.

79 "Big federal-local drug sweep brings 26 Philadelphia arrests," *Los Angeles Times*, February 19, 1987.

80 Quoted in Christine Chinlund, "Bush says opponent owes victims apology," *Boston Globe*, October 8, 1988.

81 David Hoffman, "Bush attacks Dukakis as the 'furlough king'; Republican seeks to direct attention away from Quayle's debate performance," *Washington Post*, October 8, 1988.

82 Bush and Jackson quoted in Christine C. Lawrence, "Parties fighting hard for lead on drug issue," *Congressional Quarterly Weekly Report*, vol. 46, no. 25, June 18, 1988, p. 3.

83 Quoted in "Election-year anti-drug bill enacted," *Congressional Quarterly Almanac*, vol. 44, 1989, p. 86.

84 Ibid., and "Law/Judiciary," *Congressional Quarterly Almanac*, vol. 44, 1989, p. 61.

85 "Election-year anti-drug bill enacted," *Congressional Quarterly Almanac*, vol. 44, 1989.

86 Michael Isikoff, "Drug buy set up for Bush speech: DEA lured seller to Lafayette Park," *Washington Post*, September 22, 1989; for more detail, see Baum, *Smoke and Mirrors*.

87 "Legislative summary: Law/Judiciary," *Congressional Quarterly Weekly Report*, vol. 47, no. 48, December 2, 1989, p. 3307.

88 "1990 Crime Act: major provisions," *Congressional Quarterly Almanac*, vol. 46, 1991, p. 499.

89 Bureau of Justice Statistics, cited in "Drug conviction up 161%," *USA Today*, July 24, 1989.

90 Chapin Wright, "NY's dubious drug distinction," *Newsday*, May 11, 1990.

91 California statistics from Michael Tackett, "'Tough' drug stance overwhelms U.S. prisons. Series: System Overload," *Chicago Tribune*, November 9, 1990; and Figure 6.7 in John Irwin and James Austin, *It's about Time: America's Imprisonment Binge*, second edition (Belmont, CA: Wadsworth Publishing, 1997), p. 151.

92 Tackett, "'Tough' drug stance."

93 "Clinton returns to Arkansas for execution," *San Francisco Chronicle*, January 25, 1992.

94 Sharon LaFraniere, "Governor's camp feels his record on crime can stand the heat," *Washington Post*, October 5, 1992.

95 "Reno named first woman attorney general," *Congressional Quarterly Almanac*, vol. 49, 1994, p. 306.

96 Quoted in Carolyn Skorneck, "House OK's '3 strikes' legislation: death penalty ordered for almost 70 crimes," *News Tribune* (Tacoma), April 22, 1994.

97 "Lawmakers enact $30.2 billion anti-crime bill," *Congressional Quarterly Almanac*, vol. 49, 1994, p. 273; for more detail see PL 103–322, September 13, 1994, 108 Stat. 1796.

98 "Crime bill provisions," *Congressional Quarterly Almanac*, vol. 49, 1994, p. 287.

99 Ibid., pp. 287–94.

4 DISCIPLINE IN PLAYLAND, PART I – ZERO TOLERANCE: THE SCIENCE OF KICKING ASS

1 "Ratmen of Baltimore go rat 'fishing' again," *New York Times*, May 5, 1995.

2 William Bratton, phone interview, August 1997.

3 That experiment divided the city into four areas and applied different forms of policing to each. The results were mostly ambiguous, though one thing was clear: fear of crime seemed unaffected by police practices. For a concise overview of the Police Foundation's history, see Thomas J. Deakin, "The Police Foundation, a special report," *FBI Law Enforcement Bulletin*, November 1986.

4 James Q. Wilson and George Kelling, "Broken windows," *Atlantic Monthly*, March 1982.

5 William Bratton, with Peter Knobler, *Turnaround: How America's Top Cop Reversed the Crime Epidemic* (New York: Random House, 1998), pp. 145–6.

6 Ibid., p. 176; for a more jaundiced view of the subterranean arms race, see Wendell Jamieson, "Firepower cops and 9 mm. guns: sidearmed and dangerous – are NY cops gun crazy after switch to 9 mms?" *Newsday*, June 4, 1995.

7 Bratton and Knobler, *Turnaround*, p. 152.

8   Ibid., p. 154.

9   Anyone who regularly traveled through central Brooklyn in the early nineties will recall these rather chilling displays, or see Bratton and Knobler, *Turnaround*, p. 159.

10   Daniel Machalaba, "Mobile homes: transit systems face burden of providing last-resort shelter," *Wall Street Journal*, July 18, 1990; one account, attempting to portray farebeaters as a cross-section of the city's demographic, nonetheless revealed that nearly half of the ten prisoners interviewed, while waiting to be moved to a processing center, were absolute paupers, "their pockets empty of a single penny or identification or any other latchkey to the social order" – Barry Bearrak, "The lowest crime in New York," *Los Angeles Times*, June 4, 1991.

11   Katherine Foran, "Group protests sweeps of subway homeless," *Newsday*, August 23, 1990.

12   "TA: felony crimes in subway fell 15.7%," *Newsday*, May 24, 1994.

13   Both quoted in Bruce Frankel and John Larrabee, "NYC hires away 'Babe Ruth' of police chiefs," *USA Today*, December 3, 1993.

14   Bratton and Knobler, *Turnaround*.

15   Alexander Cockburn, "Beat the devil," *The Nation*, January 23, 1995; Robert McFadden, "Two officers wounded as snipers ring in '94 with 100 rounds," *New York Times*, January 2, 1994.

16   Bratton and Knobler, *Turnaround*, p. 166.

17   John Maher, "NYPD beats the blues," *Irish Times*, June 15, 1996.

18   William Bratton, phone interview, August 1997.

19   Ibid.

20   Mayor Rudolph W. Giuliani, Congressional testimony to the House Committee on Government Reform, Thursday, March 13, 1997 10:30, copyright 1997, by Federal Document Clearing House, Inc.

21   Bratton and Knobler, *Turnaround*, p. 212; "get off . . .," quoted in Steve Fainaru, "NYC begins crackdown on truants," *Boston Globe*, April 7, 1994.

22   George Jordan, "City's tough cell: balancing arrests with jail crowding," *Newsday*, February 9, 1994.

23   Quoted in William K. Rashbaum, "Bratton plans truancy crackdown," *Newsday*, January 24, 1994.

24   "Police strategy no. 2: curbing youth violence in the schools on the streets," New York Police Department, 1994.

25   Fainaru, "NYC begins crackdown."

26   For the real deal on school violence and militarization, see John Devine, *Maximum Security: The Culture of Violence in Inner City Schools* (Chicago: University of Chicago Press, 1996).

27   "Police strategy no. 2," pp. 25, 30.

28   Mark Schoofs, "Beat it: the city's moral fixation: pushing porn out of town," *Village Voice*, June 27, 1995.

29   Derek Alger, "Soliciting is a losing proposition: anti-prostitution team takes cars, publishes names of would-be Johns," *Newsday*, November 15, 1994.

30   Kit R. Ronane, "Prostitutes on wane in New York streets but take to Internet," *New York Times*, February 23, 1998.

31   "Truants to be handcuffed," *The Guardian*, February 10, 1994; Joe Sciacca, "Evans vows own war on squeegee men," *Boston Herald*, April 21, 1994; Bruce Frankel, "Teen crime surge sparks crackdown," *USA Today*, March 17, 1994.

32   "Fight crime now" (Editorial), *Wall Street Journal*, February 24, 1994.

33   Arthur Spiegelman, "Gotham taking streets back: new mayor touting 'right of safety'; crackdown begins on petty thugs," *San Francisco Examiner*, January 16, 1994.

34 "Police strategy no. 1: getting guns off the streets of New York," New York Police Department, 1994; Charles Nicodemus, "City continues to set pace in seizing guns," *Chicago Sun-Times*, January 26, 1997.

35 Believe it or not, between 1989 and 1994 the New York State auctioned off confiscated guns after the weapons were no longer needed for evidence. As one would expect these guns inevitably showed up at other crime scenes, some in as little time as one day. See James Dao, "Used state guns wind up in bad hands, study says," *New York Times*, May 20, 1994.

36 "Police strategy no. 3: driving drug dealers out of New York," New York Police Department, 1994.

37 "A death on Staten Island: 2 paths cross on familiar ground," *New York Times*, May 15, 1994.

38 Quoted in Bratton and Knobler, *Turnaround*, p. 229.

39 "A death," *New York Times*, May 15, 1994; Robert D. McFadden, "Grand jury won't file charges against police in S.I. man's death," *New York Times*, December 9, 1994.

40 Curtis Rist, "Outrage on SI: death in scuffle with cops sparks protests," *Newsday*, April 30, 1994.

41 George L. Kelling, "Is busting small drug dealers worth it? Yes," *Newsday*, May 29, 1994.

42 Robin Pogrebin, "After an arrest, melee erupts near S.I. project, " *New York Times*, May 20, 1996.

43 "Protests continue in East Flatbush," *New York Times*, June 16, 1996; Charles Baillou, "Senseless Flatbush police killing still drawing protests," *New York Amsterdam News*, September 14, 1996.

44 Adam Nossiter, "Families of 2 killed in police incidents protest," *New York Times*, October 12, 1995.

45 Crime rates were starting to fall from the unprecedented heights of the early 1990s even before quality of life policing became vogue, but the policing revolution has, despite what its detractors say, been closely associated with a precipitous drop in violence and mayhem.

46 For a full accounting of the alternative theories, see James Lardner, "Can you believe the New York miracle?" *New York Review of Books*, August 14, 1997; one major problem for zero tolerance boosters is explaining why crime is also down in cities that don't pursue quality of life enforcement and don't have Comstat meetings. For a detailed deconstruction of zero tolerance triumphantalism, see Elliot Currie, "The scalpel not the chainsaw, the U.S. experience with public order," *City*, no. 8, 1998.

47 John Marzulli, "Subway crime stats error cost cop big R & R," *New York Daily News*, September 1, 1998.

48 Fox Butterfield, "False crime figures worry police officials," *San Francisco Chronicle*, August 3, 1998; these problems came to light after John Timoney, who was Bratton's number two man in New York, took the reins in Philadelphia in March of 1998.

49 Statistics from Cynthia Tuker, "Rogue cops may ruin a good thing," *San Francisco Chronicle*, August 23, 1997; David Rohde, "Crackdown on minor offenses swamps New York City courts," *New York Times*, February 2, 1999.

50 John Marzulli, "Crime dips 10%, slays 24%," *New York Daily News*, August 5, 1998; in fact the victory over crime in New York created such a stir that a jealous Giuliani eventually canned Bratton in late 1996.

51 Michael Fletcher, "Changes in police tactics trigger charges of brutality," *Washington Post*, April 27, 1997.

52 Cited in Peter Mancuso, "Law and order: is police brutality on the rise? Civilian complaints about cops have skyrocketed this year," *Newsday*, November 20, 1994.

53 Quentin Letts, "Tough guy with ruthless approach to low-lifes and ineffective cops," *Times* (UK), January 29, 1996.

54 Christian Parenti, "The revolution in American policing: the science of kicking ass," *Z Magazine*, December 1997.

55 Peter Hermann, "Police to begin ticketing in Oct.; limited experiment targets minor crimes in three districts," *Baltimore Sun*, September 18, 1996.

56 Interview with Lt. Gary McLhenny, Baltimore Police Department, President of Baltimore's Fraternal Order of Police Lodge, August 1997; on Frazier's final capitulation, Kris Antonelli, "Making quick work of crime," *Baltimore Sun*, February 17, 1997.

57 Joanna Daemmrich, "Law and order: Schmoke and Bell differ on 'zero tolerance,'" *Baltimore Sun*, January 26, 1997; also Peter Hermann, "Tape stokes furor over deadly force," *Baltimore Sun*, August 18, 1997.

58 Khara Coleman, "Chiefs swear by local policing: N.O., Boston say stats make case," *New Orleans Times-Picayune*, June 23, 1998.

59 Interview with Mary Howell, August 1997.

60 Story relayed by Mary Howell, interview.

61 By the summer of 1998 the justice department was even pressuring the New Orleans mayor to impose a consent decree forcing remediation of epidemic police brutality. See Bruce Alpert and Bill Walsh, "On the Hill: news from around the Louisiana Delegation and nation's capital," *New Orleans Times-Picayune*, July 19, 1998.

62 "Shielded from justice, police brutality and accountability in the United States," Human Rights Watch, New York, June 1998, p. 251.

63 Janna Griffith of the Indianapolis Police Department Public Affairs Office, phone interview, August 19, 1997; "Street sweep initiative begins today," press release, from the Indianapolis Police Department, June 19, 1997.

64 Sheila Kennedy of the Indiana Civil Liberties Union, phone interview, August 20, 1997.

65 "Calm follows violence: silent protest against police force turns to melee," *Indianapolis News*, July 27, 1995.

66 John Krull, "A mess on the street," *Indianapolis News*, July 28, 1995; "2 days of stone throwing," *New York Times*, July 29, 1995.

67 James Gillaspy, "Neighborhood a casualty of war on drugs: police chief acknowledges that some suspects may have been mistreated as part of crackdown," *Indianapolis Star*, July 28, 1995.

68 "Picking up the pieces of unrest: calm returns as city cleans up and reflects on the week," *Indianapolis Star*, July 29, 1995.

69 Mary Beth Schneider, "It's not been one of mayor's better weeks: it started with a poll showing Goldsmith and O'Bannon even and ended with a police flap," *Indianapolis Star*, September 15, 1996; Susan Schramm, "Mayor is spared from testifying in brawl lawsuit," *Indianapolis Star*, August 18, 1998.

70 Gerry Lanosga, "Police dispute gun data: officers say results of city's project not accurate," *Indianapolis News*, May 18, 1995.

71 Hudson Institute crime specialist Ed McGarrell, quoted in Susan Schramm, "Cities try targeting petty crimes to reduce major ones," *Indianapolis Star*, July 27, 1997.

72 Ibid.

73 Robert N. Bell, "Police want to build up neighborhoods: prosecutor, sheriff, IPD chief tell Northsiders that policies will help residents help themselves," *Indianapolis Star*, May 12, 1997.

74 R. Joseph Gelarden, "Police saturate area of sisters' beatings: officers boost traffic patrols, go door-to-door on near Northside in search of a suspect," *Indianapolis Star*, May 27, 1998.

75 James A. Gillaspy, "Decrease in crime offset by violence: total was down nearly 5 percent in 1997, but serious offenses, such as murder and assault, were up," *Indianapolis Star*, June 7, 1998.

76 Andrea Neal, "Difference between blacks, whites grows: economic disparity in state widened in '80s as high-paying jobs vanished," *Indianapolis Star*, September 15, 1992.

77 On the Midwestern gang scene, see John M. Hagedon, *People and Folks: Gangs, Crime and the Underclass in a Rustbelt City* (Chicago: Lake View, 1988).

78 Dan Carpenter, "City's blacks pay the price in the name of progress," *Indianapolis Star*, February 12, 1991.

79 Chief Robert Olson, Minneapolis Police Department, phone interview, August 1997.

80 Stanley Cohen, *Visions of Social Control* (Cambridge: Polity Press, 1985).

81 See Tony Platt, *Child Savers: The Invention of Delinquency* (Chicago: University of Chicago Press, 1969); Cohen, *Visions of Social Control*.

82 Bryan Brown, Anaheim District Attorney's Office, phone interview, August 1997.

83 Lt. McLhenny interview.

5 DISCIPLINE IN PLAYLAND, PART II – POLICING THE THEMEPARK CITY

1 "In the soup," *The Economist*, September 11, 1993, p. 24.

2 Quoted in Chester Hartman, *The Transformation of San Francisco* (Totowa, NJ: Rowman and Allanheld, 1984), p. 51.

3 According to one report, some 2.1 billion square feet of new space was constructed during the 1980s; almost 45 percent of the office space ever built in the US was built in the 1980s. In 1990 the national vacancy rate was 18 percent, well above the historical average of 6 percent. Of the 5.6 billion square feet of prime office space available in 1990, about one billion square feet was vacant. The excess capacity was endemic until the end of the nineties boom. See the Cognetics report cited in David L. Knight, "Commercial office space in northern Michigan," *North Force Magazine*, January 1, 1991.

4 For an excellent, detailed yet broad study of gentrification, read Neil Smith, *The New Urban Frontier: Gentrification and the Revanchist City* (London: Routledge, 1996).

5 Sharon Zukin, "Urban lifestyles: diversity and standardization in spaces of consumption," *Urban Studies*, vol. 35, no. 5–6, May 1998.

6 Ibid.

7 "Back from the brink," *The Economist*, April 17, 1993, p. 29.

8 Bill Lubinger, "Downtown dream unveiled: panel urges $3 billion in projects dramatic lakefront – new convention center – more places to live," *Plain Dealer*, May 14, 1998.

9 Dan Levy, "Sony has big plans for Yerba Buena: entertainment center on the drawing board," *San Francisco Chronicle*, November 15, 1995; Gerald D. Adams, "Super playground near finished: high tech meets art at $56 million children's center," *San Francisco Examiner*, December 7, 1997; "Pizzeria owner fights city over Moscone expansion: invested $2 million and took 15–year lease in building S.F. plans to raze," *San Francisco Examiner*, March 2, 1998; the convention center alone is expected to cost tax payers $3 million a year in subsidies.

10 Lawrence Tabak, "Wild about convention centers," *Atlantic Monthly*, April 1994, p. 28.

11 Due to the sophisticated nature of computer games and Hollywood special effects, entertainment is now one of the driving forces behind technological innovation. And major industrialists like Iaccoca are investing heavily in the booming economy of culture. See "The entertainment economy," *Business Week*, March 14, 1994, p. 58.

12 Quoted in Sharon Zukin, "Cultural strategies of economic development and the hegemony of vision", paper presented at Social Justice and the City: An Agenda for the New Millennium, Oxford University, 14–15 March 1994, p. 14.

13 Douglas Martin, "Package deal is offered to lure tourists to Big Apple," *New York Times*, May 12, 1994; for a concise cultural history of Times Square, see Marshall Berman, "Signs of the Times: the lure of 42nd Street," *Dissent*, fall 1997.

14 Becky Aikman, "Remaking a classic," *Newsday*, April 27, 1997.

15 Ibid.

16 Quoted in Beth Shuster, "Living in fear," *Los Angeles Times*, August 23, 1998.

17 Quoted in ibid.

18 Judith Evans, "D.C. wants to join the boom for BIDs; improvement districts' accomplishments cited," *Washington Post*, January 13, 1996.

19 Marvine Howe, "Business group seeks to extend sphere to shelter," *New York Times*, May 15, 1994.

20 This scene, and much of what follows, is based on my own first experience as an activist with Street Watch and first-hand reporting for WBIA, Pacifica Network News, and *Z Magazine*, in the spring of 1994.

21 Based on interviews with Grunberg and a tour of Saint Agnes in spring 1994.

22 Christian Parenti, "Sidewalk mercenaries vs. homeless," *Z Magazine*, November 1994.

23 "'They're in the security guard business, not homeless outreach,' said HUD assistant secretary Andrew Cuomo." See "Wake-up call: BIDs are not above the law," *Newsday*, July 7, 1995.

24 Karen Rothmyer, "City to oversee BID finances," *Newsday*, April 22, 1995; Dan Barry and Thomas Lueck, "Control sought on districts for businesses," *New York Times*, April 2, 1998.

25 Thomas Lueck, "Business improvement district at Grand Central is dissolved," *New York Times*, July 30, 1998; "Business district vows to fight city's order to shut it down," *New York Times*, July 31, 1998; "The Grand Central B.I.D. war," *New York Times*, August 1, 1998.

26 Mike Ivey, "'Street ambassadors a great idea for downtown," *Capital Times* (Madison), August 4, 1998.

27 Ibid.; see also Judith Evans, "D.C. wants to join the boom for BIDs; improvement districts' accomplishments cited," *Washington Post*, January 13, 1996.

28 Economic Research Associates, "1989 survey of San Francisco visitors: summary report," prepared for San Francisco Convention and Visitors Bureau, May 1990, p. 13.

29 Carlin Dee, director of the Downtown Association, interview, July 24, 1995.

30 Robert F. Begley, executive director of the Hotel Council of San Francisco, interview, July 24, 1995.

31 Kent Sims, "San Francisco's homeless problem," Mayor's Office of Economic Planning and Development, April 1992, p. 1; Sims expressed similar views in two taped interviews, but I cite his white paper because it is available for review.

32 Ibid., p. 3. Sims cited the source of almost all the statistics given in his paper, except for these figures on the economic impact of homelessness. Homeless advocates, such as Paul Boden of the Coalition on Homelessness, contest Sims' figures as inflated.

33 San Francisco Police Department, memorandum, from Commander Dennis Martel, August 6, 1993.

34   See Janet Abu-Lughod, *From Urban Village to East Village: The Battle for New York's Lower East Side* (Oxford: Blackwell, 1994).

35   Shawn Kennedy, "Riot police remove 31 squatters from two East Village buildings," *New York Times*, May 31, 1995; Wilbert A. Tatum, "Squatter removal: by the dawn's early light," *New York Amsterdam News*, June 3, 1995.

36   James Ledbetter, "Press clips," *Village Voice*, June 27, 1995.

37   Steven Wishnia, "Blocked out," *Village Voice*, July 18, 1995.

38   Ibid.

39   Ledbetter, "Press clips."

40   Wishnia, "Blocked out."

41   Dan Morrison, "Squatters booted," *Newsday*, August 14, 1996.

42   Thomas J. Lueck, "Police evict squatters from three city-owned tenements in the East Village," *New York Times*, August 14, 1996.

43   M. J. Neuberger, "El finito on East 13th Street," *Village Voice*, August 27, 1996.

44   Sarah Ferguson, "Under siege: can the East Village survive another purge?" *Village Voice*, August 27, 1996.

45   Ibid.

46   Sarah Ferguson, "Up in the smoke: city razes squat, despite court injunction," *Village Voice*, February 25, 1997.

47   Dennis Hevesi, "New York may use industrial zones as shelters sites," *New York Times*, May 15, 1994; James Rutenberg, "New homes for the homeless?" *Our Town*, May 18, 1994, p. 15.

48   Camilo Jose Vergara, "New York's new ghettos," *The Nation*, June 17, 1991, p. 806.

49   Matthew Purdy, "1993 homicides fewer but more clustered in New York City," *New York Times*, January 10, 1994; Gary Pierre, "Fewer killings tallied in '93 in New York," *New York Times*, January 2, 1994, p. 19.

50   Frank Lombardi, "Latest crackdown targets bus drivers," *New York Daily News*, July 30, 1998.

51   Christopher Drew and Andy Newman, "Taxi crackdown could backfire, critics warn," *New York Times*, August 31, 1998; Mike Allen, "Protesters on City Hall steps have declaration for Giuliani," *New York Times*, July 5, 1998.

52   Frank Lombardi, "Blizzard of summonses blankets city," *New York Daily News*, May 20, 1998; Robert Polner, "Mayor's moods swing policy," *Newsday*, March 30, 1998.

53   Charles W. Bell, "Black Israelites muffled," *New York Daily News*, April 18, 1998.

54   Conversation with Stephen Duncombe, September 1998.

55   Kit R. Roane, "Preparing for the worst, Giuliani is to build blastproof shelter," *New York Times*, June 13, 1998.

56   Michael Cooper, "Officers in Bronx fire 41 shots, and an unarmed man is killed," *New York Times*, February 5, 1999.

57   David Kocieniewski, "Success of elite police unit exacts a toll on the streets," *New York Times*, February 15, 1999.

58   Ginger Thompson, "1,000 rally to condemn shooting of unarmed man by police," *New York Times*, February 8, 1999.

59   Kevin Flynn, "Police killing draws national notice," *New York Times*, February 8, 1999.

60   Paul Zielbauer, "FBI examines site in Bronx where police fatally shot unarmed man," *New York Times*, February 18, 1999.

61   Kit R. Roane, "Mayor says officers' new ammunition will be safer," *New York Times*, February 14, 1999.

62   Ron Scherer, "Backlash builds over police tactics," *Christian Science Monitor*, March 19, 1999.

63 Alissa J. Rubin, "Clinton cites police brutality, seeks more funds for officer training," *Los Angeles Times*, March 14, 1999.

64 Larry Bivins, "Police brutality reporting has not fulfilled promise of anti-crime bill," Gannett News Service, March 5, 1999.

6 CARRYING THE BIG STICK: SWAT TEAMS AND PARAMILITARY POLICING

1   This section is based on first-hand reporting and interviews sighted below. The spokeswoman is quoted in Charles McCarthy, "Officers target of gunfire in several recent incidents," *Fresno Bee*, May 5, 1994.

2   Quoted in Bill Hazlett, "Police specialists – grim training aimed at saving lives," *Los Angeles Times*, October 29, 1972; *The Iron Fist and the Velvet Glove*, Center for Research on Criminal Justice, 1977.

3   Peter B. Kraska and Victor E. Kappler, "Militarizing American police: the rise and normalization of paramilitary units," *Social Problems*, vol. 44, no. 1, February 1997, pp. 1–18; on the culture of paramilitary policing, see Peter Kraska, "Enjoying militarism: political/personal dilemmas in studying US police paramilitary units," *Justice Quarterly*, vol. 13, no. 3, September 1996, pp. 405–29. It is worth noting that Kraska is one of the only sociologists studying paramilitary policing units in a systematic and critical fashion. My understanding of tactical policing is indebted to his writing and an interview.

4   Fresno had a 13.9 percent unemployment in 1998. See George Hostetter, "Fresno-area jobless rate worst in the state," *Fresno Bee*, February 18, 1998.

5   Based on interviews with Homer Leija, of Barrios Unidos, and with Officer Michael Manfredi of the Fresno PD, October 1998. In Fresno, the local version of this state-wide war among Latino gangs had, and has, a few unique features: for example, most *norteño* (normally allied to the superstructure of *La Familia*) tend to affiliate with the Bull Dogs, a Central Valley meta-gang, allegedly formed in prison by *vatos* from Fresno, which now has local, autonomous sets throughout Fresno, Visalia, and the rest of the valley.

6   Calkins, "Fed up with gangs, Fresno sends in SWAT units," *Sacramento Bee*, December 17, 1994.

7   Charles McCarthy, "Officers target of gunfire in several recent incidents," *Fresno Bee*, May 5, 1994.

8   Calkins, "Fed up with gangs."

9   Royal Calkins and Cristina Medina, "SWAT team members take back Fresno streets," *Fresno Bee*, December 17, 1994.

10 Ibid.

11 Interviews with Homer Leija, director of Barrios Unidos, October 1998, and Lt. John Fries, September 1998.

12 The following section is based on interviews and first-hand observation of the VSCU, who allowed me to ride with them, in October 1998.

13 Information regarding the imprisonment of veteran gang members comes from interviews with VCSU officers and Donna Hardina *et al.*, "Examination of gang membership in a multi-ethnic urban neighborhood," unpublished paper from Department of Social Work, California State University, Fresno, 1997.

14 Fresno, like every jurisdiction, is riven with petty jealousies and ferocious competition between agencies and within agencies. One VCSU sergeant said that "when things get too slow the guys [on the VCSU] are just at each other's throats. They're all type-A, highly competitive personalities."

15 Kimi Yoshino, "Questions swirl around Valley's officer-involved shootings," *Fresno Bee*, July 6, 1998.

16 These figures provide by public information officer Lt. Fries, October 1998.

17 These numbers come from the NAACP, interview with Johnny Nelum, president of the local Fresno chapter of the NAACP, September 1998.

18 Statistics provided by FPD grant coordinator Sam Mahtab, Lt. John Fries, and Mike Johnson, senior budget analyst for the city of Fresno, phone interviews, October 1998.

19 Interviews with community members, sheriff's deputies; statistics from Jim Steinberg, "The crime fight behind the numbers – it's your call," *Fresno Bee*, September 30, 1996.

20 Interview with Lt. Jim Kerns, Fresno County Sheriff's Department, October 5, 1998; on SSU, interview with Lt. Martin Rivera, of MAGEC, October 26, 1998. For a fascinating political history of the California Department of Corrections' secret police forces, see Jo Durden-Smith, *Who Killed George Jackson?* (New York: Alfred Knopf, 1976) and Citizens Research and Investigation Committee and Louis Tackwood, *The Glass House Tapes* (New York: Avon, 1973).

21 Mark Arax, "Agencies fight gangs with MAGEC crime," *Los Angeles Times*, February 2, 1998.

22 Interview with Lt. Martin Rivera.

23 Cyndee Fontana, "Fresno County making inroads in the battle against gangs," *Fresno Bee*, July 20, 1997.

24 Interview with Lt. Marin Rivera.

25 For the California law, see *California Penal Code, Street Terrorism Enforcement and Prevention Act, Chapter 11 section 186.20–186.27*. A growing number of states also have "gang enhancement status," for example Utah, Arizona, Tennessee, and Florida have laws similar to California's.

26 Interview with Lt. Martin Rivera.

27 Ibid.

28 For a good discussion of this phenomenon, see chapter 5, John Hagan, *Crime and Disrepute* (Thousand Oaks, CA: Pine Forge Press, 1994).

29 Leija interview.

30 "Report attacks use of gang injunctions," *Fresno Bee*, May 29, 1997; "False premise, false promise: the Blythe Street gang injunction and its aftermath," American Civil Liberties Union, 1997.

31 Quoted in Nina Siegal, "Ganging up on civil liberties," *Progressive*, October 1, 1997.

32 In civil court guilt is proven upon "a preponderance of the evidence." In criminal court the standard is the familiar "beyond a reasonable doubt."

33 Dave Harmon, "Suspects of crime face new legal tool," *Austin American-Statesman*, July 3, 1998.

34 Mike Males and Dan Macallair, "The impact of juvenile curfews in California," The Justice Policy Institute, June 1998; also see Jim Steinberg, "Curfews don't cut crime, study says: officials say report findings are misleading," *Fresno Bee*, June 21, 1998. The study reported that San Francisco, with a curfew but no youth curfew arrests, had a youth property felony rate nearly matching Fresno County's, thus suggesting that curfews have little if any real impact on crime. Most youth crime occurs between 3 p.m. and 8 p.m.

35 For example of the SWAT parade cover, see Mark Arax, "Farm town's SWAT team leaves it a costly legacy," *Los Angeles Times*, April 5, 1999.

36 "Early-morning raids swift, without warning: most residents in homes were still asleep," *News Tribune* (Tacoma, WA), July 19, 1998.

37 Jane Stancill, "Authorities say search warrant for street block was necessary," *News & Observer* (Raleigh, NC) November 19, 1990.

38 *Barnett vs. Karipnos*, 1995, cited in Kraska and Kappler, "Militarizing American police"; Joyce Clark, "Suit over drug raid settled for $200,000," *News & Observer* (Raleigh, NC), February 22, 1996.

39 Julie Powers, "Agents who killed hostage face SBI inquiry: family gets $250,000 payment," *News & Observer* (Raleigh, NC), March 5, 1993; Peter Cassidy, "The rise in paramilitary policing," *Covert Action Quarterly*, fall 1997.

40 Donald W. Patterson, "Bookmobile gets new life on cop team," *Greensboro News & Record*, March 17, 1993.

41 Kathleen Cei, "Commando cops," *New Haven Advocate*, April 16, 1998.

42 Testimony before San Francisco Police Commission, November 4, 1998.

43 Ibid.

44 Newscast: "Use of SWAT teams up greatly across the country," *CBS Evening News*, broadcast Monday, December 8, 1997.

45 Scott Sandlin, "Navy unit, APD sued for drug raid death," *Albuquerque Journal*, October 7, 1992. An example of more standard military training for SWAT took place in Pittsburgh during June 1997 and involved fourteen army helicopters and 200 special forces troops. See Dana Priest "Inside America: manoeuvres in the dark," *The Guardian*, April 15, 1997.

46 Karen Alexander, "2 cities settle Pratt lawsuits: 92 SWAT raid left Everett woman dead," *Seattle Times*, October 20, 1995.

47 "Review of slaying urged," *Greensboro News & Record*, September 8, 1998; "Police shooting draws protests," *Greensboro News & Record*, September 7, 1998.

48 "Greenville County deputies defend actions," *The Herald* (Rock Hill, SC), September 17, 1998.

49 M. Floyd Hall, "Bethlehem 1 dead after fire guts home raided by Bethlehem police," *Allentown Morning Call*, April 24, 1997.

50 Jerry Bier, "Dinuba family awarded $12.5 million," *Fresno Bee*, March 13, 1999.

51 Steve Shoup, "Board seeks info on cop raids," *Albuquerque Journal*, April 17, 1997.

52 Cindy Glover, "Residents ask open hearing on shooting," *Albuquerque Journal*, February 4, 1997.

53 Gregory R. Chin, "SWAT team shoots 75 rounds to kill suspected dealer, age 73," *Miami Times*, March 21, 1996.

54 Hector Castro, "Shooting review yields new checklist," *News Tribune* (Tacoma, WA), September 25, 1998.

55 It is worth noting that in the UK the police often feel no urgency to storm barricaded suspects, as long as the suspect does not have a hostage. In one case during the mid nineties British police built a wall around a suspect's house, blocking his visibility, and waited two weeks for him to emerge, which he did.

56 Brian M. Trotta, "SWAT experts: officers in shooting undertrained," *Hartford Courant*, December 5, 1996. Compare the treatment received with that dispensed to a heavily armed, homicidal Mr. John du Pont. During a 48-hour stand-off, police allowed du Pont to "take a night's sleep, having promised that they would not try to arrest him as he rested. They also gave him a telephone wake-upcall the next morning": Quentin Letts, "Police 'showing du Pont favours,'" *The Times* (UK), January 31, 1996.

57 Dana Calvo and Robert George, "Miami man receives his death wish," *Sun-Sentinel* (Fort Lauderdale), October 16, 1998.

58   Bill Teeter, "'Friendly fire' cited in shootout: officer hurt; suspect's gun not used, reports say," *Fort Worth Star-Telegram*, October 7, 1998.

59   Ryan Slattery, "SWAT member shot by officer," *Press-Enterprise* (Riverside, CA), September 24, 1998.

60   James S. Sotos, "Cop-on-cop violence: city faces liability in officer's death," *Chicago Daily Law Bulletin*, vol. 144, no. 119, June 18, 1998; Hilart E. MacGregor, "Family of slain officer can sue city, court rules," *Los Angeles Times*, May 29, 1998.

61   Scott Hadly,"DA report on slaying faults police and victim, *"Los Angeles Times*, March 15, 1997; "Oxnard SWAT team looks inward," *Los Angeles Times*, August 31, 1997.

62   Lewis Griswold, "SWAT action resulting in 2 deaths questioned," *Fresno Bee*, January 20, 1998.

63   Lauren Dodge, "3 police officers shot in Portland, 1 fatally," *Seattle Post-Intelligencer*, January 28, 1998; Erin Hoover, "More equality in ranks brings with it more risks," *Portland Oregonian*, January 28, 1998.

64   Steve Marshall, "L.A. cops get 600 M-16s to help even odds on street," *USA Today*, September 17, 1997.

65   Tom Hallman, Jr., "Assault on community policing," *Portland Oregonian*, April 19, 1998.

66   Kevin Krause, "Sheriff beefs up deputies' arsenal: 25 semiautomatic rifles on order," *Sun-Sentinel* (Fort Lauderdale), August 28, 1997.

67   "Apopka police sargents to get assault weapons," *Orlando Sentinel*, September 13, 1998; Kevin P. Connolly, "Police in Apopka add more firepower: patrol sargents will soon be packing semiautomatic assault weapons instead of shotguns," *Orlando Sentinel*, September 13, 1998.

68   Henry Lee, "Pair awards $408,000 after being shot by Pinole police," *San Francisco Chronicle*, February 13, 1999.

69   Peter Cassidy, "Police take military turn counter to other image as neighborhood peace-keepers," *Boston Globe*, January 11, 1998.

70   Lee Hancock, "Smith County sheriff unveils armored unit, military personnel carriers add weight to war on crime," *Dallas Morning News*, April 10, 1997.

71   David Haase, "Surplus bayonets used as tools, not weapons, police say," *Indianapolis Star*, November 7, 1997.

72   Derrick DePledge, "Lawmen rake in free military-surplus gear," *Star-Ledger* (Newark, NJ), November 23, 1997.

73   Kraska and Kappler, "Militarizing American police," p. 12.

74   J. David McCrery, "The role of the inner perimeter," *Tactical Edge*, summer 1996, p. 30.

75   Ed Sanow, "12 gauge quick shok Sabot slug," *SWAT*, November 1998, p. 26.

76   Capt. Roy Hudson, "The future of SWAT in law enforcement," *Tactical Edge*, fall 1997, p. 20.

77   Several interviewees from southwest Fresno expressed this sentiment to me over the phone in September 1998, and several *Fresno Bee* articles on policing contain similar comments.

78   Interview with Lt. Greg Coleman, September 1998.

79   Michel Foucault, *Discipline and Punish: The Birth of the Prison* (New York: Vintage, 1979), p. 30; and special thanks to Ruthie Gilmore for helping me clarify my thinking regarding the politics of terror.

80   Ibid., p. 138.

81   Ibid., p. 49.

7 REPATRIATING *LA MIGRA*'S WAR: THE MILITARIZED BORDER COMES HOME

1 Interviews with witnesses and victims of the raid, January 1998; "Survey of the Chandler Police Department-INS/Border Patrol joint operation," the Office of the Attorney General Grant Wood, Civil Rights Division (Arizona), November 1997. Interestingly, the AG's report found that the Chandler raid was just an extreme episode within an ongoing campaign to pacify and then redevelop Chandler's downtown, so that it would be "the jewel of the East Valley."

2 Ibid., pp. 12-14.

3 Ibid., p. 21.

4 Interview with Alberto Esparza, January 1998.

5 Robbie Sherwood, "Chandler police demand apology for 'racist' remark," *Arizona Republic*, December 9, 1997.

6 "INS fact book," US Department of Justice Immigration and Naturalization, 1997, p. 33.

7 Margaret Ramirez, "'96 immigration law causing rise in deportations," *Los Angeles Times*, September 22, 1998.

8 Michelle Mittlestadt, "Refugee tells committee of mistreatment by INS," *Orange County Register*, September 17, 1998.

9 See "The United States of America rights for all," Amnesty International, October 1998, chapter 5.

10 Saskia Sassen, *The Mobility of Labor and Capital: A Study in International Investment and Labor Flow* (Cambridge: Cambridge University Press, 1988).

11 Public Law 104-208, 110 stat. 3009 (September, 30, 1996); Public Law 104-132, 110 stat. 1214 (April 24, 1996).

12 Susan Gilmore, "New laws pose challenge to thousands of immigrants," *Seattle Times*, March 12, 1998.

13 Barry Newman, "Bad form, how a Canadian man married an American – and got deported," *Wall Street Journal*, May 28, 1998.

14 Margaret Ramirez, "Immigration law separates Valley pair," *Los Angeles Times*, September 22, 1998.

15 Sarah Huntley, "Families protest deportation rules," *Tampa Tribune*, October 31, 1998.

16 Rene Romo, "Protests demand end to INS raids," *Albuquerque Journal*, October 15, 1998.

17 Bob Ortega, "Last call: Texas agents spark outcry in roundup of legal immigrants," *Wall Street Journal*, October 12, 1998; David L. Marcus, "Three times and out: some face deportation for repeat drunken driving," *Boston Globe*, October 14, 1998.

18 Ortega, ibid.

19 Quoted in Timothy J. Dunn, *The Militarization of the U.S.–Mexico Border 1978–1992: Low-Intensity Conflict Doctrine Comes Home* (Austin, TX: CMAS Books, 1996), p. 114.

20 Interview, Mike Connell, Chief Border Patrol agent, INS El Paso sector, February 1998.

21 Interview, Jesus Rodriguez, public affairs officer, INS El Paso sector, February 1998.

22 Interview with Rosemary Moreno, El Concilio Immigration Project, for KPFA radio, April 5, 1998; Robert Rodriguez, "Teen deported from Roosevelt High returned to mother," *Fresno Bee*, April 9, 1998; Pablo Lopez, "Law officials defend arrests at Roosevelt High," *Fresno Bee*, April 4, 1998.

23 I once traveled by bus from Guatemala City to San Francisco, California, via El Paso, and encountered only one checkpoint, located deep in Arizona and run by the US Border Patrol.

24 Interview with Jesus Rodriguez, public affairs officer, INS El Paso sector, February 1998.

25 Conversation with Jeremy Warren San Diego, Federal Public Defender, January 1998.

26 Interview with Michael Flynn, February 1998.

27 Interview, Richard Roger, Director of the INS LA District Office, February 1998.

28 Special Order No. 40, Office of the Chief of Police, November 27, 1979 (provided by LAPD public relations officer, Mike Partain, February 1998).

29 Dan Kraut, "INS hopes to deport 200 NJ criminal gang members in Passaic on list," *The Record* (Northern New Jersey), April 3, 1998.

30 William Branigin, "INS pursuing aliens in urban gangs; new immigration law aids agents in drive to put criminals out of the country," *Washington Post*, May 2, 1997.

31 Krystyna Slivinski, "INS partnership anchors war on gangs," *Chicago Tribune*, September 2, 1997.

32 Jennifer Bjorhus, "Joint effort by police, INS concern immigrant-rights groups," *Portland Oregonian*, November 2, 1997.

33 Interview with Virginia Kice, INS Western Region spokeswoman, February 1998.

34 Doris Meissner, Commissioner, Immigration and Naturalization Service, Congressional testimony before the Committee on Appropriations, Subcommittee on Commerce, Justice, State and the Judiciary, April 10, 1997; much of the following section is based on a series of interviews with numerous INS officials.

35 Richard Benke, "Database files faces, fingerprints of illegal immigrants," *Denver Post*, June 21, 1998; INS press office statistic.

36 David Lyon, *The Electronic Eye: The Rise of Surveillance Society* (Minneapolis: University of Minnesota Press, 1994).

37 Interview with Michael Flynn, Assistant Director for Investigations in the INS's Western Region, February 1998.

38 Ibid.

39 Ibid.

40 Teresa Malcolm, "Mexican workers deported after filing complaint," *National Catholic Reporter*, October 16, 1998.

41 "Portrait of injustice: the impact of immigration raids on families, workers and communities," Report by National Raids Task Force of the National Network for Immigrant and Refugee Rights, October 1998, pp. 33–5.

42 Ibid., pp. 36–8.

43 "Community development – changes in Nebraska's and Iowa's counties with large meat packing plant workforces," United States General Accounting Office, Report to Congressional Requesters, February 27, 1998, p. 38.

44 "Operation Prime Beef," INS fact sheet, September 1998, p. 1.

45 For more on "employer sanctions" as employer leverage over labor, see David Bacon, "Immigration laws abused," *San Francisco Chronicle*, October 20, 1998.

46 "125 arrested in Nebraska immigration raid," *New York Times*, March 5, 1995.

47 Interview with Roberto Martinez, American Friends Service Committee, February 1998.

48 Curtis Hubbard, "Feds target Hispanic workers," *Jackson Hole Guide*, August 28, 1996; Tom Hacker, "Jackson raids net more than more than 100 illegal workers," *Star Tribune* (Jackson Hole), August 27, 1996.

49 "Agent fired during raid on migrants, report finds," *New York Times*, December 12, 1997.

50 Evelyn Nieves, "INS raid reaps many, but sows pain," *New York Times*, November 20, 1997; "Portrait of injustice," pp. 19–20.

51 Louis Freedberg and Ramon G. McLeod, "The other side of the law," *San Francisco Chronicle*, October 13, 1998.

52 For examples of white immigrants surviving INS raids unmolested, see "Portrait of Injustice."

53 This account is based on first-hand reporting conducted during December 1997.

54 "INS fact book," US Department of Justice, Immigration and Naturalization, 1997, p. 33.

55 "Border Patrol plans to buy up to 45 new helicopters," *Helicopter News*, July 19, 1996; "Border Patrol will bypass surplus aircraft, buy new machines," *Helicopter News*, April 26, 1996.

56 For an over-view of how the military sees its counter-narcotics role after the murder of Esequiel Hernandez, see Stacey Evers, "USA treads a fine line over counter-narcotics operations," *Jane's Defense Weekly*, September 10, 1997.

57 For a resumé of National Guard anti-drug activities on the US–Mexico border, see Ronald E. Brooks, Past President, California Narcotic Officers Association, Congressional testimony, House Sub-committee for National Security, International Affairs and Criminal Justice, May 14, 1997.

58 Testimony of H. Allen Holmes, Assistant Secretary of Defense for Special Operations/ Low Intensity Conflict, House Judiciary Committee, July 20, 1995; cited in Jose Palafox, "Militarizing the border," *Covert Action Quarterly*, spring 1996.

59 Dunn, *The Militarization of the U.S.–Mexico Border*, pp. 133–5.

60 Interview with Lieutenant Colonel Bill Riechret, Joint Task Force-Six, February 1998.

61 Major Christopher M. Schnaubelt, "Interagency command and control: planning for counter-drug support," *Military Review*, vol. 76, no. 5, October–September 1996, p. 16.

62 Col. Bruce Cucuel, quoted in Evers, "USA treads a fine line."

63 Lt. Col. John B. Hunt, "OOTW: a concept in flux," *Military Review*, vol. 76, no. 5, September–October 1996, p. 5.

64 Lt. Charles J. Dunlap, Jr., " The origins of the American military coup of 2012," *Parameters* (winter) 1992–93: pp. 2–20; Lt. Colonel Scott Anderson, chief of staff for the US Marine Corps Warfare Laboratory in Quantico Virginia, and the officer in charge of the "Urban Warrior Games" in Oakland, assured Jose Palafox and me that Dunlap's article was "very widely read" and it is essentially *the* argument against military involvement in domestic policing. Interview with Lt. Colonel Scott Anderson, March 17, 1999.

65 Interview, Lt. Colonel Reichret, Joint Task Force-Six, February 1998.

66 This is from a list published in *Resister* (Special Forces underground newsletter), vol. 2, no. 2, fall 1995, and then confirmed in an interview with Maureen Bosch, JTF-6 press liaison, January 1998.

67 Christopher M. Schaubelts, "Lessons in command and control from the Los Angeles riots," *Parameters*, vol. 23, no. 2, summer 1997, pp. 88–109.

68 Interview with Lt. Colonel Reichret, Joint Task Force Six, February 1998; for a detailed explanation of HIDTA, see "Drug control – an overview of US counterdrug intelligence activities," United States General Accounting Office, June 25, 1998, pp. 79–84.

69 Interview with Roberto Martinez, February 1998.

70 David Reyes, "A checkpoint reprieve for commuters' immigration," *Los Angeles Times*, April 22, 1997; "New lane opens at I-5 checkpoint," *San Diego Union-Tribune*, July 1, 1997.

8 THE RISE OF BIG HOUSE NATION: FROM REFORM TO REVENGE

1 See Steven R. Donziger, ed., *The Real War on Crime: The Report of the National Criminal Justice Commission* (New York: Harper Perennial, 1996), statistical chart, p. 32.

2   *Sixth Annual Report of LEAA*, US Department of Justice (Washington, DC: Government Printing Office, 1974), p. 4; for examples of treatment programs, see the *Third Annual Report of LEAA*, US Department of Justice, (Washington, DC: Government Printing Office, 1971), pp. 76–7.

3   Stan Cohen, *Visions of Social Control: Crime Punishment and Classification* (Polity Press: Cambridge, 1985).

4   On construction, see the *Second Annual Report of LEAA*, US Department of Justice (Washington, DC: Government Printing Office, 1970), p. 25; this is not to say that *no* new prisons were built, just that most of the LEAA resources went towards rationalizing existing institutions.

5   For a history of Southern penology, see Alex Lichtenstein, *Twice the Work of Free Labor* (New York: Verso, 1996).

6   National Advisory Commission on Criminal Justice Standards and Goals, *A National Strategy to Reduce Crime* (Washington, DC: Government Printing Office, 1973); *Second Annual Report of LEAA*, US Department of Justice (Washington, DC: Government Printing Office, 1970), p. 7.

7   Eric Cummins, *The Rise and Fall of California's Radical Prison Movement* (Stanford, CA: Stanford University Press, 1994).

8   Malcolm M. Feeley and Edward R. Rubin, "Judicial policy making and prison reform," unpublished manuscript, April 1996; William Banks Taylor, *Brokered Justice: Race, Politics, and Mississippi Prisons 1798–1992* (Columbus: Ohio State University Press, 1993); David M. Oshinsky, *Worse than Slavery: Parchment Farm and the Ordeal of Jim Crow Justice* (New York: Free Press, 1996).

9   "Concrete mama: prison profiles from Walla Walla," presentation by Ed Mead and Bo Brown, at Critical Resistance, Beyond the Prison Industrial Complex Conference, September 23–25, 1998, University of California, Berkeley; "tough fag" quote relayed by Daniel Burton-Rose, who is writing a book on the George Jackson Brigade.

10 Quoted in Bert Useem and Peter Kimball, *States of Siege: US Prison Riots, 1971–1982* (Oxford: Oxford University Press, 1989), p. 37.

11 Ibid.

12 Riots have a way of concentrating the minds of prison officials and liberal lawyers on the outside who might otherwise ignore the big house. Attica created conjugal visits for New York inmates. And officials there found visits helpful in managing the population and credited them with having cut the recidivism rate by 10 percent. Even the ghastly and politically stunted Santa Fe, New Mexico, riot, in which inmates killed perceived snitches and sex offenders, won New Mexico prisoners conjugal visits; see Kit Miniclier, "Trailers give inmates cozy setting for family visits: N.M. program helps prisoners keep outside ties," *Denver Post*, November 9, 1992.

13 *Source Book, 1995*, Bureau of Justice Statistics (Washington, DC: Government Printing Office, 1996), Table 6.33, p. 568.

14 Charles Murray, *Losing Ground: American Social Policy, 1950–1980* (New York: Basic Books, 1984); Michael Katz, *The Undeserving Poor: From the War on Poverty to the War on Welfare* (New York: Pantheon Books, 1989).

15 George Gilder, *Wealth and Poverty* (New York: Basic Books, 1981).

16 Lawrence Mead, *Beyond Entitlement: The Social Obligations of Citizenship* (New York: Free Press, 1986), pp. 13, 84–5.

17 See Katherine Beckett, *Making Crime Pay: Law and Order in Contemporary American Politics* (New York: Oxford University Press, 1997).

18 Joan Petersilia, "Crime and punishment in California," in James Stineberg *et al.*, eds., *Urban America: Policy Choices for Los Angeles and the Nation* (Santa Monica: RAND, 1992), p. 187.

19 Barbara A. Nadel, "Prison sightings: a rundown of the factors that go into site selection and development of correctional facilities," *Planning*, vol. 61, no. 6, June 1995, pp. 2–3.

9 PRISON AS ABATTOIR: OFFICIAL TERROR

1 See discussion of "The SHU syndrome," in Terry Kupers, *Prison Madness: The Mental Health Crisis Behind Bars and What We Must Do About It* (San Francisco: Jossey-Bass, 1998).

2 This video, obtained as part of a lawsuit filed by the Tate family, has been incorporated into the documentary, *Maximum Security University*, 1997. Available from California Prison Focus, San Francisco, CA.

3 Mark Arax and Mark Gladstone, "Prison officials to revise policy on deadly force," *Los Angeles Times*, October 24, 1998.

4 Mark Arax and Mark Gladstone "Only California uses deadly force in inmate fights," *Los Angeles Times*, October 18, 1998.

5 Ibid.

6 Mark Arax, "Prison told to resume mixing gang rivals," *Los Angeles Times*, Thursday, August 22, 1996.

7 Andy Furillo, "Many causes but few solutions to prison race war," *Sacramento Bee Sunday*, October 20, 1996.

8 These gang fault lines are based on interviews with prisoners, conducted by the author, during research trips on behalf of California Prison Focus.

9 That phrase is quoted in the documentary, *Maximum Security University*, 1998.

10 Quoted in Mark Arax and Mark Gladstone "Only California uses deadly force in inmate fights" *Los Angeles Times*, October 18, 1998.

11 "California Department of Corrections, five-year facilities master plan 1995–2000," California Department of Corrections, 1995, pp. 2–6.

12 Quoted in Reynolds Holding, "Prison chief denies link between violence, budget" *San Francisco Chronicle*, Tuesday, November 19, 1996.

13 Kathleen Connolly, Lea McDermid, Vincent Schiraldi, and Dan Macallair, "From classrooms to cell blocks: how prison building affects education and African American enrollment," Center on Juvenile and Criminal Justice, October 1996.

14 Pamela J. Podger and Royal Calkins, "Prison supervisor's tip spawned FBI inquiry," *Fresno Bee*, October 29, 1994; "FBI probes fatal shootings of prison inmates by guards," *San Francisco Examiner*, October 28, 1994.

15 Podger and Calkins, "Prison supervisor's tip"; Pamela J. Podger, "Corcoran whistle-blower deals with consequences two years later," *Fresno Bee*, November 3, 1996; Reynolds Holding, "State sends investigators to Corcoran," *San Francisco Chronicle*, November 8, 1996. Richard Caruso found that his difficulties extended into other agencies when his attempts to obtain employment with a Bay Area county jail system were quashed. See Bernadette Tansey, "Whistle-blower sues after sheriff's office job is denied," *San Francisco Chronicle*, September 29, 1998.

16 Kim Christensen and Marc Lifsher, "Under the gun," *Orange County Register*, October 23, 1994.

17 Kim Christensen and Marc Lifsher, "Prison guards: licensed to kill?" *Orange County Register*, October 23, 1994.

18   Marc Lifsher, "Suit accuses prison officials of cover-up in fatal shooting," *Orange County Register*, April 1, 1995.

19   Mark Arax, "Policy of mixing prison gangs under study," *Los Angeles Times*, Sunday, August 25, 1996.

20   Mark Arax, "8 prison officials fired over beating of black inmates," *Los Angeles Times*, April 11, 1996.

21   *Madrid vs. Gomez*, 889 F Supp. 1146 (N.D. Cal. 1995), see Findings of Fact.

22   Mark Arax, "Ex-guard tells of brutality, code of silence at Corcoran Prison," *Los Angeles Times*, July 6, 1998.

23   Marx Arax, "Tales of brutality behind bars," *Los Angeles Times*, Wednesday, August 21, 1996.

24   Jan Summerfield, "Inmates' lifestyles are far too lavish to be a deterrent," (Letters) *Fresno Bee*, December 9, 1995.

25   Marylee N. Reynolds, "Back on the chain gang," *Corrections Today*, vol. 58, no. 2, April 1, 1996.

26   "Sex behind bars: lawmakers rein in dubious prisoner 'right,' " Editorial, *San Diego Union-Tribune*, July 20, 1996; see also "California briefly," *Orange County Register*, November 21, 1998. The state first instituted such visits in 1968. The policy was further solidified in 1975 with the creation of the Prisoners' Bill of Rights. See Nancy Hill-Holtzman, "21st State Senate District," *Los Angeles Times*, March 15, 1996; Rich Harris, "Three strikes, conjugal visits bills derailed," Associated Press Political Service, April 23, 1997.

27   Michael Sangiacomo, "Still bitter recovery taking time in Lucasville," *Plain Dealer*, Cleveland, April 10, 1994; "News from every state," *USA Today*, February 5, 1996; Richard P. Jones, "Phase-in advocated," *Milwaukee Journal Sentinel*, February 17, 1996; Paul Wright, Prisons change weight-lift policy," *Baton Rouge Advocate*, August 15, 1997; "Prison weight lifting is a nonsense issue," in Daniel Burton-Rose, Dan Pens, and Paul Wright, eds., *The Celling of America: An Inside Look at the US Prison Industry* (Monroe, ME: Common Courage Press, 1998).

28   Don Hannula, "Pumping iron in prison: much ado about nothing," *Seattle Times*, February 16, 1995; Rep. Steve Chabot, "No pumping iron behind federal prison bars," *Houston Chronicle*, March 14, 1995; David Foster, "Prison weightlifting perks weigh on legislators' minds," *Los Angeles Times*, June 4, 1995.

29   Dan Morain, "More inmate privileges fall in get-tough drive," *Los Angeles Times*, February 9, 1998.

30   "California inmates donating their hair to sick children who need wigs," CDC Press Release, February 18, 1998, #98–03. So far there are no plans for tattoos to be made into lampshades or for gold fillings to be extracted.

31   Charlotte Lowe, "Crackdown on prisoners' possessions," *Tucson Citizen*, February 18, 1994.

32   Ed Penhale, "Jail is so tough inmates want to work on chain gang," *Milwaukee Journal Sentinel*, October 30, 1997; "Juvenile chain gangs, tent jails planned," *Arizona Republic*, August 31, 1997; "Chain gangs put in place by Lewis County sheriff," *Seattle Post-Intelligencer*, August 18, 1997.

33   Richard P. Jones, "50,000-volt stun belts to control chain gang," *Chicago Sun-Times*, June 3, 1997.

34   Paul Wright, "Prison Litigation Reform Act passed," *Prison Legal News*, July 1996.

35   Public Law 104–134, Sec. 806.

36   Wright, "Prison litigation."

37   Public Law 104–134, SEC. 804.

38   "Prison Litigation Reform Act news," *Prison Legal News*, June 1998.

39   "UNICOR worker receives $928.32 for lost hand," *Prison Legal News*, October 1998.

40   Wright, "Prison litigation."

41   Ibid.

42   Terry L. Stewart, Congressional testimony on "Judicial activism," US Senate, Subcommittee on the Constitution, Federalism and Property Rights, July 15, 1997.

43   Dan Pens, "Arizona DOC paralegal fraud: law libraries closed, replaced by scam artists," *Prison Legal News*, October 1998.

44   "Arizona paralegals obstruct court access," *Prison Legal News*, October 1998.

45   Thomas D. Elias, "California inmates' perks being lifted: prisoners and rights groups cry foul," *Washington Times*, March 1, 1998.

46   "Idaho law libraries closed, pillaged," *Prison Legal News*, August 1998.

47   Rhonda Cook, "Inmates' attorneys criticized: state-approved group gives prisoners bad advice, legal expert says," *Atlanta Constitution*, November 11, 1998.

48   Anti-Terrorism and Effective Death Penalty Act of 1996, Public Law 104–132, April 24, 1996.

49   For a comprehensive overview of education in prisons and Pell grants, see James S. Kunen, "Teaching prisoners a lesson," *New Yorker*, July 10, 1995.

50   Conversations with Ted Hamm, former instructor at San Quentin, July 1998.

51   "A study released in 1991 by the New York State Department of Corrections Services, for example, found that male inmates who completed one or more years of higher education in prisons had a recidivism rate four years after their release, more than 20 percent lower than the average for all male inmates. The Office of Research and Evaluation at the Federal Bureau of Prisons last year [1994] reported a similar drop in recidivism among prisoners released in 1987 who had completed one or more education courses at any level during each six month period they were in prison" (Kunen, "Teaching prisoners," p. 36).

52   Scott Dyer, "House committee kills 'prison reform' package," *Baton Rouge Advocate*, May 15, 1997.

53   Adrian Lomax, "Captive audience," *In These Times*, June 14, 1998.

54   On the role of the press and prison movements in the 1960s, see Eric Cummins, *The Rise and Fall of California's Radical Prison Movement* (Stanford, CA: Stanford University Press, 1994).

10 BALKANS IN A BOX: RAPE, RACE WAR, AND OTHER FORMS OF MANAGEMENT

1   Andrew Gumbel, "Guards charged in rape case at jail in Los Angeles," *The Independent* (UK), October 12, 1998.

2   Mark Arax, "Ex-guard tells of brutality, code of silence at Corcoran Prison," *Los Angeles Times*, July 6, 1998.

3   Mark Arax and Mark Gladstone, "5 charged in Corcoran Prison rape inquiry," *Los Angeles Times*, October 9, 1998.

4   Ibid.

5   Wilbert Rideau, "Sexual jungle," in Wilbert Rideau and Ron Wikberg, *Life Sentences: Rage and Survival Behind Bars* (New York: Times Books, 1992); "Inmate victimization," chapter 9 in Hans Torch, *Living in Prison: The Ecology of Survival* (New York: Free Press, 1977); for the ultimate overview of every aspect of male prison rape, including the accounts of rape victims, see Stop Prison Rape's *Amicus* brief in support of Petitioner, *Farmer vs. Brennan*, No. 92–7247, Supreme Court of the United States, October Term, 1993; see also Jennifer Gronerman, "Love behind bars," *Village Voice*, May 13, 1997.

6 Study of the Nebraska prison system by Cindy Struckman-Johnson, "Sexual coercion reported by men and women in prison,"*Journal of Sex Research*, vol. 33, no. 1, 1996, pp. 67–76; Mary Dallao, "Fighting prison rape: how to make your facility safer," *Corrections Today*, vol. 58, no. 7, December 1, 1996.

7 Wayne Wooden and Jay Parker.

8 *Amicus* brief, *Farmer vs. Brennan*; for an account of rape as a tool in juvenile facilities, see Dwight Edgar Abbot, with Jack Carter, *I Cried, You Didn't Listen: A Survivor's Exposé of the California Youth Authority* (Los Angeles: Feral House, 1991).

9 Robert W. Dumond, "The sexual assault of male inmates in incarcerated settings," *International Journal of the Sociology of Law*, 1992, vol. 20, pp. 135–57.

10 Charles M. Sennott, "Prison's hidden horror," *Boston Globe*, May 1, 1994.

11 Ibid.

12 Ibid.

13 David Cray, "Prison-rape quote slows extradition," *Seattle Times*, October 30, 1997.

14 Greg Burton, "Prison rapes covered up, inmates say; prison rapes covered up, inmates charge," *Salt Lake Tribune*, November 9, 1997.

15 Charles M. Sennott and Zachary R. Dowdy, "Prison rape cry recanted amid surgery and a suicide," *Boston Globe*, December 7, 1994.

16 James Gillaspy, "Evidence is missing in prison rape case," *Indianapolis Star*, June 8, 1996.

17 *Farmer vs. Brennan*, No. 92–7247.

18 *Blucker vs. Washington et al.*, 95C50110, US District Court, Northern District of Illinois; Michael Pearson, "Jury awards no damages in Illinois prison rape lawsuit," Associated Press, August 29, 1997; "No award in prison rape case," *St. Louis Post-Dispatch*, August 30, 1997; "Damages denied in prison rape," *Chicago Tribune*, August 29, 1997.

19 Wilbert Rideau, "Sexual jungle," p. 79.

20 Ann Landers, "Issue of prison rape provokes outrage, avalanche of mail," *Los Angeles Daily News*, October 29, 1995; this extended series of letters to Ann Landers regarding prison rape included submissions from current and former prisoners, vengeful members of the public, guards, and even Cindy Struckman-Johnson, Ph.D., University of South Dakota, who conducted the above-mentioned study of rape in a Nebraska prison.

21 Lee H. Bowker, *Prison Victimization* (New York: Elsevier, 1980), esp. chapter 7.

22 A friend, fellow writer, and former prisoner tells me that in the federal joint he served in there was very little rape, in part because there were so many freelance male prostitutes willing to service many customers. Conversation, December 1998.

23 Ibid., p. 70.

24 Donald Tucker, "A punk's song," in Anthony M. Scacco, Jr., ed., *Male Rape: A Casebook of Sexual Aggressions* (New York: AMS Press, 1982), pp. 77–8. Donald Tucker is the *nom de plume* of Stephen Donaldson, founder of Stop Prison Rape.

25 Herman "Hooks" Wallace, letter to Scott Flemming, November 5, 1998.

26 For inmate-on-inmate rape in women's prisons, see chapter 2, "The victims," in Carl Weiss and James Friar, *Terror in the Prisons: Homosexual Rape and Why Society Condones It* (Indianapolis: Bobbs-Merrill, 1974); for an overview of corrections officers' abuse of the female captives, see "All too familiar: sexual abuse of women in US state prisons," Human Rights Watch, Woman's Rights Project, September 1996.

27 Interviews with Brenda Smith, esq., Executive Director of the National Women's Law Center, February 1998; *Women of the District of Columbia Department of Corrections vs. District of Columbia*, Civ. A. No. 93–2052 9(USDC); Toni Locy, "Suit tells of reluctant cell block striptease," *Washington Post*, December 15, 1997.

28 Smith interview; *Women vs. DC*.

29   Quoted in Christopher D. Cook and Christian Parenti, "Rape camp USA," *In These Times*, December 1998.

30   Steven A. Holmes, "Rape case underscores problems for prisons," *Arizona Republic*, January 6, 1997; Susie Steckner, "Inmate recalls horrors, sex abuse 'added punishment,'" *Arizona Republic*, March 16, 1997.

31   Bobbie Stein, "Sexual abuse: guards let rapists into women's cells," *The Progressive*, July 1, 1996; Emelyn Cruz Lat, "Sex-slave suit forces reforms at prisons," *San Francisco Examiner*, March 3, 1998.

32   Christy Oglesby, "Crossing the line: officers suspected of forcing sex," *Atlanta Journal*, March 5, 1997.

33   Maureen O'Hagan, "Private affairs," *Willamette Weekly*, October 22, 1997.

34   Certified statement by Barrilee A. Banister, no date, submitted to *Prison Legal News* in 1998.

35   "All too familiar," Human Rights Watch, p. 2.

36   Darrell K. Gilliard and Allen J. Beck, "Prisoners in 1994," *Bureau of Justice Statistics Bulletin*, August 1995, p. 5.

37   Kathleen Maguire and Ann L. Pastore, eds., *Source Book of Criminal Justice Statistics 1995* (Washington, DC: Bureau of Justice Statistics, Government Printing Office, 1996), Table 6.33.

38   60 Minutes, CBS, "Profile: La Eme; the Mexican Mafia uses its power and influence inside California prisons and in the outside world," broadcast Sunday, February 23, 1997.

39   Daniel B. Wood, "To keep peace, prisons allow race to rule," *Christian Science Monitor*, September 16, 1997; on the breakdown of older more structured gangs and the rise of looser more fractured associations, see Geoffrey Hunt *et al.*, "Changes in prison culture: prison gangs and the case of the 'Pepsi generation,'" *Social Problems*, vol. 40, no. 3, August 1993, pp. 398–409.

40   Willie Wisely, "Corcoran Prison: sex, lies and videotape," *Prison Legal News*, October 1998.

41   Daniel B. Wood, "To keep peace, prisons allow race to rule," Christian Science Monitor, September 16, 1997; conversations with gang truce organizer Dewayne Holmes, 1997–98.

42   Ibid.

43   On the end of *de jure* segregation, see Eric Cummins, *The Rise and Fall of California's Radical Prison Movement* (Stanford, CA: Stanford University Press, 1994), chapter 4.

44   Composite history drawn from: "Prison gangs: their extent, nature and impact on prisons," US Department of Justice, Office of Legal Policy, July 1985, pp. 89–114; John Irwin, *Prisons in Turmoil* (Boston: Little, Brown, 1980); quote from Joan W. Moore, *Homeboys: Gangs, Drugs and Prison in the Barrios of Los Angeles* (Philadelphia, PA: Temple University Press, 1978), p. 155.

45   Brian Kahn and R. Neil Zinn, "Prison gangs in the community," a briefing document for the Board of Corrections, June 14, 1978, Appendix B, pp. 85B–92B.

46   Paper in the personal collection of William Hankins, cited in Cummins, *The Rise and Fall*, pp. 139–40.

47   George Ramos, "US uses racketeering law to fight Mexican Mafia court: wide ranging trial targets 13 alleged members. Defense attorneys dispute that prison gang even exists," *Los Angeles Times*, December 2, 1996; "US got life terms for 10 Mexican Mafia members and may continue its offensive," *Los Angeles Times*, September 21, 1997. An interesting twist to the cinematic life of the Eme was the suit filed by Joe "Pegleg" Morgan. Although of Slavic descent, Morgan grew up in the predominantly Latino East Side of Los Angeles, spoke fluent Spanish and identified with Latino culture and was reputed to have been a founding member of the Mexican Mafia. Morgan alleged that Olmos had based a character on him without

permission. Morgan died in, and sued from, the Security Housing Unit in Pelican Bay State Prison in 1993. "Joe Morgan: obituary," *San Francisco Chronicle*, November 11, 1993; Jesse Katz, "Reputed Mexican Mafia leader dies in prison at 64," *Los Angeles Times*, November 10, 1993.

48 Robert J. Lopez and Jesse Katz, "Mexican Mafia tells gangs to halt drive-bys," *Los Angeles Times*, September 26, 1993.

49 Peter Y. Hong, "Rise in killings may mean gang truce is over," *Los Angeles Times*, October 6, 1995.

50 Maria Alicia Gaura, "Blood brothers, the killing started when Nuestra Familia gang leaders felt their influence in San Jose waning, prosecutors say," *San Francisco Chronicle*, June 29, 1997.

51 Interview with Bryan Perry, officer with the California Department of Corrections Special Services Unit, December 1998.

52 Quoted in Cummins, *The Rise and Fall*, p. 137.

53 See the epilogue in Abbot, *I Cried, You Didn't Listen*.

54 See the BGF interview cited in Cummins, *The Rise and Fall*, p. 236.

55 Ibid.

56 Brian Kahn and R. Neil Zinn, "Prison gangs in the community," a briefing document for the Board of Corrections, June 14, 1978, p. 32.

57 Andy Furillo, "Black prison gang moves in on cocaine trade," *Los Angeles Times*, May 21, 1985.

58 "Prison gangs," US Department of Justice, July 1985, p. 102.

59 Erik Ingram, "3 are charged in guard death at San Quentin," *San Francisco Chronicle*, December 3, 1985; the jailhouse armouring story was related to me by several former convicts.

60 Lonn Johnston and Clarence Johnson, "Confession in slaying of Newton," *San Francisco Chronicle*, August 26, 1989; Eric Malinic and Mark Stein, "Suspect admits killing Newton, police report," *Los Angeles Times*, August 26, 1989; Dean Congbalay and L. A. Chung, "Top security for suspect in Huey Newton slaying," *San Francisco Chronicle*, August 29, 1989; Will Jones, "Newton's killer guilty of 1st-degree murder," *Oakland Tribune*, October 10, 1991; "Newton's killer sentenced to 32 years to life," *San Francisco Examiner*, December 3, 1991; investigators with California Prison Focus met and interviewed Robinson in 1997 and subsequently.

61 This was relayed to me by attorney Erica Ettelson, who interviewed Robinson on behalf of California Prison Focus, January 1997.

62 Conversations with gang truce activist Dewayne Holmes, 1997.

63 For a detailed account of the Consolidated Crip Organization, see the last four chapters of Sanyika Shakur, *Monster: The Autobiography of an LA Gang Member* (New York: Penguin Books, 1993).

64 "Prison gangs," Department of Justice, July 1985; also see Cummins, *The Rise and Fall*.

65 Russell Working, "Tattoos: required reading for prison guards," *Seattle Times*, October 5, 1986.

66 Brian Kahn and R. Neil Smith, "Prison gangs in the community," a briefing document for the Board of Corrections, 1978, p. 57.

67 Interview with anonymous white inmate in general population, conducted during a legal investigation with California Prison Focus, January 1997.

68 Interview with anonymous inmate at Pelican Bay, conducted during a legal investigation with California Prison Focus, January 1997.

69 Interview with Brian Perry, December 1998.

70 See Florida Department of Corrections' "Gang and security threat group awareness" web page, 1998.

71 Stephen Green, "Members of Aryan gang called cunning, violent," *Sacramento Bee*, April 1, 1990.

72 Interview with Bryan Perry, officer with the California Department of Corrections Special Services Unit, December 1998.

73 Shakur, *Monster*, p. 339, described the 415s as the main plumbers in Soledad – and thus the primary provisioners of hacksaw blades.

74 Andy Furillo, "Tense Lassen Prison one of most dangerous," *Sacramento Bee*, March 23, 1998.

75 Wood, "To keep peace."

76 Ibid.

77 John L. Spain, "Coming to terms with race," *Sun Reporter* (San Francisco), July 4, 1996.

78 "All things considered," National Public Radio, February 23, 1999.

79 Denny Walsh, "Convict bests guard in court, own lawyer in rights case," *Sacramento Bee*, November 24, 1998.

80 John Mitchell and Josh Meyer, "Gang bullets pierce Santa Monica's image violence: as turf wars cross city lines, officials seek to reassure residents and visitors of their safety," *Los Angeles Times*, October 29, 1998.

81 Willie Wisely, "Racism in the ranks," *Prison Legal News*, August 1998.

82 This was the general assesment of more than a dozen prisoners interviewed in February 1999.

83 Corey Weinstein and Eric Cummins, "The crime of punishment: Pelican Bay Maximum Security Prison," in Elihu Rosenblatt, ed., *Criminal Injustice: Confronting the Prison Crisis* (Boston: South End, 1996).

84 "Cold storage: super-maximum security confinement in Indiana," Human Rights Watch, 1997; for more on brutality in the SHU, see Weinstein and Cummins, "The crime of punishment."

85 Interview with Dr. Terry Kupers, expert witness on psychological effects of SHUs, June 1998.

86 See Michael Ignatieff, *A Just Measure of Time: The Penitentiary in the Industrial Revolution 1750–1850* (New York: Pantheon, 1978).

87 Cummins, *The Rise and Fall*.

88 "Security Housing Units (SHUs) within the California Department of Corrections," attachment of news release #96–039, CDC, 1996.

89 This section is based on interviews with prisoners in the Corcoran and Pelican Bay SHUs, and on "Challenging gang validation in California," photocopied documents compiled by attorney Graham Noyes, 1998.

90 This is based on a series of first-hand interviews with HIV-positive prisoners in the Corcoran SHU and the California Prison for Women, conducted by the author, while working as a California Prison Focus investigator, July 24, 1998.

91 For full accounting of the debriefing policey, see *Castillo vs. Gomez*, Civil No. C-94–2847 CW, United States District Court for the Northern District of California, 1995.

92 Andy Furillo, "Deal to undermine prison gang might help solve slayings," *Sacramento Bee*, February 2, 1998; also confirmed by interviews with anonymous AB associated in the SHU during California Prison Focus research trip, January 1997. Mike Davis was the first to make the point about CDC strategy as a cause of violence; see Mike Davis, *Ecology of Fear: Los Angeles and the Imagination of Disaster* (New York: Metropolitan Books, 1998), chapter 7.

93 Jeffrey Reiman calls this process of successful growth by way of "failed" policy the "Pyrrhic defeat." Unlike the Pyrrhic victory in which the cost of winning is as great as the cost of defeat, the Pyrrhic defeat is a loss which entails secret or hidden victories. See Jeffrey Reiman, *The Rich Get Richer and the Poor Get Prison: Ideology, Class and Criminal Justice*, third edition (New York: Macmillan, 1990).

94 California Legislative Analyst's Office, Analysis of the 1998–99 Budget Bill.

11 BIG BUCKS FROM THE BIG HOUSE: THE PRISON INDUSTRIAL COMPLEX AND BEYOND

1   Economic data on Crescent City comes from interviews with staff of the Del Norte County Assessor's Office, January–February 1996.

2   John David, "Building prisons is bad investment," *Charleston Gazette*, December 22, 1995.

3   Eric Lotke, "The prison-industrial complex," *Multinational Monitor*, November 1, 1996.

4   Miller has made such comments in interviews, but for his full analysis, see Jerome Miller, *Search and Destroy: African American Males in the Criminal Justice System* (New York: Cambridge University Press, 1996).

5   Patricia J. Malin, "A new prison for Rome," *Central New York Business Journal*, vol. 10, no. 9, April 29, 1996.

6   Teena Hammond, "Inland Empire focus: prisons and prosperity," *Business Press* (Ontario, CA), November 4, 1996.

7   Ibid.

8   "New prison to bring jobs to South Bay," *Sun-Sentinel* (Fort Lauderdale), May 26, 1995; Randy Gragg, "A high-security, low-risk investment: private prisons make crime pay," *Harper's Magazine*, August 1, 1996.

9   Scott L. Miley, "New prison down to 2 possible homes: Madison and Miami Counties remain in running for medium-security facility," *Indianapolis Star*, December 21, 1995; Virginia Young, "Rural towns eager to house new prison," *St. Louis Post-Dispatch*, February 6, 1994.

10   Barbara A. Nadel, "Prison sightings: a rundown of the factors that go into site selection and development of correctional facilities," *Planning*, vol. 61, no. 6, June 1995.

11   Don Terry, "Town pins its economic hopes on new prison," *Seattle Times*, January 3, 1993.

12   Tom Shales, " 'Nation': with malice toward all," *Washington Post*, July 19, 1994.

13   Allen Palmer, "In Canon City, prisons accepted as a way of life: economic security has its drawbacks," *Denver Post*, August 16, 1998.

14   "New prison pushes town into housing shortage," *Fort Worth Star-Telegram*, July 17, 1992.

15   Mike Lewis, "Governor grants financial help to Valley prison cities," *Fresno Bee*, October 13, 1997.

16   Jeffrey Leib, "Jobs booming in Colo. corrections field: tougher sentencing laws swell inmate rolls, spur 4 new prisons," *Denver Post*, June 22, 1992.

17   Fox Butterfield, "With a little help from the movies and TV, a subject that once got no respect attracts students," *New York Times*, December 5, 1998.

18   Tim Novak, "Edgar: new prisons add jobs for whites – few minorities are in jail sites, governor says," *St. Louis Post-Dispatch*, August 3, 1993. It is important to note that this is not always the pattern. In many prisons guards are a very divers lot.

19   Chris Bryson, "Crime pays for those in the prison business," *National Times*, September 1996; Ken Silverstein, "America's private gulag," *Prison Legal News*, June 1997; Stephen Handelman, "Prisons for profit," *Toronto Star*, September 25, 1994.

20   Eric Schlosser, "The prison industrial complex," *Atlantic Monthly*, December 1993.

21   "Letter to our shareholders," Corrections Corporation of America 1997 Annual Report.

22   Paulette Thomas, "Making crime pay: triangle of interests creates infrastructure to fight lawlessness," *Wall Street Journal*, May 12, 1994.

23   Lotke, "The prison-industrial complex."

24   Tom Humphrey, "Private prison backers adopting new tack," *Knoxville News-Sentinel*, November 22, 1998.

25 Testimony of Timothy P. Cole, Chairman, Wackenhut Corrections Corporation, before the Committee on the Judiciary United States Senate, Washington, DC, 27 July 1995; testimony of J. Michael Quinlan, before the House Subcommittee on Public Buildings and Economic Development, February 26, 1998.

26 Andrew Billen, "A man called Wackenhut," *The Observer*, November 3, 1996; Gragg, "A high-security, low-risk investment."

27 Thomas, "Making crime pay."

28 Bryson, "Crime pays for those in the prison business."

29 See, for example, anything written by Morgan Reynolds of the Dallas-based National Center for Policy Analysis and Texas A&M University, or Charles W. Thomas of Private Corrections Project Center for Studies in Criminology & Law, University of Florida, Gainesville; or the nauseatingly ebullient Fox Butterfield, "Private Tennessee prison is praised in state studies, *New York Times*, August 19, 1995. Recently Butterfield has adopted a more critical stance toward private prisons.

30 "Private and public prisons – studies comparing operational costs and/or quality of service," United States General Accounting Office (Washington, DC: Government Printing Office, August 16, 1996), p. 7.

31 Ibid., p. 20.

32 Silverstein, "America's private gulag."

33 Bates, *op. cit.*

34 Quoted in Mark Tatge, "Employees criticize privately run prison: guards, others leaving, calling facility unsafe," *Plain Dealer*, August 30, 1998.

35 Shirley Downing, "Officials still seek causes of riots at two prisons: FCI reports 'semi-lockdown'; Mason facility back to normal," *Memphis Commercial Appeal*, October 31, 1995; Shirley Downing and Bartholomew Sullivan, "Prison riot unleashes questions," *Memphis Commercial Appeal*, November 13, 1995.

36 MaryAnn Spoto, "Victim saw jail officer during day of beatings," *Star-Ledger* (Newark, NJ), February 4, 1998; David Stout, "Detention jail called worse than prison," *New York Times*, June 19, 1995.

37 Martin Weil, "Six D.C. inmates escape Ohio prison," *Washington Post*, July 26, 1998; Ann Fisher, "Questions raised over thwarted prison inspection," *Columbus Dispatch*, May 8, 1998: "CCA prison off to a rocky start," *Prison Legal News*, October 1997.

38 Eleena de Lisser, "Prison's woes spur sell-off in CCA shares," *Wall Street Journal Europe*, July 29, 1998.

39 Cheryl W. Thompson, "Ohio sours on prison managed by private firm; D.C. inmates live in troubled facility," *Washington Post*, October 19, 1998.

40 Quotes from "CCA-run prison under attack by former employees," *The Tennessean*, August 31, 1998; Tatge, "Employees criticize privately run prison."

41 Tatge, "Employees criticize privately run prison."

42 Cheryl W. Thompson, "Report galvanizes D.C. prison critics," *Washington Post*, December 10, 1998.

43 Michael Scott and Janet Tebben, "Prison project: annexation clears the way," *Tribune Chronicle* (Warren, OH), March 29, 1996; Mark Tatge, "Private prisons: a growth industry; Youngstown lock-up would be Ohio's first," *Plain Dealer*, December 26, 1995; Cheryl W. Thompson, "Ohio issues restraining order for prison firm; control of facility cannot be changed," *Washington Post*, November 19, 1998.

44 "Schools in crisis," *Cincinnati Post*, September 20, 1996. Around the same time drug treatment and poison controls services were also being slashed. Sue MacDonald, "Poison hotline: not just for emergencies, it's a source for prescription drugs and substance abuse information," *Cincinnati Enquirer*, March 19, 1996.

45 Dan Egbert, "Ohio CCA facility hit by inmates' lawsuit," *Nashville Banner*, November 24, 1997; Mark Tatge, "Prison control bill dies in Senate: private operator blocks attempt at regulation," *Plain Dealer*, November 25, 1997.

46 Humphrey, "Private prison backers adopting new tack."

47 Kim Bell, "Missouri says Texas attack was planned: distance makes keeping track of out-of-state inmates difficult," *St. Louis Post-Dispatch*, August 24, 1997.

48 "Shakedown; closer look at a private prison in Texas that videotaped guards' abuse of inmates," Dateline NBC, Tuesday, September 23, 1997.

49 Barbara Hoberock, "Removal of inmates not linked to tape," *Tulsa World*, August 21, 1997; "Guard in jail video guilty of past beating," *Austin American-Statesman*, August 21, 1997.

50 Greg Jaffe and Rick Brooks, "Hard time: violence at prison run by Corrections Corp. irks Youngstown, Ohio," *Wall Street Journal*, August 5, 1998.

51 "Prison supervisor ordered inmate beating, N.M. finds," *Denver Post*, November 28, 1998.

52 "Corrections officials to seek money to send more inmates out of state $3.2 million request includes funds to move 519 additional prisoners," *Milwaukee Journal Sentinel*, November 27, 1998; "FBI probe at prison praised lawyer claims client beaten at CCA facility," *The Tennessean*, November 12, 1998.

53 "Inmate abuse denied by prison in Tennessee: complaints probably groundless, Wisconsin official says," *Wisconsin State Journal*, October 8, 1998; Richard P. Jones, "State now admits private prison abuse: seven employees of corrections firm fired as result of Tennessee incident," *Milwaukee Journal Sentinel*, November 11, 1998.

54 Jaffe and Brooks, "Hard time: violence at prison run by Corrections Corp."

55 "Former High Plains officials regroup: company applies to open private youth prison under new name," *Denver Rocky Mountain News*, November 8, 1998; Jaffe and Brooks, "Hard time: violence at prison run by Corrections Corp."

56 Bonna M. De la Cruz, "Sundquist offers private-prison rules," *The Tennessean*, December 19, 1998.

57 Andy Furillo, "Prison officers' union on a roll," *Sacramento Bee*, October 12, 1998.

58 John Hurst, "The big house that Don Novey built," *Los Angeles Times*, February 6, 1994; Craig Marine, "Up from the Hole State prison guards' powerful leader now a heavyweight in political ring," *San Francisco Examiner*, June 26, 1994.

59 Furillo, "Prison officers' union on a roll."

60 Bruce Shapiro, "Victims and vengeance: why the victims' rights amendment is a bad idea," *The Nation*, February 10, 1997; Tupper Hull, "Prison guards' union helps victims' groups: lobbying for tough laws, more prisons, aided by financial contributions," *San Francisco Examiner*, September 19, 1994; Erin McCormick, "The price of power Top 10 special interest groups lavish millions on elected officials to steer the course of state in their direction," *San Francisco Examiner*, November 1, 1998.

61 Bill Ainsworth, "Guard union opens doors to Davis in snub of rival," *San Diego Union-Tribune*, October 5, 1998.

62 Daniel B. Wood, "Private prisons, public doubts: as California's first big private prison goes up, questions surface on profits vs. safety," *Christian Science Monitor*, July 21, 1998; Andy Furillo, "Effort to block private prisons dies in Senate," *Sacramento Bee*, June 17, 1998.

63 Max Vanzi, "Firm's plans is news to prison officials corrections: state says it is unaware of proposal to build a private facility in California City. Sen. Polanco backs the idea," *Los Angeles Times*, August 2, 1997.

64 David Judson, "Guards' union attacks prison privatization," Gannett News Service, May 6, 1998.

65 Peter Durantine, "Ridge now against private firm to run a new prison," *Pittsburgh Post-Gazette*, February 27, 1997.

66 "Governor waffles on private prison plan. The proposal: build them in Wisconsin," *Wisconsin State Journal*, December 9, 1998.

67 Laura LaFay, "Private VA. prison targeted by group of public workers: the emphasis is placed on profit rather than safety, the group says," *Virginian-Pilot and the Ledger-Star*, Norfolk, VA, May 14, 1998; Robynn Tysver, "State workers decry for-profit prisons," *Omaha World-Herald*, May 14, 1998; "Prison guards in union call privatization bad idea for Iowa," *Omaha World-Herald*, May 13, 1998.

68 Ann Fisher, "Correction officers protest push for private prisons," *Columbus Dispatch*, March 18, 1998.

69 Alex Friedman, "Tennessee prison privatization bill fails to pass," *Prison Legal News*, September 1998; Bonna M. De la Cruz, "Corrections officers plan prison privatization protest," *The Tennessean*, October 15, 1998.

70 Christian Parenti, "Making prison pay," *The Nation*, January 29, 1996; Christian Parenti, "Pay now, pay later," *The Progressive*, July 1996; "Prisons punish inmates because of 'negative' news stories," press release, Society of Professional Journalists, Wednesday, September 10, 1997.

71 Public Law 96–157 (codified at 18 U.S.C. 1761(c) and 41 U.S.C. 35); George E. Sexton *et al.*, "Work in American prisons: joint ventures with the private sector," series: NIJ Program Focus (Washington, DC: Government Printing Office, November 1995); for a basic overview of prison labor, see Parenti, "Making prison pay" and "Pay now, pay later."

72 Interview with Brad Haag, UniGroup Spokesperson, June 1995.

73 Testimony of David A. Smith, Director of the Public Policy Department, American Federation of Labor and Congress of Industrial Organizations, on Prison Industry Programs, before the House Committee on Education and the Workforce Subcommittee on Oversight and Investigations, August 5, 1998.

74 Correction Industries Association, First Quarterly Report, 1998.

75 Guy Gugliotta, "From federal prisons to an agency near you," *Washington Post*, July 15, 1997.

76 Jeff Erlich, "Competing with convicts," *Government Executive*, June 1, 1997; for more on Unicor, see Vince Beiser, "Look for the prison label: America puts its inmates to work," *Village Voice*, May 21, 1996.

77 Robert J. Verdeyen, "Correctional industries: making inmate work productive," *Corrections Today*, August 1, 1995.

78 "Reforming the Prison Industry Authority," California Legislative Analyst's Office, April 30, 1996, p. 9; PIA official cook their books and brag efficiency to the press. Journalist on both the left and right often repeat such claims without checking for verification, such as outside audits.

79 Dan Pens, "Virginia prisons 'wide open to business,'" *Prison Legal News*, November 1998; Laura LaFay, "State prisons broke laws, lost money, while others benefited from jail labor," *Virginian-Pilot and the Ledger-Star*, June 28, 1998.

80 Matthew T. Clarke, "State auditor blasts Texas correctional industries," *Prison Legal News*, November 1998.

81 Sam Whiting, "Prisoners at work: inmates learn silk screening in for-profit partnership program," *San Francisco Chronicle*, October 24, 1996; interview with Darren Angus, proprietor of Inkarcerated, November 1996.

82 Interview with Jeff Thompson, Chief Legislative Advocate for the California Correctional Peace Officers Association, February 1997; also interviews and conversation with Moreen Blonian, Director, California Joint Venture Program, August 1995, February 1996.

83 Interviews with Moreen Blonian, Director, California Joint Venture Program, August 1995 and February 1996.

84 For more on resistance by convict workers, see "Minnesota prisoners strike for minimum wage," *Prison Legal News*, July 1996; James Quigley, "Florida PRIDE employees denied minimum wages," *Prison Legal News*, February 1998; Daniel Burton-Rose, "Work strike suppressed and sabotaged in Ohio," *Prison Legal News*, May 1998; "Texas prison labor union," *Prison Legal News*, May 1998.

85 Ron Schere, "Jailhouse capitalism stirs revolt," *Christian Science Monitor*, November 10, 1998.

86 Ibid.

87 Frank Swoboda, "Military-glove suppliers protest prison competitor; with captive work force, Unicor can undercut contractors," *Washington Post*, June 10, 1997.

88 Catherine Strong, "Coalition battles to overturn prison monopoly; Rep. Peter Hoekstra and others want private furniture companies to have less restrictions in winning government contracts," *Grand Rapids Press*, July 5, 1998; Joseph T. Hallinan, "Hard labor at $7 an hour," *Boston Globe*, August 23, 1998; for examples of small business organized to oppose prison industries, see Kenton H. Pattie, "Prison industry programs," Congressional testimony, August 5, 1998.

89 Joseph T. Hallinan,"Hard labor at $7 an hour," *Boston Globe*, August 23, 1998.

90 Gugliotta, "From federal prisons to an agency near you."

91 See, for example, Terry Kupers, *Prison Madness: The Mental Health Crisis Behind Bars and What We Must Do About It* (San Francisco: Jossey-Bass, 1999), pp. 266–9. Kuper's book is excellent but its short analysis of the prison industrial complex could be broader.

92 The impulse to focus on interest groups as opposed to the *general logic of class society* is born of the great tradition of American red baiting. A very concrete, journalistic, "anti-corporate" critique is unpopular but politically acceptable. However, a more abstract and organic critique of capitalist *society as a whole* rings the deep emotional, non-rational, bells of our almost Pavlovian anti-communism. Ironically red baiting, which often uses the trope of economic determinism, forces leftists into a simplistic lobbying and interest-group-focused style of analysis that is itself far more "economistic" than most Marxist class analysis, which takes into account more than the paper trails of campaign contributions.

93 Robert Cherry, "Black men still jobless," *Dollars & Sense*, November 1, 1998.

94 Ibid.

95 William Julius Wilson, *When Work Disappears: The World of the New Urban Poor* (New York: Vintage, 1996), p. 146.

96 Scott Shepard, "Household incomes up, but troubling gaps remain," *Atlanta Constitution*, September 25, 1998.

97 US census 1997 annual report, cited in Jim Lobe, "Economy-U.S.: slight reduction in poverty in 1997," Inter Press Service, September 24, 1998.

98 Marc Mauer and Tracy Huling, "Young black Americans and the criminal justice system: five years later," Sentencing Project Report, 1995.

99 Marc Mauer, "Americans behind bars: U.S. and international rates of incarceration, 1995," Sentencing Project Report, 1997.

INDEX